D0425345

If found, please return to:

_____

_____

_____

_____

Reward: $ _____

THE LONELINESS OF THE LONG-DISTANCE CARTOONIST

ALSO BY ADRIAN TOMINE

FICTION

Sleepwalk and Other Stories

Summer Blonde

Shortcomings

Killing and Dying

NONFICTION

Scenes from an Impending Marriage

ILLUSTRATION

New York Drawings

JUVENILIA

32 Stories: The Complete *Optic Nerve* Mini-Comics

Scrapbook (Uncollected Work: 1990–2004)

For Nora and May

That's like being the most famous badminton player.
—DANIEL CLOWES,
on being one of the most famous cartoonists

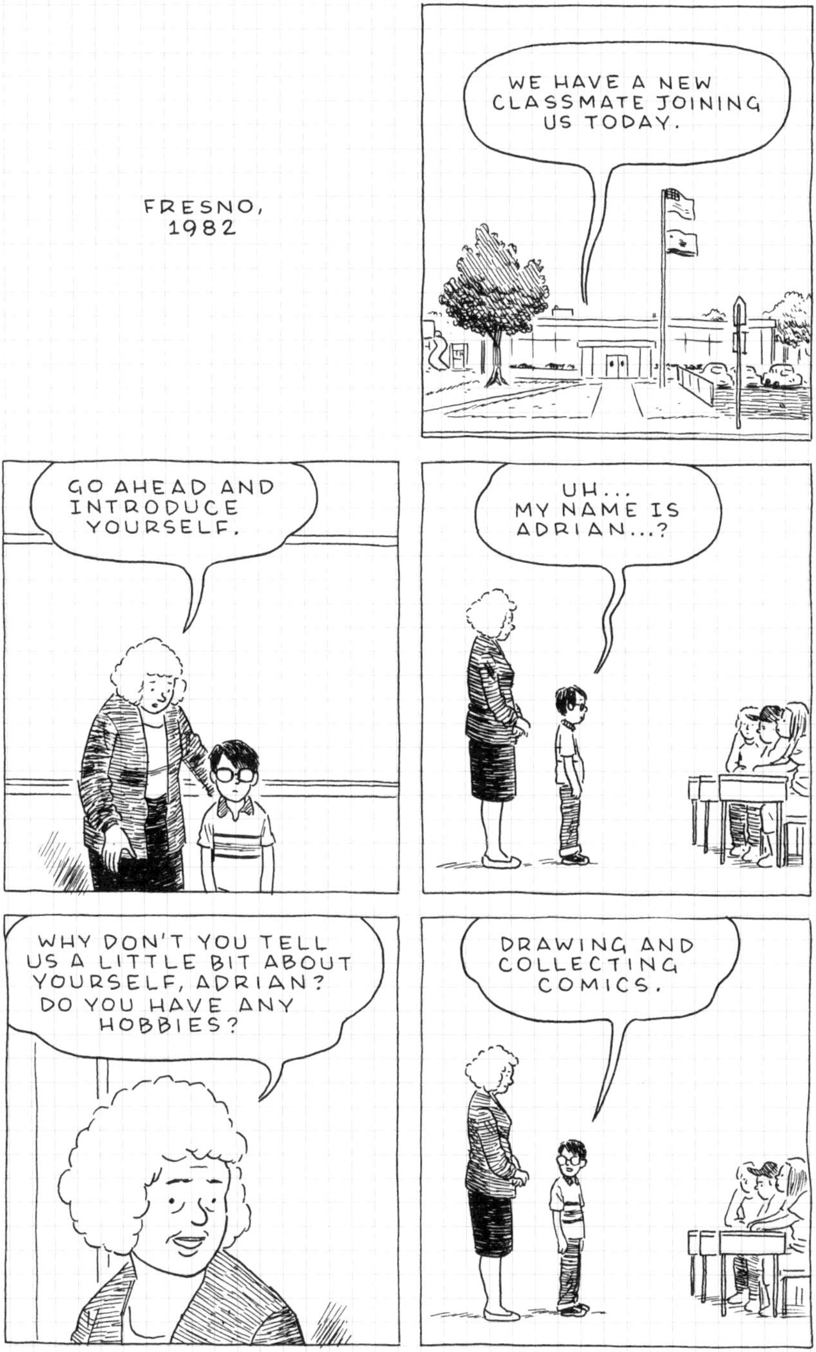
FRESNO, 1982
WE HAVE A NEW CLASSMATE JOINING US TODAY.
GO AHEAD AND INTRODUCE YOURSELF.
UH... MY NAME IS ADRIAN...?
WHY DON'T YOU TELL US A LITTLE BIT ABOUT YOURSELF, ADRIAN? DO YOU HAVE ANY HOBBIES?
DRAWING AND COLLECTING COMICS.

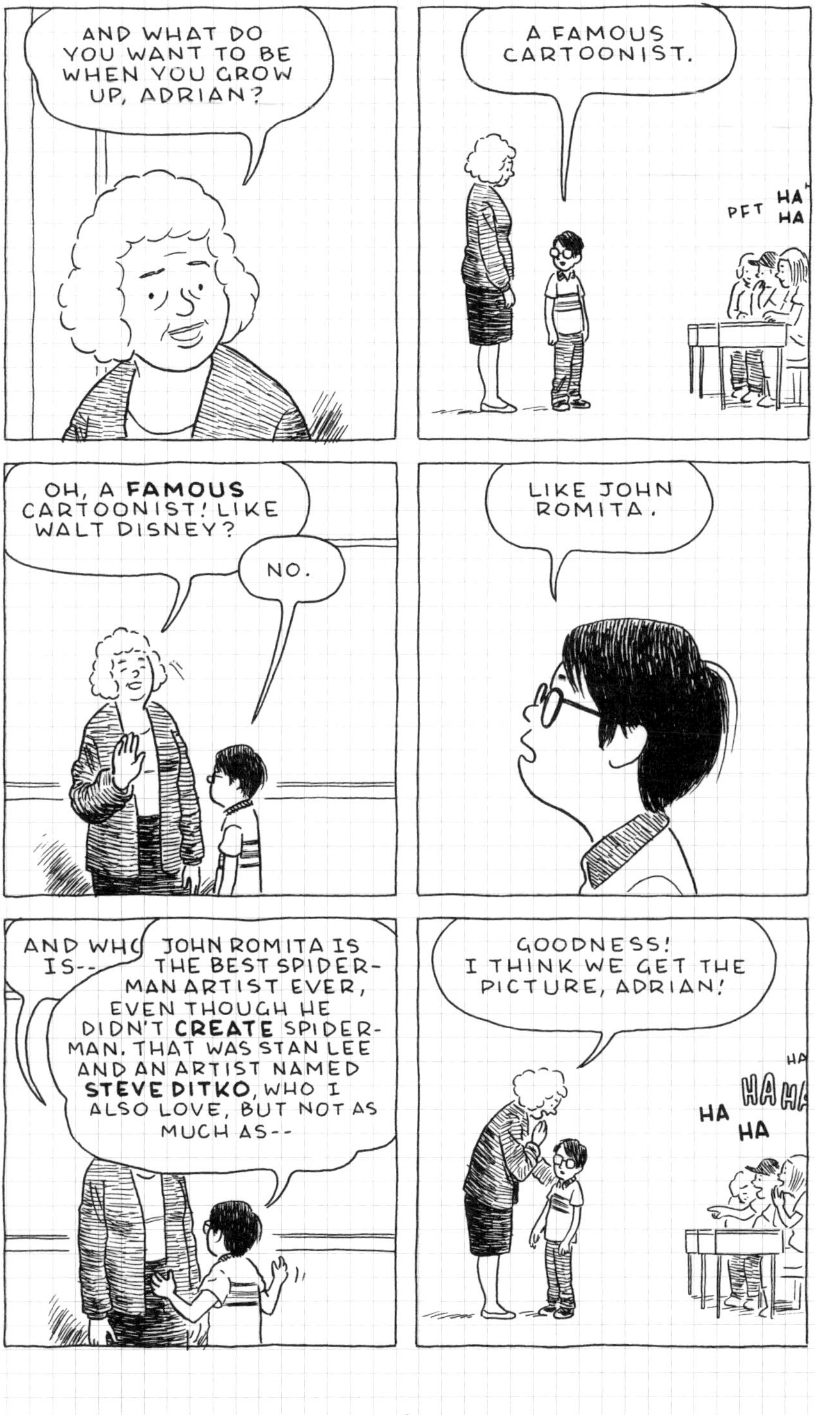
AND WHAT DO YOU WANT TO BE WHEN YOU GROW UP, ADRIAN?
A FAMOUS CARTOONIST.
PFT
HA HA
OH, A **FAMOUS** CARTOONIST! LIKE WALT DISNEY?
NO.
LIKE JOHN ROMITA.
AND WHO IS--
JOHN ROMITA IS THE BEST SPIDER-MAN ARTIST EVER, EVEN THOUGH HE DIDN'T **CREATE** SPIDER-MAN. THAT WAS STAN LEE AND AN ARTIST NAMED **STEVE DITKO**, WHO I ALSO LOVE, BUT NOT AS MUCH AS--
GOODNESS! I THINK WE GET THE PICTURE, ADRIAN!
HA
HAHA
HA
HA

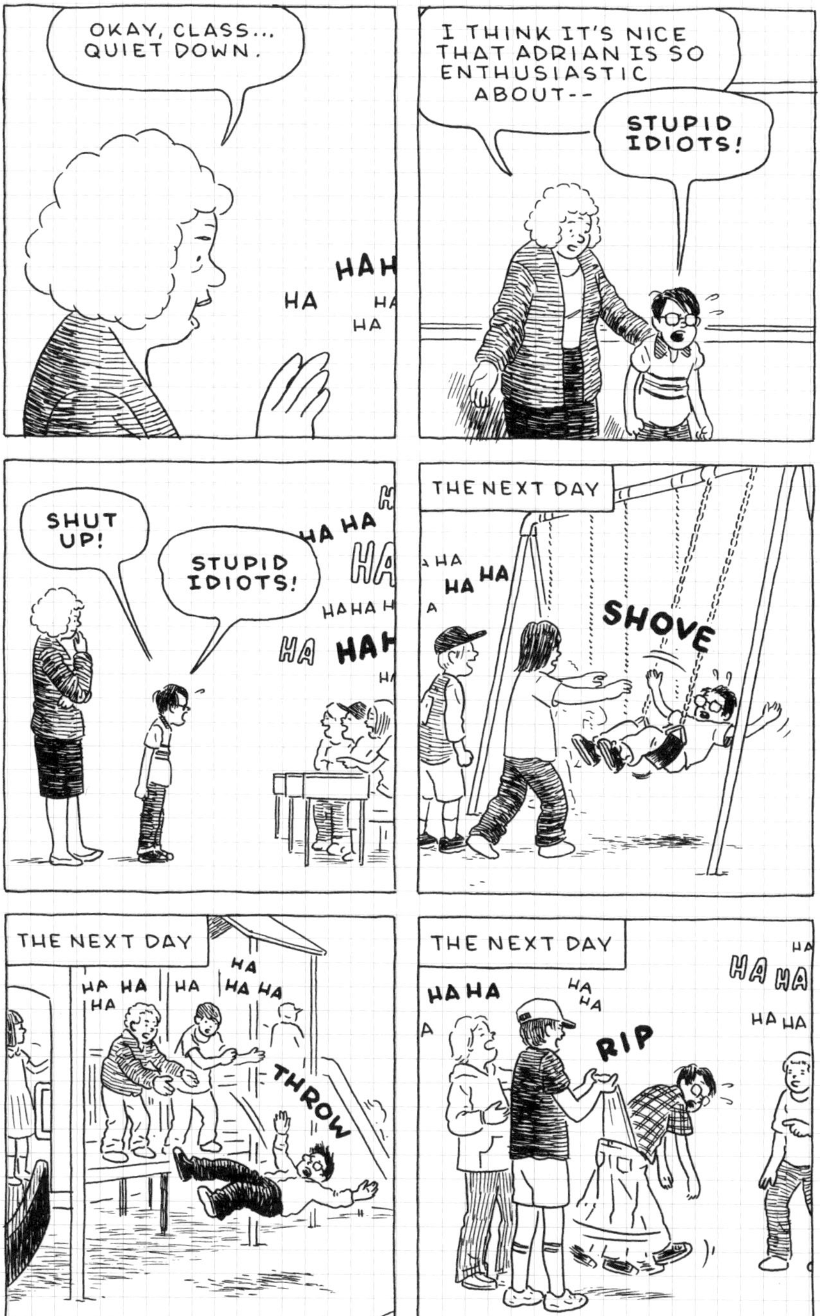
OKAY, CLASS... QUIET DOWN.
HAH
HA
HA
HA
I THINK IT'S NICE THAT ADRIAN IS SO ENTHUSIASTIC ABOUT--
STUPID IDIOTS!
SHUT UP!
STUPID IDIOTS!
HA HA
HA
HAHA
HA
HAH
THE NEXT DAY
HA
HA HA
SHOVE
THE NEXT DAY
HA HA
HA
HA
HA HA HA
HA
THROW
THE NEXT DAY
HA HA
HA HA
RIP
HA HA
HA HA

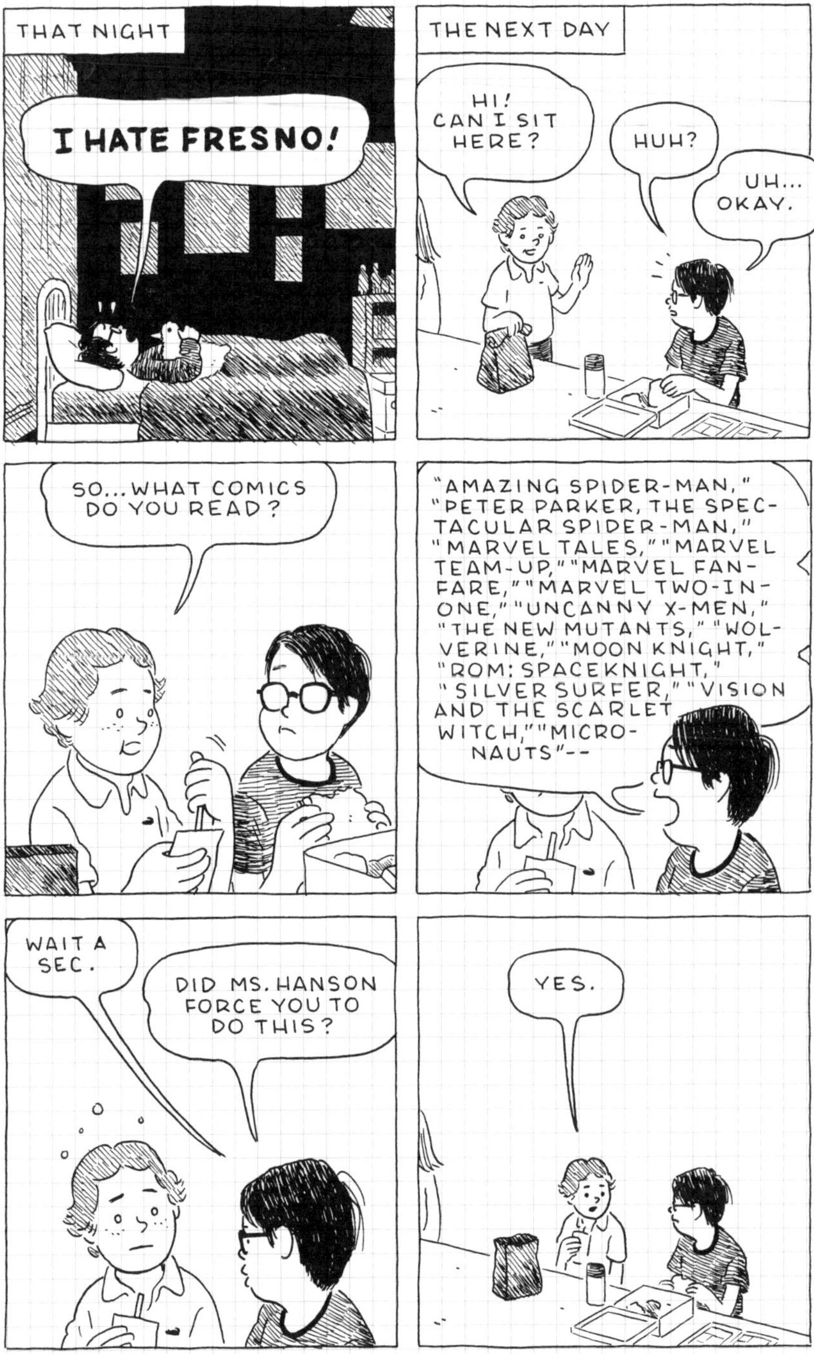
THAT NIGHT
I HATE FRESNO!
THE NEXT DAY
HI! CAN I SIT HERE?
HUH?
UH... OKAY.
SO... WHAT COMICS DO YOU READ?
"AMAZING SPIDER-MAN," "PETER PARKER, THE SPECTACULAR SPIDER-MAN," "MARVEL TALES," "MARVEL TEAM-UP," "MARVEL FANFARE," "MARVEL TWO-IN-ONE," "UNCANNY X-MEN," "THE NEW MUTANTS," "WOLVERINE," "MOON KNIGHT," "ROM: SPACEKNIGHT," "SILVER SURFER," "VISION AND THE SCARLET WITCH," "MICRONAUTS"--
WAIT A SEC.
DID MS. HANSON FORCE YOU TO DO THIS?
YES.

ADRIAN TOMINE

THE LONELINESS OF THE
LONG–DISTANCE CARTOONIST

DRAWN & QUARTERLY

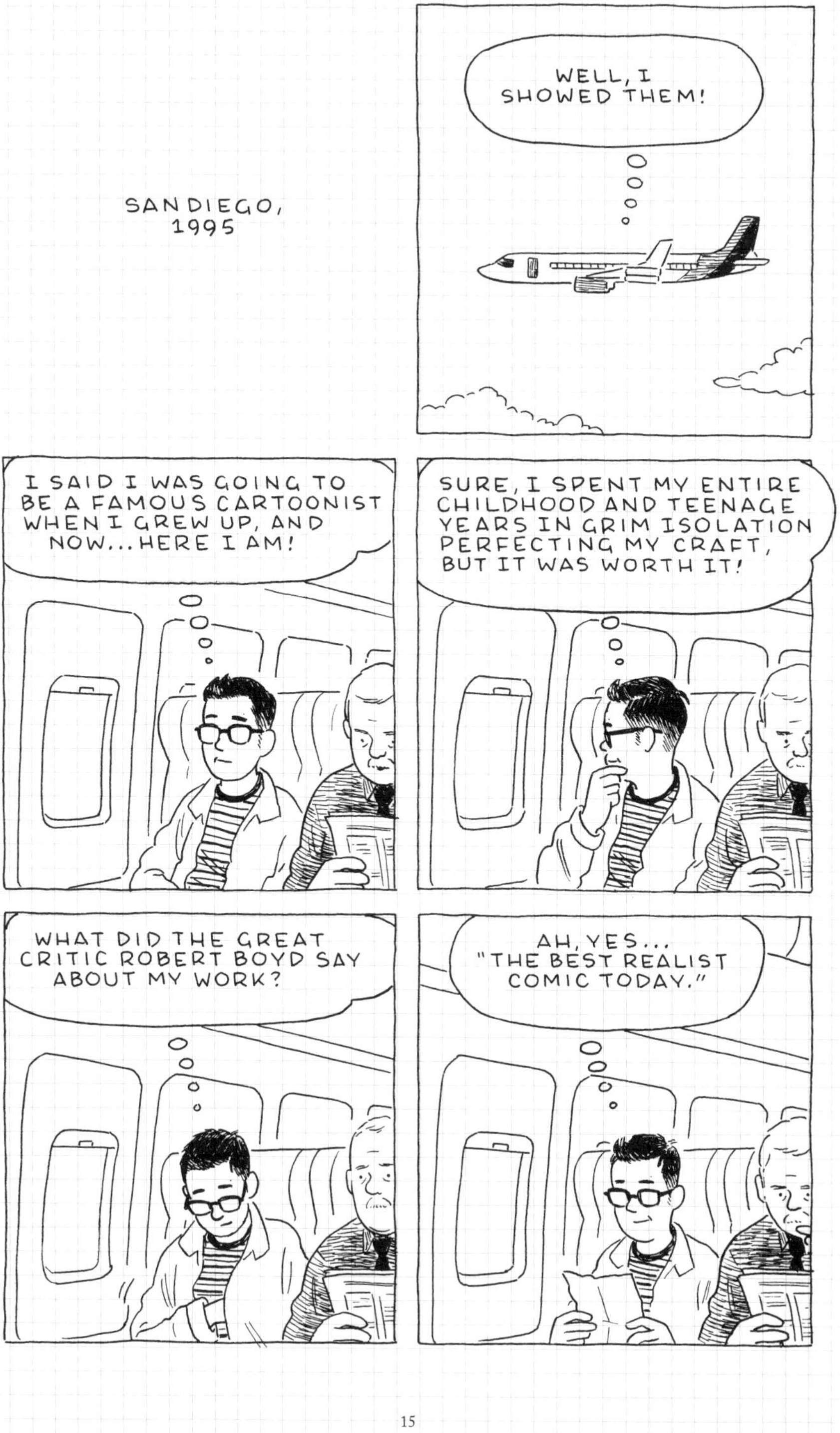
SAN DIEGO, 1995
WELL, I SHOWED THEM!
I SAID I WAS GOING TO BE A FAMOUS CARTOONIST WHEN I GREW UP, AND NOW... HERE I AM!
SURE, I SPENT MY ENTIRE CHILDHOOD AND TEENAGE YEARS IN GRIM ISOLATION PERFECTING MY CRAFT, BUT IT WAS WORTH IT!
WHAT DID THE GREAT CRITIC ROBERT BOYD SAY ABOUT MY WORK?
AH, YES... "THE BEST REALIST COMIC TODAY."

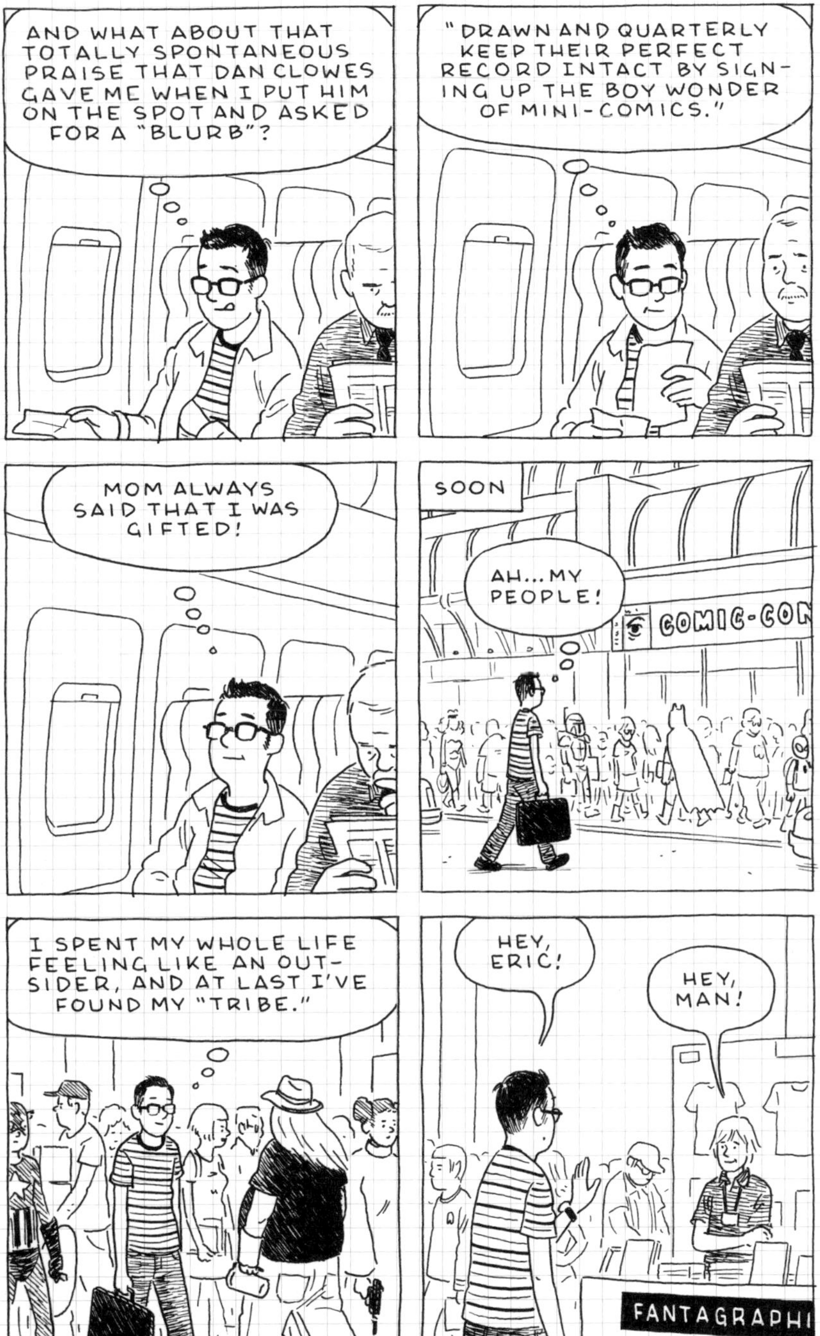
AND WHAT ABOUT THAT TOTALLY SPONTANEOUS PRAISE THAT DAN CLOWES GAVE ME WHEN I PUT HIM ON THE SPOT AND ASKED FOR A "BLURB"?
"DRAWN AND QUARTERLY KEEP THEIR PERFECT RECORD INTACT BY SIGNING UP THE BOY WONDER OF MINI-COMICS."
MOM ALWAYS SAID THAT I WAS GIFTED!
SOON
AH... MY PEOPLE!
COMIC-CON
I SPENT MY WHOLE LIFE FEELING LIKE AN OUTSIDER, AND AT LAST I'VE FOUND MY "TRIBE."
HEY, ERIC!
HEY, MAN!
FANTAGRAPHI

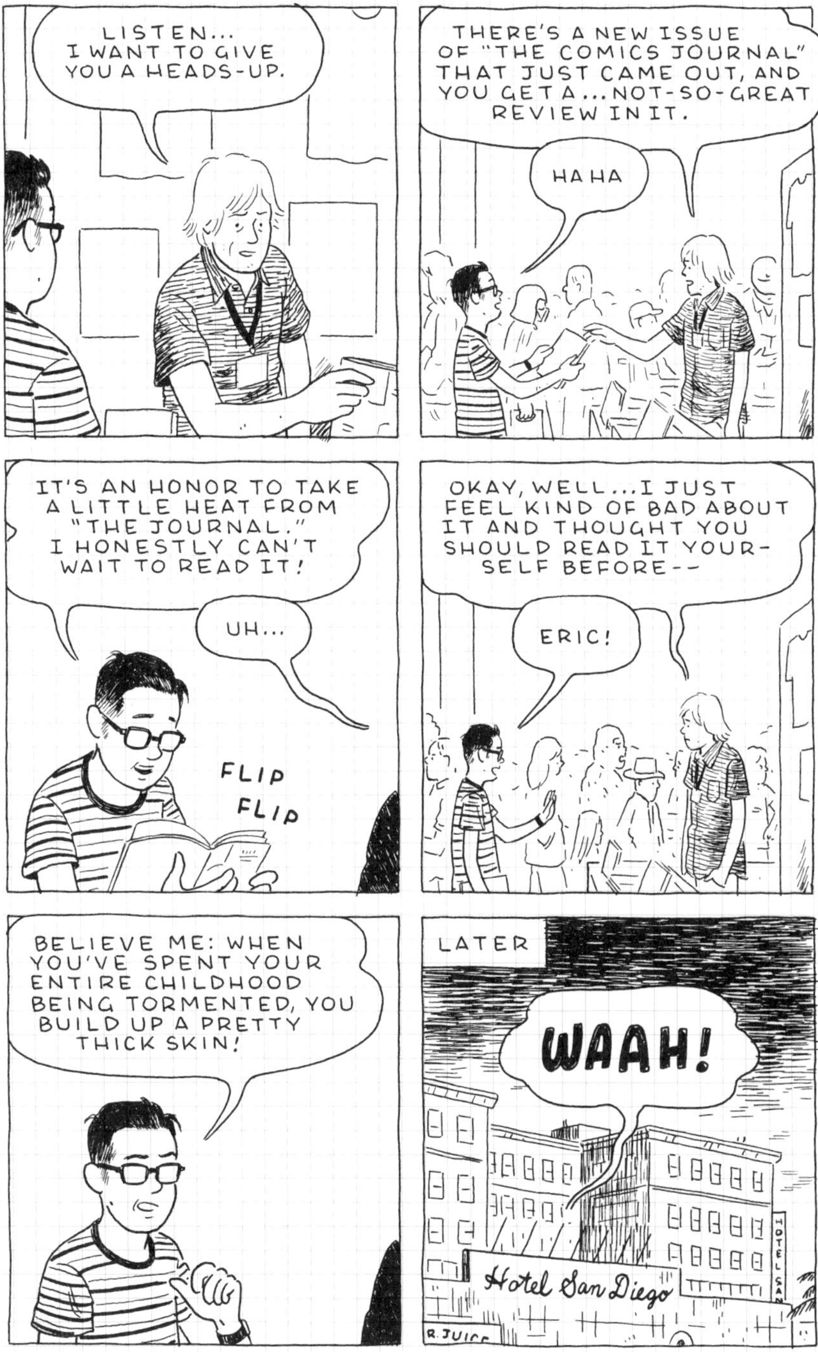
LISTEN... I WANT TO GIVE YOU A HEADS-UP.
THERE'S A NEW ISSUE OF "THE COMICS JOURNAL" THAT JUST CAME OUT, AND YOU GET A... NOT-SO-GREAT REVIEW IN IT.
HA HA
IT'S AN HONOR TO TAKE A LITTLE HEAT FROM "THE JOURNAL." I HONESTLY CAN'T WAIT TO READ IT!
UH...
FLIP
FLIP
OKAY, WELL... I JUST FEEL KIND OF BAD ABOUT IT AND THOUGHT YOU SHOULD READ IT YOURSELF BEFORE--
ERIC!
BELIEVE ME: WHEN YOU'VE SPENT YOUR ENTIRE CHILDHOOD BEING TORMENTED, YOU BUILD UP A PRETTY THICK SKIN!
LATER
WAAH!
Hotel San Diego
HOTEL SAN

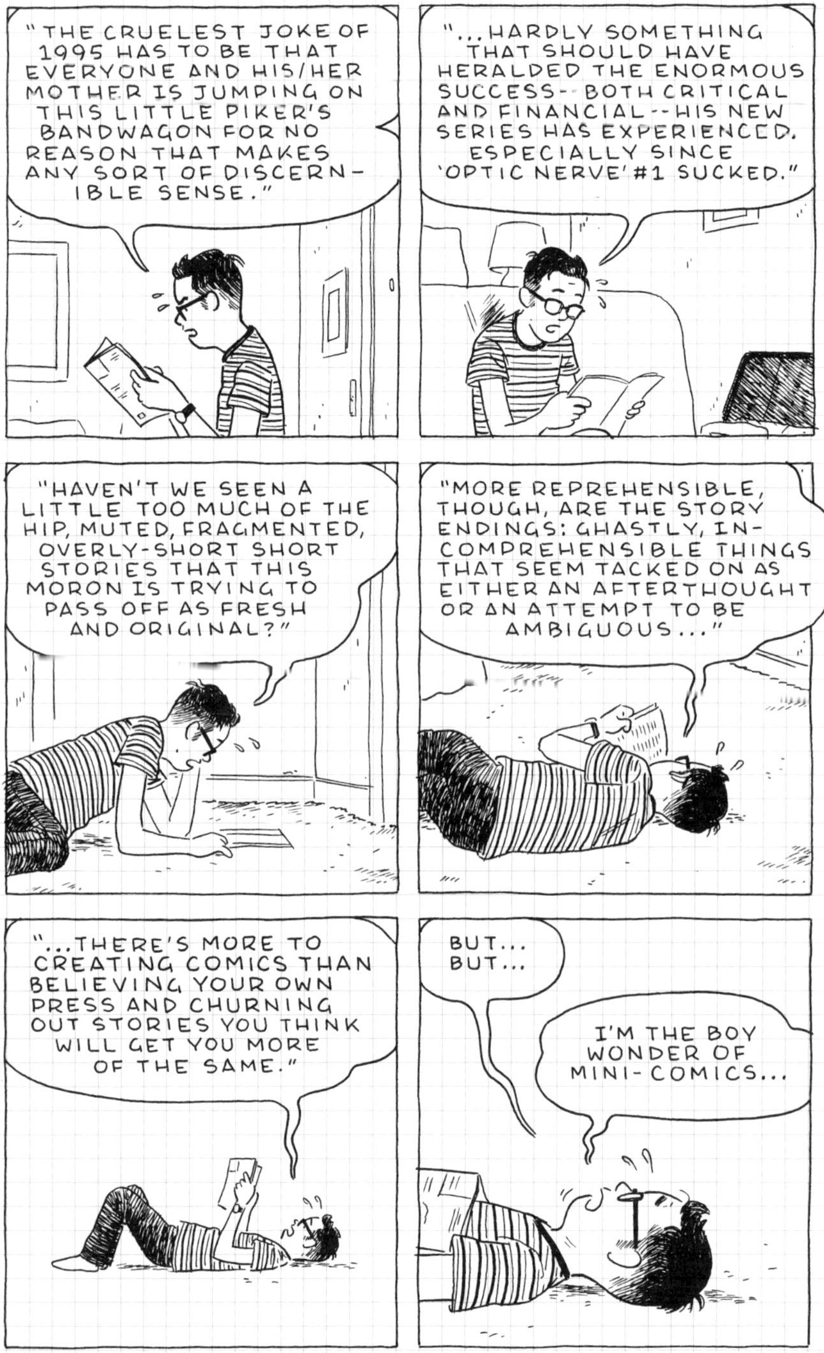
"THE CRUELEST JOKE OF 1995 HAS TO BE THAT EVERYONE AND HIS/HER MOTHER IS JUMPING ON THIS LITTLE PIKER'S BANDWAGON FOR NO REASON THAT MAKES ANY SORT OF DISCERN-IBLE SENSE."
"...HARDLY SOMETHING THAT SHOULD HAVE HERALDED THE ENORMOUS SUCCESS--BOTH CRITICAL AND FINANCIAL--HIS NEW SERIES HAS EXPERIENCED. ESPECIALLY SINCE 'OPTIC NERVE' #1 SUCKED."
"HAVEN'T WE SEEN A LITTLE TOO MUCH OF THE HIP, MUTED, FRAGMENTED, OVERLY-SHORT SHORT STORIES THAT THIS MORON IS TRYING TO PASS OFF AS FRESH AND ORIGINAL?"
"MORE REPREHENSIBLE, THOUGH, ARE THE STORY ENDINGS: GHASTLY, IN-COMPREHENSIBLE THINGS THAT SEEM TACKED ON AS EITHER AN AFTERTHOUGHT OR AN ATTEMPT TO BE AMBIGUOUS..."
"...THERE'S MORE TO CREATING COMICS THAN BELIEVING YOUR OWN PRESS AND CHURNING OUT STORIES YOU THINK WILL GET YOU MORE OF THE SAME."
BUT... BUT...
I'M THE BOY WONDER OF MINI-COMICS...

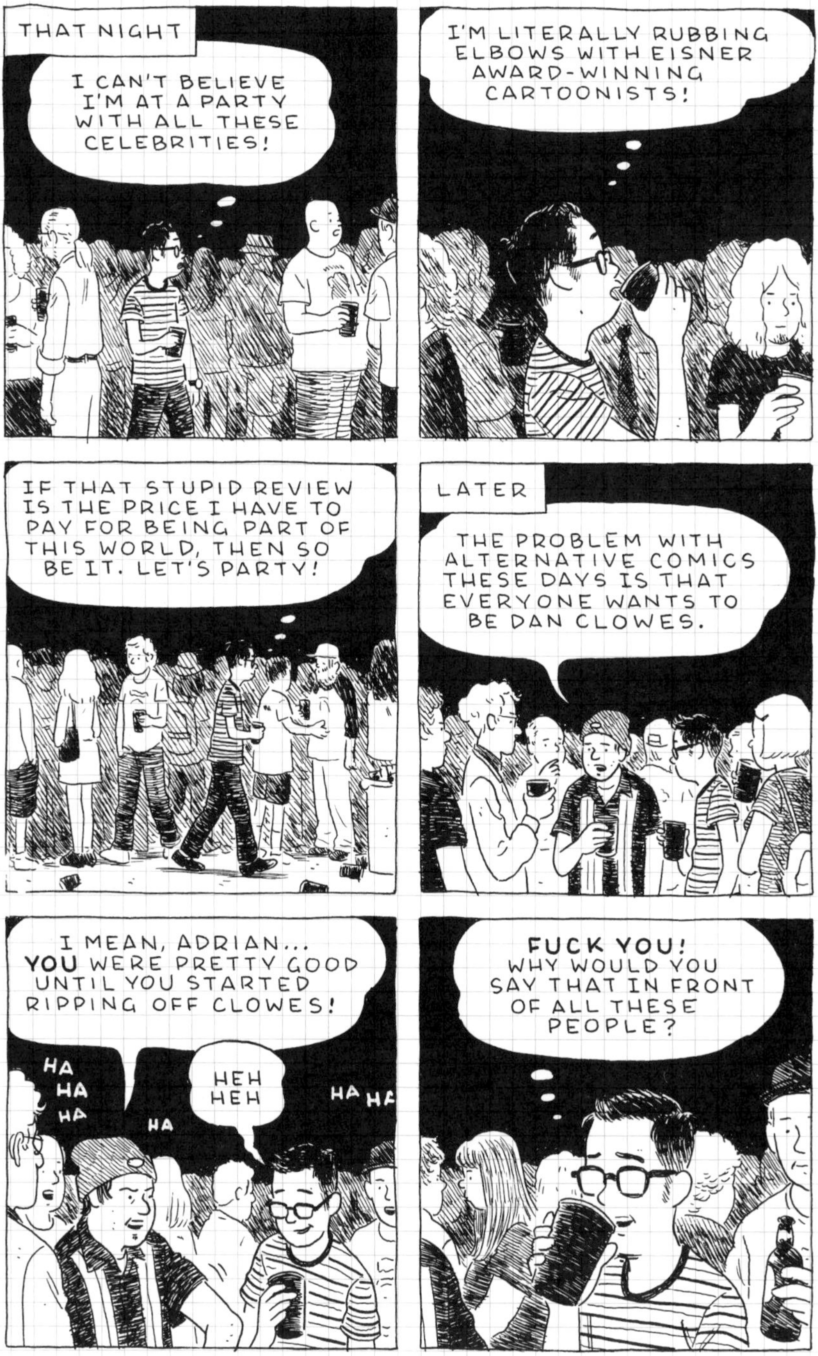
THAT NIGHT
I CAN'T BELIEVE I'M AT A PARTY WITH ALL THESE CELEBRITIES!
I'M LITERALLY RUBBING ELBOWS WITH EISNER AWARD-WINNING CARTOONISTS!
IF THAT STUPID REVIEW IS THE PRICE I HAVE TO PAY FOR BEING PART OF THIS WORLD, THEN SO BE IT. LET'S PARTY!
LATER
THE PROBLEM WITH ALTERNATIVE COMICS THESE DAYS IS THAT EVERYONE WANTS TO BE DAN CLOWES.
I MEAN, ADRIAN... **YOU** WERE PRETTY GOOD UNTIL YOU STARTED RIPPING OFF CLOWES!
HA HA HA
HA
HEH HEH
HA HA
FUCK YOU! WHY WOULD YOU SAY THAT IN FRONT OF ALL THESE PEOPLE?

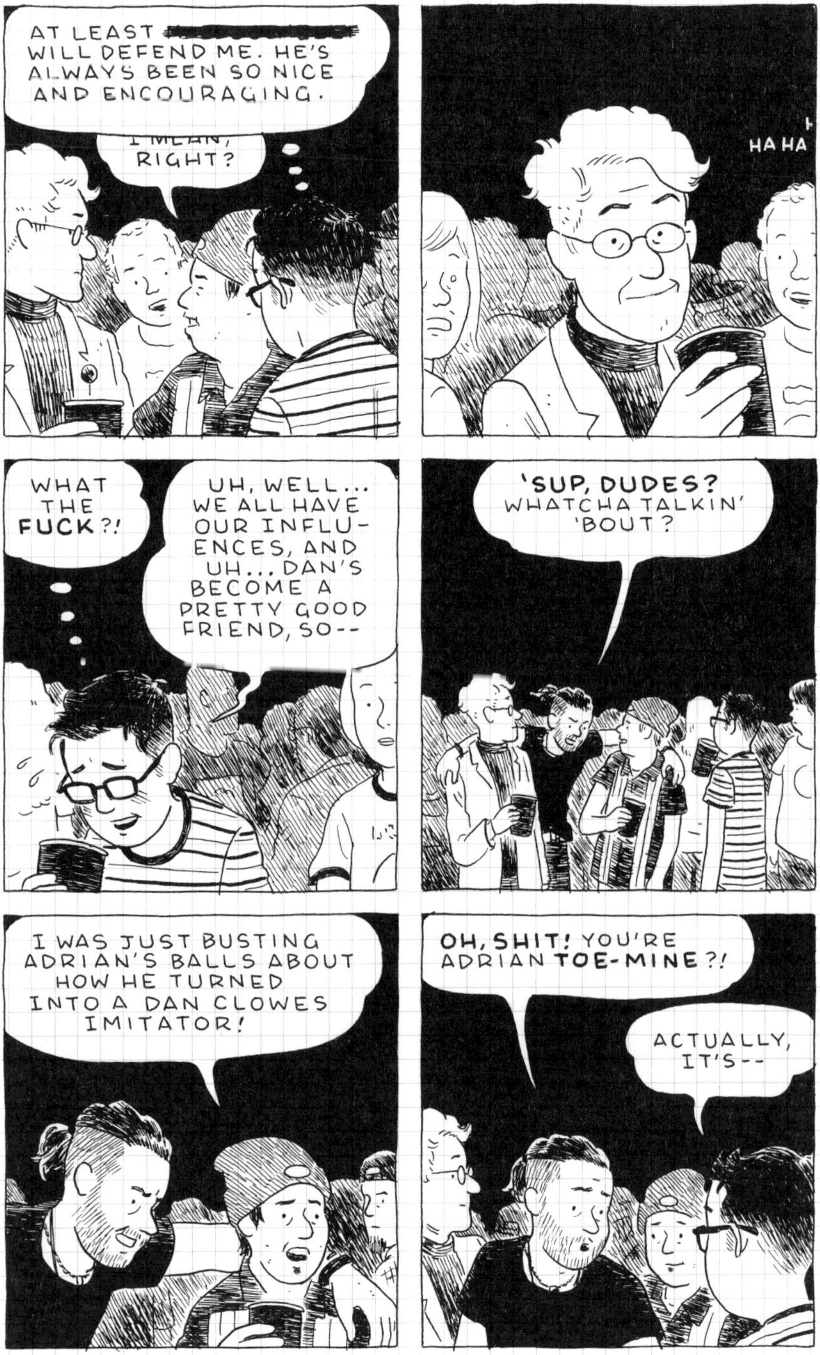
AT LEAST [redacted] WILL DEFEND ME. HE'S ALWAYS BEEN SO NICE AND ENCOURAGING.
I MEAN, RIGHT?
HA HA
WHAT THE **FUCK**?!
UH, WELL... WE ALL HAVE OUR INFLU-ENCES, AND UH... DAN'S BECOME A PRETTY GOOD FRIEND, SO--
'SUP, DUDES? WHATCHA TALKIN' 'BOUT?
I WAS JUST BUSTING ADRIAN'S BALLS ABOUT HOW HE TURNED INTO A DAN CLOWES IMITATOR!
OH, SHIT! YOU'RE ADRIAN **TOE-MINE**?!
ACTUALLY, IT'S--

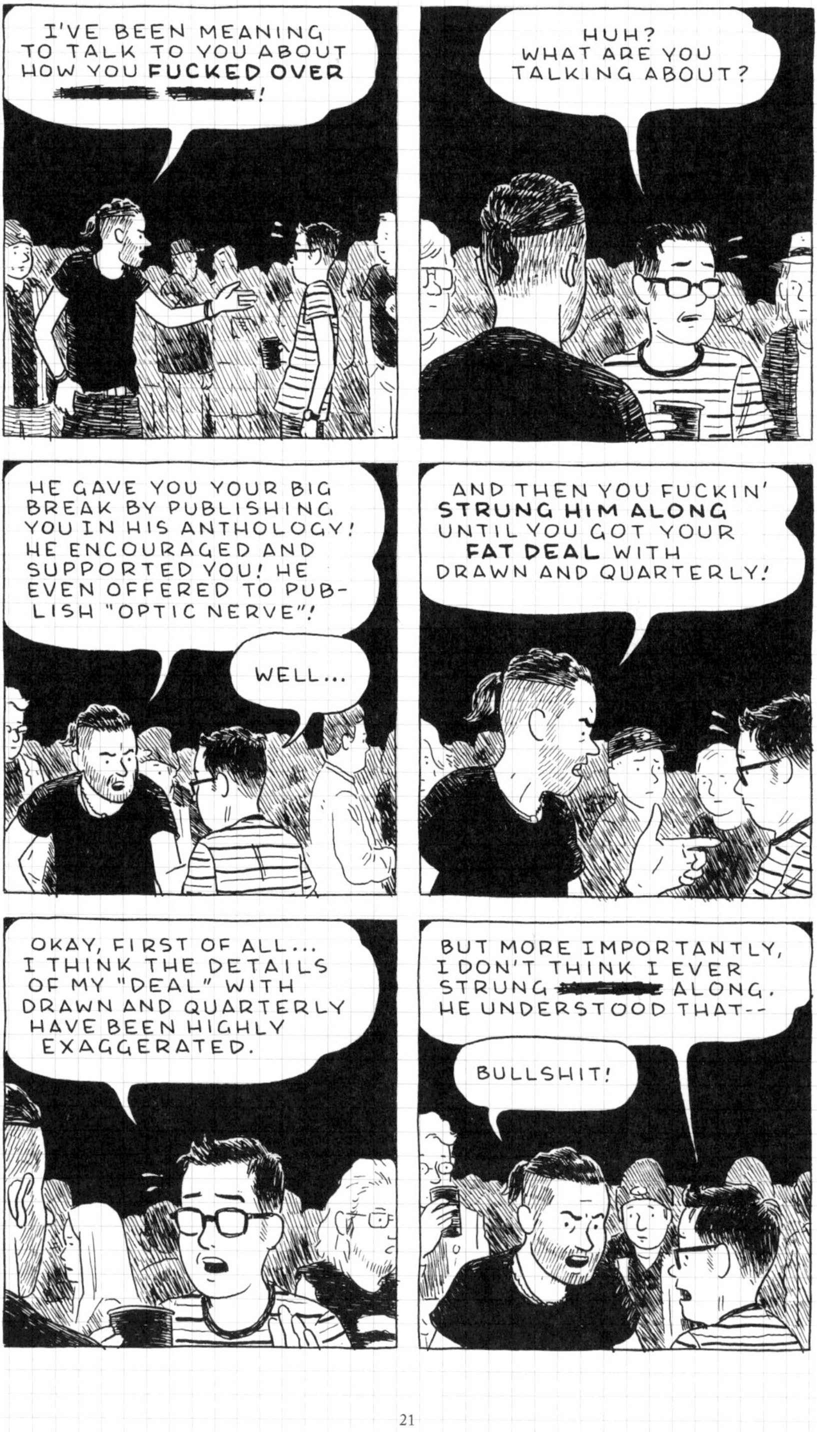
I'VE BEEN MEANING TO TALK TO YOU ABOUT HOW YOU FUCKED OVER [redacted]!
HUH? WHAT ARE YOU TALKING ABOUT?
HE GAVE YOU YOUR BIG BREAK BY PUBLISHING YOU IN HIS ANTHOLOGY! HE ENCOURAGED AND SUPPORTED YOU! HE EVEN OFFERED TO PUB-LISH "OPTIC NERVE"!
WELL...
AND THEN YOU FUCKIN' STRUNG HIM ALONG UNTIL YOU GOT YOUR FAT DEAL WITH DRAWN AND QUARTERLY!
OKAY, FIRST OF ALL... I THINK THE DETAILS OF MY "DEAL" WITH DRAWN AND QUARTERLY HAVE BEEN HIGHLY EXAGGERATED.
BUT MORE IMPORTANTLY, I DON'T THINK I EVER STRUNG [redacted] ALONG. HE UNDERSTOOD THAT--
BULLSHIT!

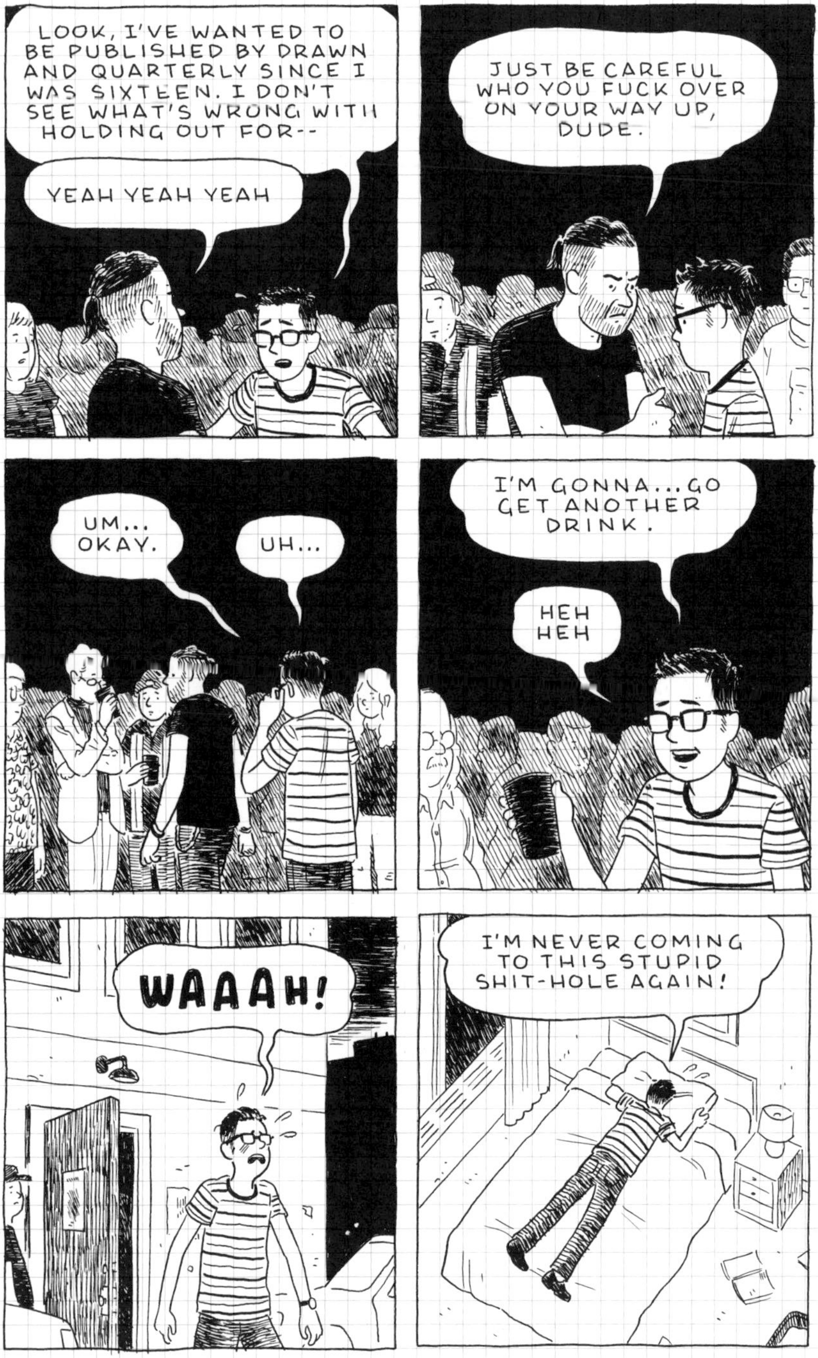
LOOK, I'VE WANTED TO BE PUBLISHED BY DRAWN AND QUARTERLY SINCE I WAS SIXTEEN. I DON'T SEE WHAT'S WRONG WITH HOLDING OUT FOR--
YEAH YEAH YEAH
JUST BE CAREFUL WHO YOU FUCK OVER ON YOUR WAY UP, DUDE.
UM... OKAY.
UH...
I'M GONNA... GO GET ANOTHER DRINK.
HEH HEH
WAAAH!
I'M NEVER COMING TO THIS STUPID SHIT-HOLE AGAIN!

SAN DIEGO, 1996

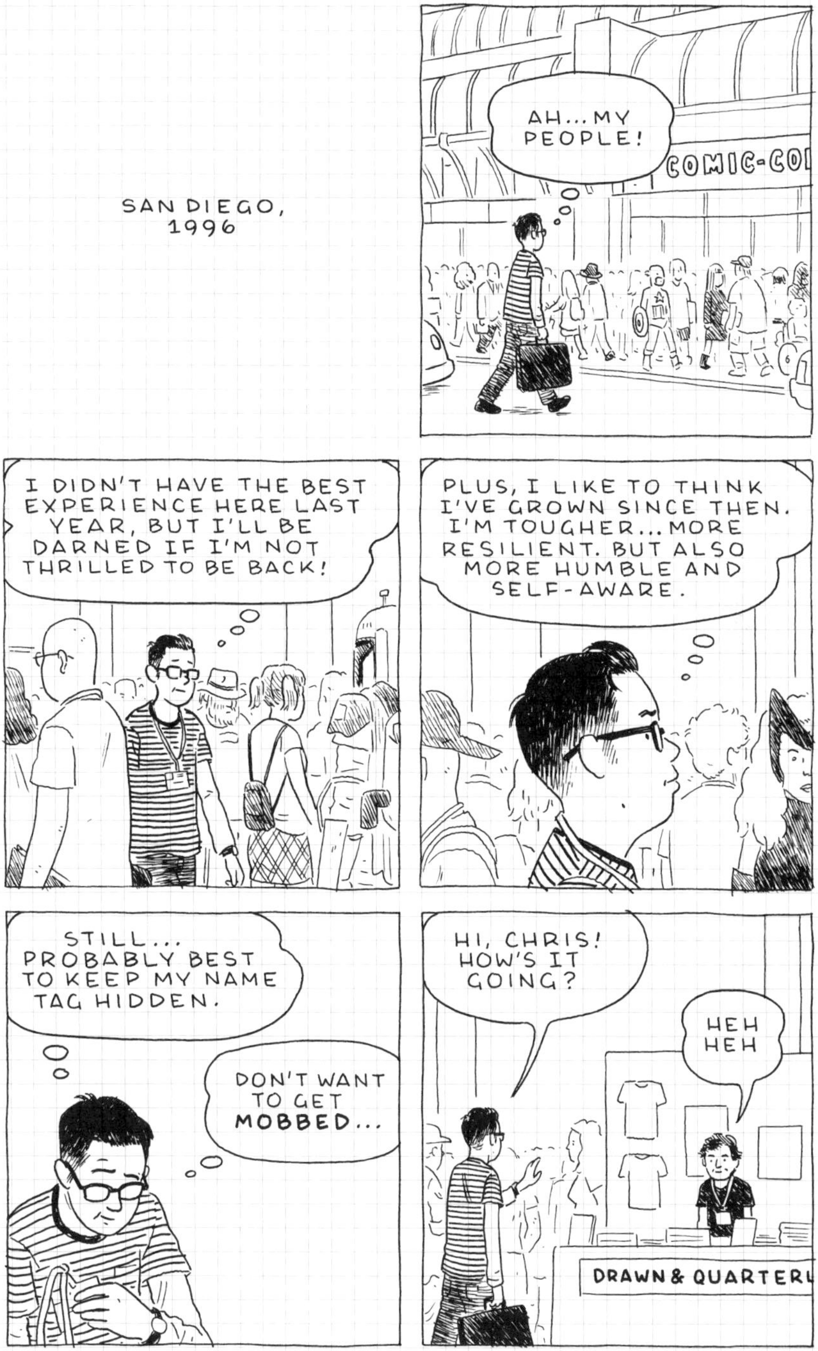
AH... MY PEOPLE!
COMIC-CO
I DIDN'T HAVE THE BEST EXPERIENCE HERE LAST YEAR, BUT I'LL BE DARNED IF I'M NOT THRILLED TO BE BACK!
PLUS, I LIKE TO THINK I'VE GROWN SINCE THEN. I'M TOUGHER... MORE RESILIENT. BUT ALSO MORE HUMBLE AND SELF-AWARE.
STILL... PROBABLY BEST TO KEEP MY NAME TAG HIDDEN.
DON'T WANT TO GET **MOBBED**...
HI, CHRIS! HOW'S IT GOING?
HEH HEH
DRAWN & QUARTERL

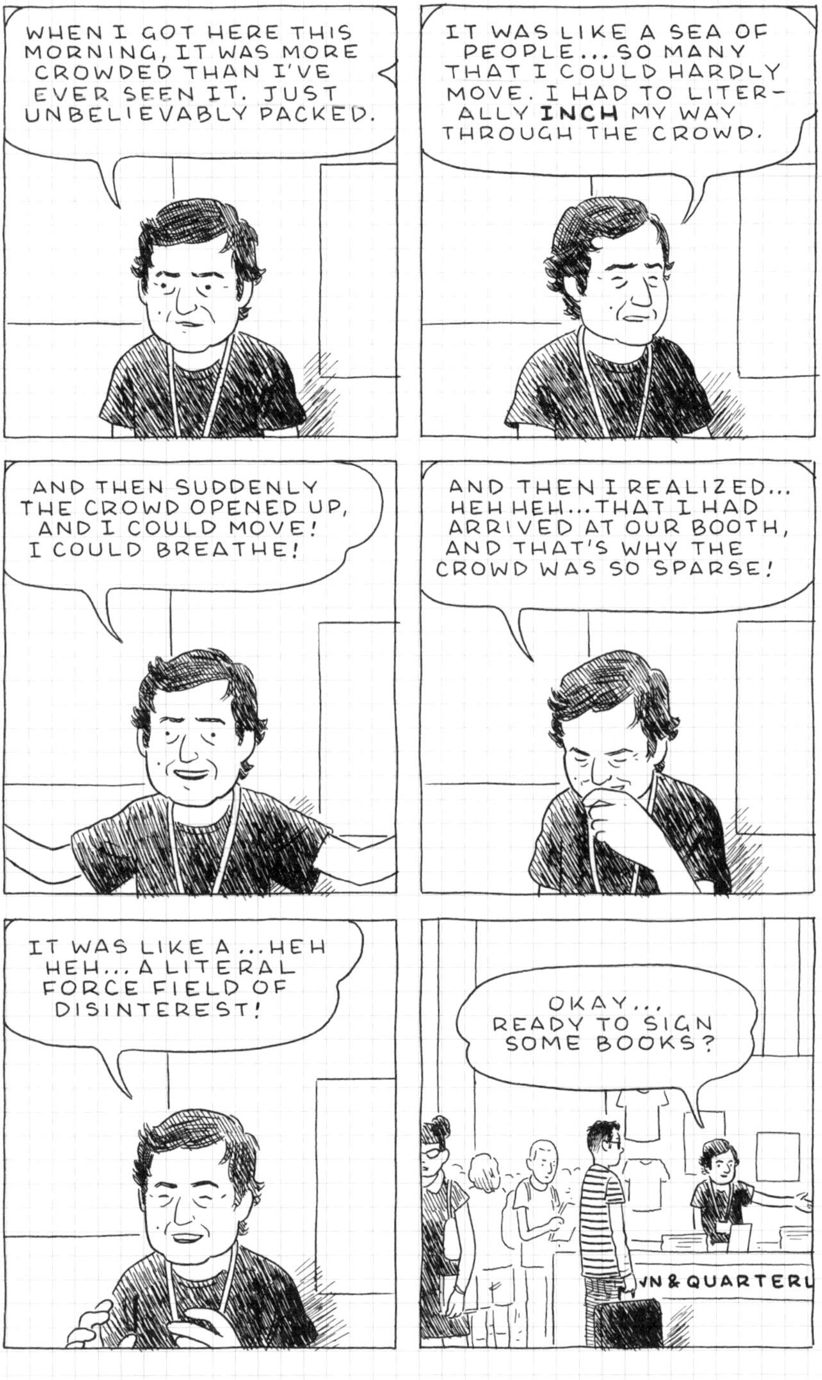
WHEN I GOT HERE THIS MORNING, IT WAS MORE CROWDED THAN I'VE EVER SEEN IT. JUST UNBELIEVABLY PACKED.
IT WAS LIKE A SEA OF PEOPLE... SO MANY THAT I COULD HARDLY MOVE. I HAD TO LITER-ALLY **INCH** MY WAY THROUGH THE CROWD.
AND THEN SUDDENLY THE CROWD OPENED UP, AND I COULD MOVE! I COULD BREATHE!
AND THEN I REALIZED... HEH HEH... THAT I HAD ARRIVED AT OUR BOOTH, AND THAT'S WHY THE CROWD WAS SO SPARSE!
IT WAS LIKE A... HEH HEH... A LITERAL FORCE FIELD OF DISINTEREST!
OKAY... READY TO SIGN SOME BOOKS?
WN & QUARTERL

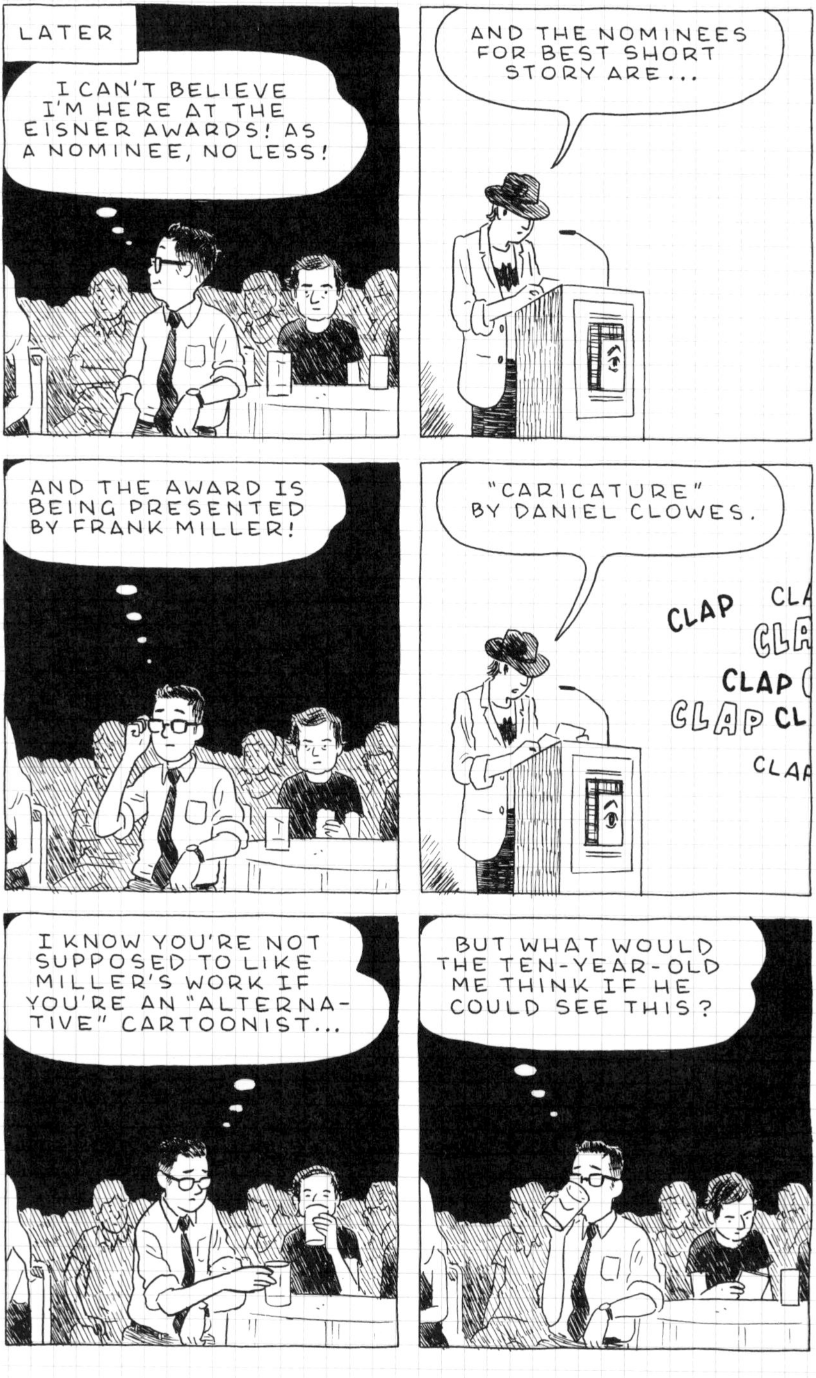
LATER
I CAN'T BELIEVE I'M HERE AT THE EISNER AWARDS! AS A NOMINEE, NO LESS!
AND THE NOMINEES FOR BEST SHORT STORY ARE...
AND THE AWARD IS BEING PRESENTED BY FRANK MILLER!
"CARICATURE" BY DANIEL CLOWES.
CLAP
CLAP
CLAP
CLAP
I KNOW YOU'RE NOT SUPPOSED TO LIKE MILLER'S WORK IF YOU'RE AN "ALTERNA-TIVE" CARTOONIST...
BUT WHAT WOULD THE TEN-YEAR-OLD ME THINK IF HE COULD SEE THIS?

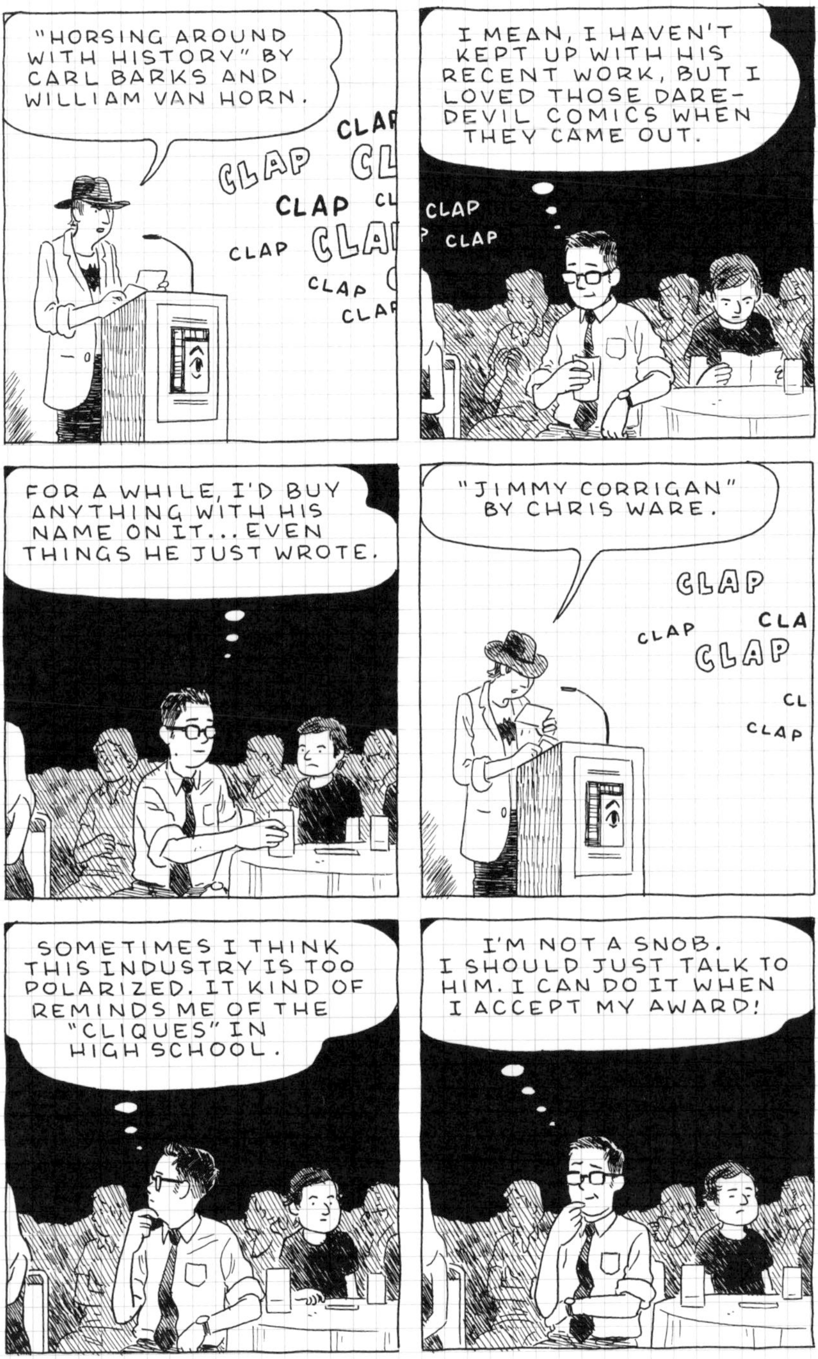
"HORSING AROUND WITH HISTORY" BY CARL BARKS AND WILLIAM VAN HORN.
CLAP CLAP CLAP CLAP CLAP
I MEAN, I HAVEN'T KEPT UP WITH HIS RECENT WORK, BUT I LOVED THOSE DARE-DEVIL COMICS WHEN THEY CAME OUT.
CLAP CLAP
FOR A WHILE, I'D BUY ANYTHING WITH HIS NAME ON IT... EVEN THINGS HE JUST WROTE.
"JIMMY CORRIGAN" BY CHRIS WARE.
CLAP CLAP CLA CLAP CL CLAP
SOMETIMES I THINK THIS INDUSTRY IS TOO POLARIZED. IT KIND OF REMINDS ME OF THE "CLIQUES" IN HIGH SCHOOL.
I'M NOT A SNOB. I SHOULD JUST TALK TO HIM. I CAN DO IT WHEN I ACCEPT MY AWARD!

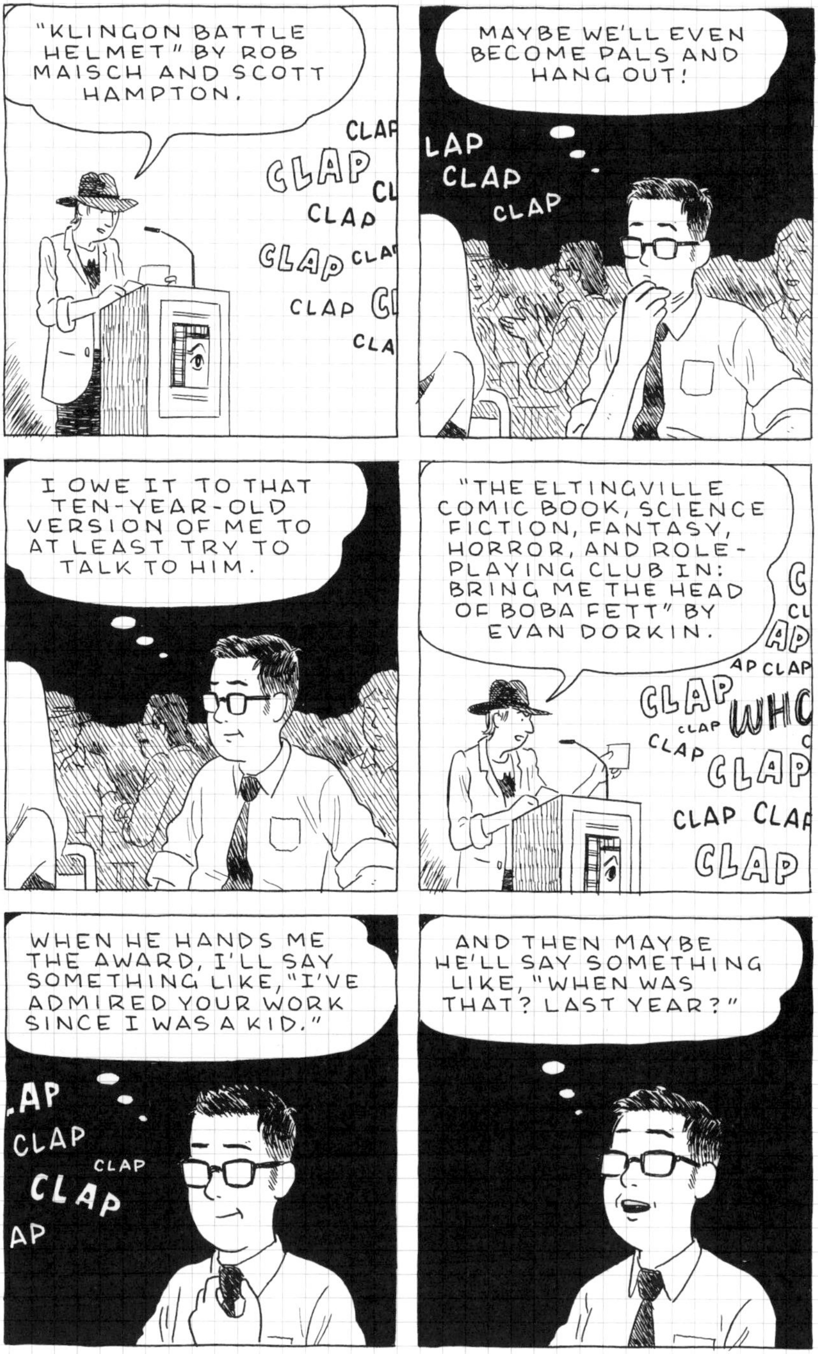
"KLINGON BATTLE HELMET" BY ROB MAISCH AND SCOTT HAMPTON.
CLAP CLAP CL CLAP CLAP CLAP CLAP CL CLA
MAYBE WE'LL EVEN BECOME PALS AND HANG OUT!
LAP CLAP CLAP
I OWE IT TO THAT TEN-YEAR-OLD VERSION OF ME TO AT LEAST TRY TO TALK TO HIM.
"THE ELTINGVILLE COMIC BOOK, SCIENCE FICTION, FANTASY, HORROR, AND ROLE-PLAYING CLUB IN: BRING ME THE HEAD OF BOBA FETT" BY EVAN DORKIN.
AP CLAP CLAP CLAP CLAP CLAP CLAP CLAP CLAP
WHEN HE HANDS ME THE AWARD, I'LL SAY SOMETHING LIKE, "I'VE ADMIRED YOUR WORK SINCE I WAS A KID."
AP CLAP CLAP CLAP AP
AND THEN MAYBE HE'LL SAY SOMETHING LIKE, "WHEN WAS THAT? LAST YEAR?"

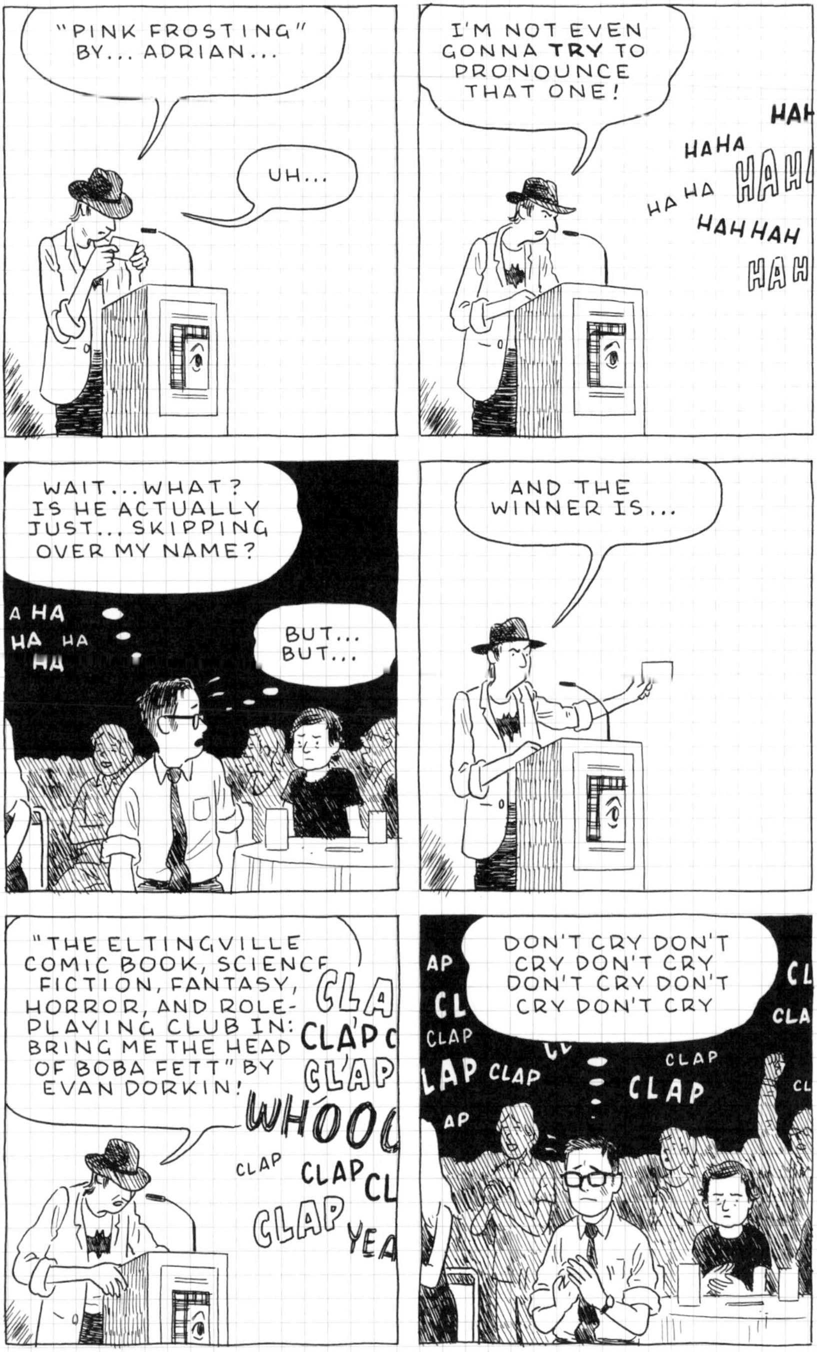
"PINK FROSTING" BY... ADRIAN...
UH...
I'M NOT EVEN GONNA TRY TO PRONOUNCE THAT ONE!
HAHA HA HA HAH HAH HAH HAH HAH
WAIT... WHAT? IS HE ACTUALLY JUST... SKIPPING OVER MY NAME?
A HA HA HA HA
BUT... BUT...
AND THE WINNER IS...
"THE ELTINGVILLE COMIC BOOK, SCIENCE FICTION, FANTASY, HORROR, AND ROLE-PLAYING CLUB IN: BRING ME THE HEAD OF BOBA FETT" BY EVAN DORKIN!
CLAP CLAP CLAP CLAP CLAP CLAP
DON'T CRY DON'T CRY DON'T CRY DON'T CRY DON'T CRY DON'T CRY DON'T CRY
CLAP CLAP CLAP CLAP CLAP

BERKELEY,
1996

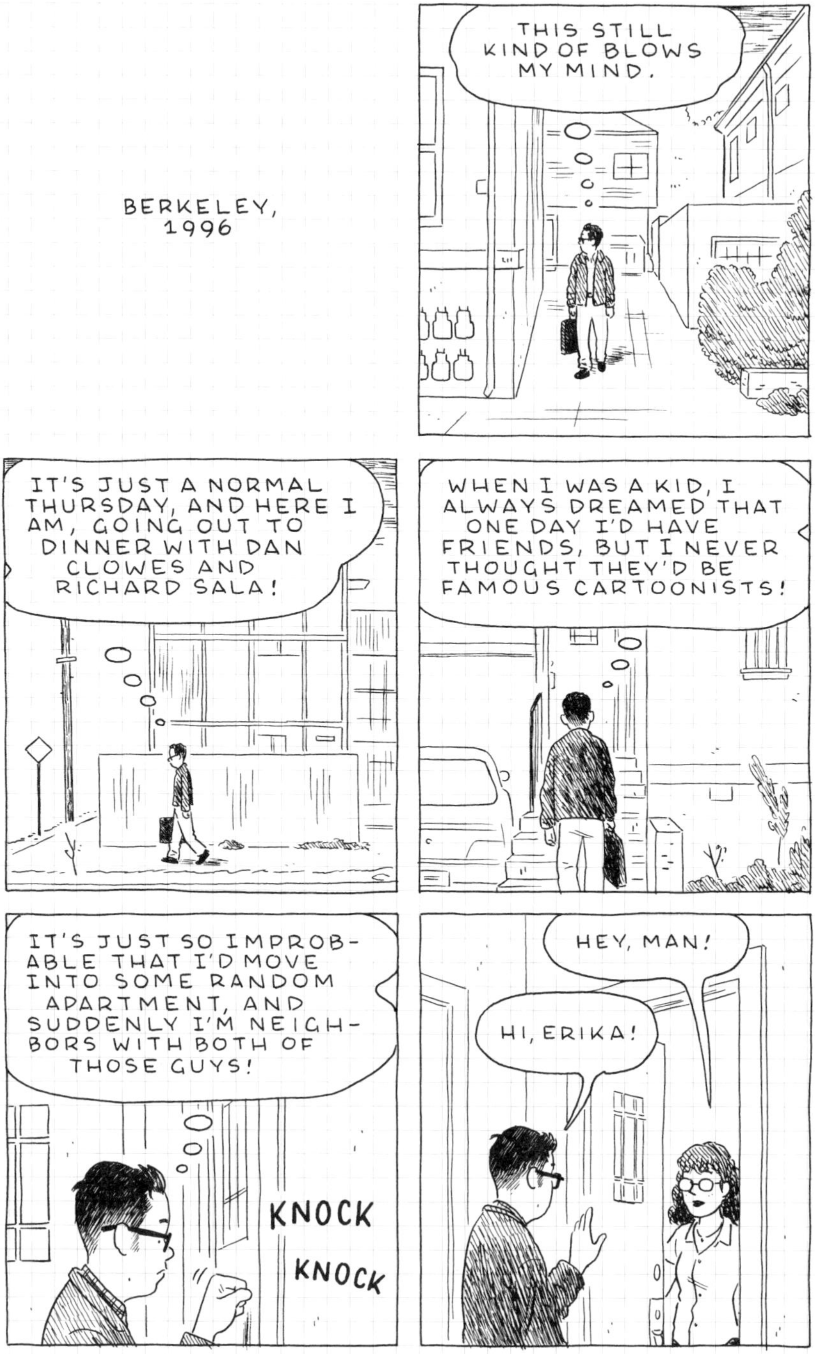
THIS STILL KIND OF BLOWS MY MIND.
IT'S JUST A NORMAL THURSDAY, AND HERE I AM, GOING OUT TO DINNER WITH DAN CLOWES AND RICHARD SALA!
WHEN I WAS A KID, I ALWAYS DREAMED THAT ONE DAY I'D HAVE FRIENDS, BUT I NEVER THOUGHT THEY'D BE FAMOUS CARTOONISTS!
IT'S JUST SO IMPROB-ABLE THAT I'D MOVE INTO SOME RANDOM APARTMENT, AND SUDDENLY I'M NEIGH-BORS WITH BOTH OF THOSE GUYS!
KNOCK
KNOCK
HEY, MAN!
HI, ERIKA!

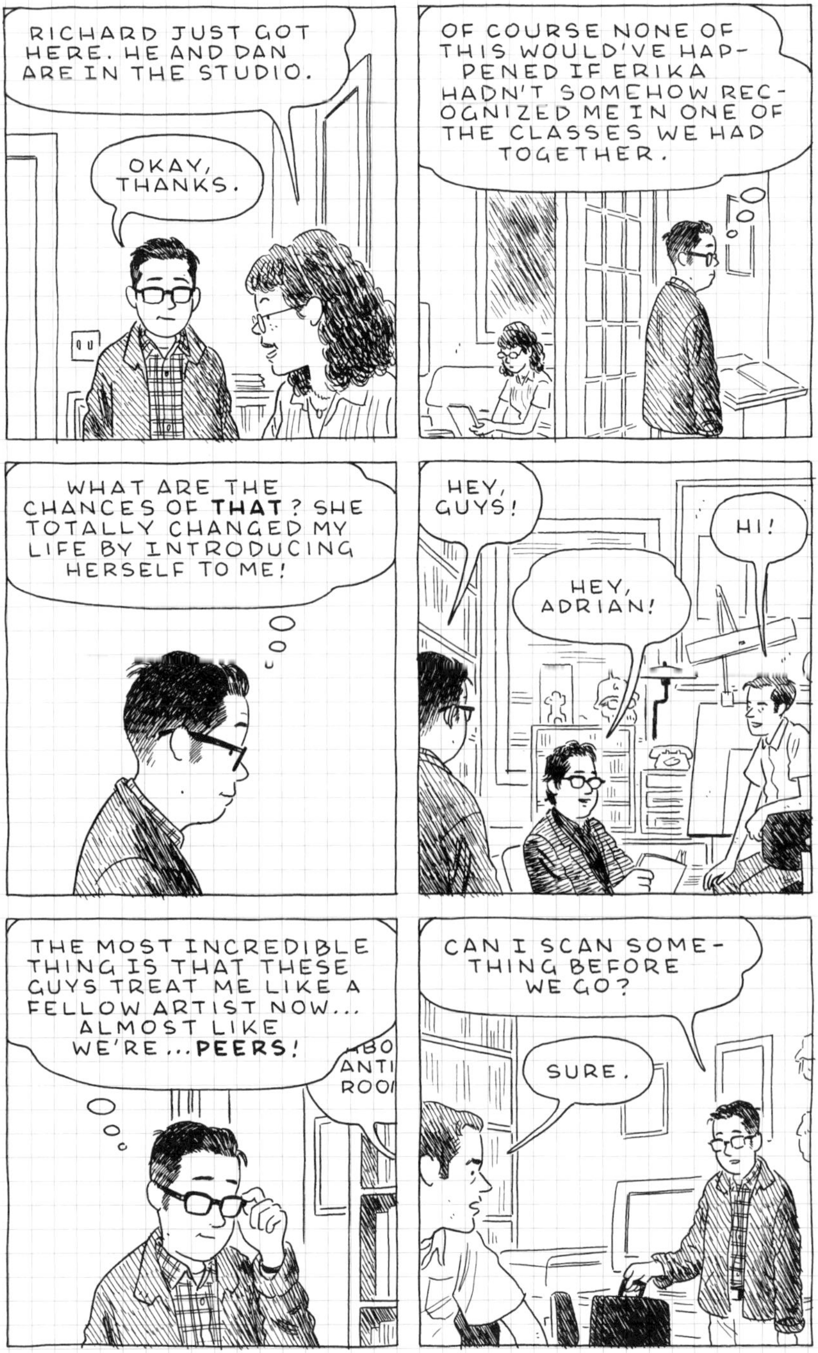
RICHARD JUST GOT HERE. HE AND DAN ARE IN THE STUDIO.
OKAY, THANKS.
OF COURSE NONE OF THIS WOULD'VE HAPPENED IF ERIKA HADN'T SOMEHOW RECOGNIZED ME IN ONE OF THE CLASSES WE HAD TOGETHER.
WHAT ARE THE CHANCES OF **THAT**? SHE TOTALLY CHANGED MY LIFE BY INTRODUCING HERSELF TO ME!
HEY, GUYS!
HI!
HEY, ADRIAN!
THE MOST INCREDIBLE THING IS THAT THESE GUYS TREAT ME LIKE A FELLOW ARTIST NOW... ALMOST LIKE WE'RE... **PEERS**!
CAN I SCAN SOMETHING BEFORE WE GO?
SURE.

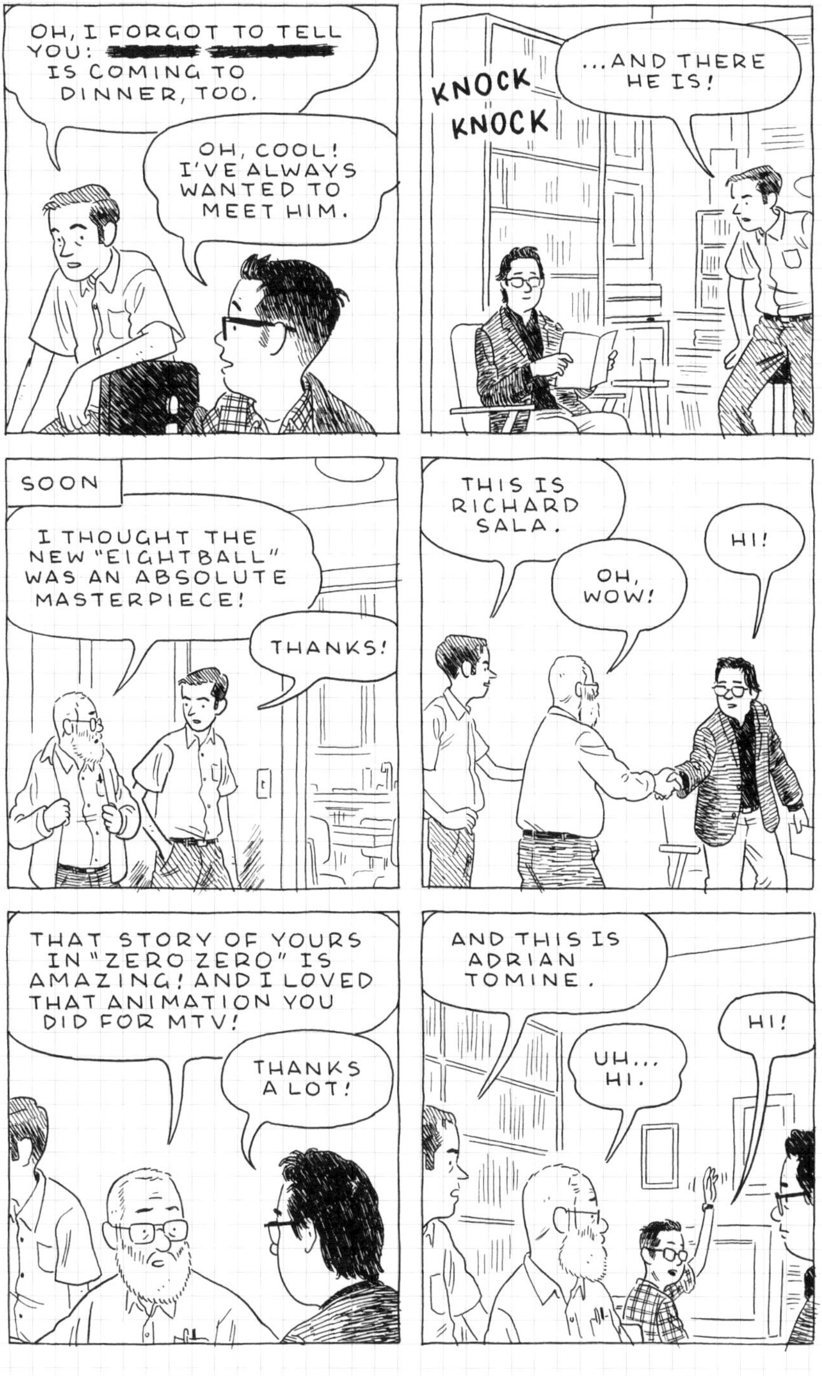
OH, I FORGOT TO TELL YOU: [redacted] IS COMING TO DINNER, TOO.
OH, COOL! I'VE ALWAYS WANTED TO MEET HIM.
KNOCK KNOCK
...AND THERE HE IS!
SOON
I THOUGHT THE NEW "EIGHTBALL" WAS AN ABSOLUTE MASTERPIECE!
THANKS!
THIS IS RICHARD SALA.
OH, WOW!
HI!
THAT STORY OF YOURS IN "ZERO ZERO" IS AMAZING! AND I LOVED THAT ANIMATION YOU DID FOR MTV!
THANKS A LOT!
AND THIS IS ADRIAN TOMINE.
UH... HI.
HI!

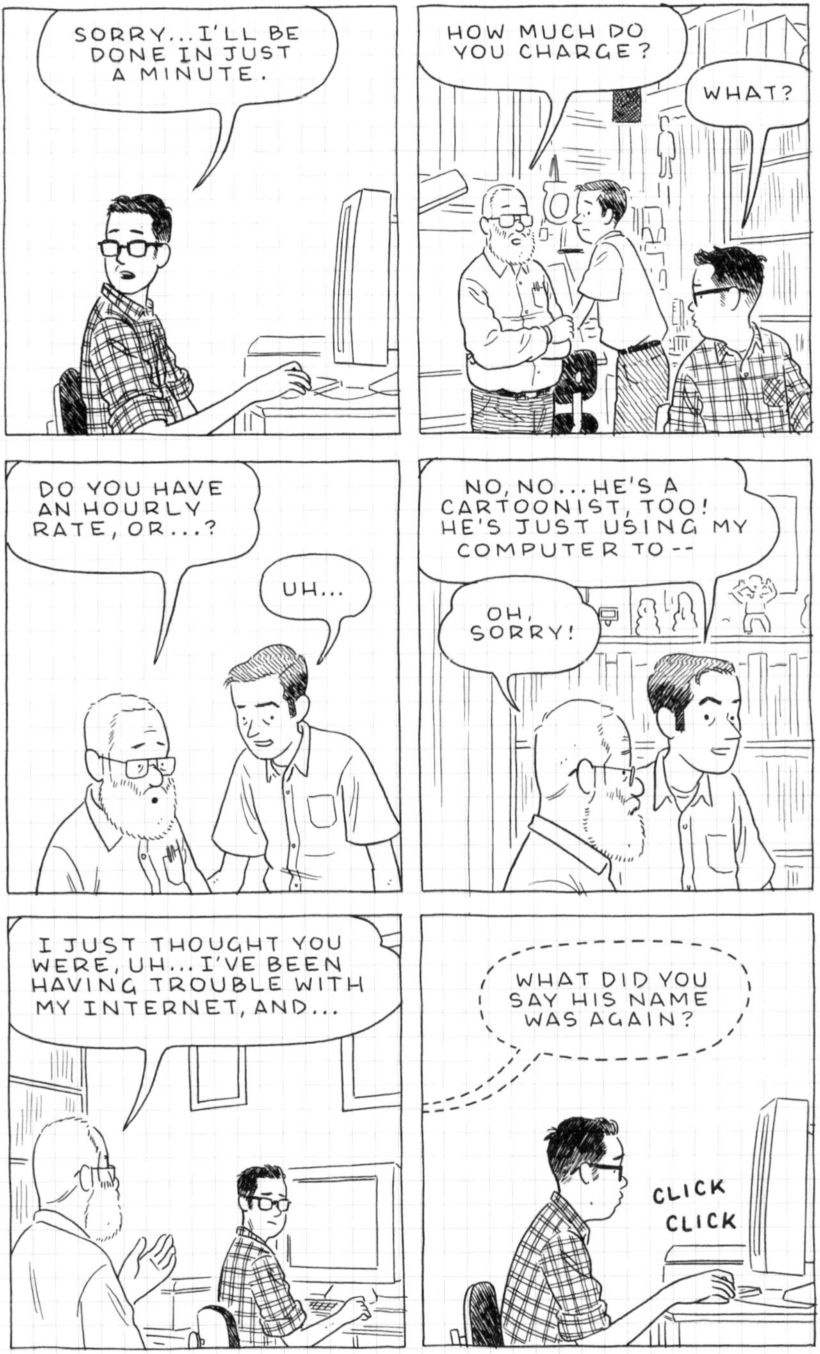
SORRY... I'LL BE DONE IN JUST A MINUTE.
HOW MUCH DO YOU CHARGE?
WHAT?
DO YOU HAVE AN HOURLY RATE, OR...?
UH...
NO, NO... HE'S A CARTOONIST, TOO! HE'S JUST USING MY COMPUTER TO--
OH, SORRY!
I JUST THOUGHT YOU WERE, UH... I'VE BEEN HAVING TROUBLE WITH MY INTERNET, AND...
WHAT DID YOU SAY HIS NAME WAS AGAIN?
CLICK
CLICK

ALBANY,
1997

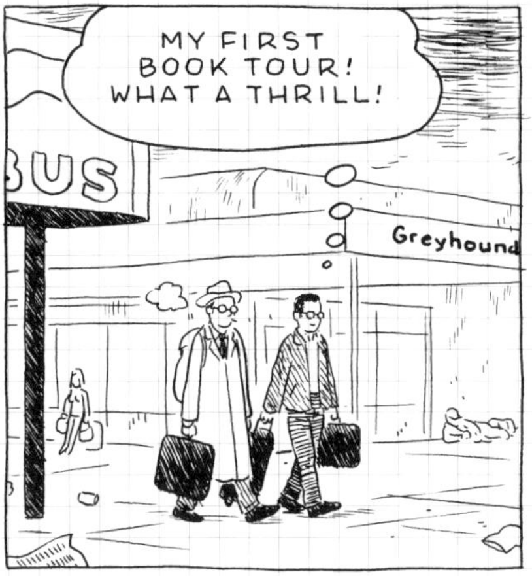
MY FIRST BOOK TOUR! WHAT A THRILL!
BUS
Greyhound

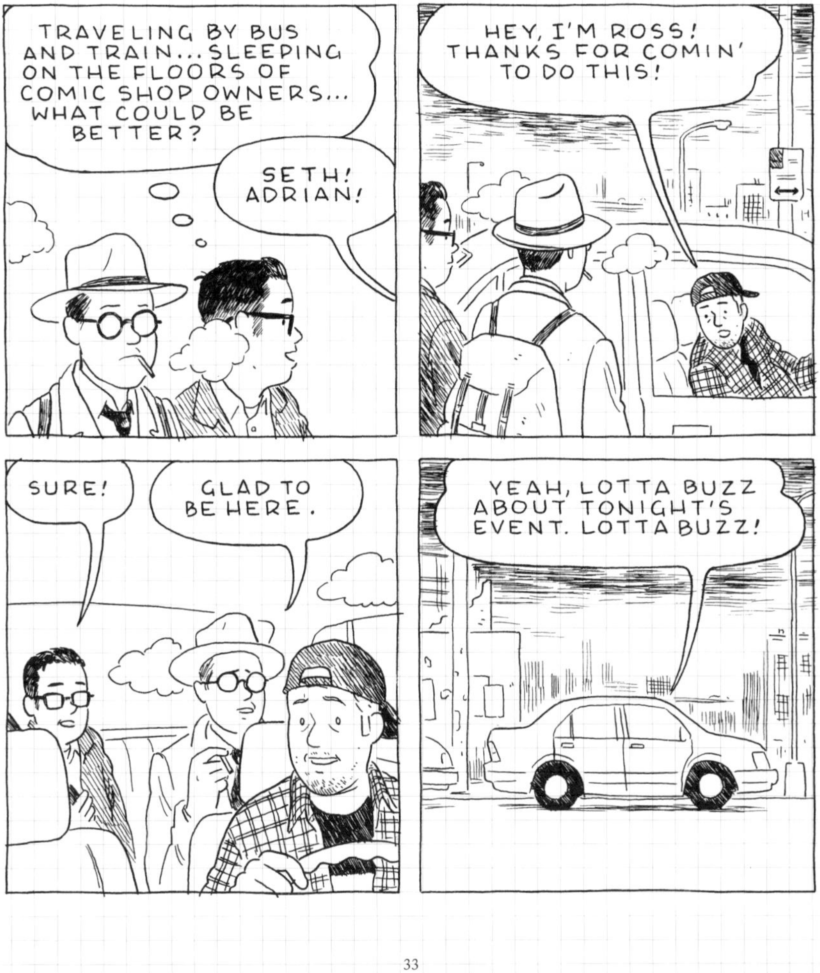
TRAVELING BY BUS AND TRAIN... SLEEPING ON THE FLOORS OF COMIC SHOP OWNERS... WHAT COULD BE BETTER?
SETH! ADRIAN!
HEY, I'M ROSS! THANKS FOR COMIN' TO DO THIS!
SURE!
GLAD TO BE HERE.
YEAH, LOTTA BUZZ ABOUT TONIGHT'S EVENT. LOTTA BUZZ!

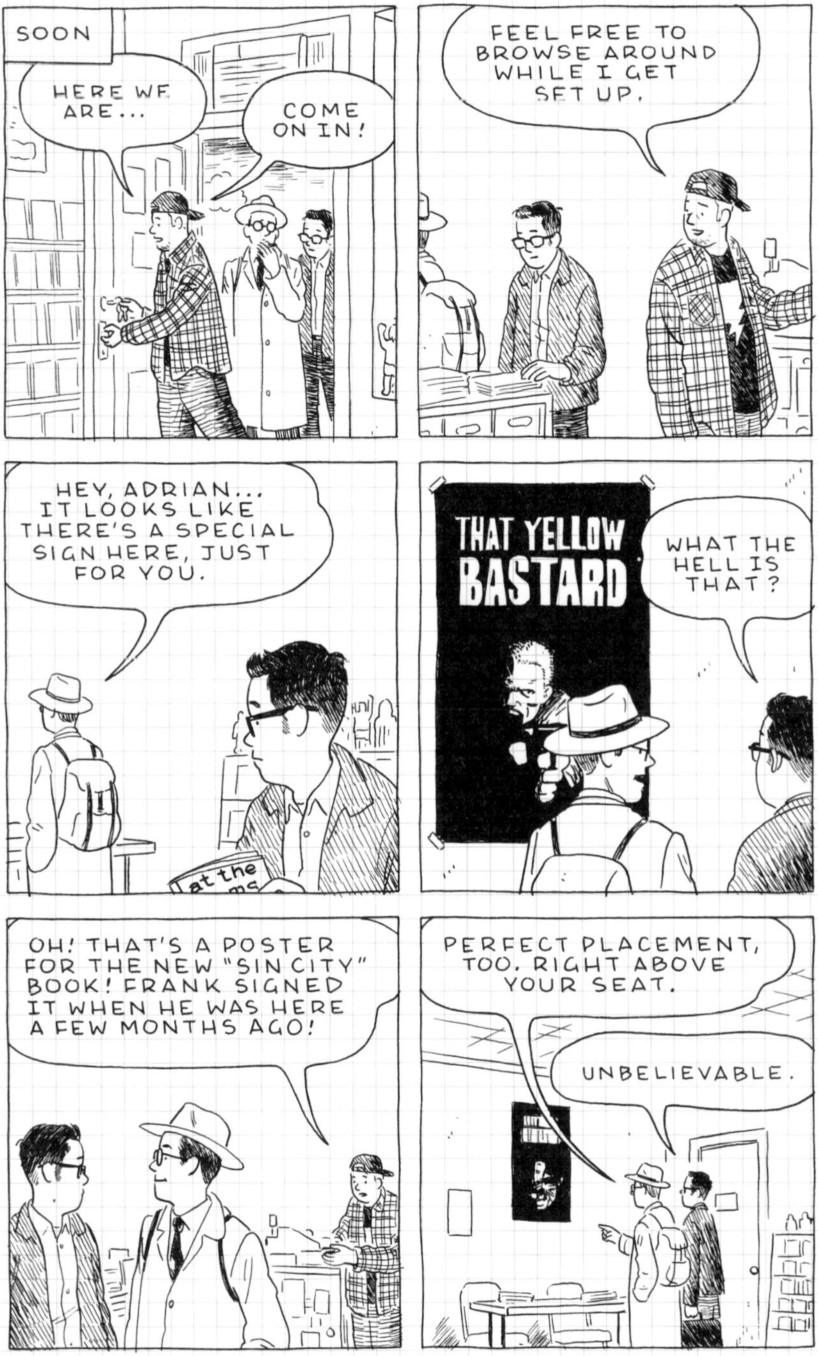
SOON
HERE WE ARE...
COME ON IN!
FEEL FREE TO BROWSE AROUND WHILE I GET SET UP.
HEY, ADRIAN... IT LOOKS LIKE THERE'S A SPECIAL SIGN HERE, JUST FOR YOU.
at the
THAT YELLOW BASTARD
WHAT THE HELL IS THAT?
OH! THAT'S A POSTER FOR THE NEW "SIN CITY" BOOK! FRANK SIGNED IT WHEN HE WAS HERE A FEW MONTHS AGO!
PERFECT PLACEMENT, TOO. RIGHT ABOVE YOUR SEAT.
UNBELIEVABLE.

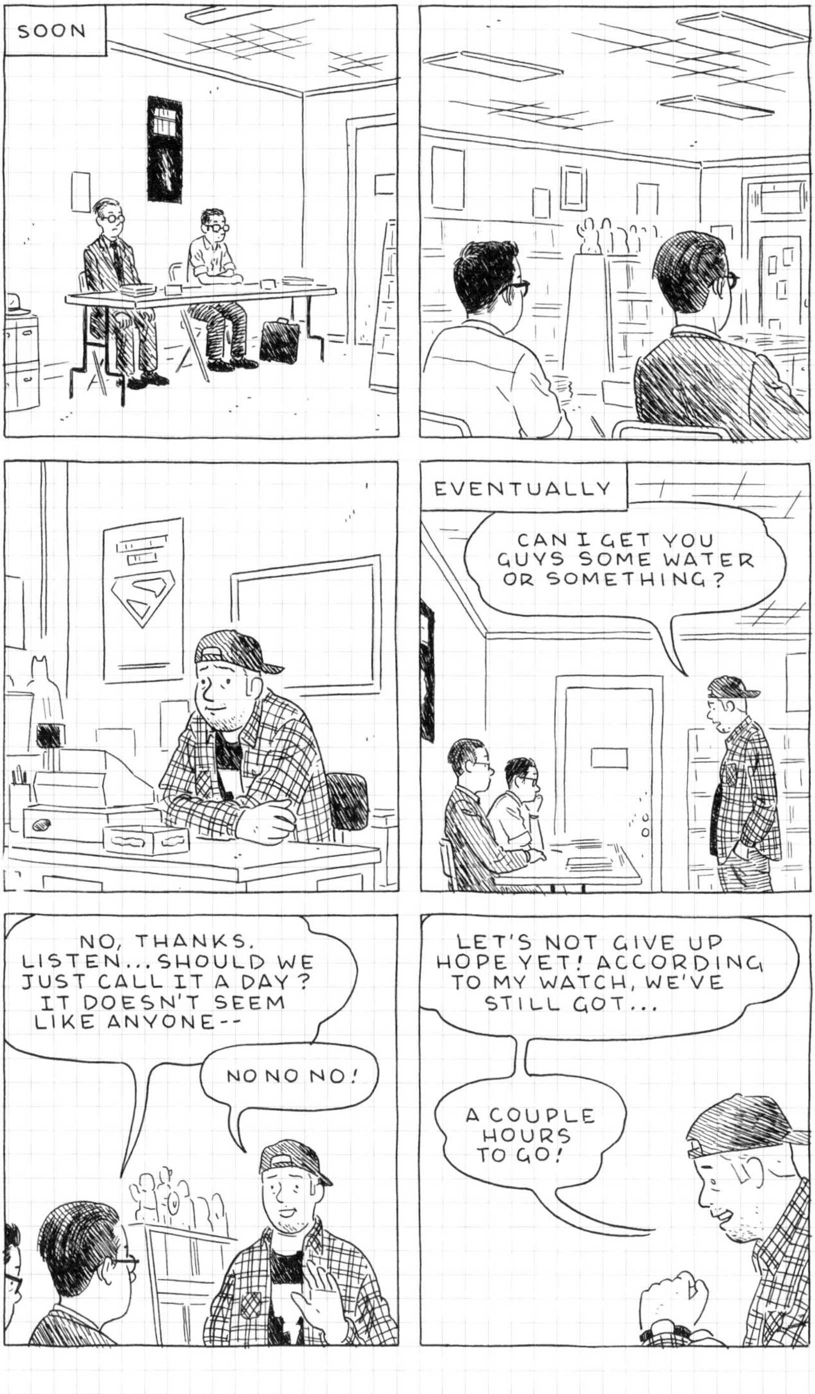
SOON
EVENTUALLY
CAN I GET YOU GUYS SOME WATER OR SOMETHING?
NO, THANKS. LISTEN... SHOULD WE JUST CALL IT A DAY? IT DOESN'T SEEM LIKE ANYONE--
NO NO NO!
LET'S NOT GIVE UP HOPE YET! ACCORDING TO MY WATCH, WE'VE STILL GOT...
A COUPLE HOURS TO GO!

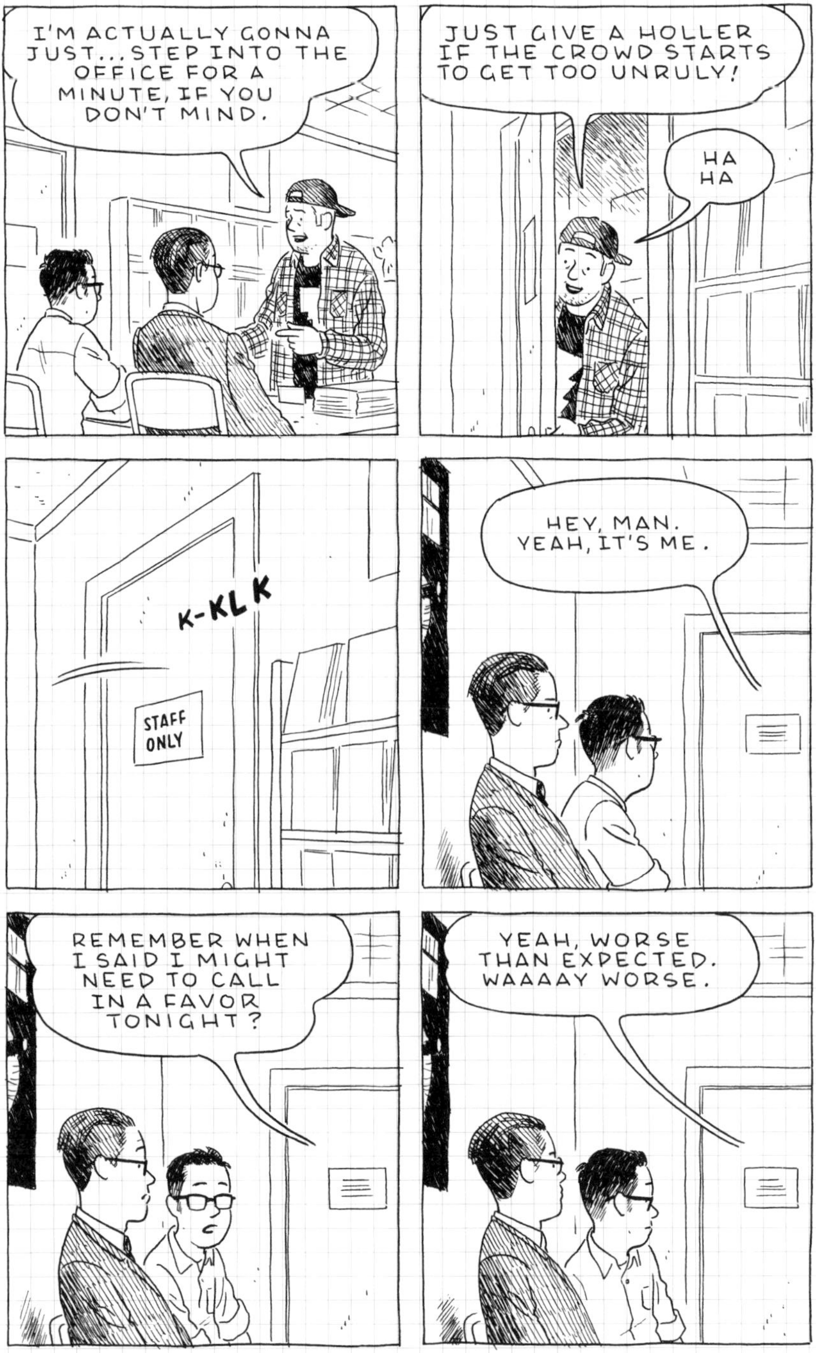
I'M ACTUALLY GONNA JUST... STEP INTO THE OFFICE FOR A MINUTE, IF YOU DON'T MIND.
JUST GIVE A HOLLER IF THE CROWD STARTS TO GET TOO UNRULY!
HA HA
K-KLK
STAFF ONLY
HEY, MAN. YEAH, IT'S ME.
REMEMBER WHEN I SAID I MIGHT NEED TO CALL IN A FAVOR TONIGHT?
YEAH, WORSE THAN EXPECTED. WAAAAY WORSE.

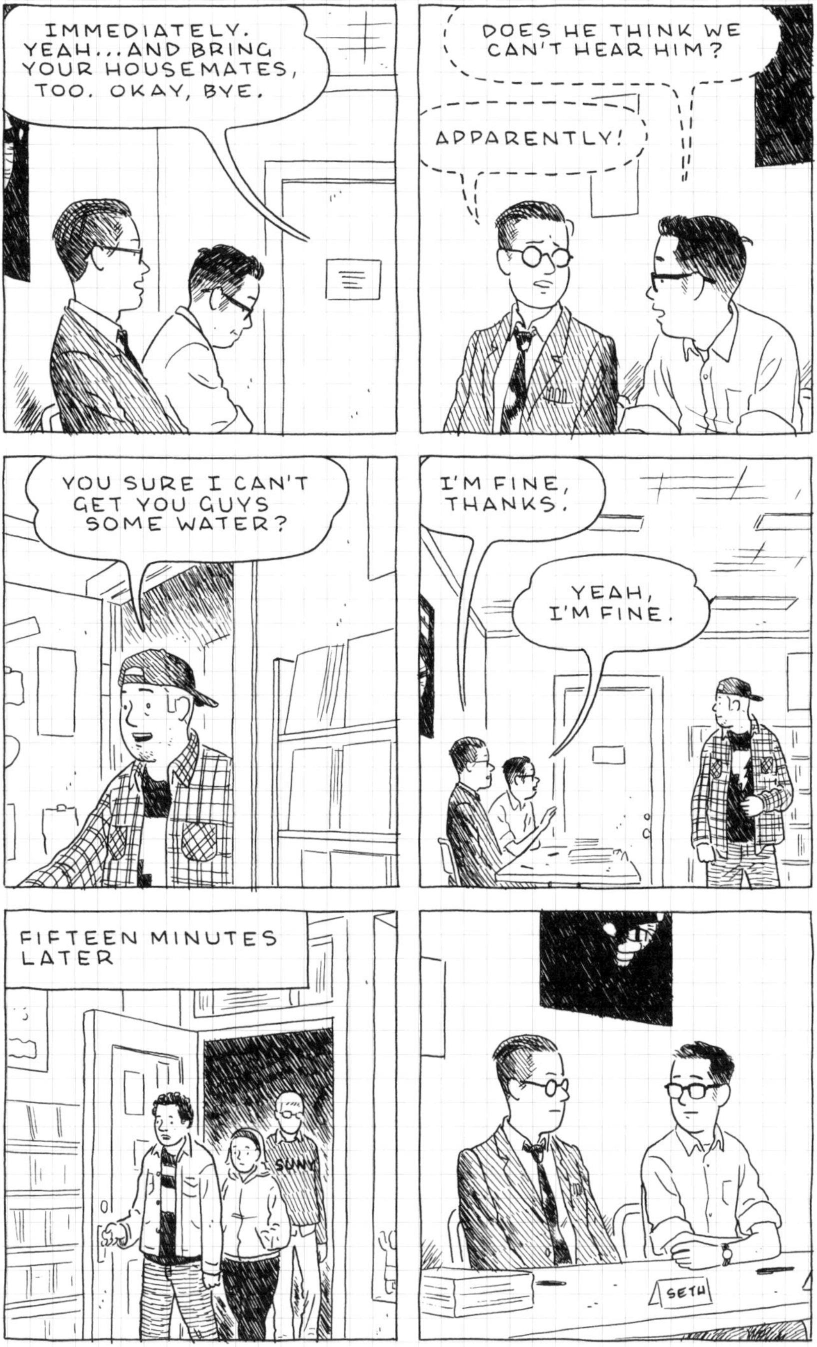
IMMEDIATELY. YEAH...AND BRING YOUR HOUSEMATES, TOO. OKAY, BYE.
DOES HE THINK WE CAN'T HEAR HIM?
APPARENTLY!
YOU SURE I CAN'T GET YOU GUYS SOME WATER?
I'M FINE, THANKS.
YEAH, I'M FINE.
FIFTEEN MINUTES LATER
SUNY
SETH

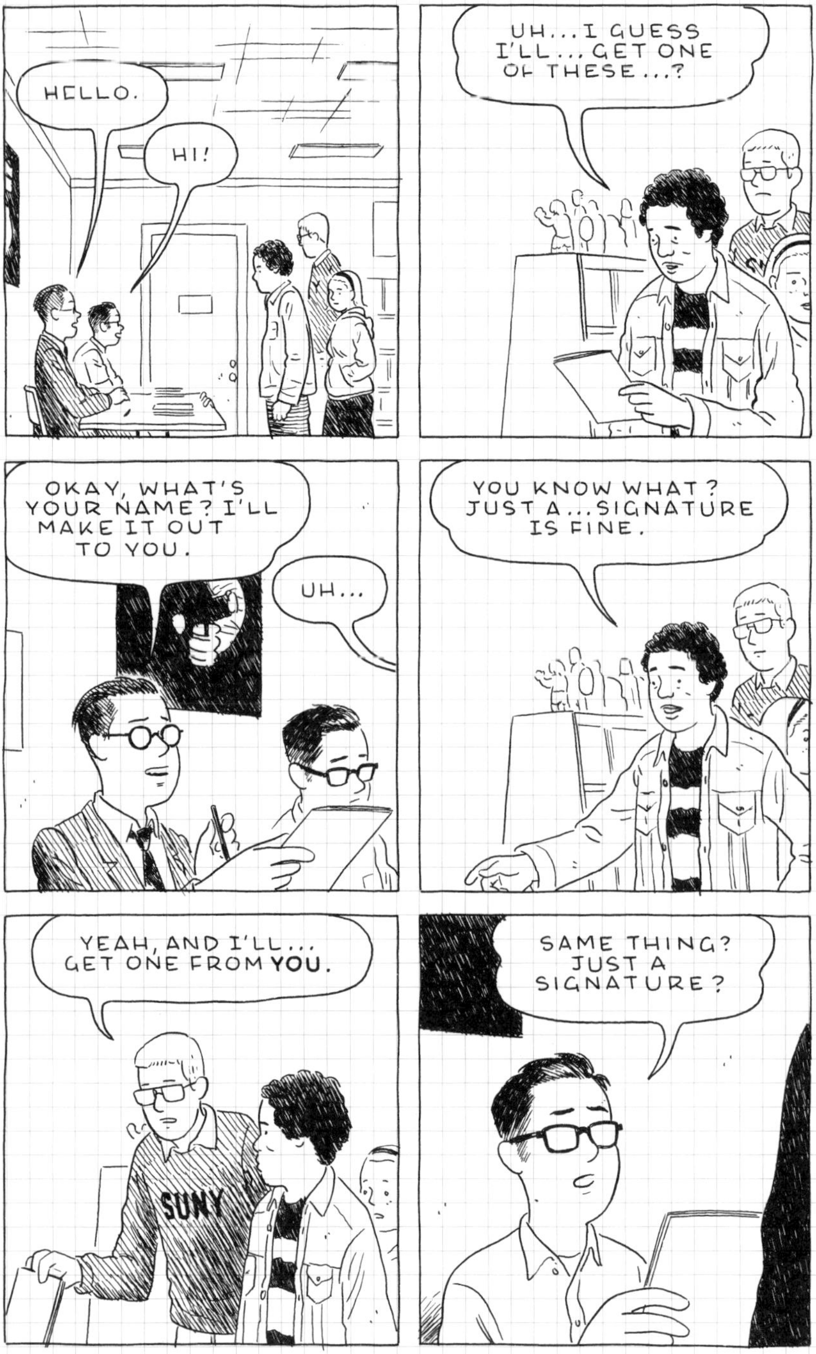
HELLO.
HI!
UH... I GUESS I'LL... GET ONE OF THESE...?
OKAY, WHAT'S YOUR NAME? I'LL MAKE IT OUT TO YOU.
UH...
YOU KNOW WHAT? JUST A... SIGNATURE IS FINE.
YEAH, AND I'LL... GET ONE FROM **YOU**.
SUNY
SAME THING? JUST A SIGNATURE?

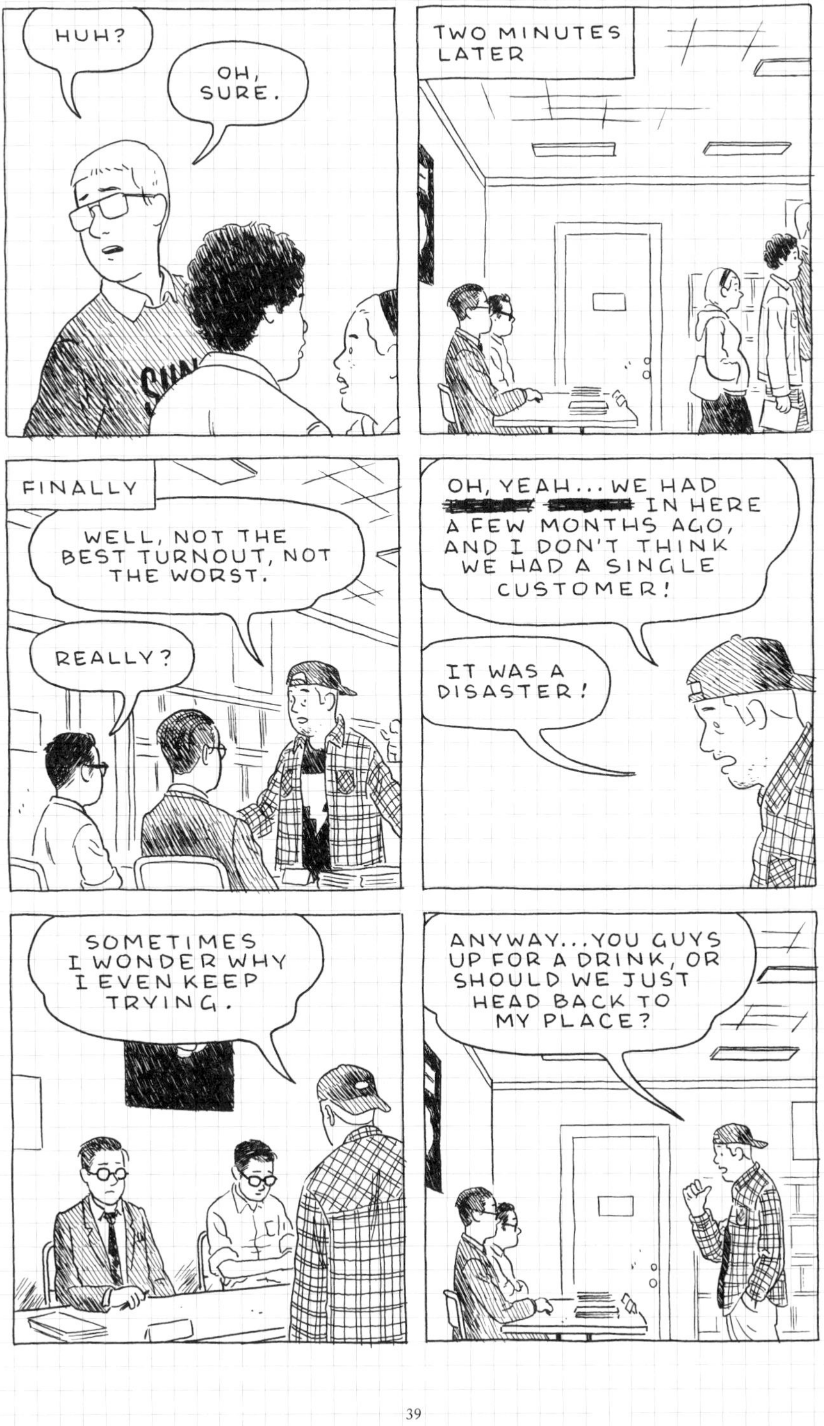
HUH?
OH, SURE.
TWO MINUTES LATER
FINALLY
WELL, NOT THE BEST TURNOUT, NOT THE WORST.
REALLY?
OH, YEAH... WE HAD [redacted] IN HERE A FEW MONTHS AGO, AND I DON'T THINK WE HAD A SINGLE CUSTOMER!
IT WAS A DISASTER!
SOMETIMES I WONDER WHY I EVEN KEEP TRYING.
ANYWAY... YOU GUYS UP FOR A DRINK, OR SHOULD WE JUST HEAD BACK TO MY PLACE?

OAKLAND AND BERKELEY, 1998

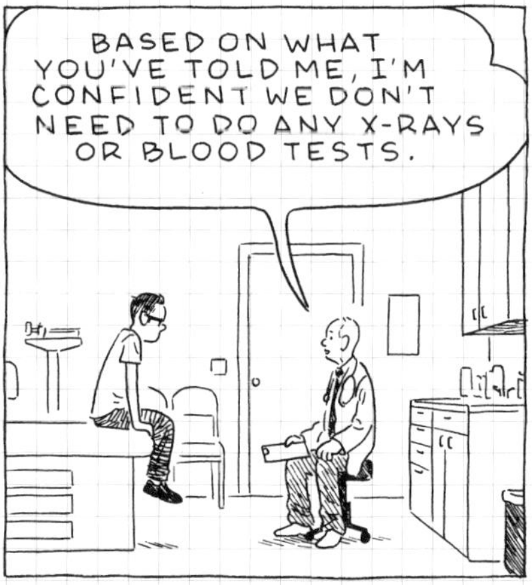
BASED ON WHAT YOU'VE TOLD ME, I'M CONFIDENT WE DON'T NEED TO DO ANY X-RAYS OR BLOOD TESTS.

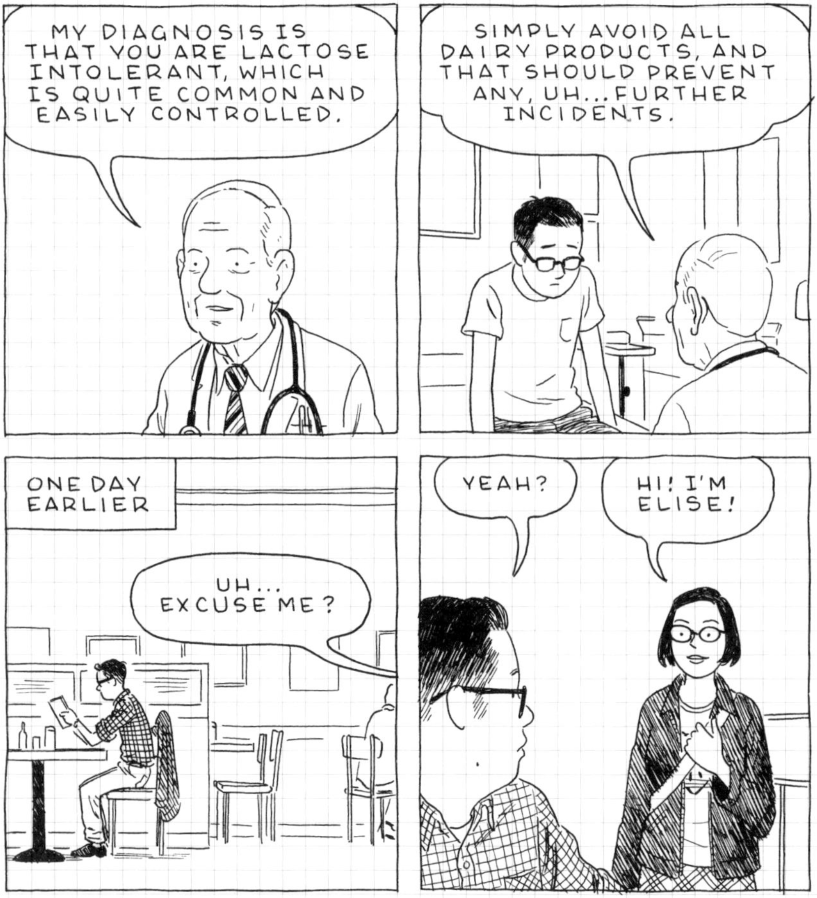
MY DIAGNOSIS IS THAT YOU ARE LACTOSE INTOLERANT, WHICH IS QUITE COMMON AND EASILY CONTROLLED.
SIMPLY AVOID ALL DAIRY PRODUCTS, AND THAT SHOULD PREVENT ANY, UH... FURTHER INCIDENTS.
ONE DAY EARLIER
UH... EXCUSE ME?
YEAH?
HI! I'M ELISE!

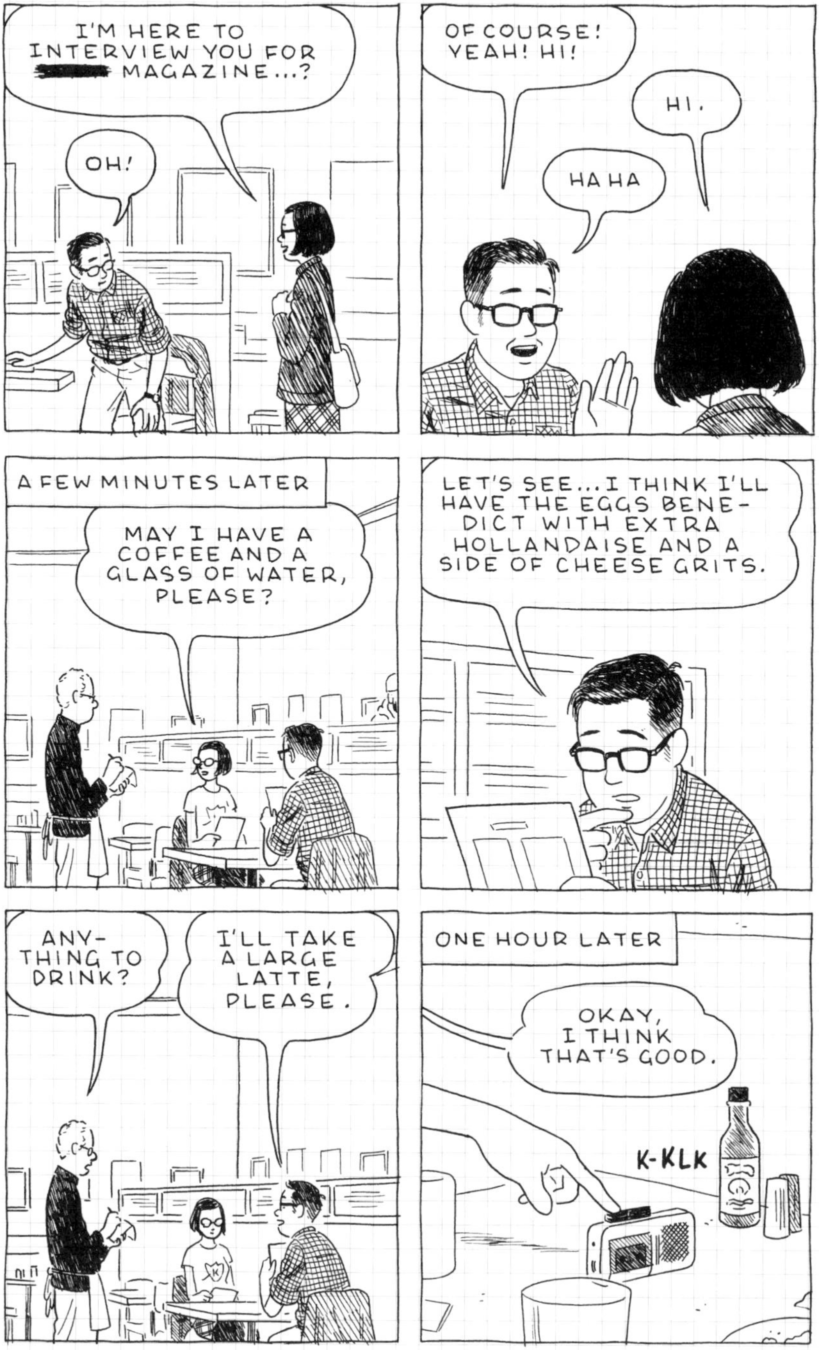
I'M HERE TO INTERVIEW YOU FOR [redacted] MAGAZINE...?
OH!
OF COURSE! YEAH! HI!
HI.
HA HA
A FEW MINUTES LATER
MAY I HAVE A COFFEE AND A GLASS OF WATER, PLEASE?
LET'S SEE... I THINK I'LL HAVE THE EGGS BENE-DICT WITH EXTRA HOLLANDAISE AND A SIDE OF CHEESE GRITS.
ANY-THING TO DRINK?
I'LL TAKE A LARGE LATTE, PLEASE.
ONE HOUR LATER
OKAY, I THINK THAT'S GOOD.
K-KLK

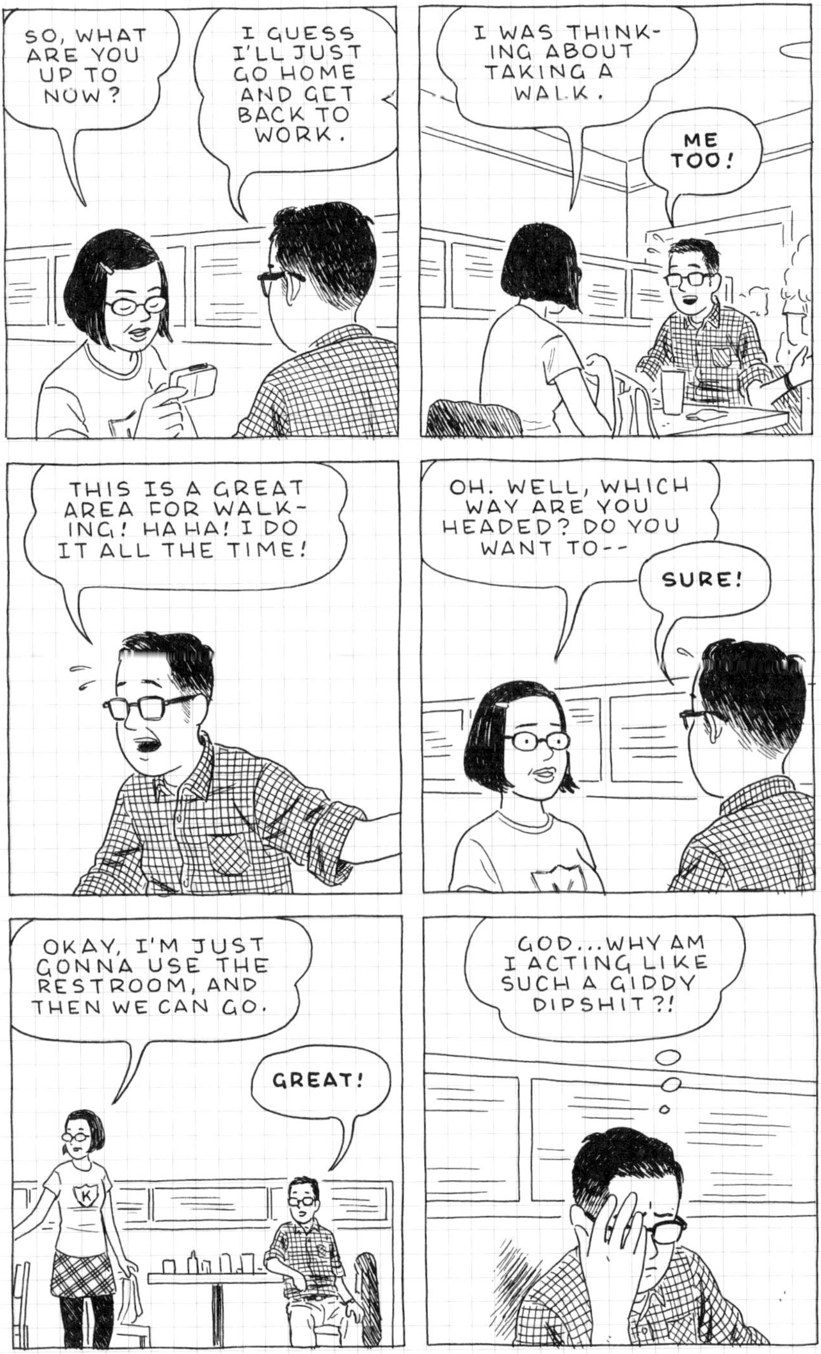
SO, WHAT ARE YOU UP TO NOW?
I GUESS I'LL JUST GO HOME AND GET BACK TO WORK.
I WAS THINKING ABOUT TAKING A WALK.
ME TOO!
THIS IS A GREAT AREA FOR WALKING! HA HA! I DO IT ALL THE TIME!
OH. WELL, WHICH WAY ARE YOU HEADED? DO YOU WANT TO--
SURE!
OKAY, I'M JUST GONNA USE THE RESTROOM, AND THEN WE CAN GO.
GREAT!
K
GOD...WHY AM I ACTING LIKE SUCH A GIDDY DIPSHIT?!

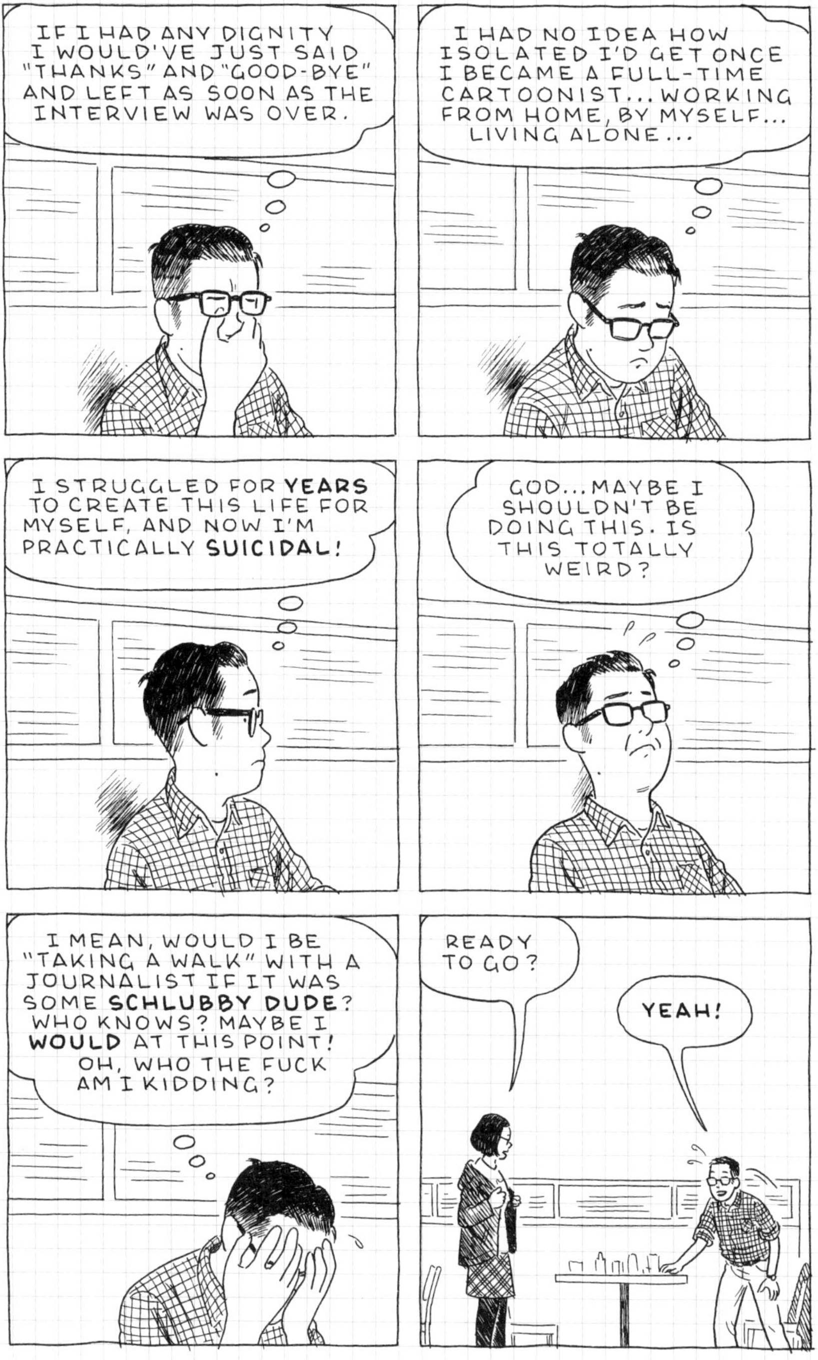
IF I HAD ANY DIGNITY I WOULD'VE JUST SAID "THANKS" AND "GOOD-BYE" AND LEFT AS SOON AS THE INTERVIEW WAS OVER.
I HAD NO IDEA HOW ISOLATED I'D GET ONCE I BECAME A FULL-TIME CARTOONIST... WORKING FROM HOME, BY MYSELF... LIVING ALONE...
I STRUGGLED FOR **YEARS** TO CREATE THIS LIFE FOR MYSELF, AND NOW I'M PRACTICALLY **SUICIDAL**!
GOD... MAYBE I SHOULDN'T BE DOING THIS. IS THIS TOTALLY WEIRD?
I MEAN, WOULD I BE "TAKING A WALK" WITH A JOURNALIST IF IT WAS SOME **SCHLUBBY DUDE**? WHO KNOWS? MAYBE I **WOULD** AT THIS POINT! OH, WHO THE FUCK AM I KIDDING?
READY TO GO?
YEAH!

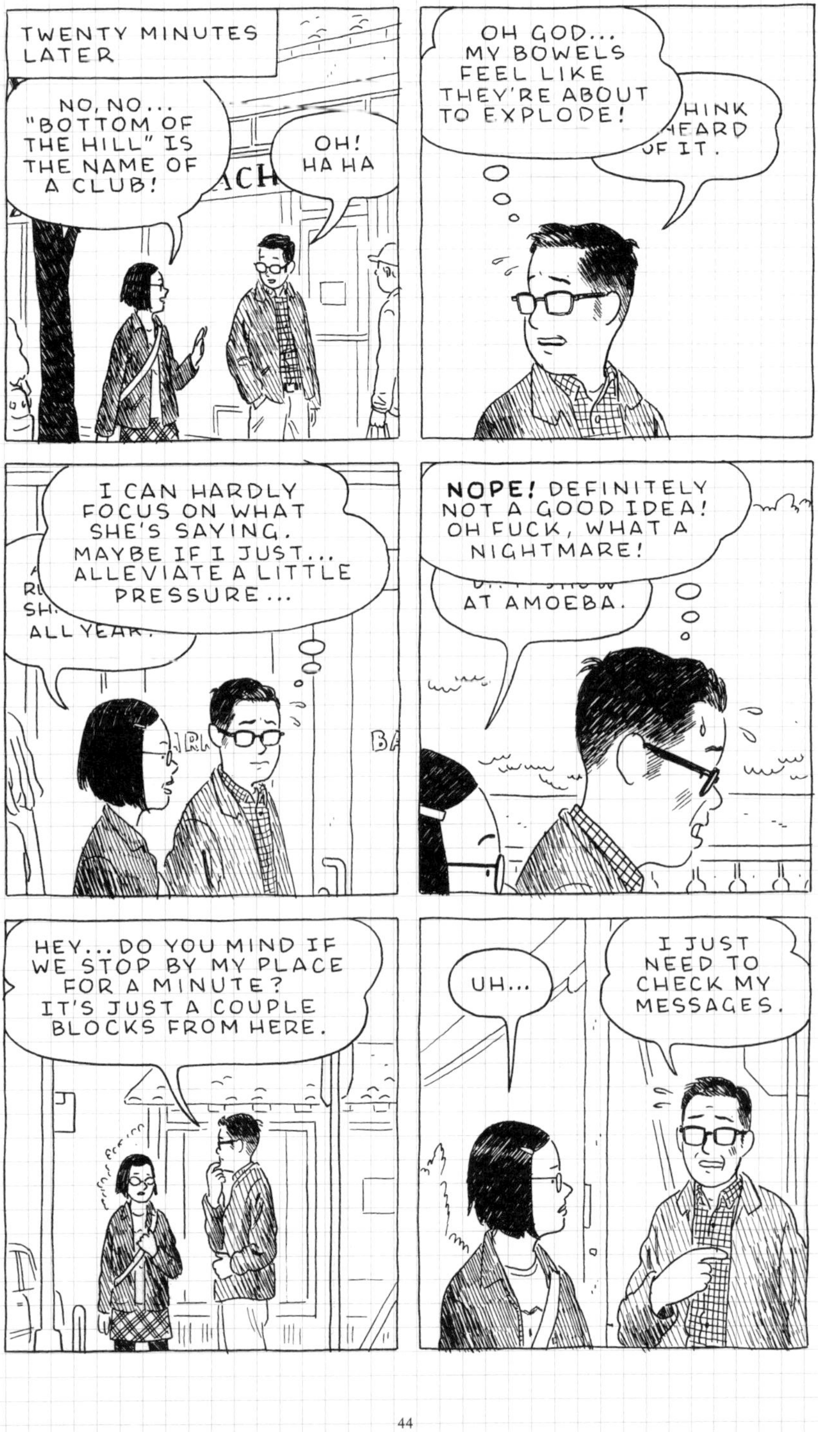
TWENTY MINUTES LATER
NO, NO... "BOTTOM OF THE HILL" IS THE NAME OF A CLUB!
OH! HA HA
OH GOD... MY BOWELS FEEL LIKE THEY'RE ABOUT TO EXPLODE!
HINK HEARD OF IT.
I CAN HARDLY FOCUS ON WHAT SHE'S SAYING. MAYBE IF I JUST... ALLEVIATE A LITTLE PRESSURE...
ALL YEAR.
NOPE! DEFINITELY NOT A GOOD IDEA! OH FUCK, WHAT A NIGHTMARE!
AT AMOEBA.
HEY... DO YOU MIND IF WE STOP BY MY PLACE FOR A MINUTE? IT'S JUST A COUPLE BLOCKS FROM HERE.
UH...
I JUST NEED TO CHECK MY MESSAGES.

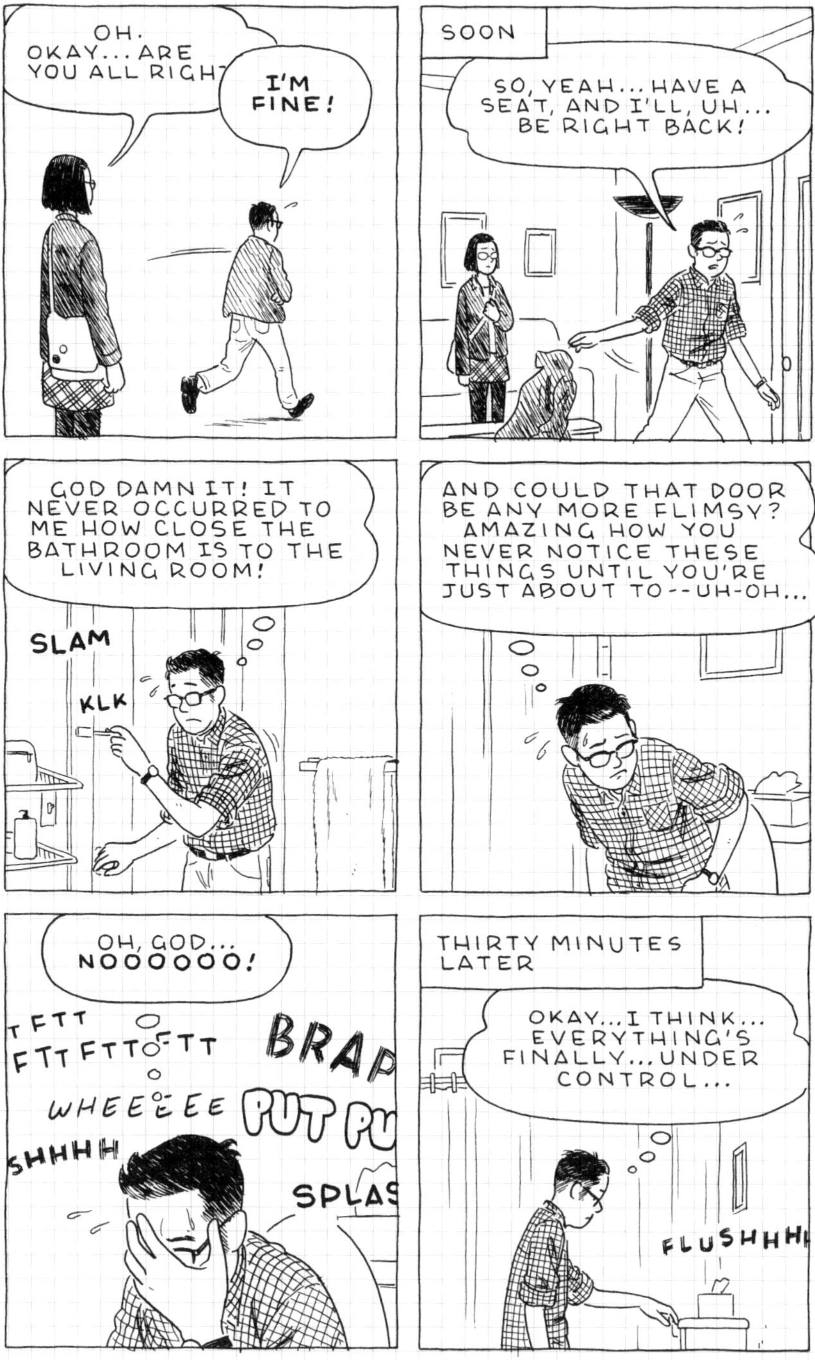
OH. OKAY... ARE YOU ALL RIGHT?
I'M FINE!
SOON
SO, YEAH... HAVE A SEAT, AND I'LL, UH... BE RIGHT BACK!
GOD DAMN IT! IT NEVER OCCURRED TO ME HOW CLOSE THE BATHROOM IS TO THE LIVING ROOM!
SLAM
KLK
AND COULD THAT DOOR BE ANY MORE FLIMSY? AMAZING HOW YOU NEVER NOTICE THESE THINGS UNTIL YOU'RE JUST ABOUT TO--UH-OH...
OH, GOD... NOOOOOO!
TFTT FTTFTTFTT
BRAP
WHEEEEEE
PUT PU
SHHHH
SPLAS
THIRTY MINUTES LATER
OKAY... I THINK... EVERYTHING'S FINALLY... UNDER CONTROL...
FLUSHHH

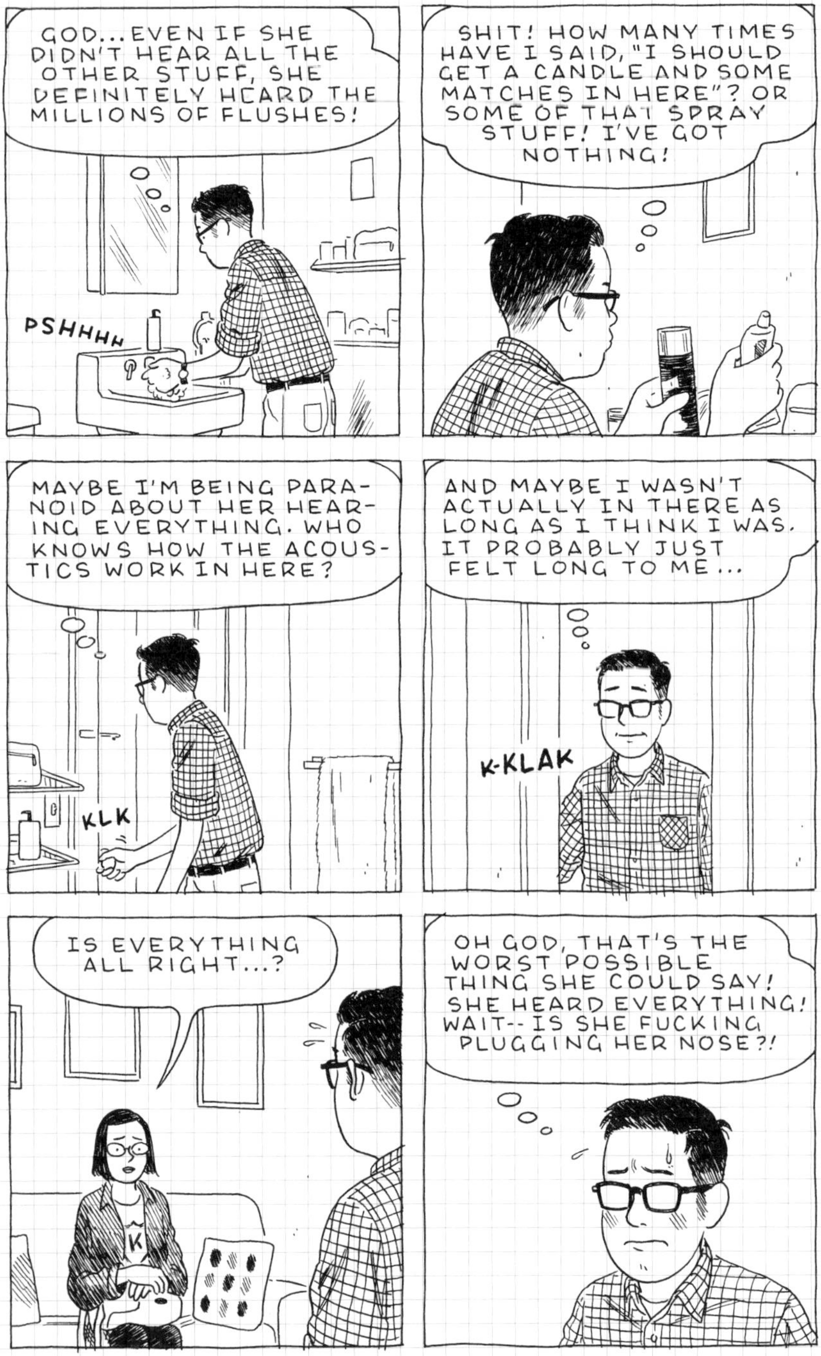
GOD... EVEN IF SHE DIDN'T HEAR ALL THE OTHER STUFF, SHE DEFINITELY HEARD THE MILLIONS OF FLUSHES!
PSHHHH
SHIT! HOW MANY TIMES HAVE I SAID, "I SHOULD GET A CANDLE AND SOME MATCHES IN HERE"? OR SOME OF THAT SPRAY STUFF! I'VE GOT NOTHING!
MAYBE I'M BEING PARANOID ABOUT HER HEARING EVERYTHING. WHO KNOWS HOW THE ACOUSTICS WORK IN HERE?
KLK
AND MAYBE I WASN'T ACTUALLY IN THERE AS LONG AS I THINK I WAS. IT PROBABLY JUST FELT LONG TO ME...
K-KLAK
IS EVERYTHING ALL RIGHT...?
K
OH GOD, THAT'S THE WORST POSSIBLE THING SHE COULD SAY! SHE HEARD EVERYTHING! WAIT-- IS SHE FUCKING PLUGGING HER NOSE?!

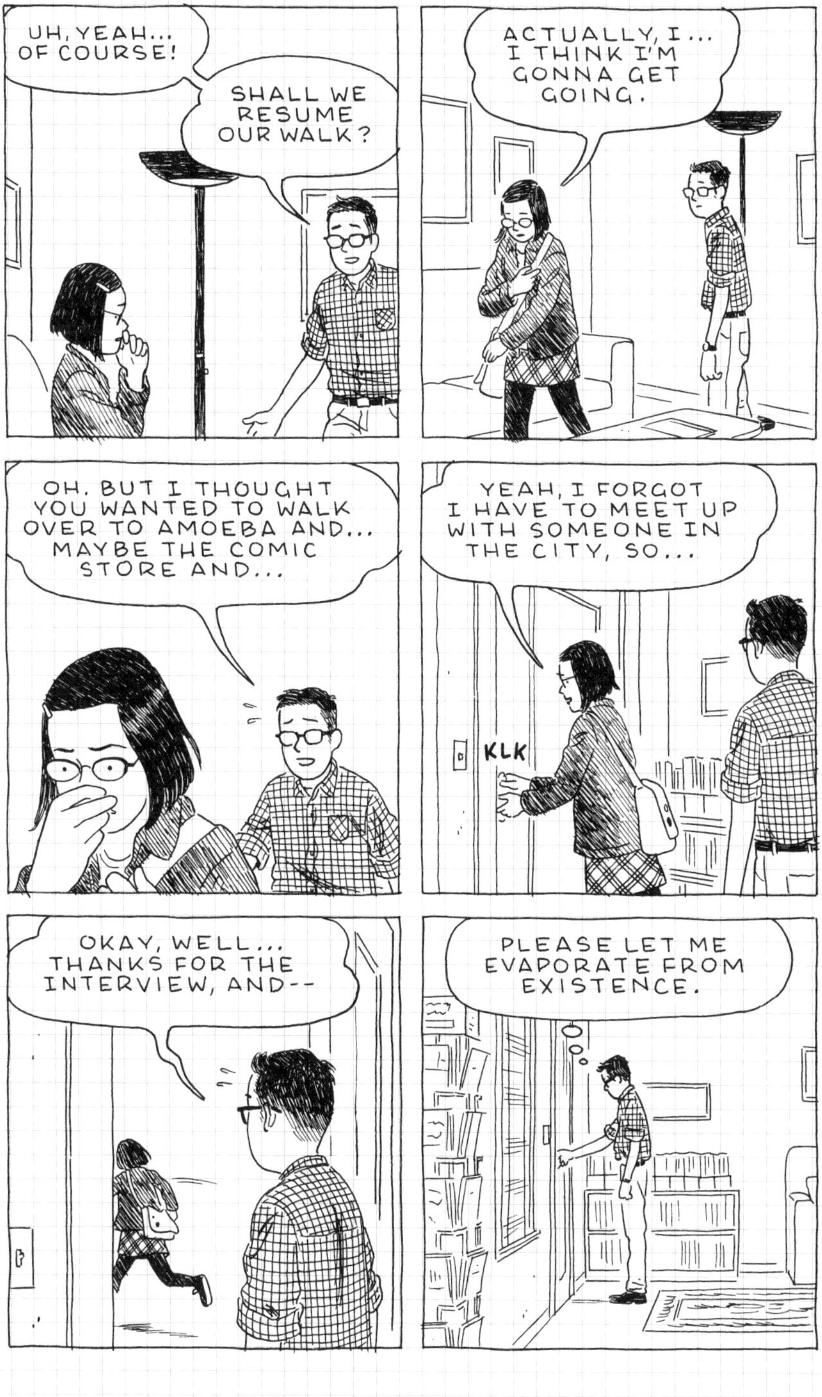
UH, YEAH... OF COURSE!
SHALL WE RESUME OUR WALK?
ACTUALLY, I... I THINK I'M GONNA GET GOING.
OH. BUT I THOUGHT YOU WANTED TO WALK OVER TO AMOEBA AND... MAYBE THE COMIC STORE AND...
YEAH, I FORGOT I HAVE TO MEET UP WITH SOMEONE IN THE CITY, SO...
KLK
OKAY, WELL... THANKS FOR THE INTERVIEW, AND--
PLEASE LET ME EVAPORATE FROM EXISTENCE.

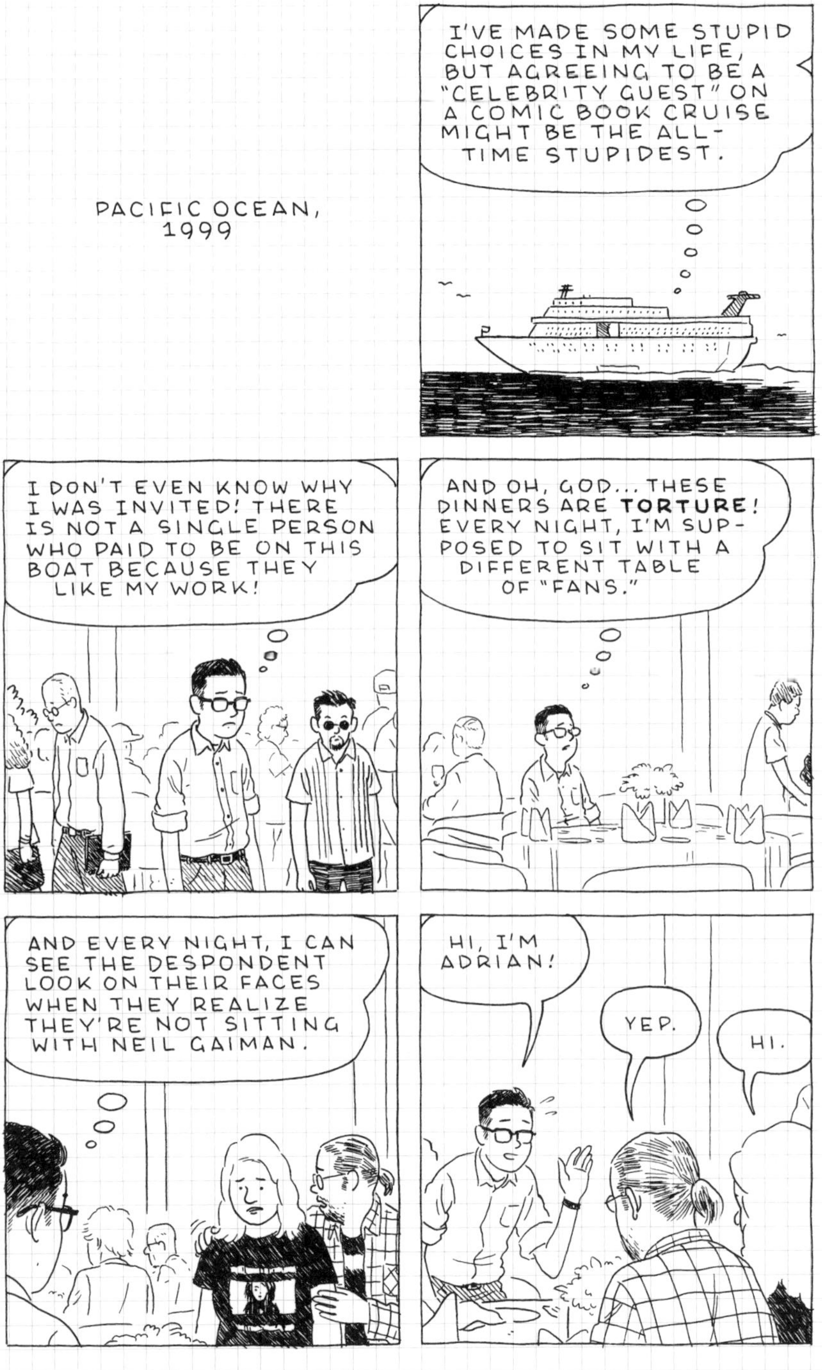

PACIFIC OCEAN, 1999
I'VE MADE SOME STUPID CHOICES IN MY LIFE, BUT AGREEING TO BE A "CELEBRITY GUEST" ON A COMIC BOOK CRUISE MIGHT BE THE ALL-TIME STUPIDEST.
I DON'T EVEN KNOW WHY I WAS INVITED! THERE IS NOT A SINGLE PERSON WHO PAID TO BE ON THIS BOAT BECAUSE THEY LIKE MY WORK!
AND OH, GOD... THESE DINNERS ARE **TORTURE**! EVERY NIGHT, I'M SUPPOSED TO SIT WITH A DIFFERENT TABLE OF "FANS."
AND EVERY NIGHT, I CAN SEE THE DESPONDENT LOOK ON THEIR FACES WHEN THEY REALIZE THEY'RE NOT SITTING WITH NEIL GAIMAN.
HI, I'M ADRIAN!
YEP.
HI.

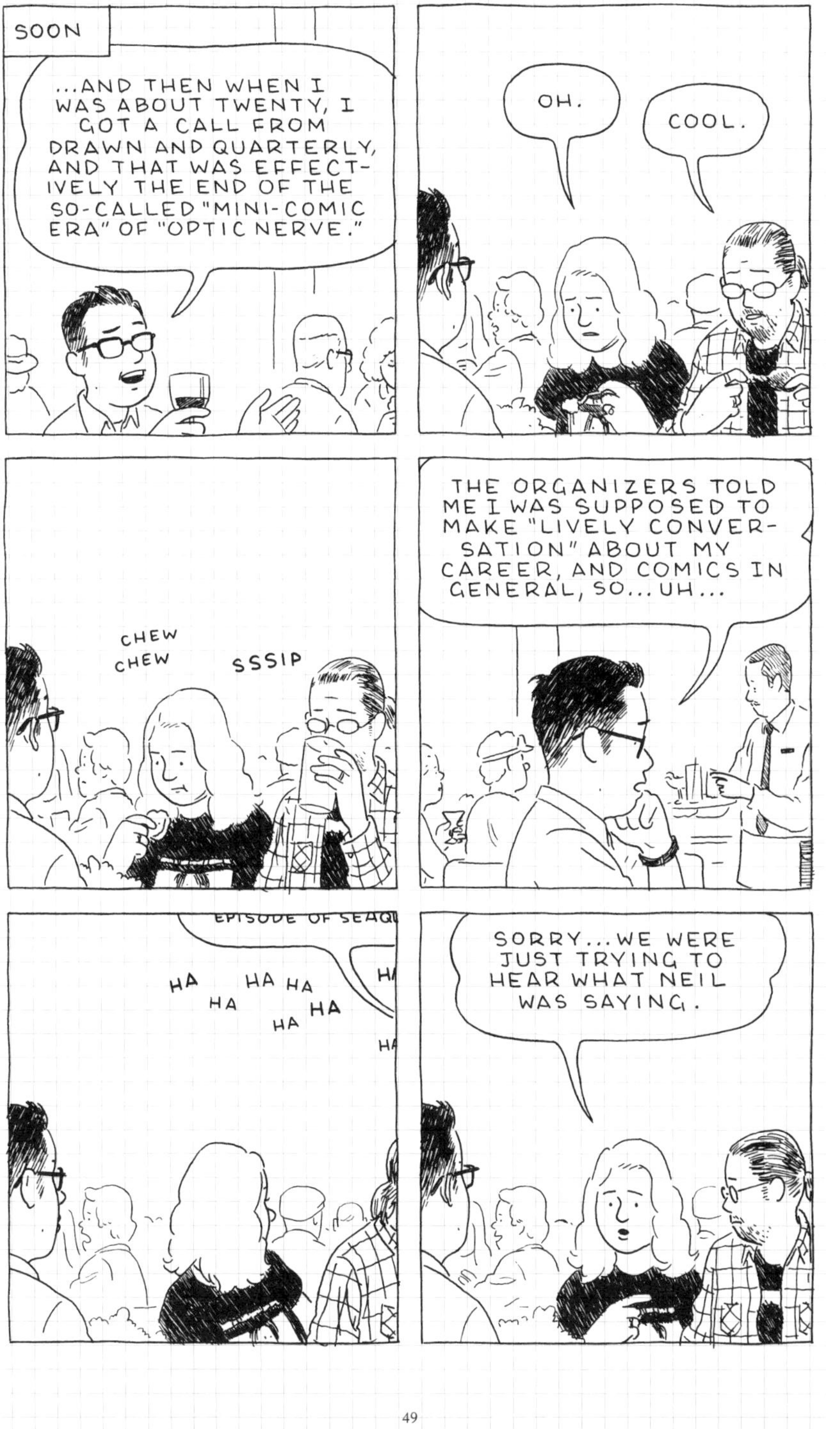
SOON
...AND THEN WHEN I WAS ABOUT TWENTY, I GOT A CALL FROM DRAWN AND QUARTERLY, AND THAT WAS EFFECTIVELY THE END OF THE SO-CALLED "MINI-COMIC ERA" OF "OPTIC NERVE."
OH.
COOL.
CHEW CHEW
SSSIP
THE ORGANIZERS TOLD ME I WAS SUPPOSED TO MAKE "LIVELY CONVERSATION" ABOUT MY CAREER, AND COMICS IN GENERAL, SO... UH...
EPISODE OF SEAQU
HA HA HA HA HA HA HA
SORRY... WE WERE JUST TRYING TO HEAR WHAT NEIL WAS SAYING.

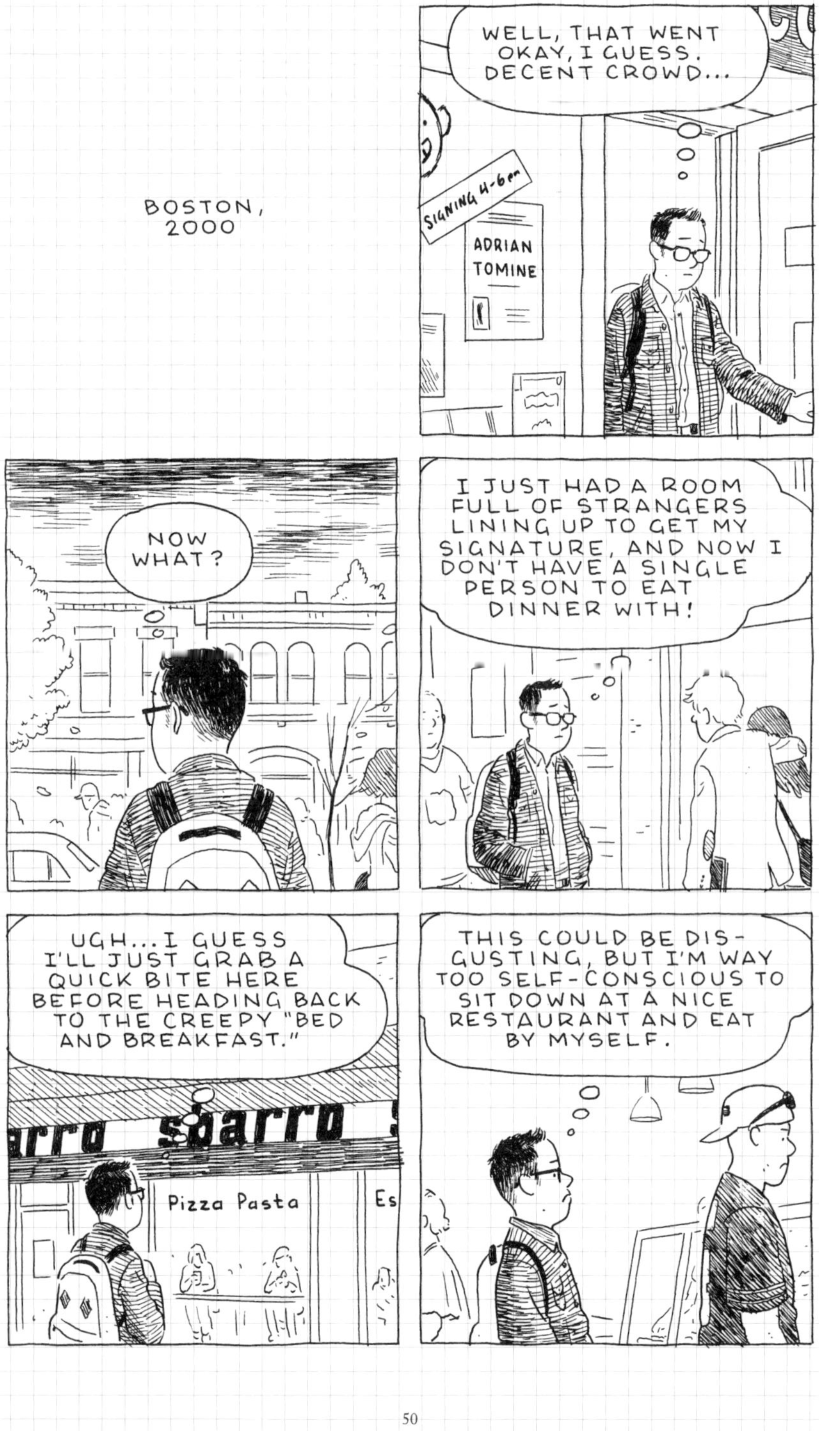
BOSTON, 2000
WELL, THAT WENT OKAY, I GUESS. DECENT CROWD...
SIGNING 4-6pm
ADRIAN TOMINE
NOW WHAT?
I JUST HAD A ROOM FULL OF STRANGERS LINING UP TO GET MY SIGNATURE, AND NOW I DON'T HAVE A SINGLE PERSON TO EAT DINNER WITH!
UGH... I GUESS I'LL JUST GRAB A QUICK BITE HERE BEFORE HEADING BACK TO THE CREEPY "BED AND BREAKFAST."
sbarro
Pizza Pasta
Es
THIS COULD BE DISGUSTING, BUT I'M WAY TOO SELF-CONSCIOUS TO SIT DOWN AT A NICE RESTAURANT AND EAT BY MYSELF.

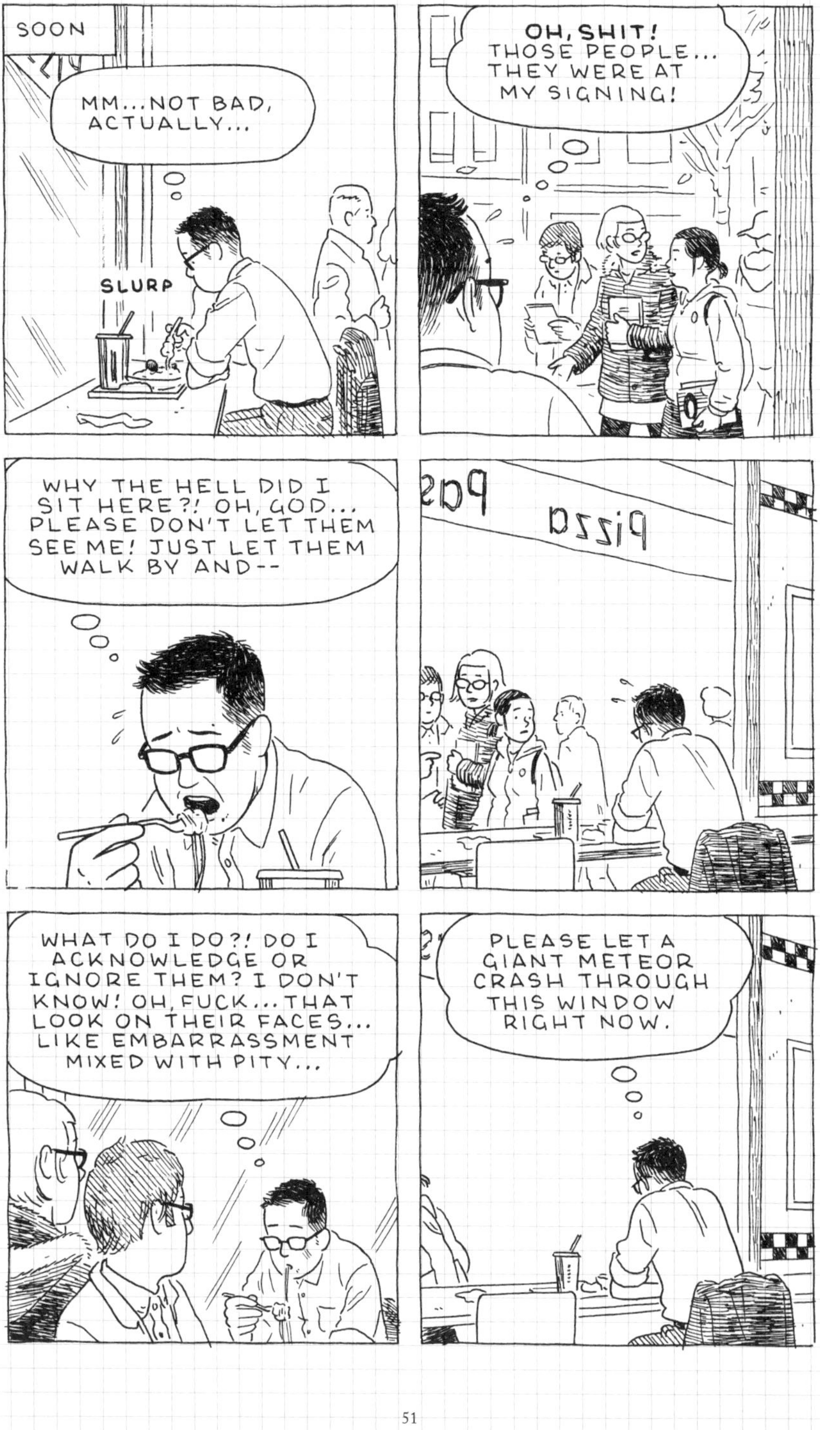
SOON
MM...NOT BAD, ACTUALLY...
SLURP
OH, SHIT! THOSE PEOPLE... THEY WERE AT MY SIGNING!
WHY THE HELL DID I SIT HERE?! OH, GOD... PLEASE DON'T LET THEM SEE ME! JUST LET THEM WALK BY AND--
WHAT DO I DO?! DO I ACKNOWLEDGE OR IGNORE THEM? I DON'T KNOW! OH, FUCK... THAT LOOK ON THEIR FACES... LIKE EMBARRASSMENT MIXED WITH PITY...
PLEASE LET A GIANT METEOR CRASH THROUGH THIS WINDOW RIGHT NOW.

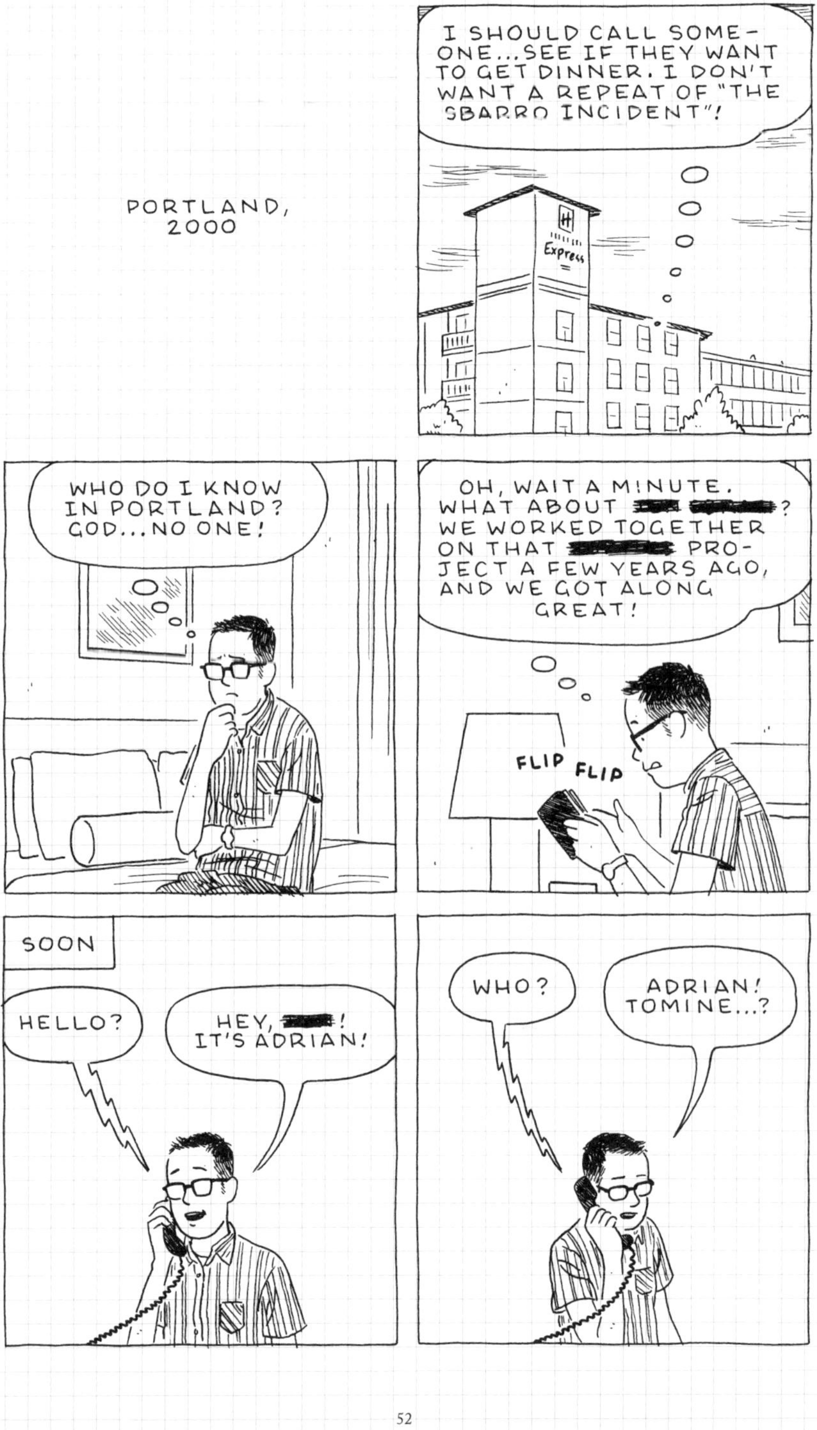
PORTLAND, 2000
I SHOULD CALL SOMEONE... SEE IF THEY WANT TO GET DINNER. I DON'T WANT A REPEAT OF "THE SBARRO INCIDENT"!
Express
WHO DO I KNOW IN PORTLAND? GOD... NO ONE!
OH, WAIT A MINUTE. WHAT ABOUT [redacted]? WE WORKED TOGETHER ON THAT [redacted] PROJECT A FEW YEARS AGO, AND WE GOT ALONG GREAT!
FLIP FLIP
SOON
HELLO?
HEY, [redacted]! IT'S ADRIAN!
WHO?
ADRIAN! TOMINE...?

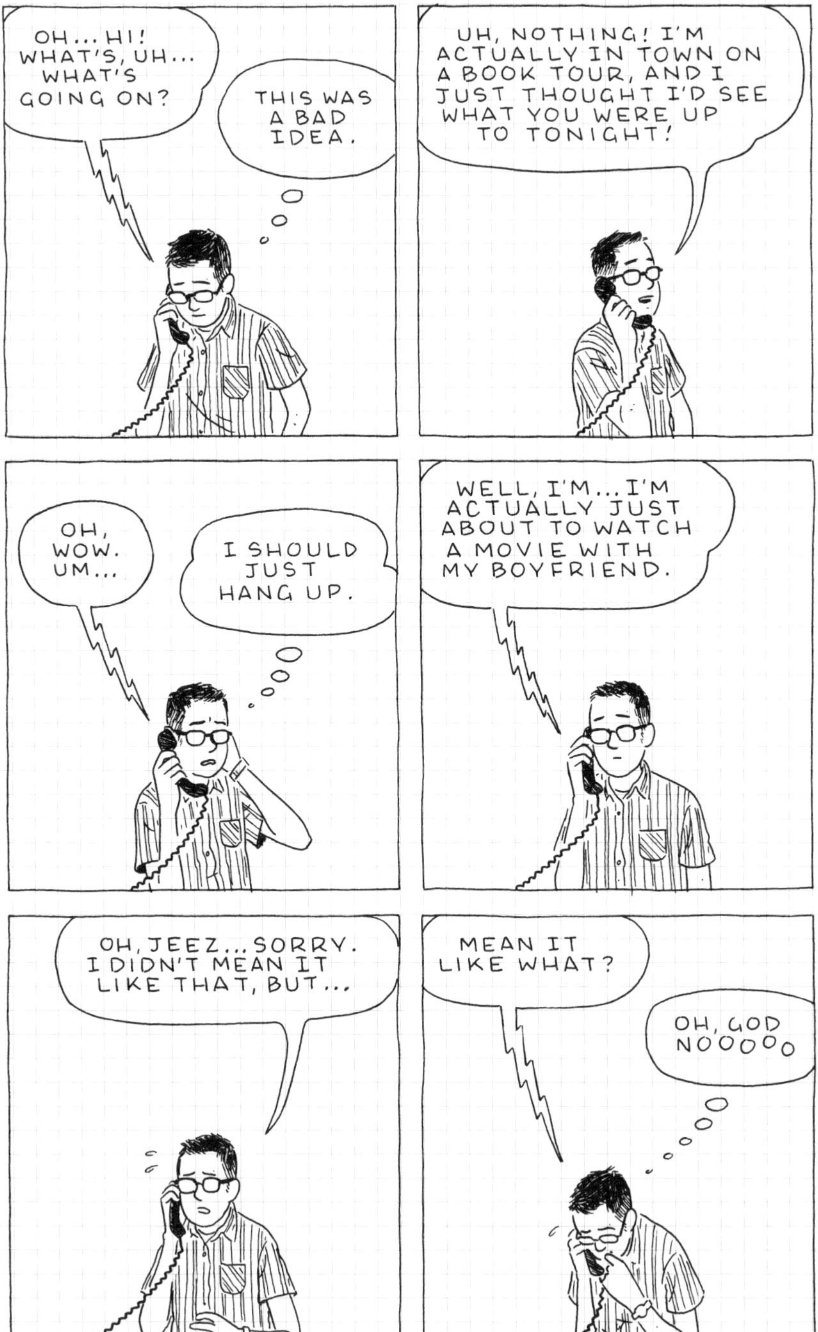

OH... HI! WHAT'S, UH... WHAT'S GOING ON?
THIS WAS A BAD IDEA.
UH, NOTHING! I'M ACTUALLY IN TOWN ON A BOOK TOUR, AND I JUST THOUGHT I'D SEE WHAT YOU WERE UP TO TONIGHT!
OH, WOW. UM...
I SHOULD JUST HANG UP.
WELL, I'M... I'M ACTUALLY JUST ABOUT TO WATCH A MOVIE WITH MY BOYFRIEND.
OH, JEEZ... SORRY. I DIDN'T MEAN IT LIKE THAT, BUT...
MEAN IT LIKE WHAT?
OH, GOD NOOOOO

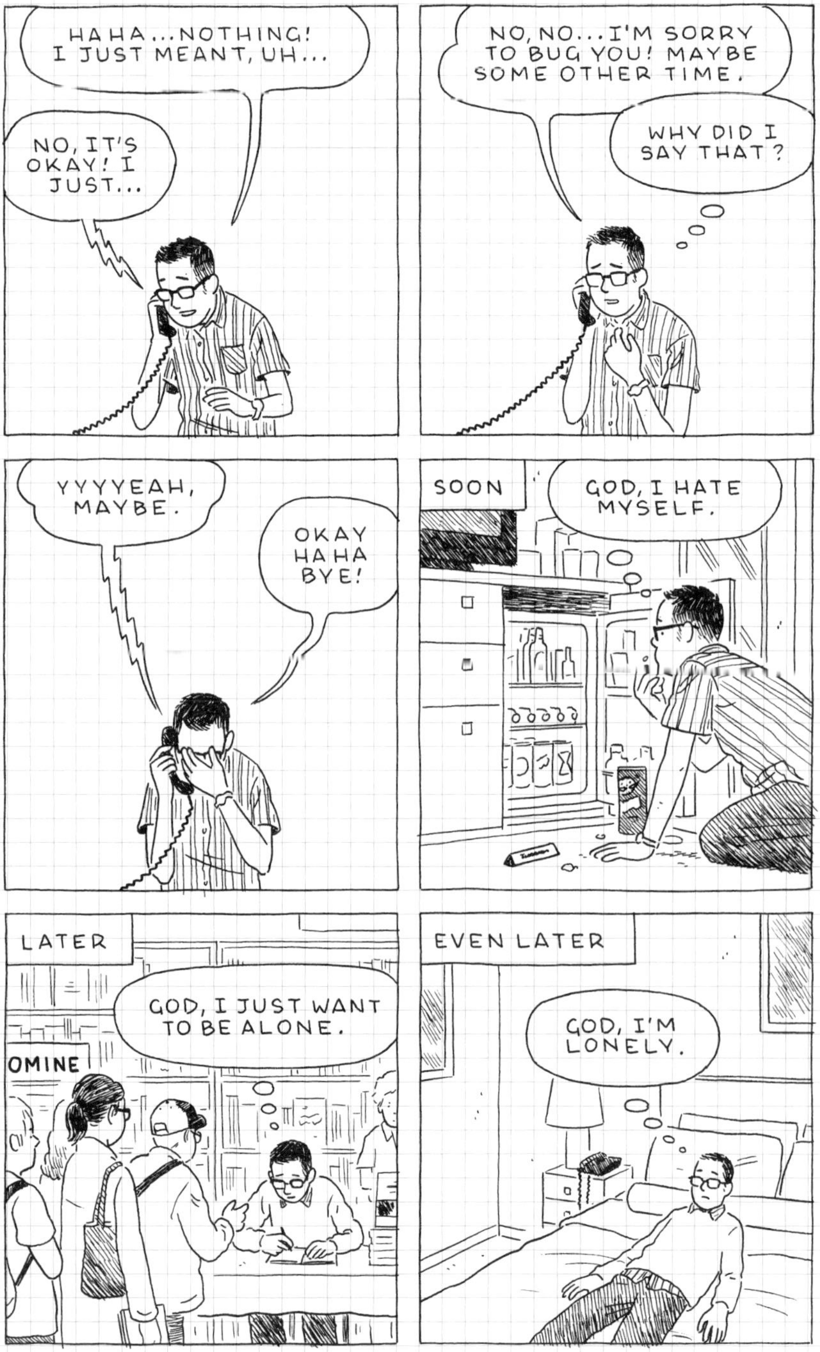
HA HA...NOTHING! I JUST MEANT, UH...
NO, IT'S OKAY! I JUST...
NO, NO...I'M SORRY TO BUG YOU! MAYBE SOME OTHER TIME.
WHY DID I SAY THAT?
YYYYEAH, MAYBE.
OKAY HA HA BYE!
SOON
GOD, I HATE MYSELF.
LATER
GOD, I JUST WANT TO BE ALONE.
OMINE
EVEN LATER
GOD, I'M LONELY.

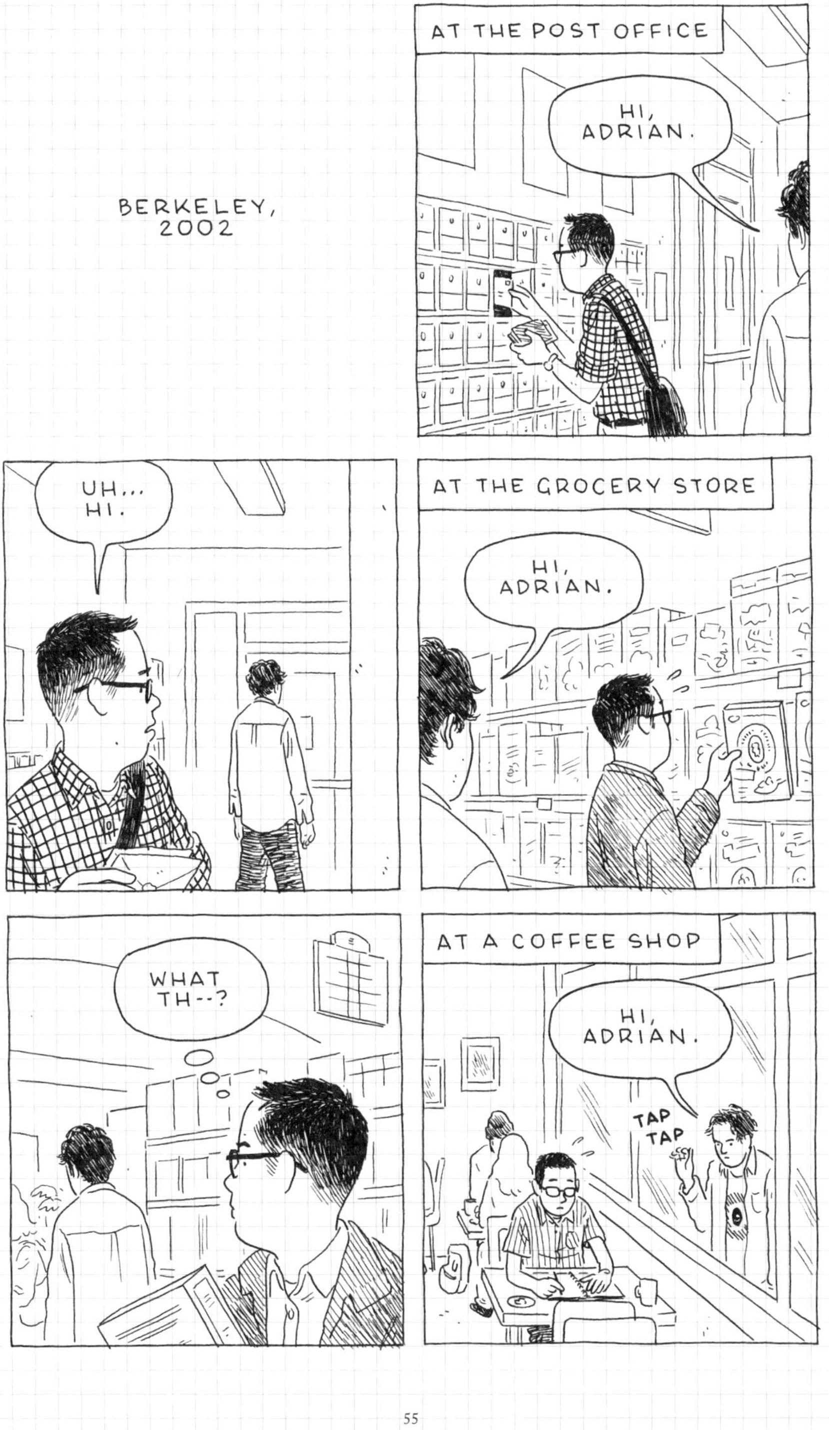
BERKELEY, 2002
AT THE POST OFFICE
HI, ADRIAN.
UH... HI.
AT THE GROCERY STORE
HI, ADRIAN.
WHAT TH--?
AT A COFFEE SHOP
HI, ADRIAN.
TAP TAP

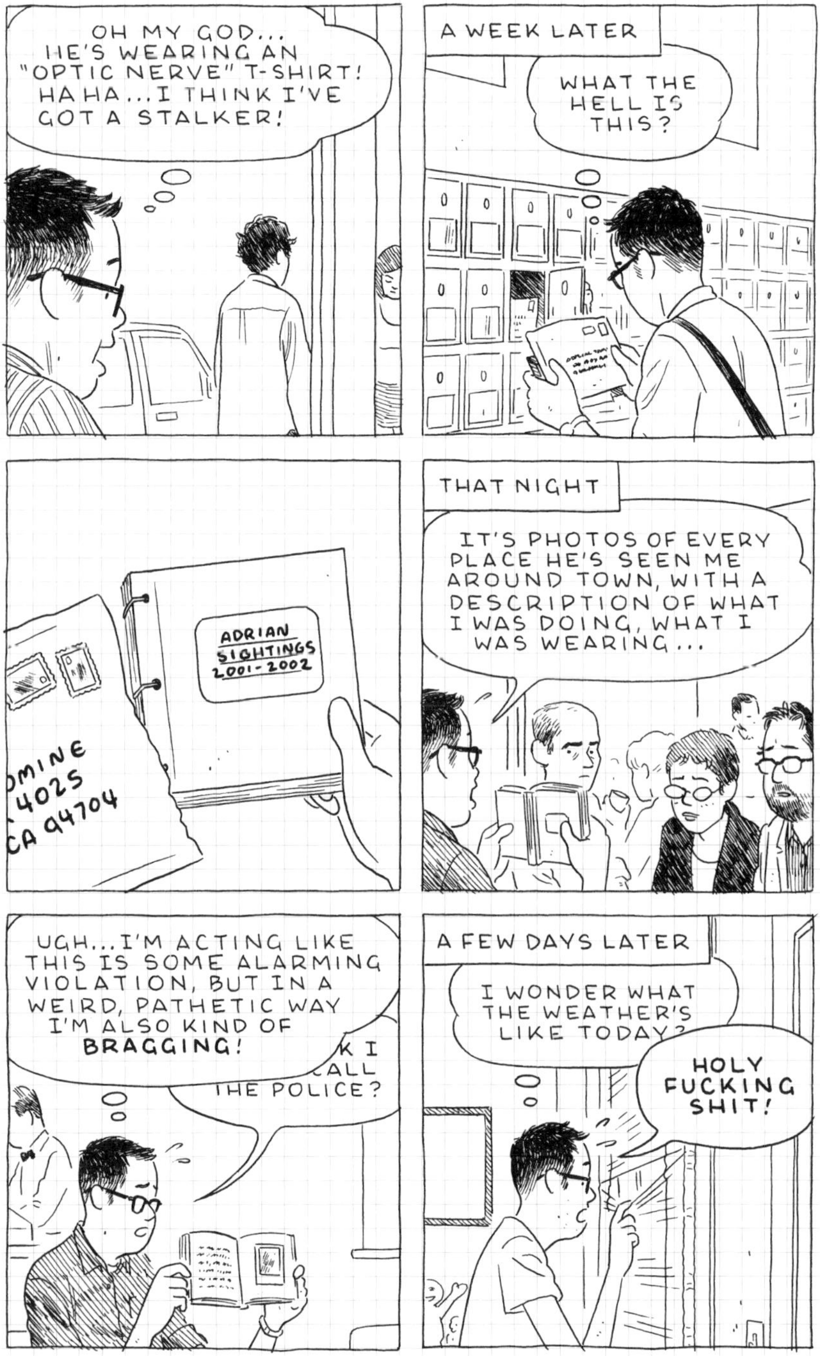
OH MY GOD... HE'S WEARING AN "OPTIC NERVE" T-SHIRT! HA HA... I THINK I'VE GOT A STALKER!
A WEEK LATER
WHAT THE HELL IS THIS?
ADRIAN SIGHTINGS 2001-2002
THAT NIGHT
IT'S PHOTOS OF EVERY PLACE HE'S SEEN ME AROUND TOWN, WITH A DESCRIPTION OF WHAT I WAS DOING, WHAT I WAS WEARING...
UGH... I'M ACTING LIKE THIS IS SOME ALARMING VIOLATION, BUT IN A WEIRD, PATHETIC WAY I'M ALSO KIND OF BRAGGING!
THE POLICE?
A FEW DAYS LATER
I WONDER WHAT THE WEATHER'S LIKE TODAY?
HOLY FUCKING SHIT!

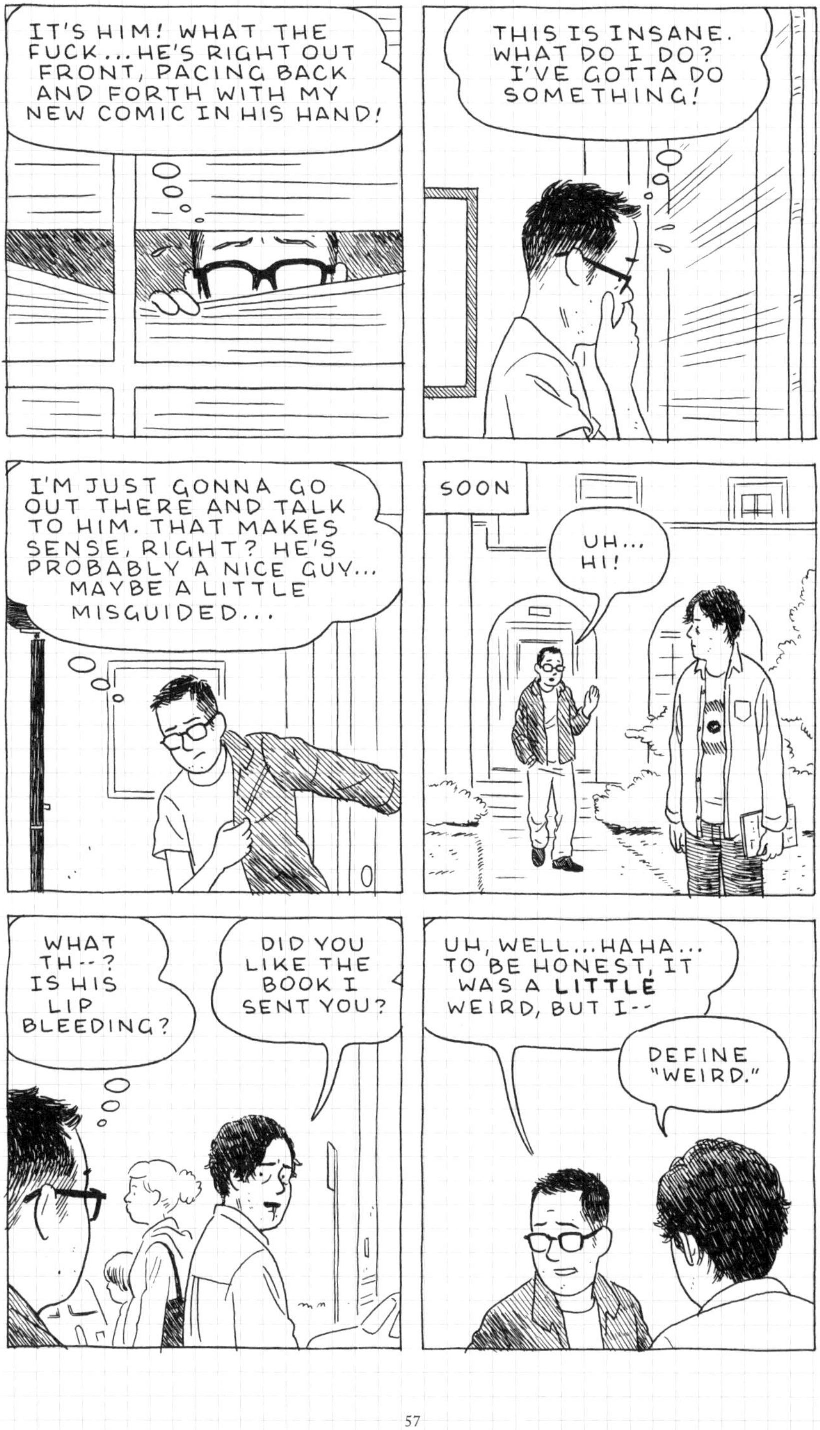
IT'S HIM! WHAT THE FUCK... HE'S RIGHT OUT FRONT, PACING BACK AND FORTH WITH MY NEW COMIC IN HIS HAND!
THIS IS INSANE. WHAT DO I DO? I'VE GOTTA DO SOMETHING!
I'M JUST GONNA GO OUT THERE AND TALK TO HIM. THAT MAKES SENSE, RIGHT? HE'S PROBABLY A NICE GUY... MAYBE A LITTLE MISGUIDED...
SOON
UH... HI!
WHAT TH--? IS HIS LIP BLEEDING?
DID YOU LIKE THE BOOK I SENT YOU?
UH, WELL...HAHA... TO BE HONEST, IT WAS A **LITTLE** WEIRD, BUT I--
DEFINE "WEIRD."

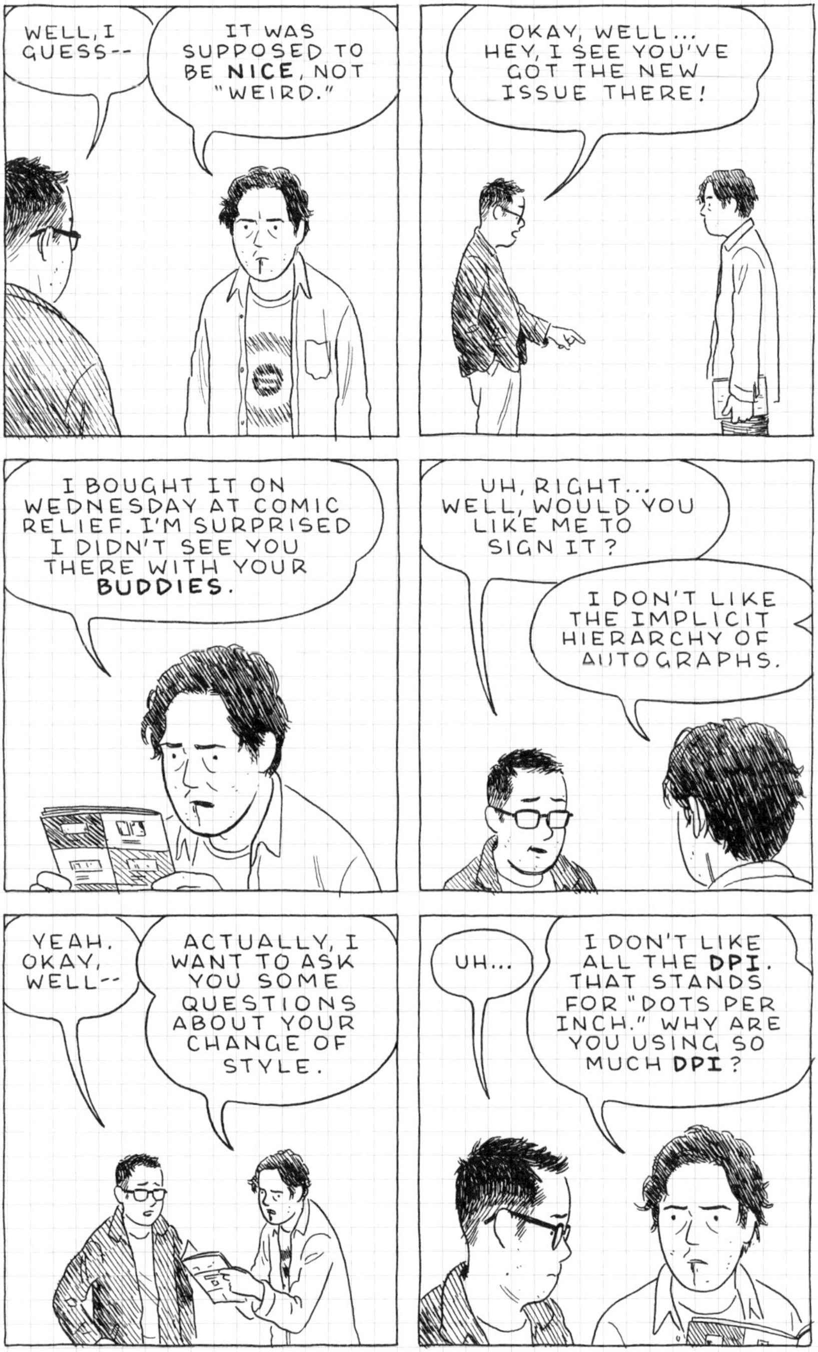
WELL, I GUESS--
IT WAS SUPPOSED TO BE NICE, NOT "WEIRD."
OKAY, WELL... HEY, I SEE YOU'VE GOT THE NEW ISSUE THERE!
I BOUGHT IT ON WEDNESDAY AT COMIC RELIEF. I'M SURPRISED I DIDN'T SEE YOU THERE WITH YOUR BUDDIES.
UH, RIGHT... WELL, WOULD YOU LIKE ME TO SIGN IT?
I DON'T LIKE THE IMPLICIT HIERARCHY OF AUTOGRAPHS.
YEAH. OKAY, WELL--
ACTUALLY, I WANT TO ASK YOU SOME QUESTIONS ABOUT YOUR CHANGE OF STYLE.
UH...
I DON'T LIKE ALL THE DPI. THAT STANDS FOR "DOTS PER INCH." WHY ARE YOU USING SO MUCH DPI?

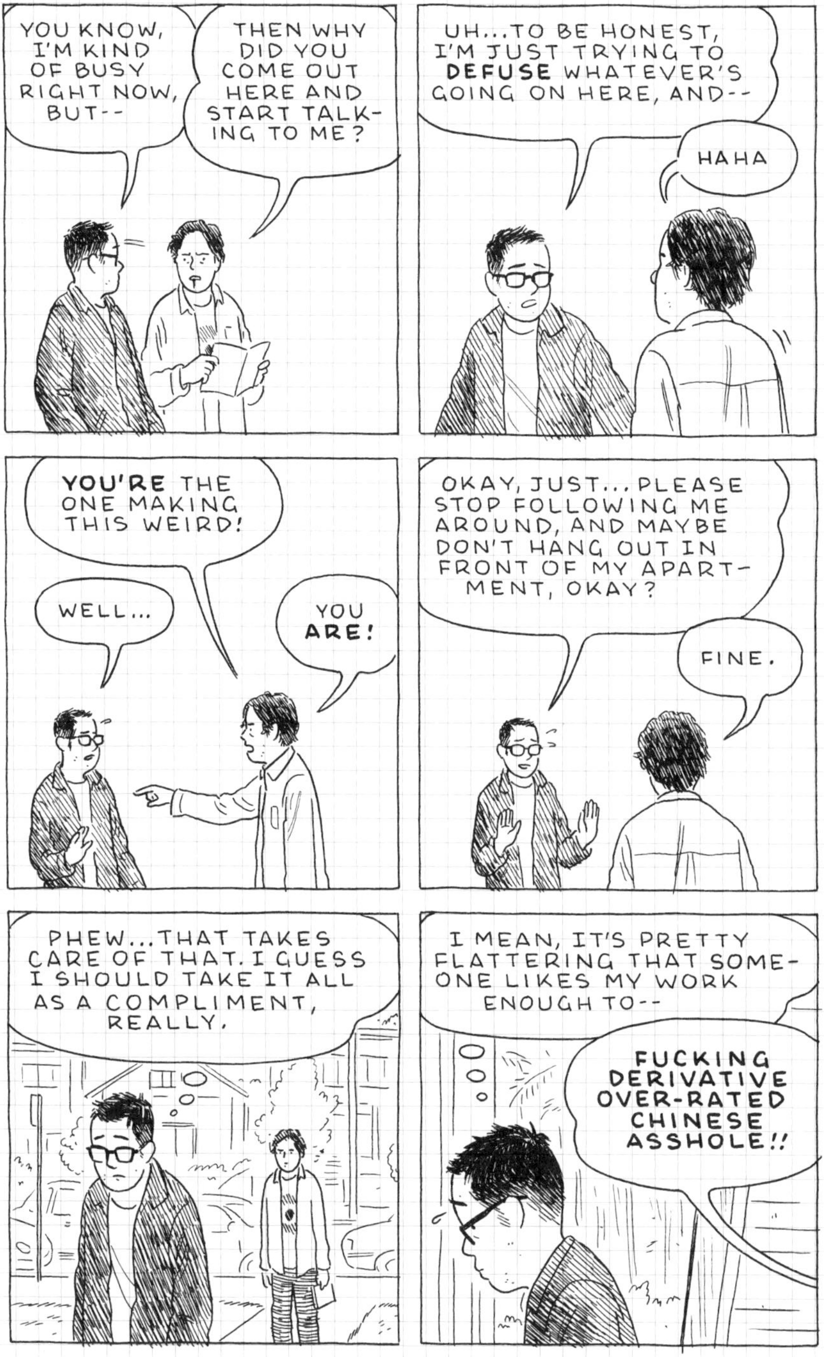
YOU KNOW, I'M KIND OF BUSY RIGHT NOW, BUT--
THEN WHY DID YOU COME OUT HERE AND START TALKING TO ME?
UH...TO BE HONEST, I'M JUST TRYING TO DEFUSE WHATEVER'S GOING ON HERE, AND--
HAHA
YOU'RE THE ONE MAKING THIS WEIRD!
WELL...
YOU ARE!
OKAY, JUST... PLEASE STOP FOLLOWING ME AROUND, AND MAYBE DON'T HANG OUT IN FRONT OF MY APARTMENT, OKAY?
FINE.
PHEW...THAT TAKES CARE OF THAT. I GUESS I SHOULD TAKE IT ALL AS A COMPLIMENT, REALLY.
I MEAN, IT'S PRETTY FLATTERING THAT SOMEONE LIKES MY WORK ENOUGH TO--
FUCKING DERIVATIVE OVER-RATED CHINESE ASSHOLE!!

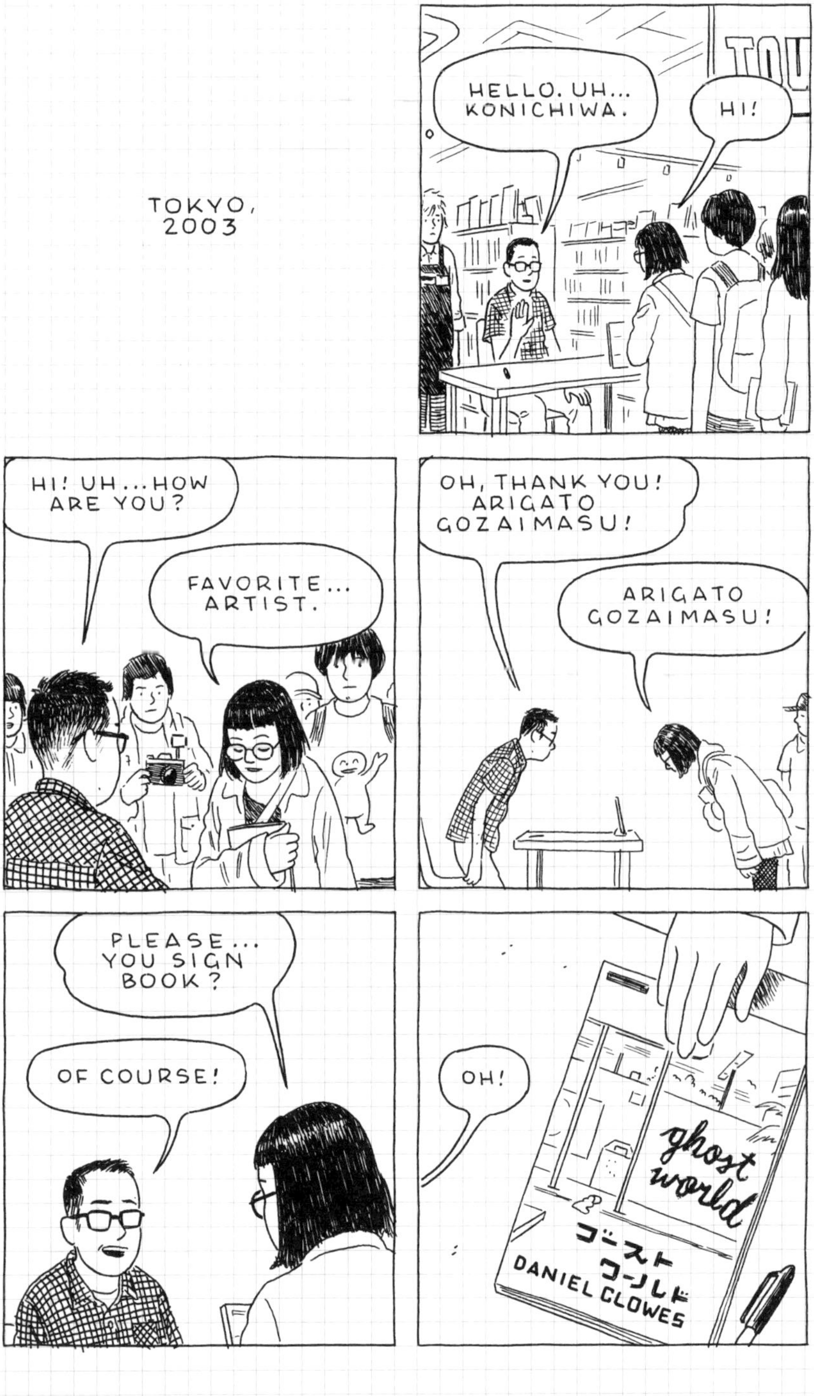
TOKYO, 2003
HELLO. UH... KONICHIWA.
HI!
HI! UH...HOW ARE YOU?
FAVORITE... ARTIST.
OH, THANK YOU! ARIGATO GOZAIMASU!
ARIGATO GOZAIMASU!
PLEASE... YOU SIGN BOOK?
OF COURSE!
OH!
ghost world
ゴースト ワールド
DANIEL CLOWES

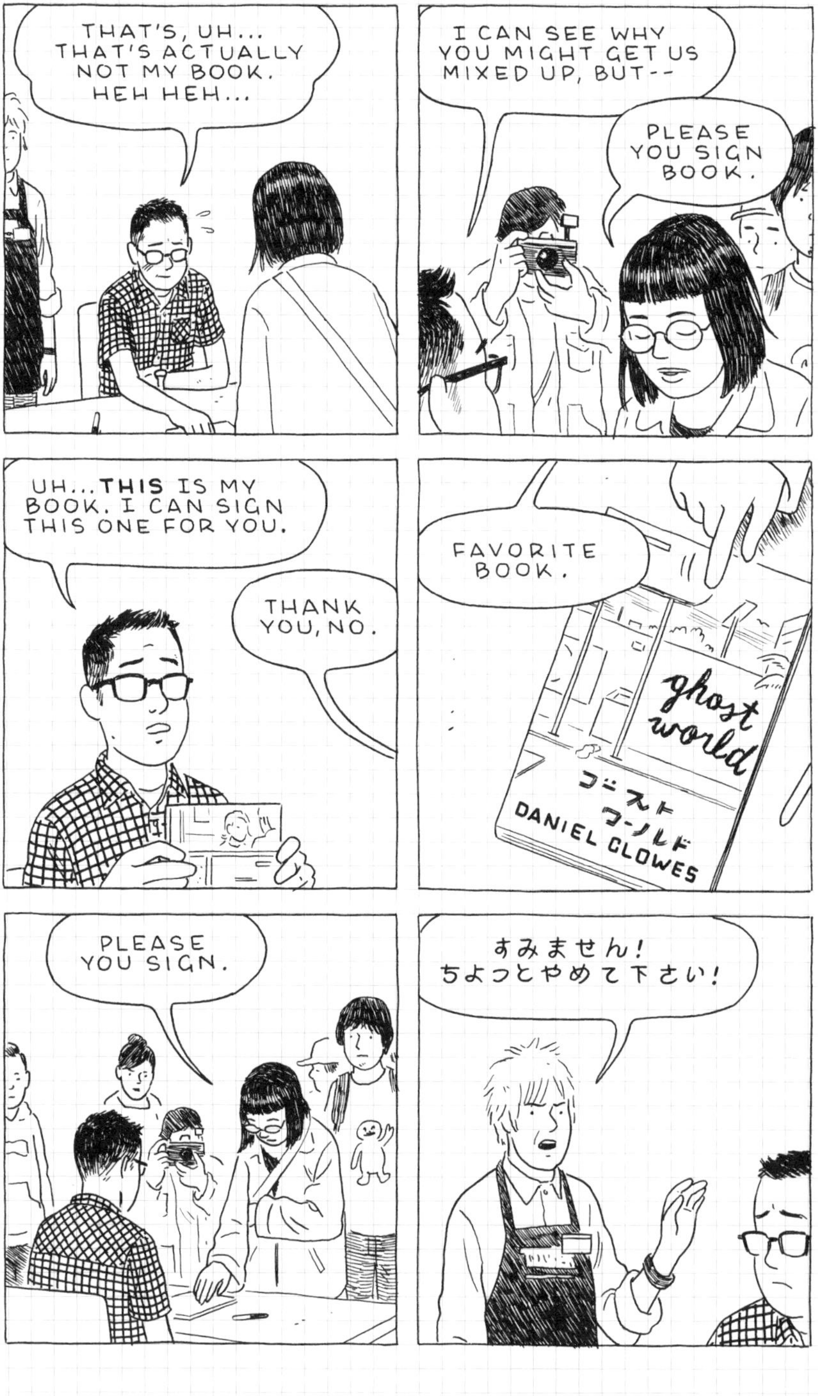
THAT'S, UH... THAT'S ACTUALLY NOT MY BOOK. HEH HEH...
I CAN SEE WHY YOU MIGHT GET US MIXED UP, BUT--
PLEASE YOU SIGN BOOK.
UH... **THIS** IS MY BOOK. I CAN SIGN THIS ONE FOR YOU.
THANK YOU, NO.
FAVORITE BOOK.
ghost world
ゴースト ワールド
DANIEL CLOWES
PLEASE YOU SIGN.
すみません!
ちよっとやめて下さい!

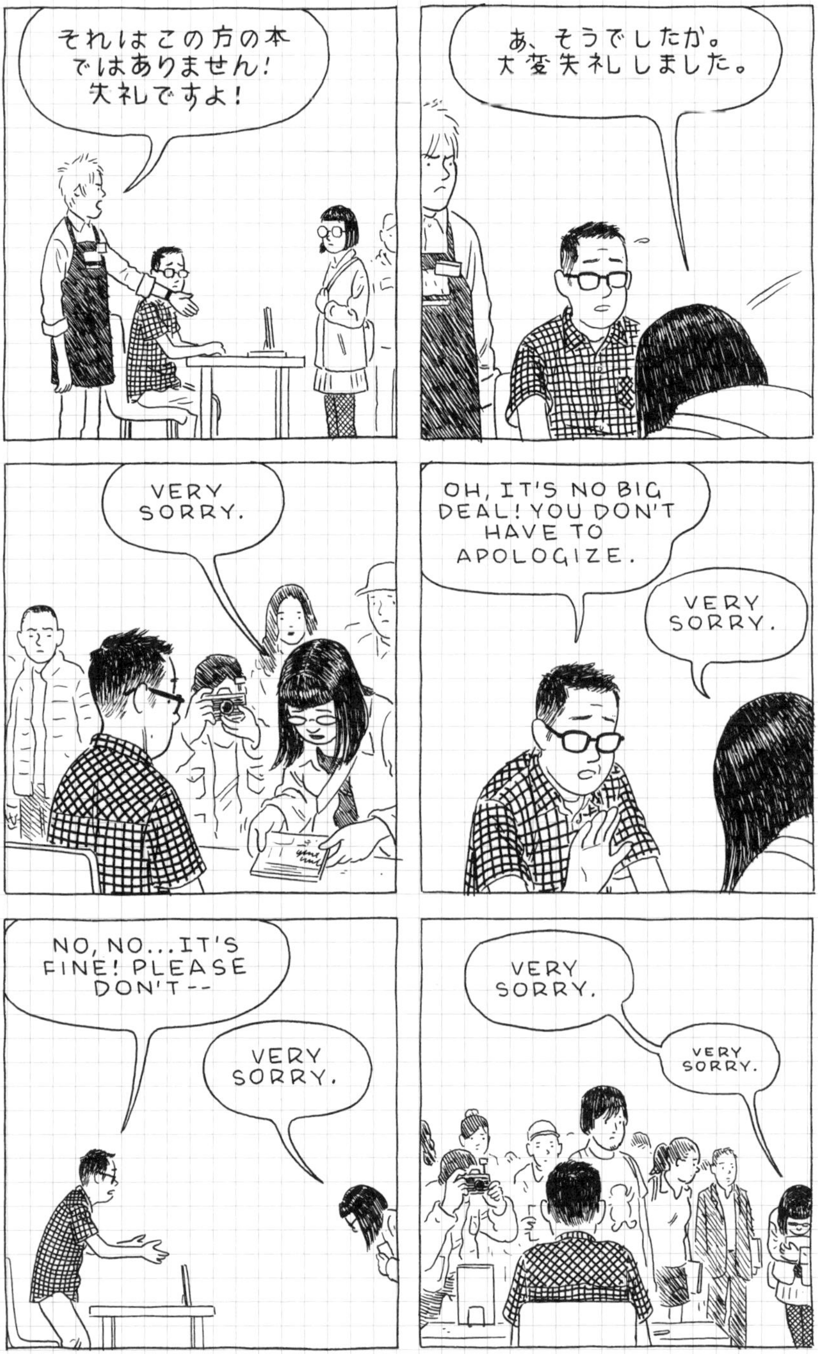
それはこの方の本
ではありません!
失礼ですよ!
あ、そうでしたか。
大変失礼しました。
VERY SORRY.
OH, IT'S NO BIG DEAL! YOU DON'T HAVE TO APOLOGIZE.
VERY SORRY.
NO, NO... IT'S FINE! PLEASE DON'T--
VERY SORRY.
VERY SORRY.
VERY SORRY.

NEW YORK, 2003

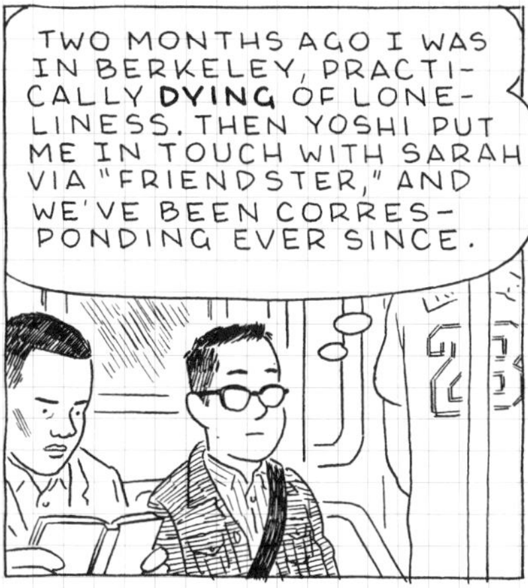
TWO MONTHS AGO I WAS IN BERKELEY, PRACTICALLY **DYING** OF LONELINESS. THEN YOSHI PUT ME IN TOUCH WITH SARAH VIA "FRIENDSTER," AND WE'VE BEEN CORRESPONDING EVER SINCE.

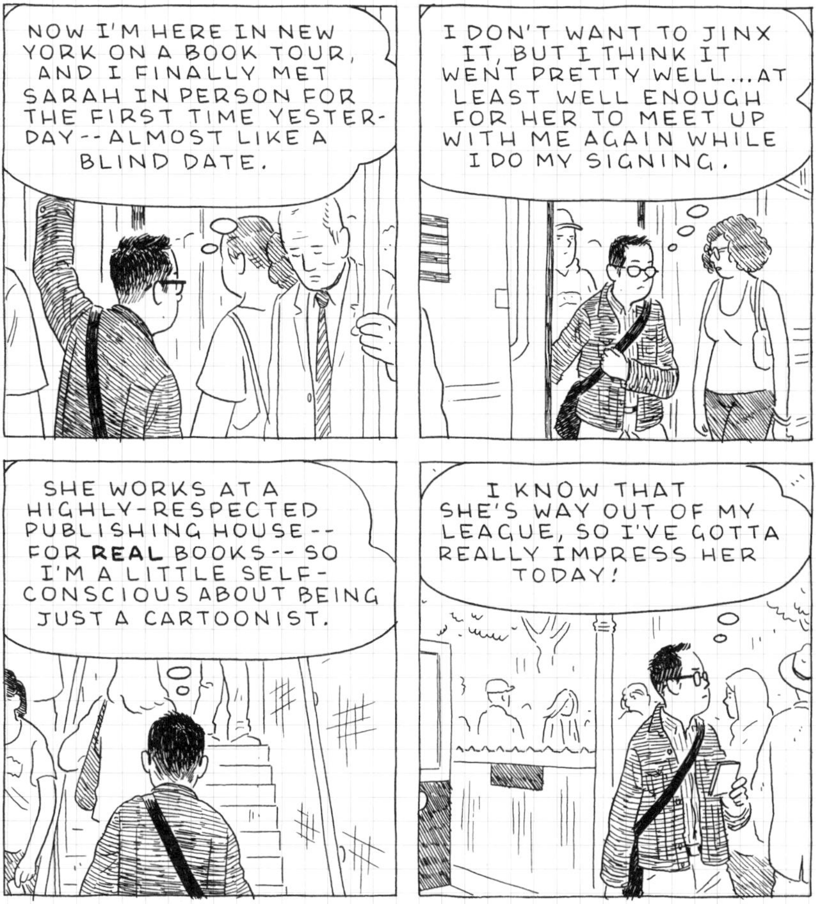
NOW I'M HERE IN NEW YORK ON A BOOK TOUR, AND I FINALLY MET SARAH IN PERSON FOR THE FIRST TIME YESTERDAY--ALMOST LIKE A BLIND DATE.
I DON'T WANT TO JINX IT, BUT I THINK IT WENT PRETTY WELL... AT LEAST WELL ENOUGH FOR HER TO MEET UP WITH ME AGAIN WHILE I DO MY SIGNING.
SHE WORKS AT A HIGHLY-RESPECTED PUBLISHING HOUSE--FOR **REAL** BOOKS--SO I'M A LITTLE SELF-CONSCIOUS ABOUT BEING JUST A CARTOONIST.
I KNOW THAT SHE'S WAY OUT OF MY LEAGUE, SO I'VE GOTTA REALLY IMPRESS HER TODAY!

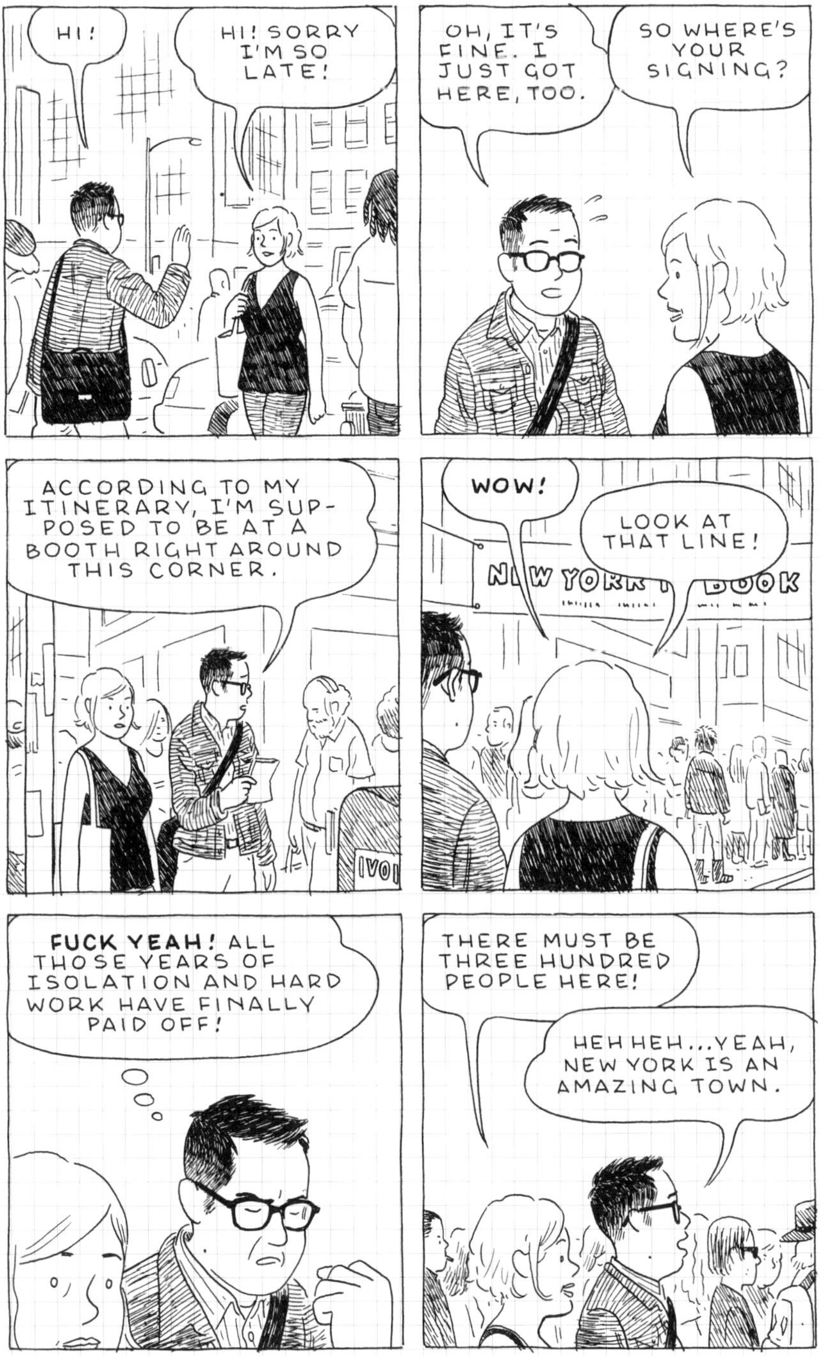
HI!
HI! SORRY I'M SO LATE!
OH, IT'S FINE. I JUST GOT HERE, TOO.
SO WHERE'S YOUR SIGNING?
ACCORDING TO MY ITINERARY, I'M SUP-POSED TO BE AT A BOOTH RIGHT AROUND THIS CORNER.
WOW!
LOOK AT THAT LINE!
FUCK YEAH! ALL THOSE YEARS OF ISOLATION AND HARD WORK HAVE FINALLY PAID OFF!
THERE MUST BE THREE HUNDRED PEOPLE HERE!
HEH HEH...YEAH, NEW YORK IS AN AMAZING TOWN.

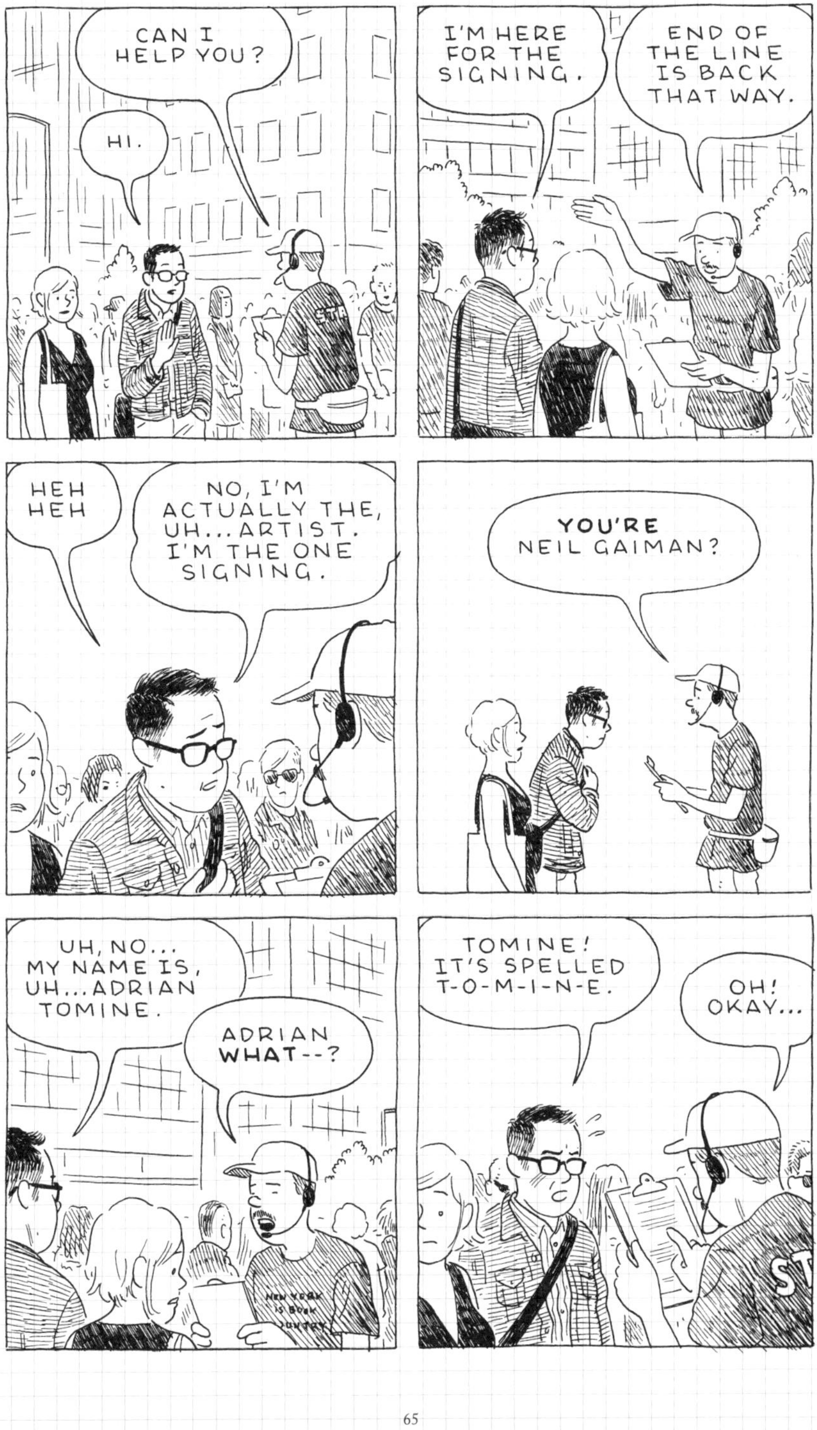
CAN I HELP YOU?
HI.
I'M HERE FOR THE SIGNING.
END OF THE LINE IS BACK THAT WAY.
HEH HEH
NO, I'M ACTUALLY THE, UH... ARTIST. I'M THE ONE SIGNING.
YOU'RE NEIL GAIMAN?
UH, NO... MY NAME IS, UH... ADRIAN TOMINE.
ADRIAN **WHAT**--?
TOMINE! IT'S SPELLED T-O-M-I-N-E.
OH! OKAY...

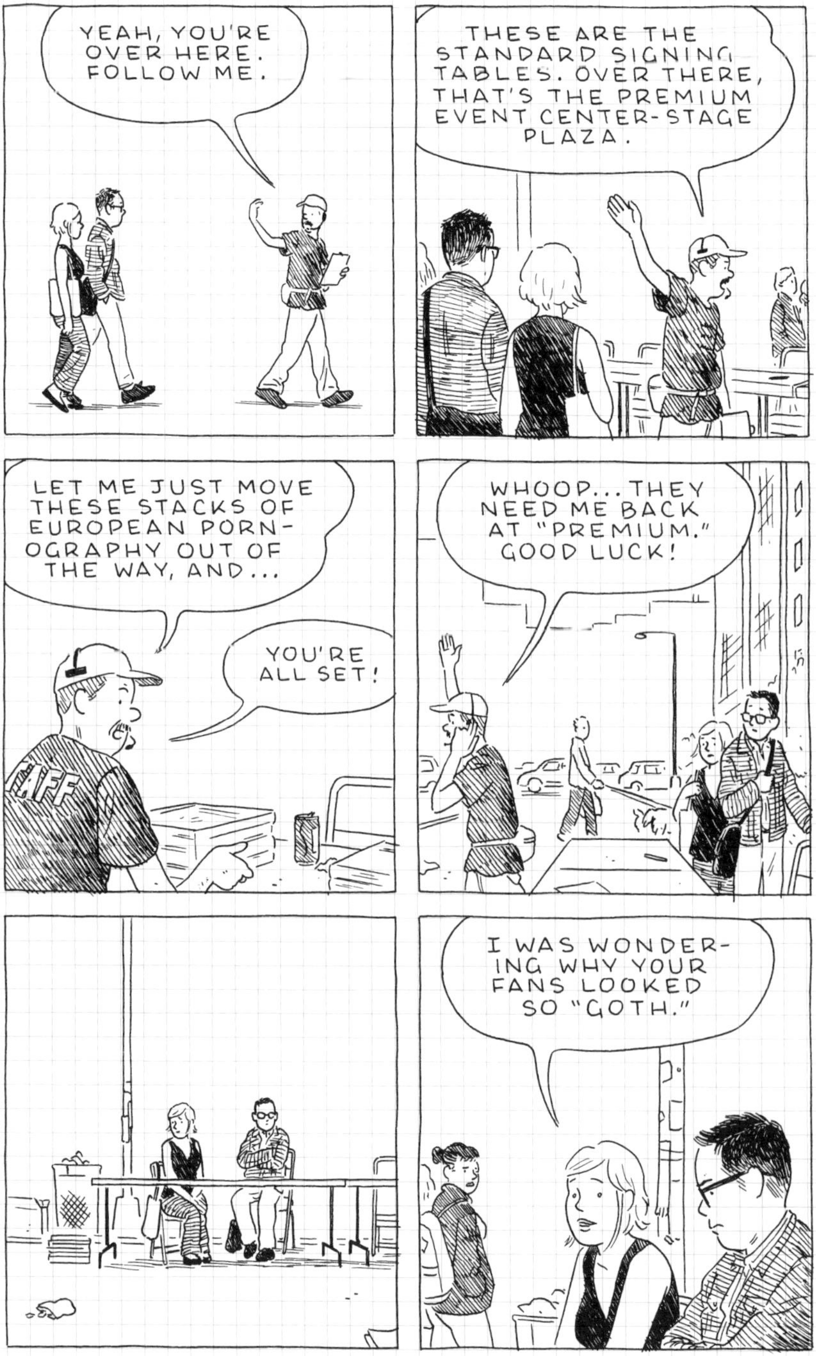
YEAH, YOU'RE OVER HERE. FOLLOW ME.
THESE ARE THE STANDARD SIGNING TABLES. OVER THERE, THAT'S THE PREMIUM EVENT CENTER-STAGE PLAZA.
LET ME JUST MOVE THESE STACKS OF EUROPEAN PORNOGRAPHY OUT OF THE WAY, AND...
YOU'RE ALL SET!
WHOOP... THEY NEED ME BACK AT "PREMIUM." GOOD LUCK!
I WAS WONDERING WHY YOUR FANS LOOKED SO "GOTH."

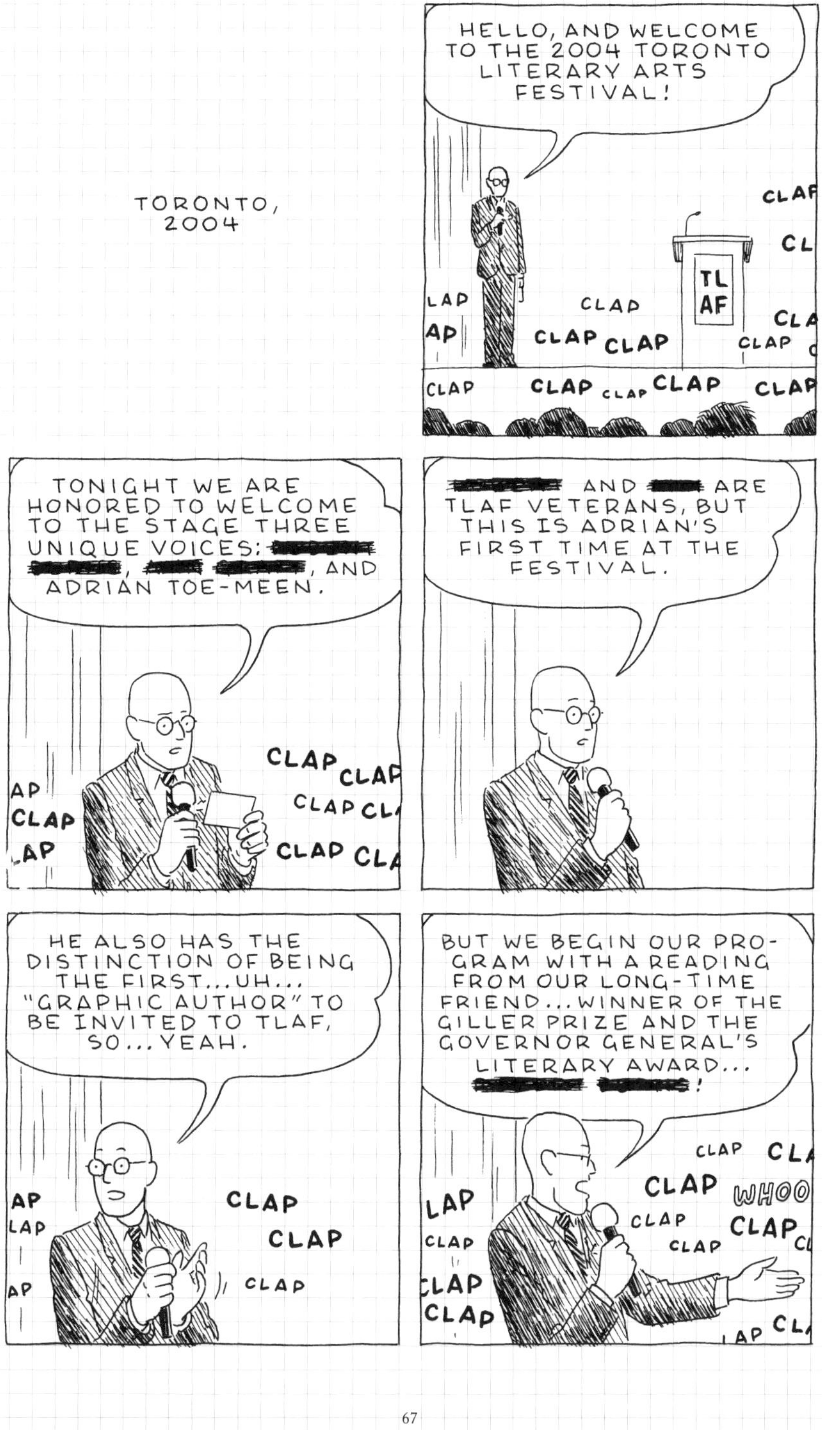
TORONTO, 2004
HELLO, AND WELCOME TO THE 2004 TORONTO LITERARY ARTS FESTIVAL!
TL AF
CLAP CLAP CLAP CLAP CLAP CLAP CLAP CLAP
TONIGHT WE ARE HONORED TO WELCOME TO THE STAGE THREE UNIQUE VOICES: [redacted], [redacted], AND ADRIAN TOE-MEEN.
CLAP CLAP CLAP CLAP
[redacted] AND [redacted] ARE TLAF VETERANS, BUT THIS IS ADRIAN'S FIRST TIME AT THE FESTIVAL.
HE ALSO HAS THE DISTINCTION OF BEING THE FIRST... UH... "GRAPHIC AUTHOR" TO BE INVITED TO TLAF, SO... YEAH.
CLAP CLAP CLAP
BUT WE BEGIN OUR PRO-GRAM WITH A READING FROM OUR LONG-TIME FRIEND... WINNER OF THE GILLER PRIZE AND THE GOVERNOR GENERAL'S LITERARY AWARD... [redacted]!
CLAP CLAP CLAP CLAP CLAP CLAP CLAP

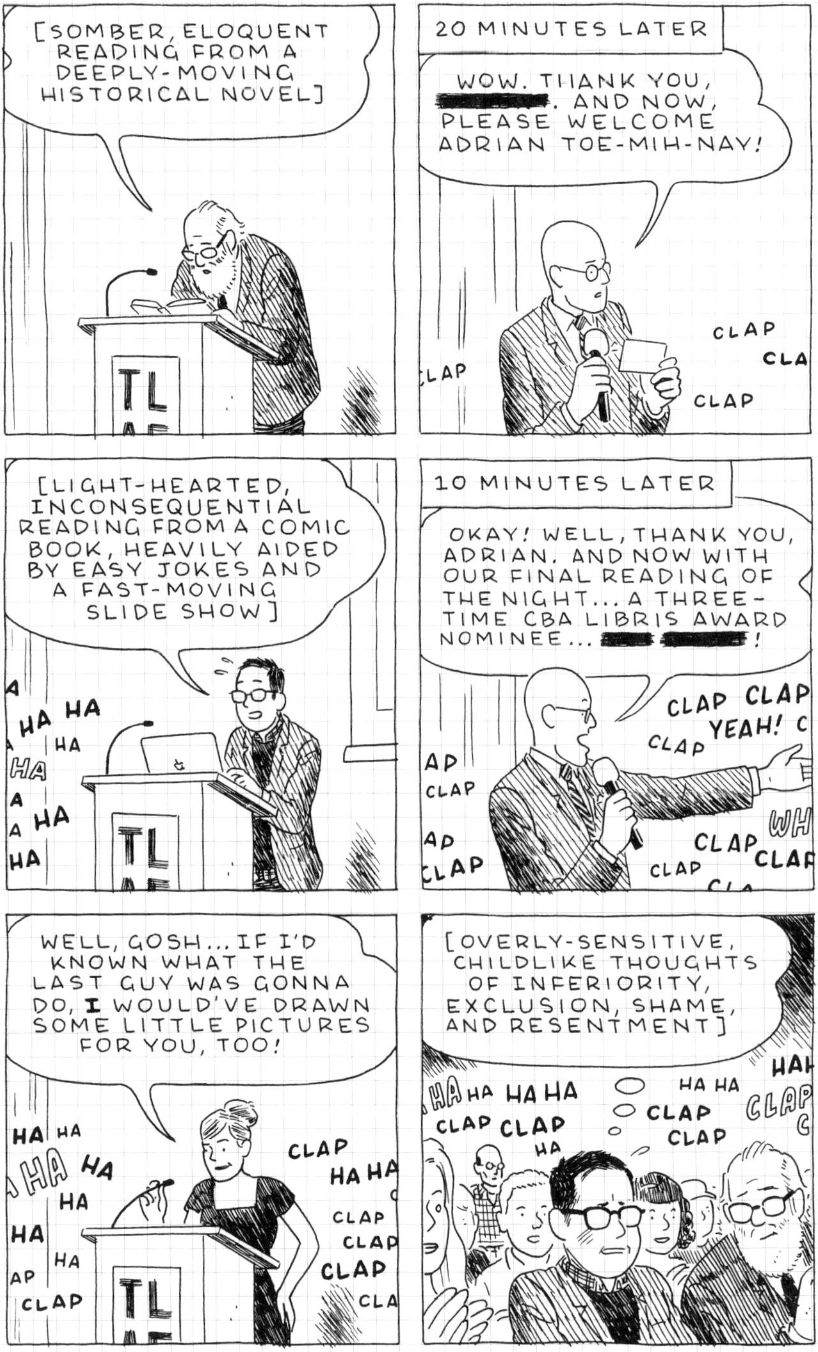
[SOMBER, ELOQUENT READING FROM A DEEPLY-MOVING HISTORICAL NOVEL]
20 MINUTES LATER
WOW. THANK YOU, [redacted]. AND NOW, PLEASE WELCOME ADRIAN TOE-MIH-NAY!
CLAP CLAP CLAP
[LIGHT-HEARTED, INCONSEQUENTIAL READING FROM A COMIC BOOK, HEAVILY AIDED BY EASY JOKES AND A FAST-MOVING SLIDE SHOW]
HA HA HA HA HA HA
10 MINUTES LATER
OKAY! WELL, THANK YOU, ADRIAN. AND NOW WITH OUR FINAL READING OF THE NIGHT... A THREE-TIME CBA LIBRIS AWARD NOMINEE... [redacted]!
CLAP CLAP YEAH! CLAP CLAP CLAP CLAP
WELL, GOSH... IF I'D KNOWN WHAT THE LAST GUY WAS GONNA DO, **I** WOULD'VE DRAWN SOME LITTLE PICTURES FOR YOU, TOO!
HA HA HA HA HA HA HA CLAP CLAP CLAP CLAP CLAP
[OVERLY-SENSITIVE, CHILDLIKE THOUGHTS OF INFERIORITY, EXCLUSION, SHAME, AND RESENTMENT]
HA HA HA HA HA HA HA CLAP CLAP CLAP CLAP HA

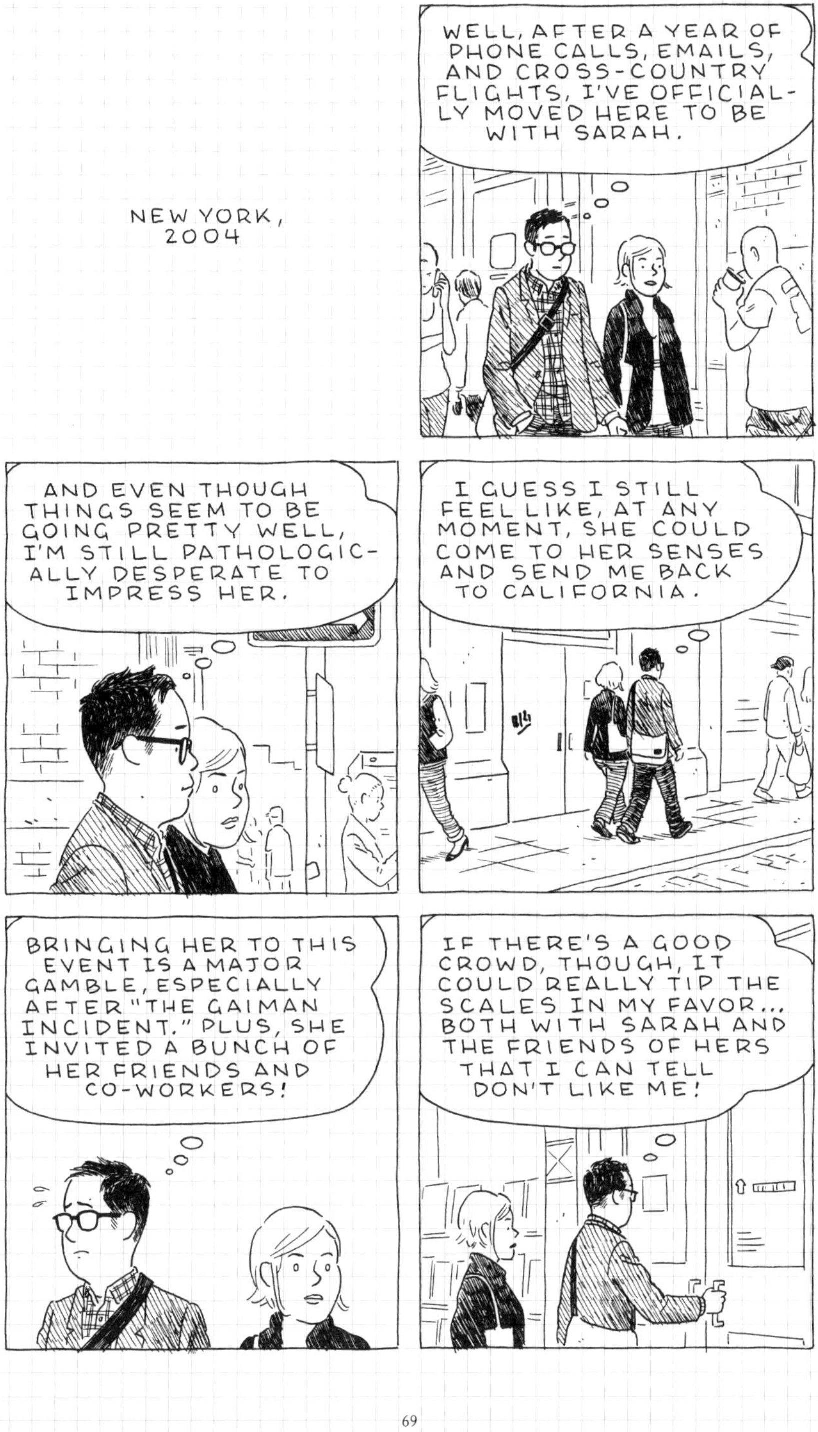
NEW YORK, 2004
WELL, AFTER A YEAR OF PHONE CALLS, EMAILS, AND CROSS-COUNTRY FLIGHTS, I'VE OFFICIALLY MOVED HERE TO BE WITH SARAH.
AND EVEN THOUGH THINGS SEEM TO BE GOING PRETTY WELL, I'M STILL PATHOLOGICALLY DESPERATE TO IMPRESS HER.
I GUESS I STILL FEEL LIKE, AT ANY MOMENT, SHE COULD COME TO HER SENSES AND SEND ME BACK TO CALIFORNIA.
BRINGING HER TO THIS EVENT IS A MAJOR GAMBLE, ESPECIALLY AFTER "THE GAIMAN INCIDENT." PLUS, SHE INVITED A BUNCH OF HER FRIENDS AND CO-WORKERS!
IF THERE'S A GOOD CROWD, THOUGH, IT COULD REALLY TIP THE SCALES IN MY FAVOR... BOTH WITH SARAH AND THE FRIENDS OF HERS THAT I CAN TELL DON'T LIKE ME!

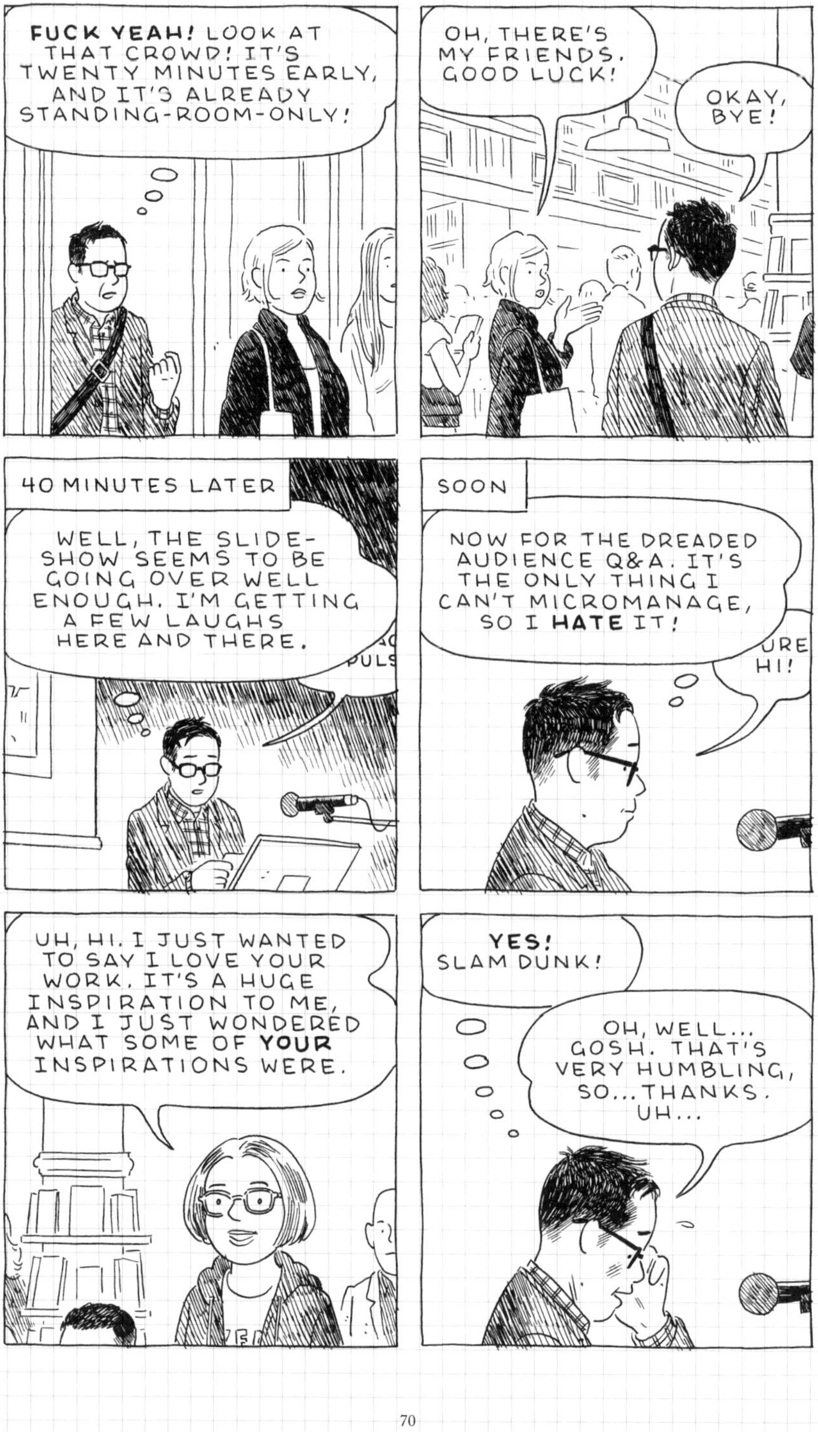
FUCK YEAH! LOOK AT THAT CROWD! IT'S TWENTY MINUTES EARLY, AND IT'S ALREADY STANDING-ROOM-ONLY!
OH, THERE'S MY FRIENDS. GOOD LUCK!
OKAY, BYE!
40 MINUTES LATER
WELL, THE SLIDE-SHOW SEEMS TO BE GOING OVER WELL ENOUGH. I'M GETTING A FEW LAUGHS HERE AND THERE.
SOON
NOW FOR THE DREADED AUDIENCE Q&A. IT'S THE ONLY THING I CAN'T MICROMANAGE, SO I HATE IT!
URE HI!
UH, HI. I JUST WANTED TO SAY I LOVE YOUR WORK. IT'S A HUGE INSPIRATION TO ME, AND I JUST WONDERED WHAT SOME OF YOUR INSPIRATIONS WERE.
YES! SLAM DUNK!
OH, WELL... GOSH. THAT'S VERY HUMBLING, SO... THANKS. UH...

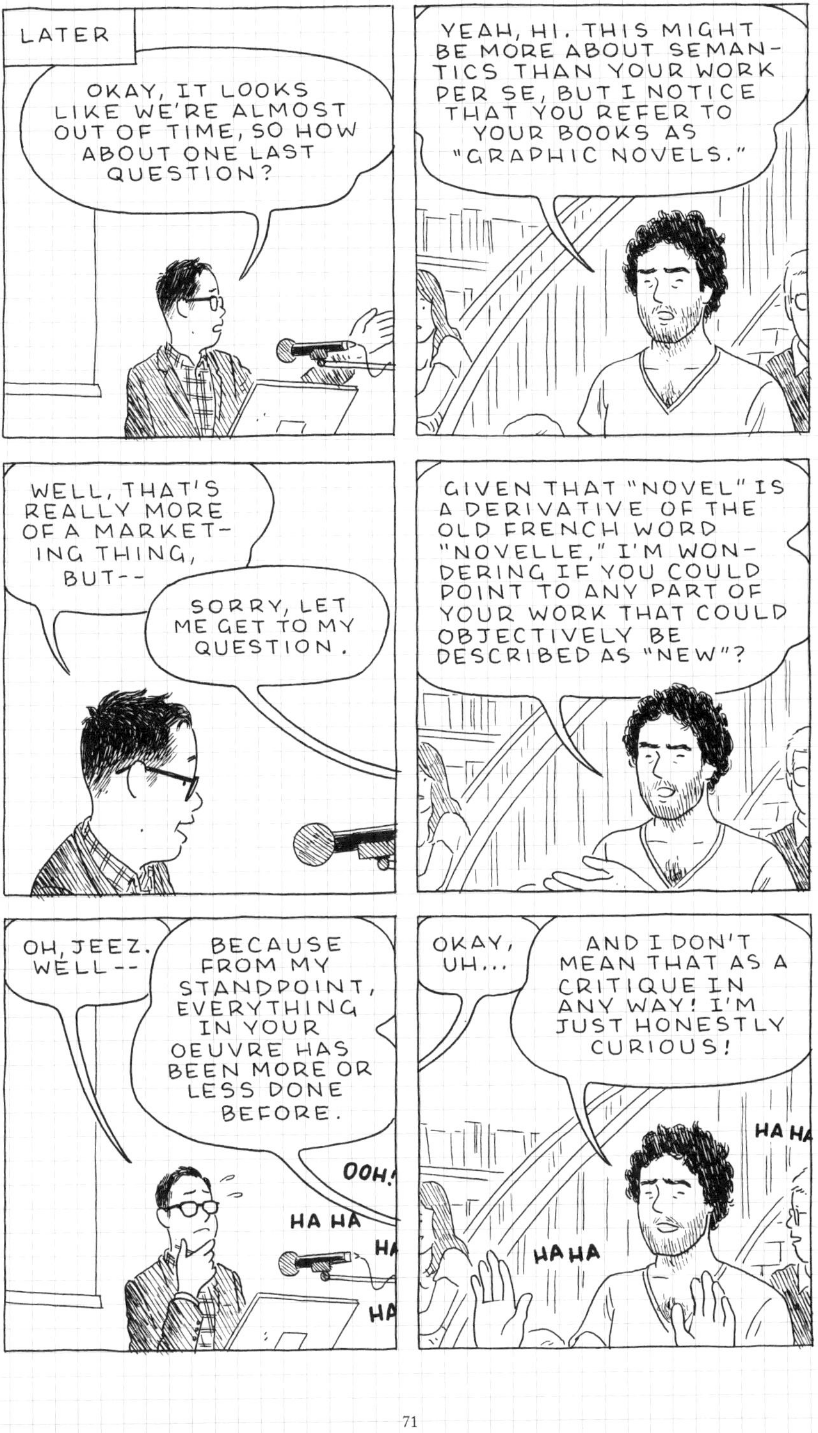
LATER
OKAY, IT LOOKS LIKE WE'RE ALMOST OUT OF TIME, SO HOW ABOUT ONE LAST QUESTION?
YEAH, HI. THIS MIGHT BE MORE ABOUT SEMANTICS THAN YOUR WORK PER SE, BUT I NOTICE THAT YOU REFER TO YOUR BOOKS AS "GRAPHIC NOVELS."
WELL, THAT'S REALLY MORE OF A MARKETING THING, BUT--
SORRY, LET ME GET TO MY QUESTION.
GIVEN THAT "NOVEL" IS A DERIVATIVE OF THE OLD FRENCH WORD "NOVELLE," I'M WONDERING IF YOU COULD POINT TO ANY PART OF YOUR WORK THAT COULD OBJECTIVELY BE DESCRIBED AS "NEW"?
OH, JEEZ. WELL--
BECAUSE FROM MY STANDPOINT, EVERYTHING IN YOUR OEUVRE HAS BEEN MORE OR LESS DONE BEFORE.
OOH!
HA HA
OKAY, UH...
AND I DON'T MEAN THAT AS A CRITIQUE IN ANY WAY! I'M JUST HONESTLY CURIOUS!
HA HA
HA HA

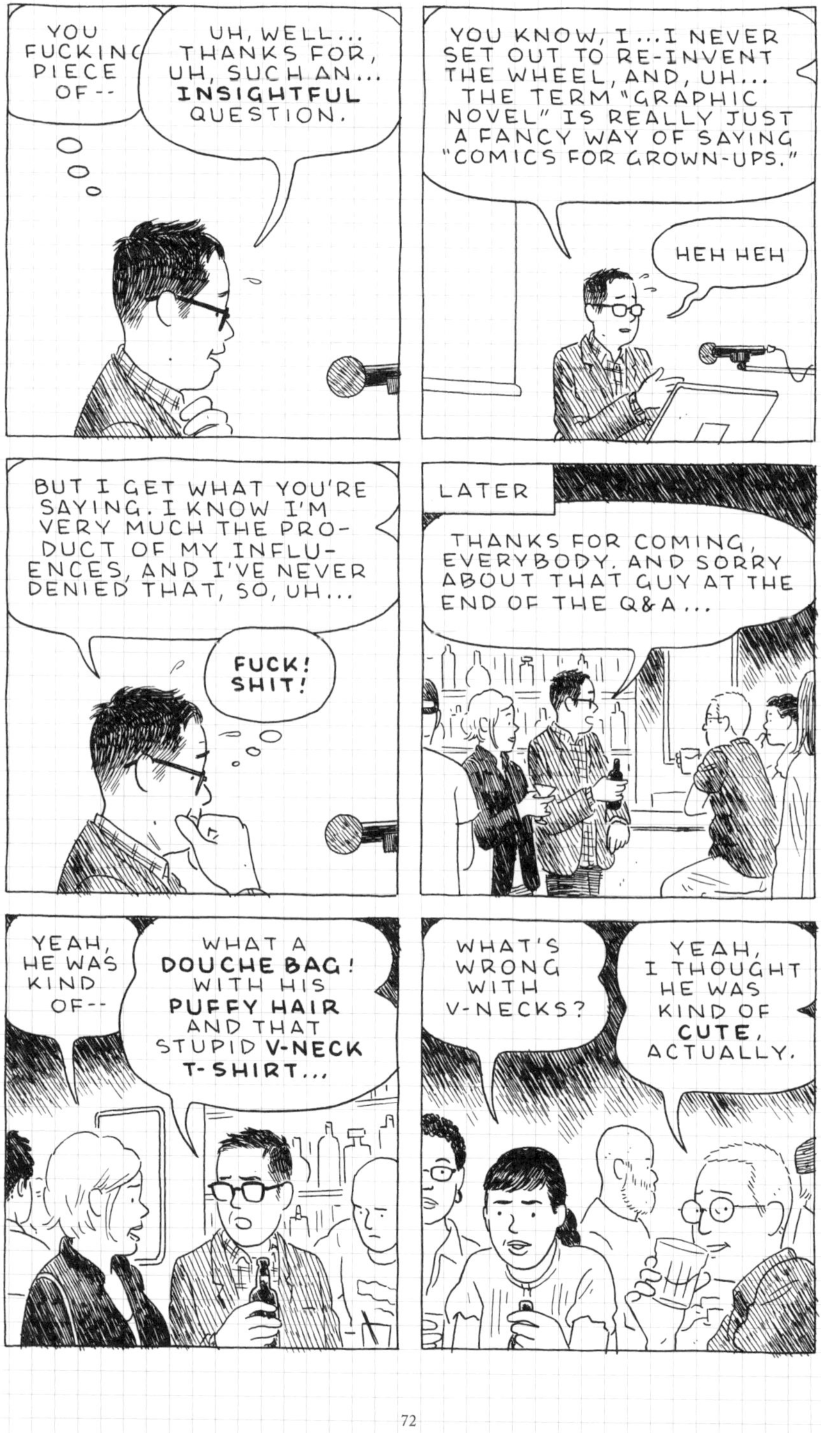
YOU FUCKING PIECE OF--
UH, WELL... THANKS FOR, UH, SUCH AN... **INSIGHTFUL** QUESTION.
YOU KNOW, I...I NEVER SET OUT TO RE-INVENT THE WHEEL, AND, UH... THE TERM "GRAPHIC NOVEL" IS REALLY JUST A FANCY WAY OF SAYING "COMICS FOR GROWN-UPS."
HEH HEH
BUT I GET WHAT YOU'RE SAYING. I KNOW I'M VERY MUCH THE PRODUCT OF MY INFLUENCES, AND I'VE NEVER DENIED THAT, SO, UH...
FUCK! SHIT!
LATER
THANKS FOR COMING, EVERYBODY. AND SORRY ABOUT THAT GUY AT THE END OF THE Q&A...
YEAH, HE WAS KIND OF--
WHAT A **DOUCHE BAG!** WITH HIS **PUFFY HAIR** AND THAT STUPID **V-NECK T-SHIRT...**
WHAT'S WRONG WITH V-NECKS?
YEAH, I THOUGHT HE WAS KIND OF **CUTE**, ACTUALLY.

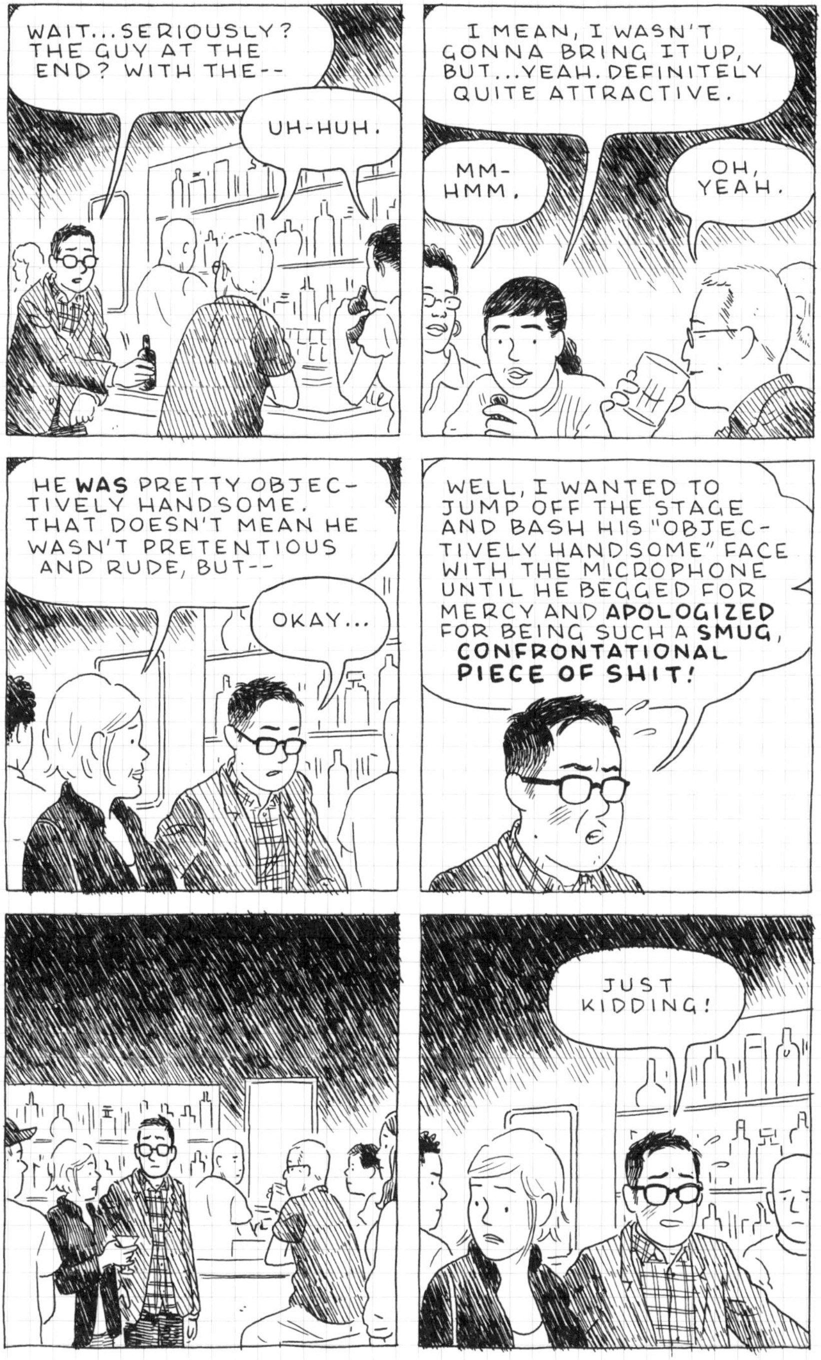
WAIT... SERIOUSLY? THE GUY AT THE END? WITH THE--
UH-HUH.
I MEAN, I WASN'T GONNA BRING IT UP, BUT... YEAH. DEFINITELY QUITE ATTRACTIVE.
MM-HMM.
OH, YEAH.
HE **WAS** PRETTY OBJECTIVELY HANDSOME. THAT DOESN'T MEAN HE WASN'T PRETENTIOUS AND RUDE, BUT--
OKAY...
WELL, I WANTED TO JUMP OFF THE STAGE AND BASH HIS "OBJECTIVELY HANDSOME" FACE WITH THE MICROPHONE UNTIL HE BEGGED FOR MERCY AND **APOLOGIZED** FOR BEING SUCH A **SMUG, CONFRONTATIONAL PIECE OF SHIT!**
JUST KIDDING!

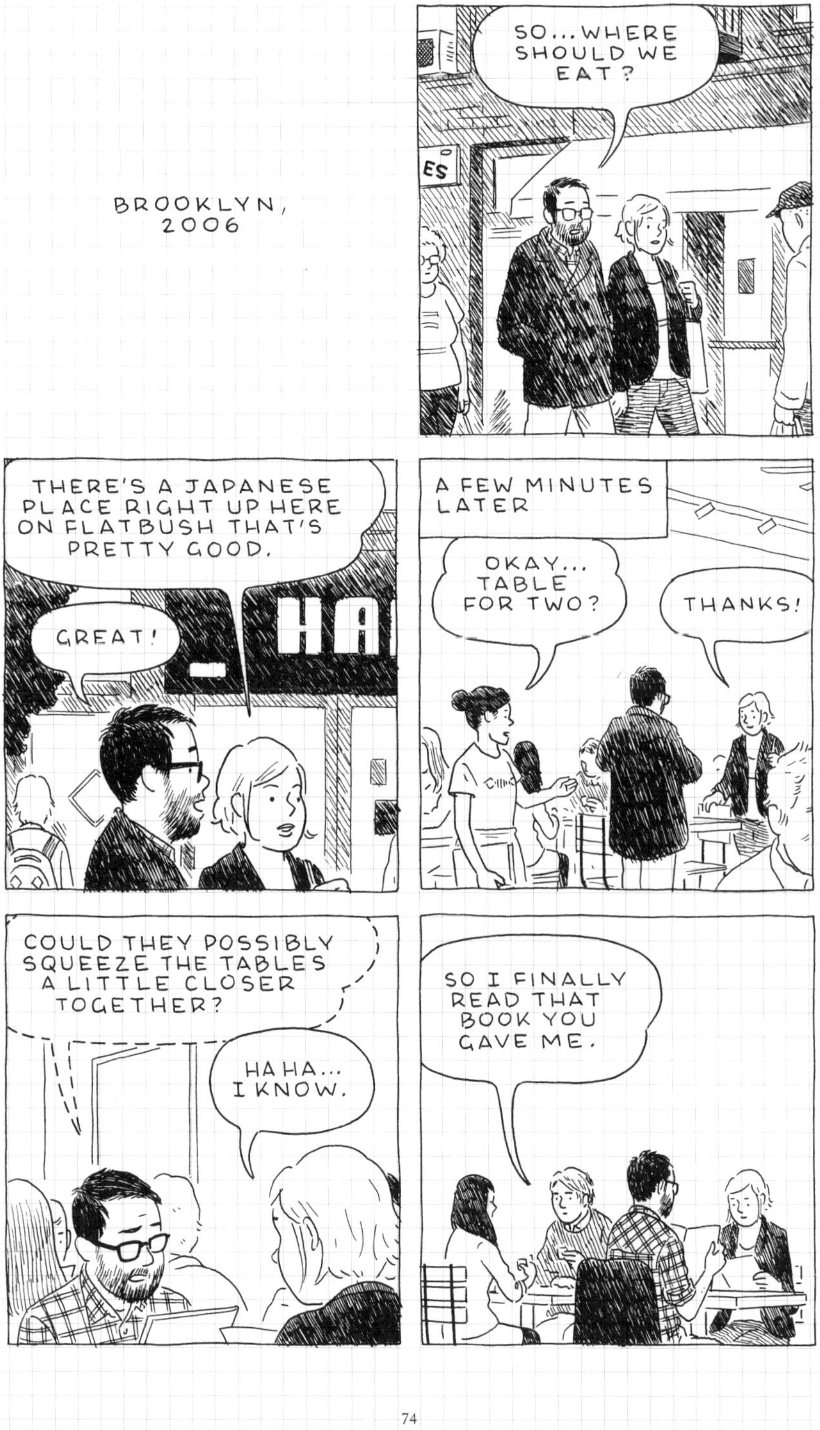
BROOKLYN, 2006
SO... WHERE SHOULD WE EAT?
THERE'S A JAPANESE PLACE RIGHT UP HERE ON FLATBUSH THAT'S PRETTY GOOD.
GREAT!
A FEW MINUTES LATER
OKAY... TABLE FOR TWO?
THANKS!
COULD THEY POSSIBLY SQUEEZE THE TABLES A LITTLE CLOSER TOGETHER?
HA HA... I KNOW.
SO I FINALLY READ THAT BOOK YOU GAVE ME.

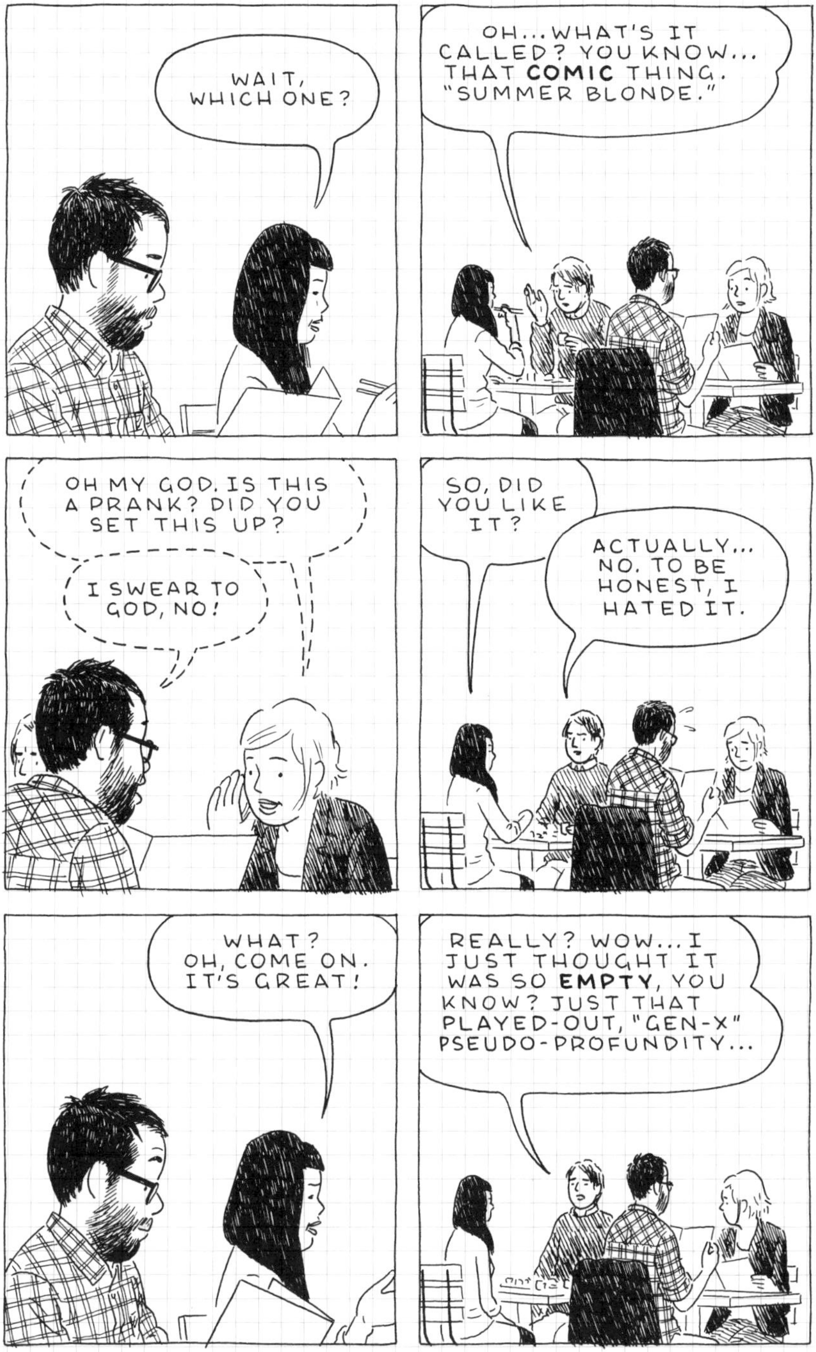
WAIT, WHICH ONE?
OH... WHAT'S IT CALLED? YOU KNOW... THAT **COMIC** THING. "SUMMER BLONDE."
OH MY GOD. IS THIS A PRANK? DID YOU SET THIS UP?
I SWEAR TO GOD, NO!
SO, DID YOU LIKE IT?
ACTUALLY... NO. TO BE HONEST, I HATED IT.
WHAT? OH, COME ON. IT'S GREAT!
REALLY? WOW... I JUST THOUGHT IT WAS SO **EMPTY**, YOU KNOW? JUST THAT PLAYED-OUT, "GEN-X" PSEUDO-PROFUNDITY...

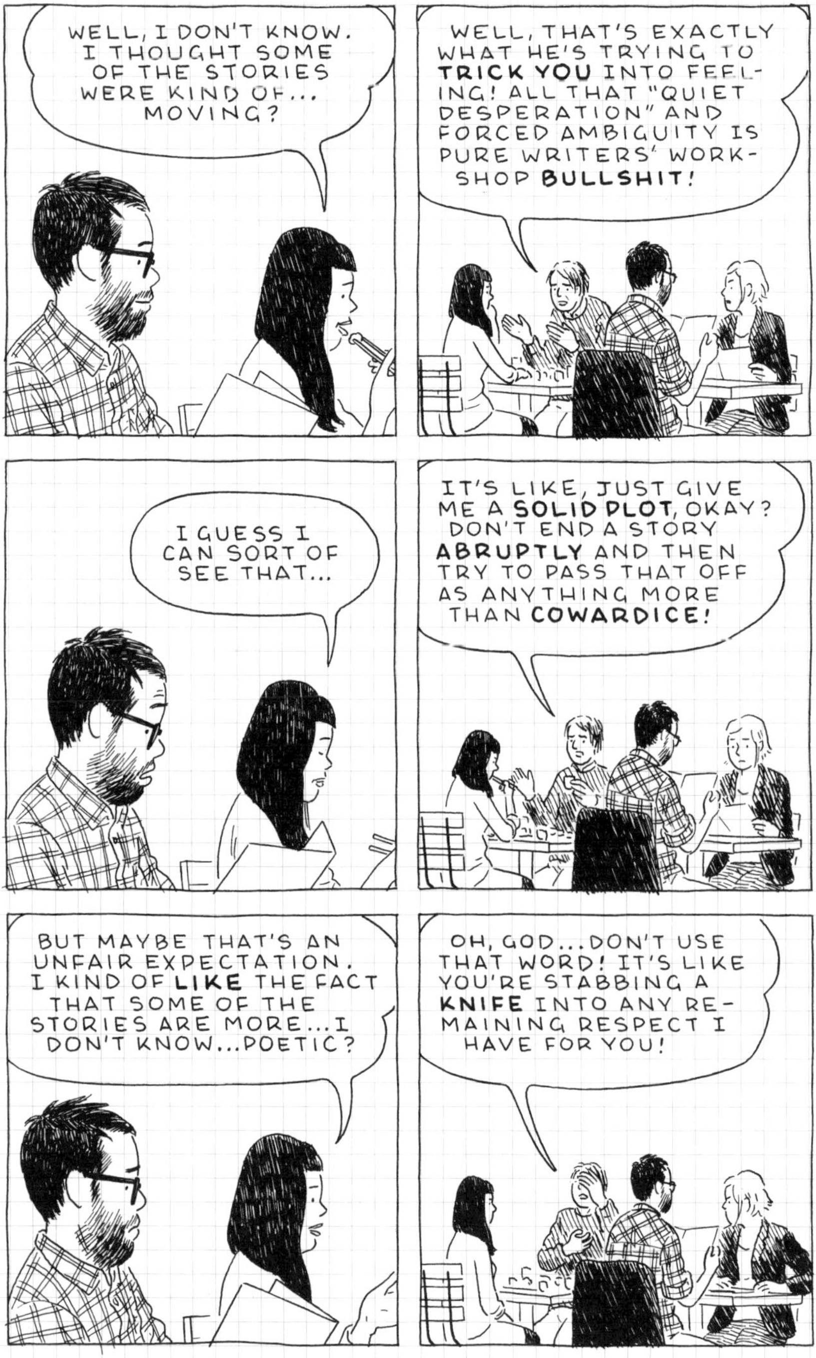
WELL, I DON'T KNOW. I THOUGHT SOME OF THE STORIES WERE KIND OF... MOVING?
WELL, THAT'S EXACTLY WHAT HE'S TRYING TO TRICK YOU INTO FEELING! ALL THAT "QUIET DESPERATION" AND FORCED AMBIGUITY IS PURE WRITERS' WORKSHOP BULLSHIT!
I GUESS I CAN SORT OF SEE THAT...
IT'S LIKE, JUST GIVE ME A SOLID PLOT, OKAY? DON'T END A STORY ABRUPTLY AND THEN TRY TO PASS THAT OFF AS ANYTHING MORE THAN COWARDICE!
BUT MAYBE THAT'S AN UNFAIR EXPECTATION. I KIND OF LIKE THE FACT THAT SOME OF THE STORIES ARE MORE... I DON'T KNOW... POETIC?
OH, GOD... DON'T USE THAT WORD! IT'S LIKE YOU'RE STABBING A KNIFE INTO ANY REMAINING RESPECT I HAVE FOR YOU!

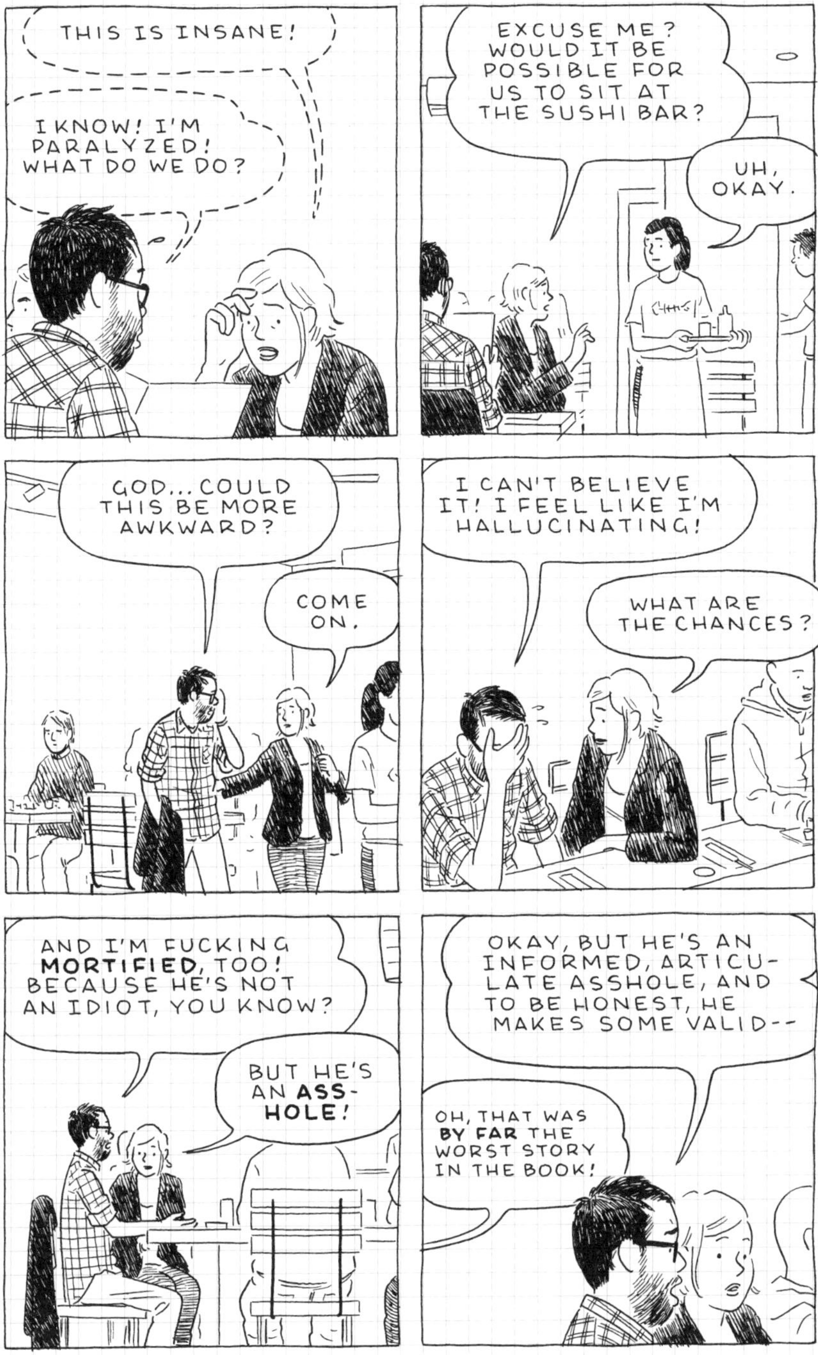
THIS IS INSANE!
I KNOW! I'M PARALYZED! WHAT DO WE DO?
EXCUSE ME? WOULD IT BE POSSIBLE FOR US TO SIT AT THE SUSHI BAR?
UH, OKAY.
GOD... COULD THIS BE MORE AWKWARD?
COME ON.
I CAN'T BELIEVE IT! I FEEL LIKE I'M HALLUCINATING!
WHAT ARE THE CHANCES?
AND I'M FUCKING **MORTIFIED**, TOO! BECAUSE HE'S NOT AN IDIOT, YOU KNOW?
BUT HE'S AN **ASS-HOLE**!
OKAY, BUT HE'S AN INFORMED, ARTICU-LATE ASSHOLE, AND TO BE HONEST, HE MAKES SOME VALID--
OH, THAT WAS **BY FAR** THE WORST STORY IN THE BOOK!

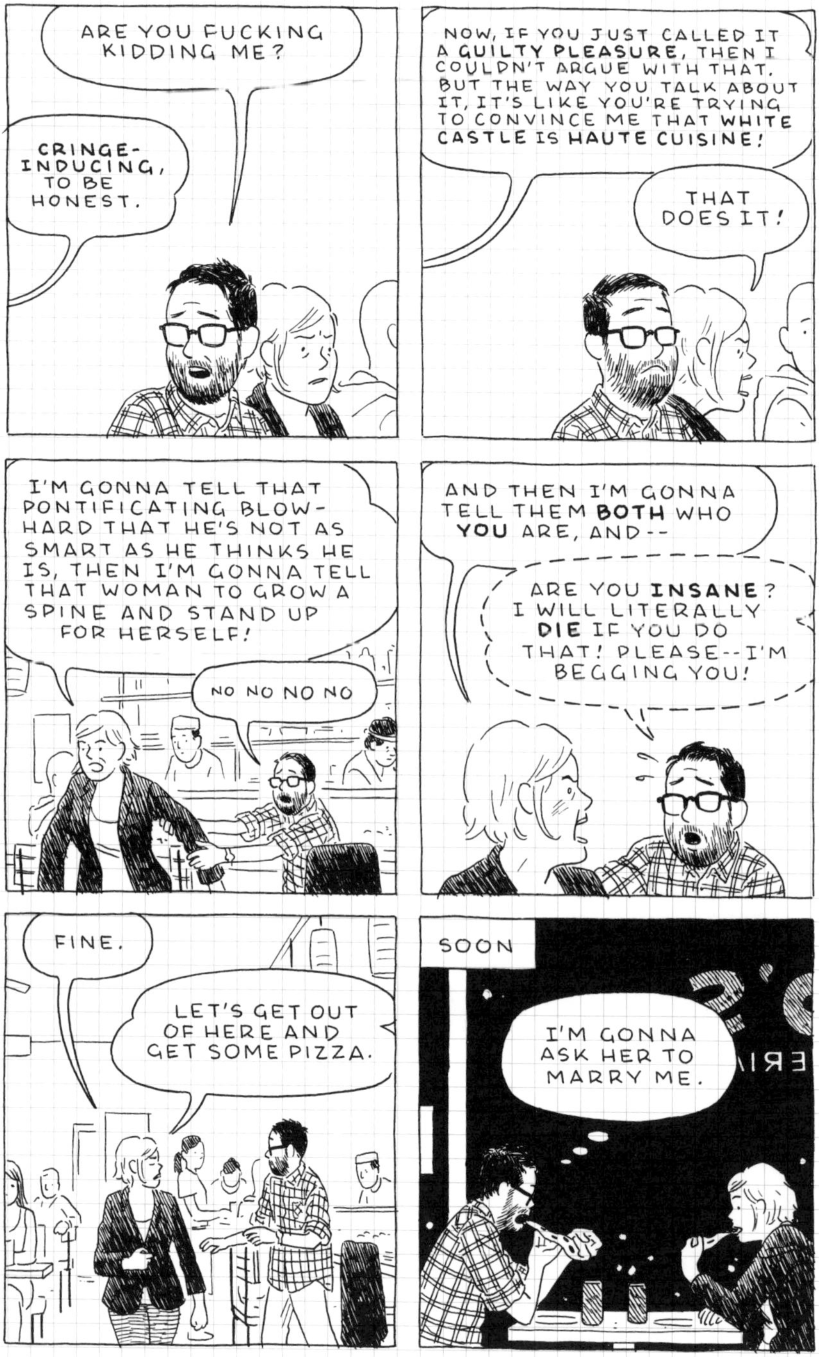
ARE YOU FUCKING KIDDING ME?
CRINGE-INDUCING, TO BE HONEST.
NOW, IF YOU JUST CALLED IT A GUILTY PLEASURE, THEN I COULDN'T ARGUE WITH THAT. BUT THE WAY YOU TALK ABOUT IT, IT'S LIKE YOU'RE TRYING TO CONVINCE ME THAT WHITE CASTLE IS HAUTE CUISINE!
THAT DOES IT!
I'M GONNA TELL THAT PONTIFICATING BLOW-HARD THAT HE'S NOT AS SMART AS HE THINKS HE IS, THEN I'M GONNA TELL THAT WOMAN TO GROW A SPINE AND STAND UP FOR HERSELF!
NO NO NO NO
AND THEN I'M GONNA TELL THEM BOTH WHO YOU ARE, AND--
ARE YOU INSANE? I WILL LITERALLY DIE IF YOU DO THAT! PLEASE--I'M BEGGING YOU!
FINE.
LET'S GET OUT OF HERE AND GET SOME PIZZA.
SOON
I'M GONNA ASK HER TO MARRY ME.

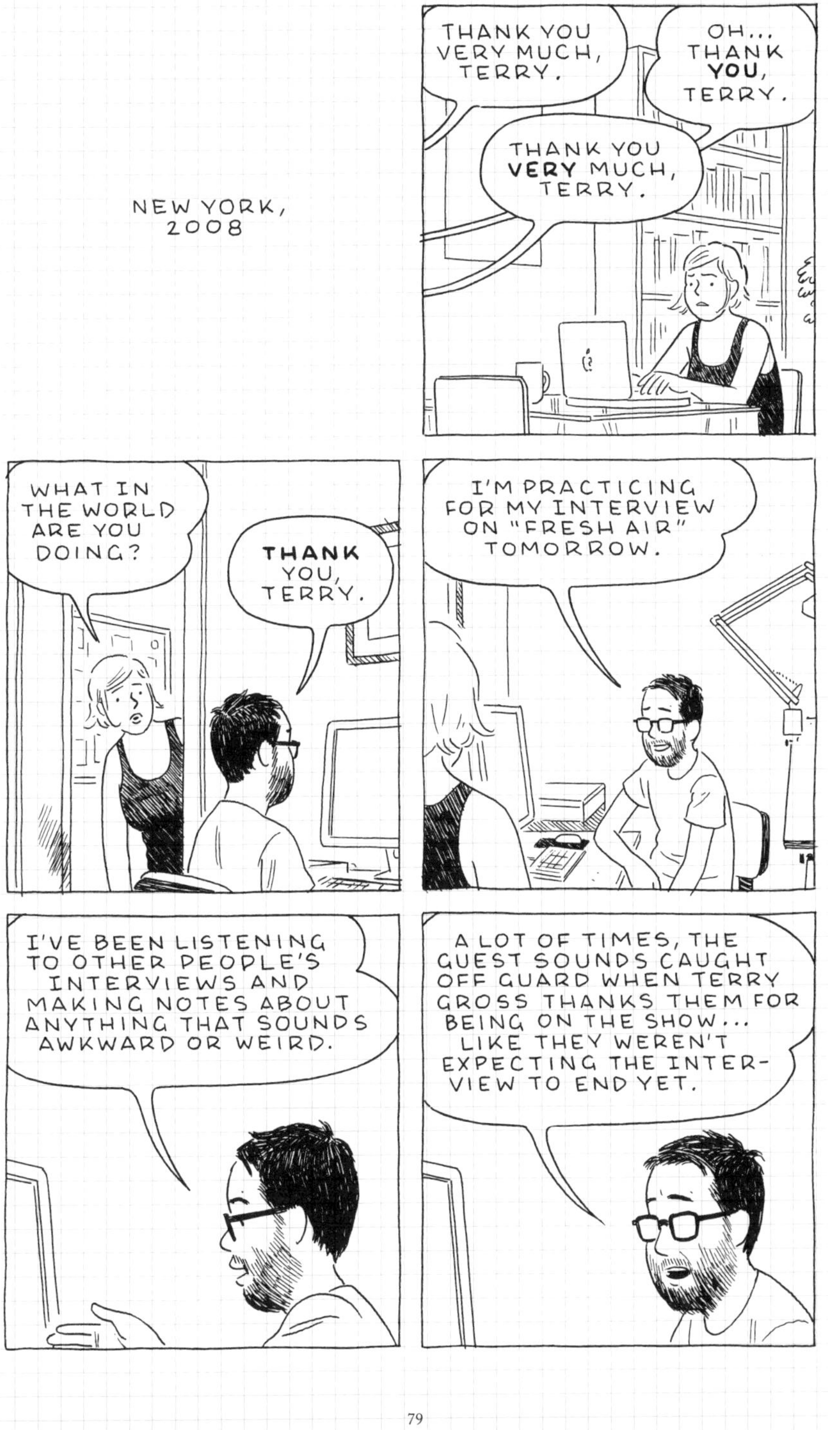
NEW YORK, 2008
THANK YOU VERY MUCH, TERRY.
OH... THANK **YOU**, TERRY.
THANK YOU **VERY** MUCH, TERRY.
WHAT IN THE WORLD ARE YOU DOING?
THANK YOU, TERRY.
I'M PRACTICING FOR MY INTERVIEW ON "FRESH AIR" TOMORROW.
I'VE BEEN LISTENING TO OTHER PEOPLE'S INTERVIEWS AND MAKING NOTES ABOUT ANYTHING THAT SOUNDS AWKWARD OR WEIRD.
A LOT OF TIMES, THE GUEST SOUNDS CAUGHT OFF GUARD WHEN TERRY GROSS THANKS THEM FOR BEING ON THE SHOW... LIKE THEY WEREN'T EXPECTING THE INTER-VIEW TO END YET.

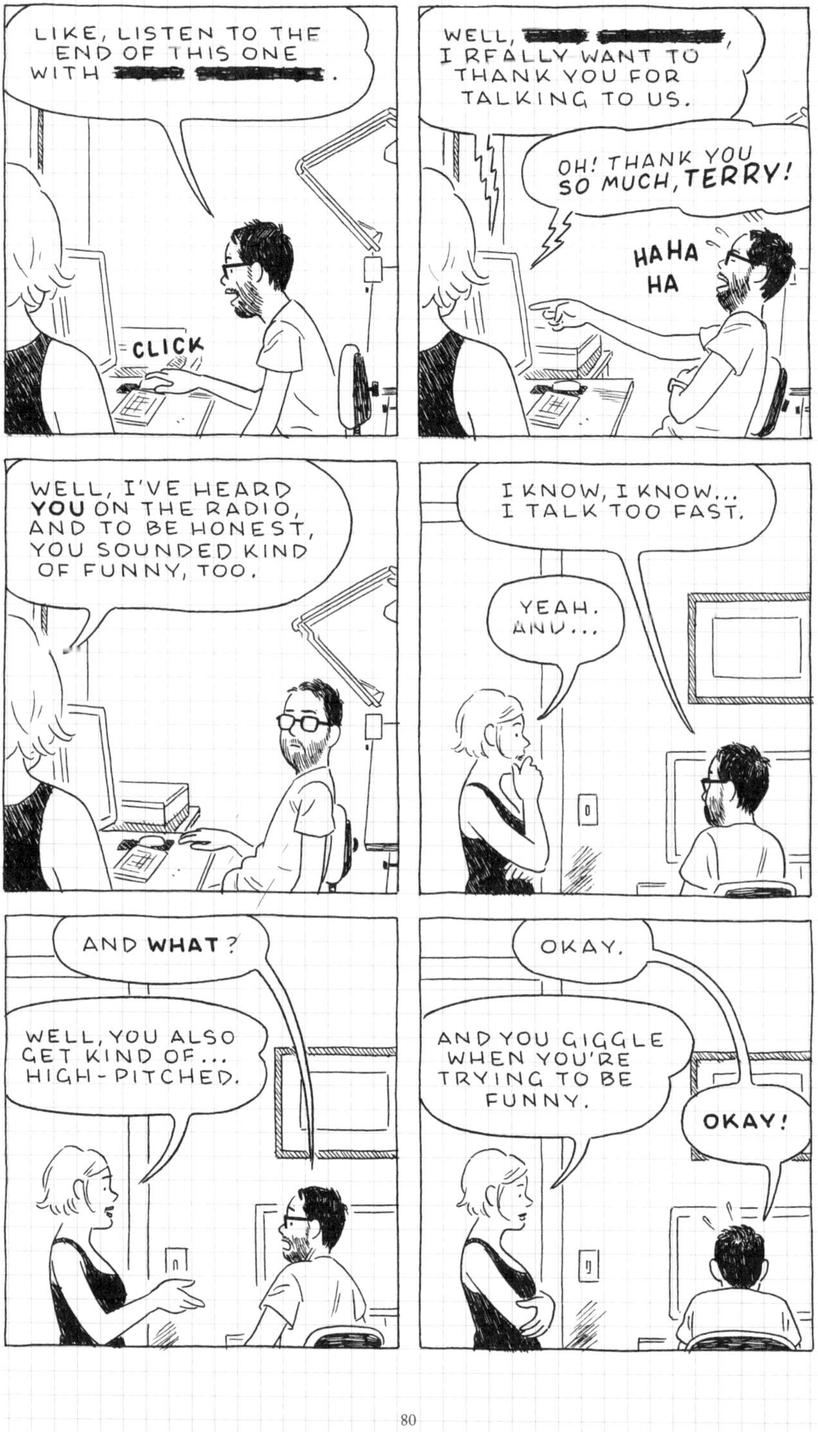
LIKE, LISTEN TO THE END OF THIS ONE WITH [redacted].
CLICK
WELL, [redacted], I REALLY WANT TO THANK YOU FOR TALKING TO US.
OH! THANK YOU SO MUCH, TERRY!
HAHA HA
WELL, I'VE HEARD YOU ON THE RADIO, AND TO BE HONEST, YOU SOUNDED KIND OF FUNNY, TOO.
I KNOW, I KNOW... I TALK TOO FAST.
YEAH. AND...
AND WHAT?
WELL, YOU ALSO GET KIND OF... HIGH-PITCHED.
OKAY.
AND YOU GIGGLE WHEN YOU'RE TRYING TO BE FUNNY.
OKAY!

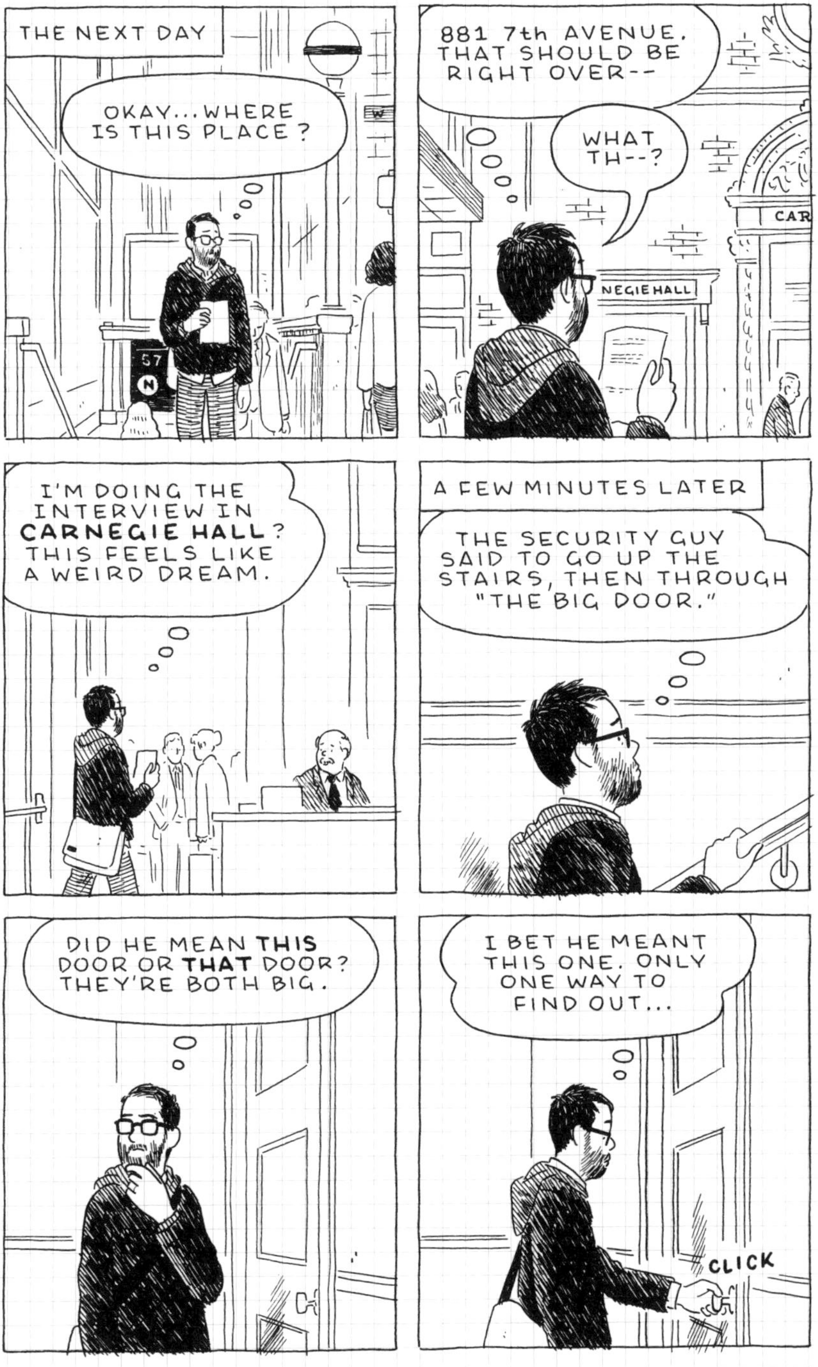
THE NEXT DAY
OKAY...WHERE IS THIS PLACE?
881 7th AVENUE. THAT SHOULD BE RIGHT OVER--
WHAT TH--?
NEGIEHALL
CAR
I'M DOING THE INTERVIEW IN **CARNEGIE HALL**? THIS FEELS LIKE A WEIRD DREAM.
A FEW MINUTES LATER
THE SECURITY GUY SAID TO GO UP THE STAIRS, THEN THROUGH "THE BIG DOOR."
DID HE MEAN **THIS** DOOR OR **THAT** DOOR? THEY'RE BOTH BIG.
I BET HE MEANT THIS ONE. ONLY ONE WAY TO FIND OUT...
CLICK

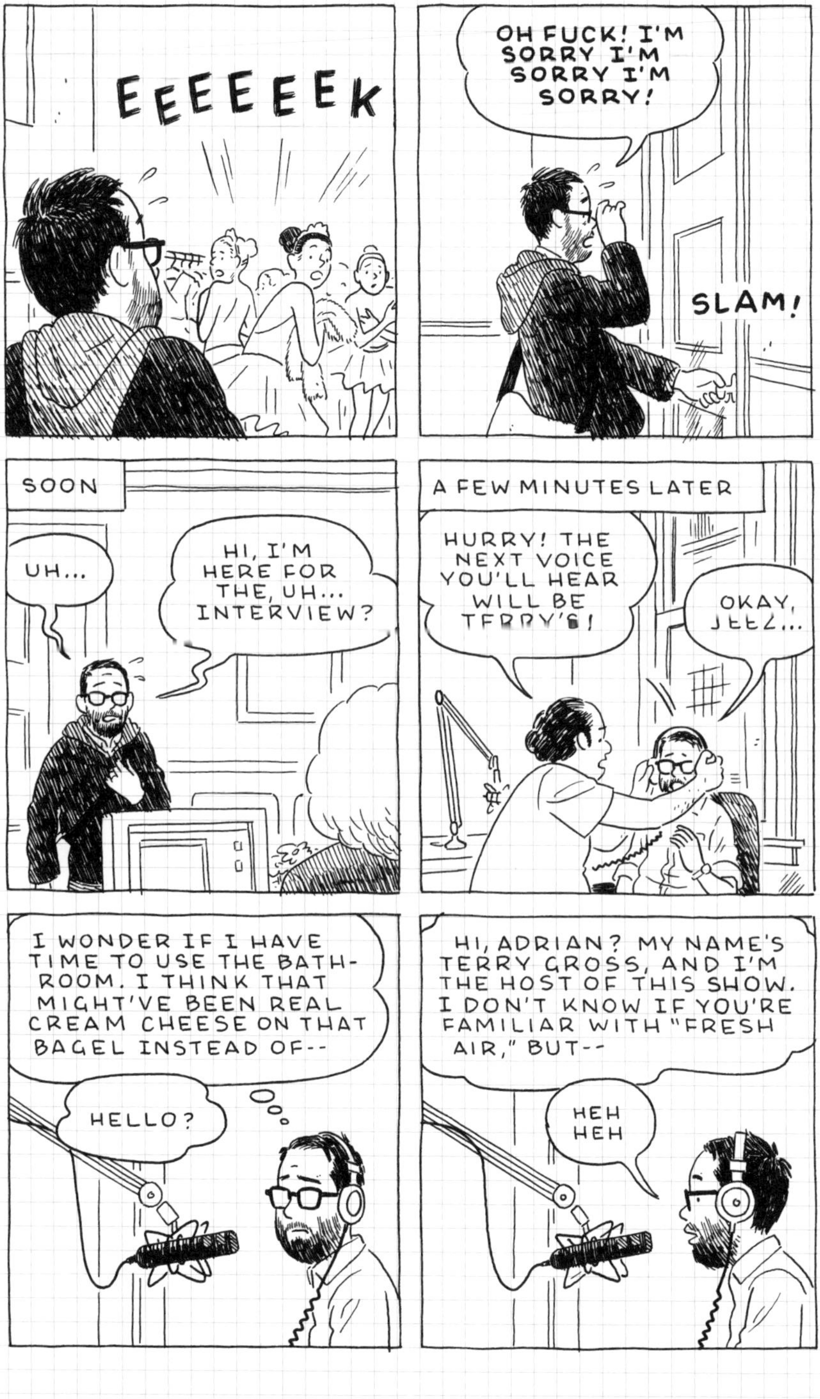
EEEEEEK
OH FUCK! I'M SORRY I'M SORRY I'M SORRY!
SLAM!
SOON
UH...
HI, I'M HERE FOR THE, UH... INTERVIEW?
A FEW MINUTES LATER
HURRY! THE NEXT VOICE YOU'LL HEAR WILL BE TERRY'S!
OKAY, JEEZ...
I WONDER IF I HAVE TIME TO USE THE BATHROOM. I THINK THAT MIGHT'VE BEEN REAL CREAM CHEESE ON THAT BAGEL INSTEAD OF--
HELLO?
HI, ADRIAN? MY NAME'S TERRY GROSS, AND I'M THE HOST OF THIS SHOW. I DON'T KNOW IF YOU'RE FAMILIAR WITH "FRESH AIR," BUT--
HEH HEH

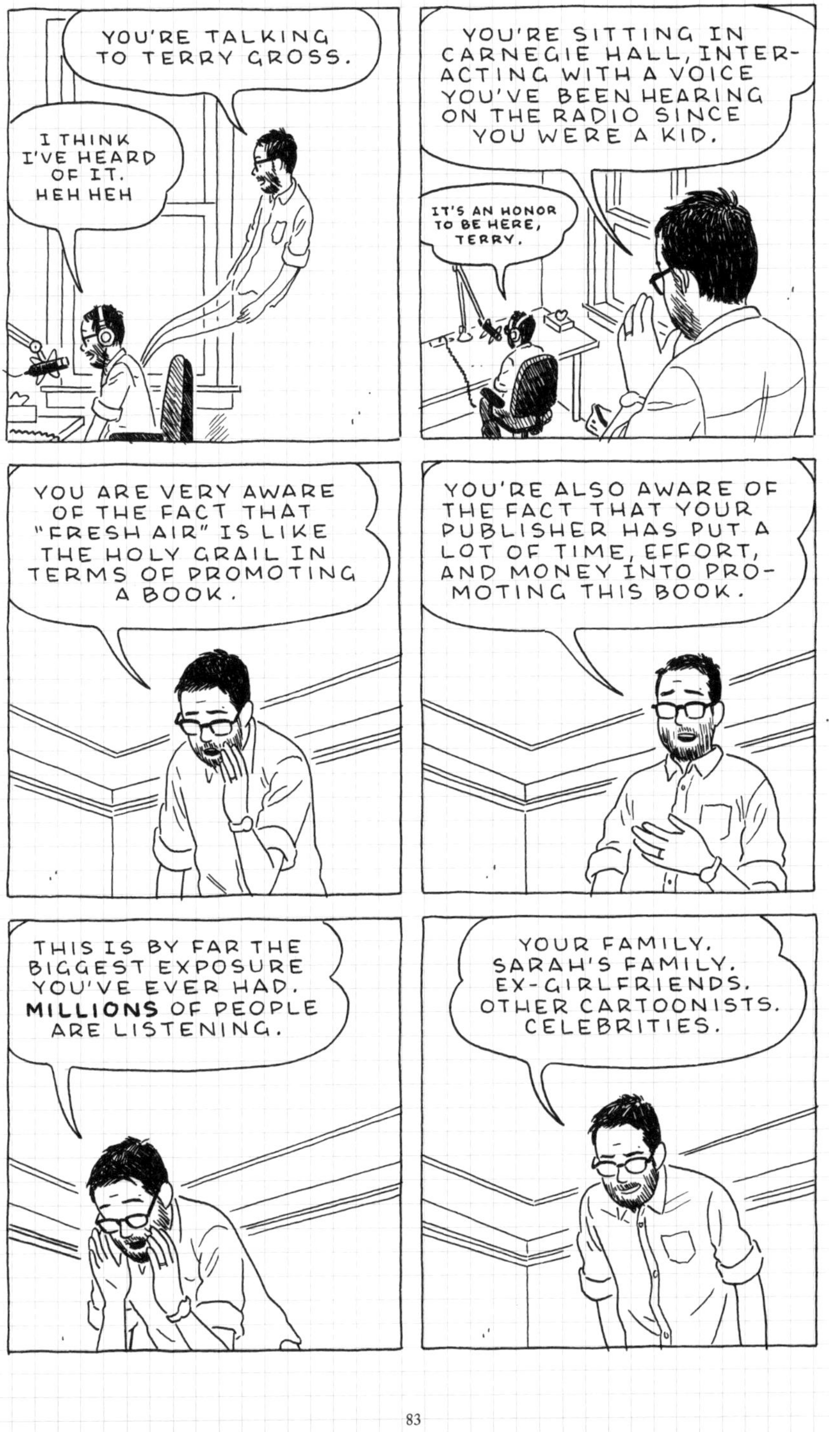
YOU'RE TALKING TO TERRY GROSS.
I THINK I'VE HEARD OF IT. HEH HEH
YOU'RE SITTING IN CARNEGIE HALL, INTERACTING WITH A VOICE YOU'VE BEEN HEARING ON THE RADIO SINCE YOU WERE A KID.
IT'S AN HONOR TO BE HERE, TERRY.
YOU ARE VERY AWARE OF THE FACT THAT "FRESH AIR" IS LIKE THE HOLY GRAIL IN TERMS OF PROMOTING A BOOK.
YOU'RE ALSO AWARE OF THE FACT THAT YOUR PUBLISHER HAS PUT A LOT OF TIME, EFFORT, AND MONEY INTO PROMOTING THIS BOOK.
THIS IS BY FAR THE BIGGEST EXPOSURE YOU'VE EVER HAD. **MILLIONS** OF PEOPLE ARE LISTENING.
YOUR FAMILY. SARAH'S FAMILY. EX-GIRLFRIENDS. OTHER CARTOONISTS. CELEBRITIES.

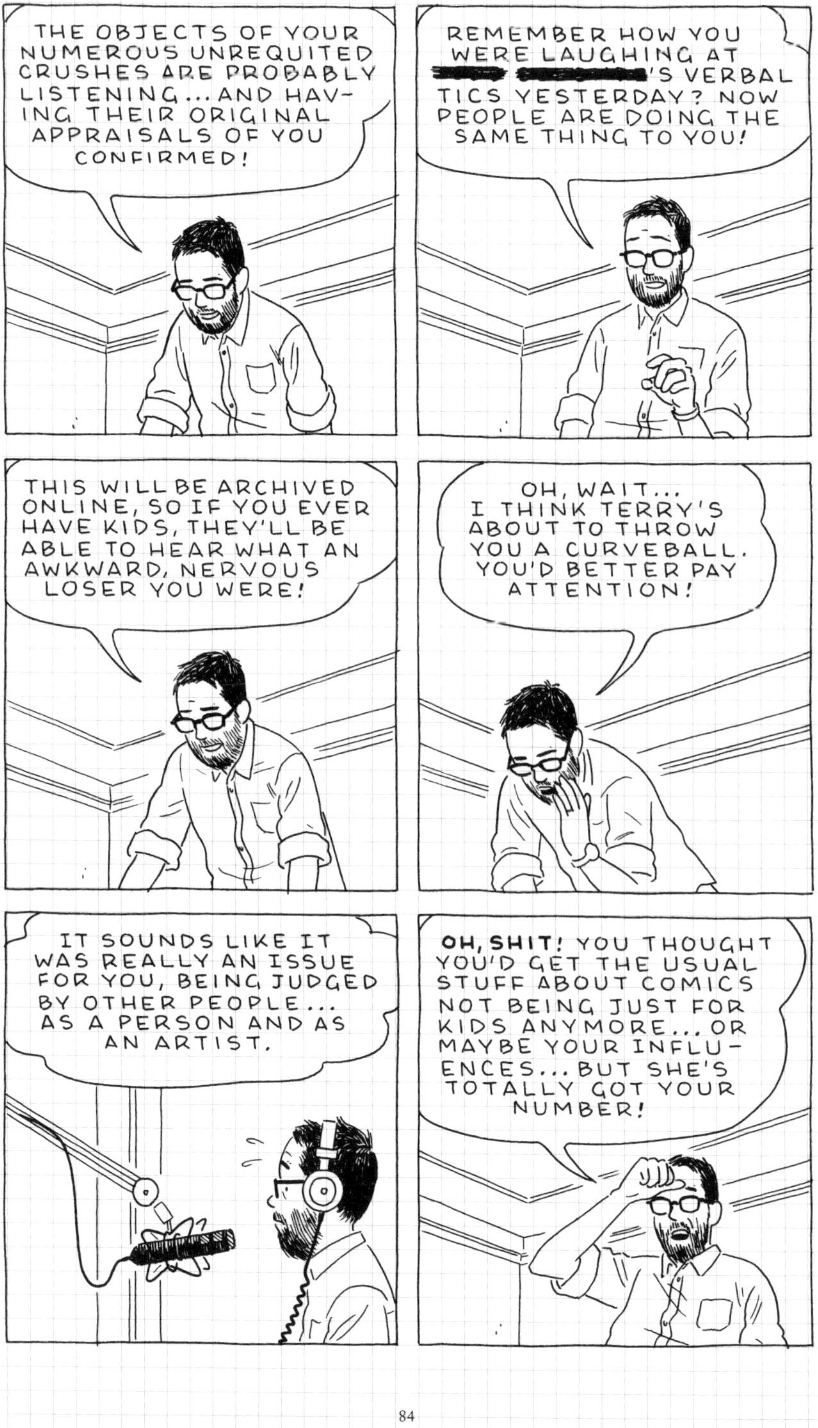
THE OBJECTS OF YOUR NUMEROUS UNREQUITED CRUSHES ARE PROBABLY LISTENING... AND HAVING THEIR ORIGINAL APPRAISALS OF YOU CONFIRMED!
REMEMBER HOW YOU WERE LAUGHING AT [redacted]'S VERBAL TICS YESTERDAY? NOW PEOPLE ARE DOING THE SAME THING TO YOU!
THIS WILL BE ARCHIVED ONLINE, SO IF YOU EVER HAVE KIDS, THEY'LL BE ABLE TO HEAR WHAT AN AWKWARD, NERVOUS LOSER YOU WERE!
OH, WAIT... I THINK TERRY'S ABOUT TO THROW YOU A CURVEBALL. YOU'D BETTER PAY ATTENTION!
IT SOUNDS LIKE IT WAS REALLY AN ISSUE FOR YOU, BEING JUDGED BY OTHER PEOPLE... AS A PERSON AND AS AN ARTIST.
OH, SHIT! YOU THOUGHT YOU'D GET THE USUAL STUFF ABOUT COMICS NOT BEING JUST FOR KIDS ANYMORE... OR MAYBE YOUR INFLUENCES... BUT SHE'S TOTALLY GOT YOUR NUMBER!

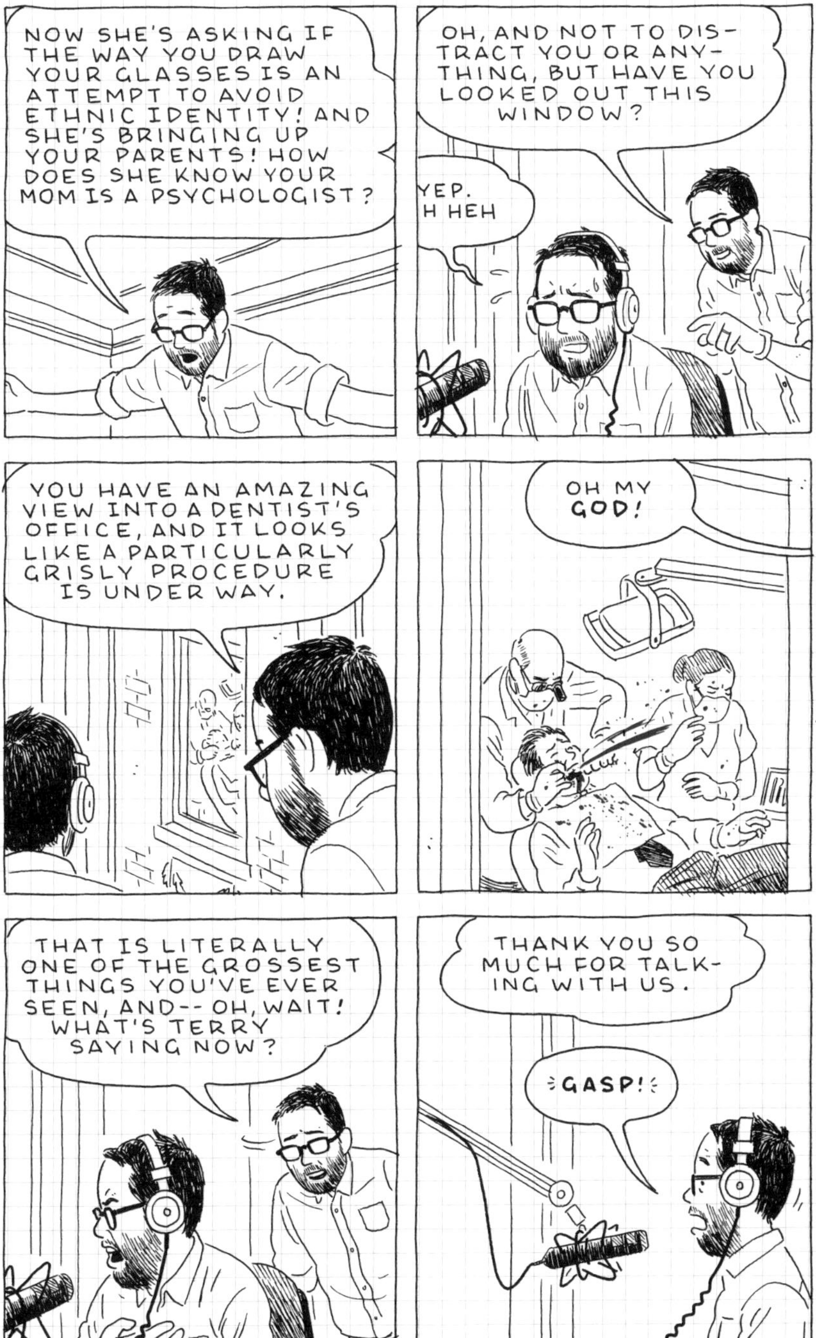
NOW SHE'S ASKING IF THE WAY YOU DRAW YOUR GLASSES IS AN ATTEMPT TO AVOID ETHNIC IDENTITY! AND SHE'S BRINGING UP YOUR PARENTS! HOW DOES SHE KNOW YOUR MOM IS A PSYCHOLOGIST?
OH, AND NOT TO DISTRACT YOU OR ANYTHING, BUT HAVE YOU LOOKED OUT THIS WINDOW?
YEP. H HEH
YOU HAVE AN AMAZING VIEW INTO A DENTIST'S OFFICE, AND IT LOOKS LIKE A PARTICULARLY GRISLY PROCEDURE IS UNDER WAY.
OH MY GOD!
THAT IS LITERALLY ONE OF THE GROSSEST THINGS YOU'VE EVER SEEN, AND-- OH, WAIT! WHAT'S TERRY SAYING NOW?
THANK YOU SO MUCH FOR TALKING WITH US.
GASP!

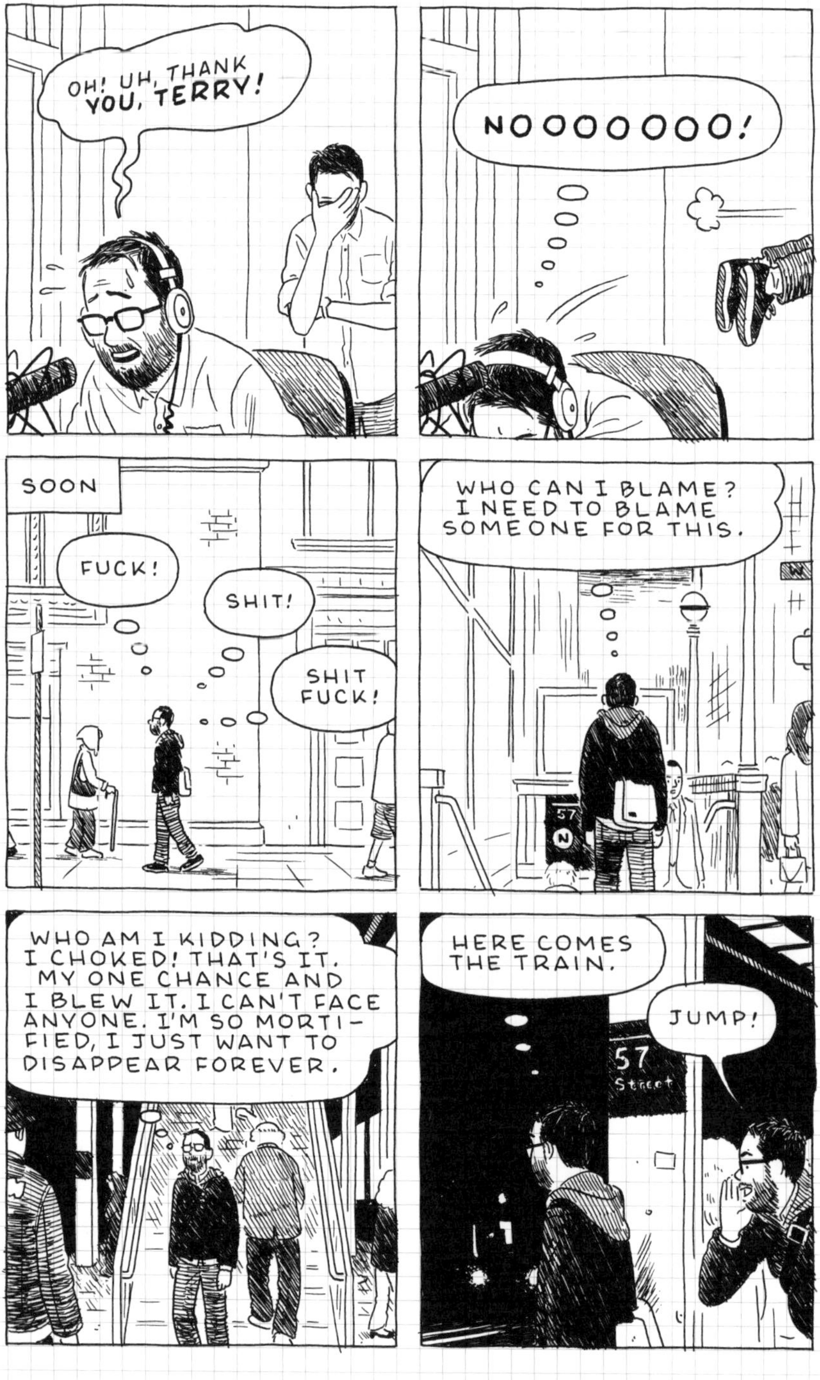
OH! UH, THANK YOU, TERRY!
NOOOOOOO!
SOON
FUCK!
SHIT!
SHIT FUCK!
WHO CAN I BLAME? I NEED TO BLAME SOMEONE FOR THIS.
WHO AM I KIDDING? I CHOKED! THAT'S IT. MY ONE CHANCE AND I BLEW IT. I CAN'T FACE ANYONE. I'M SO MORTI- FIED, I JUST WANT TO DISAPPEAR FOREVER.
HERE COMES THE TRAIN.
JUMP!
57 Street

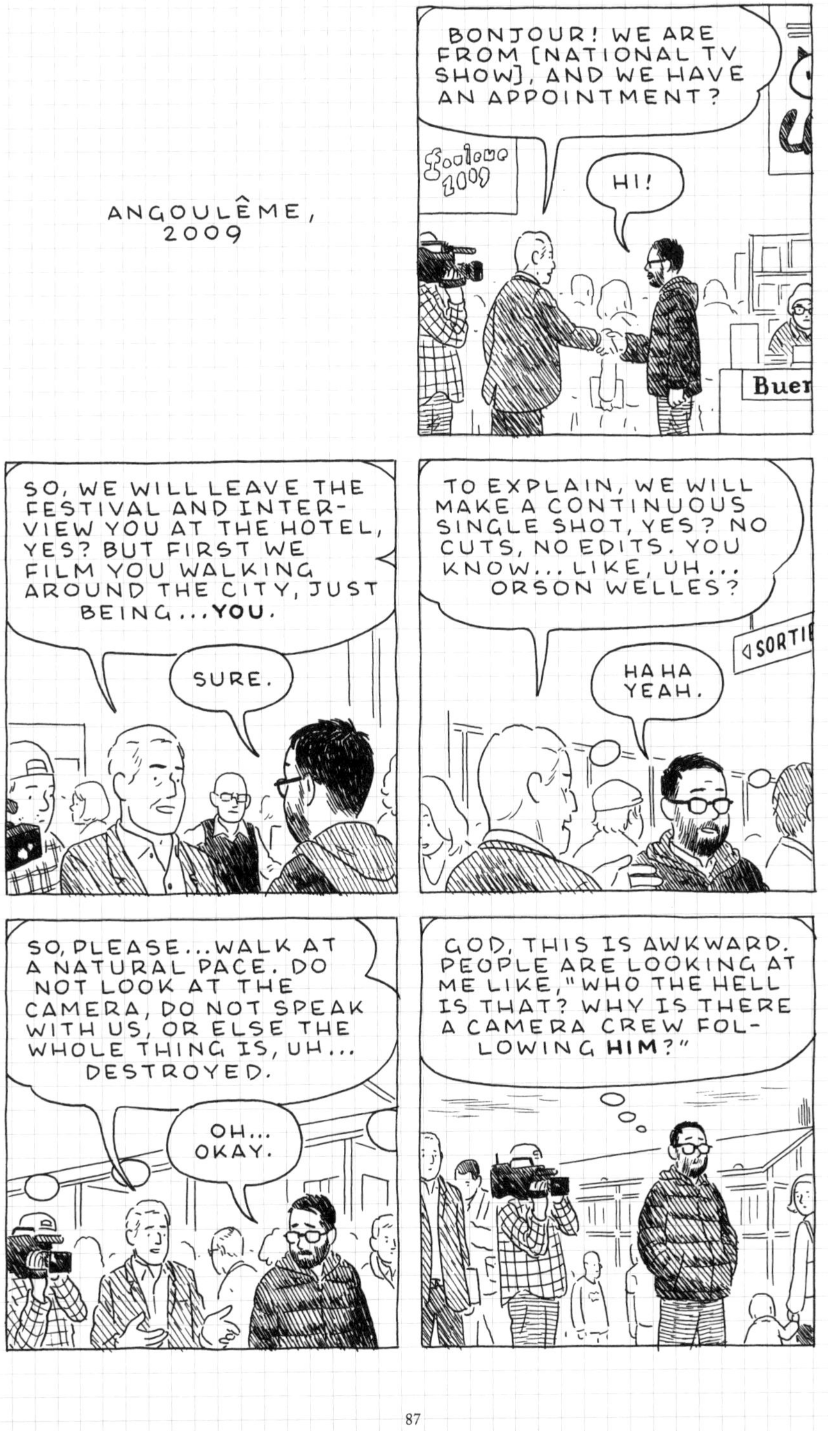
ANGOULÊME, 2009
BONJOUR! WE ARE FROM [NATIONAL TV SHOW], AND WE HAVE AN APPOINTMENT?
HI!
SO, WE WILL LEAVE THE FESTIVAL AND INTERVIEW YOU AT THE HOTEL, YES? BUT FIRST WE FILM YOU WALKING AROUND THE CITY, JUST BEING... **YOU**.
SURE.
TO EXPLAIN, WE WILL MAKE A CONTINUOUS SINGLE SHOT, YES? NO CUTS, NO EDITS. YOU KNOW... LIKE, UH... ORSON WELLES?
HA HA YEAH.
SO, PLEASE... WALK AT A NATURAL PACE. DO NOT LOOK AT THE CAMERA, DO NOT SPEAK WITH US, OR ELSE THE WHOLE THING IS, UH... DESTROYED.
OH... OKAY.
GOD, THIS IS AWKWARD. PEOPLE ARE LOOKING AT ME LIKE, "WHO THE HELL IS THAT? WHY IS THERE A CAMERA CREW FOLLOWING **HIM**?"

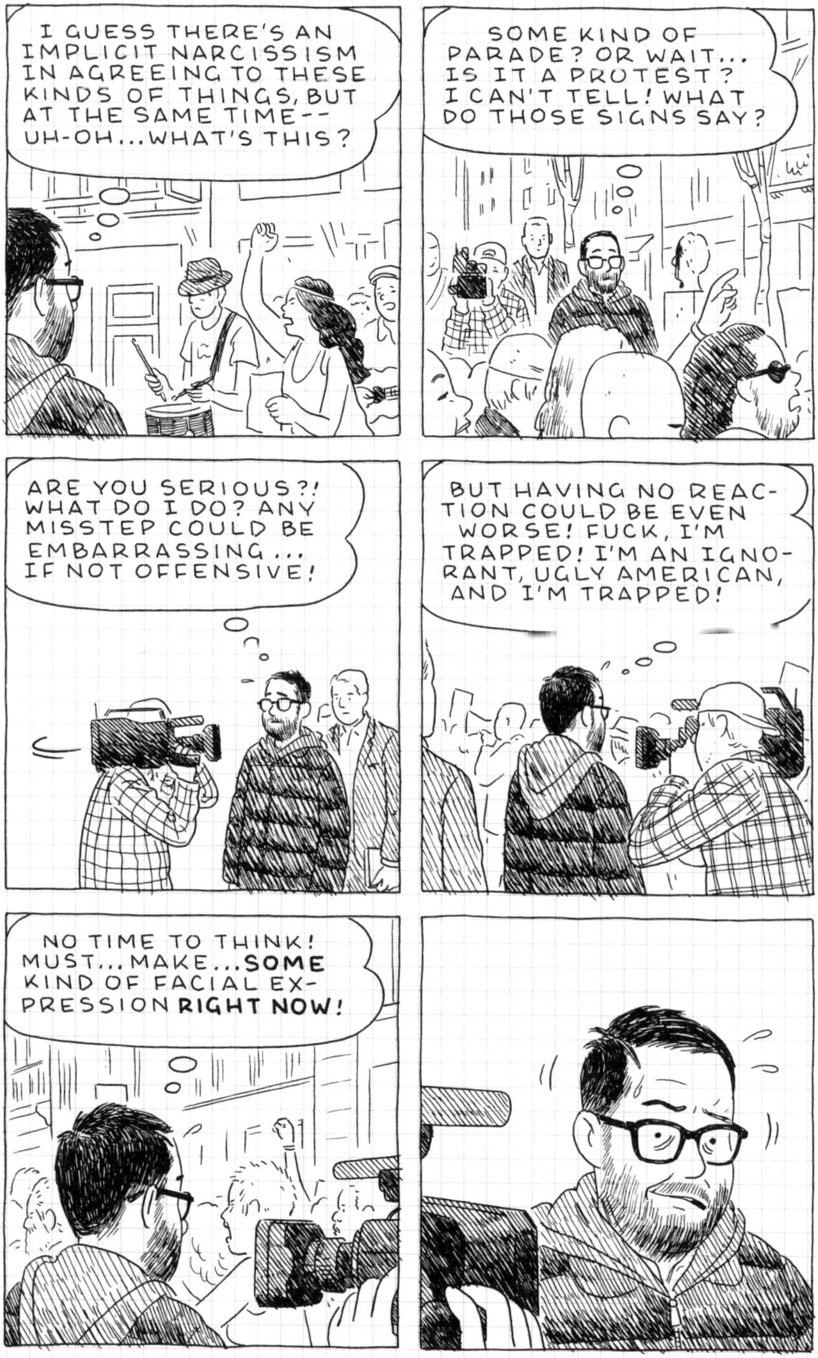
I GUESS THERE'S AN IMPLICIT NARCISSISM IN AGREEING TO THESE KINDS OF THINGS, BUT AT THE SAME TIME-- UH-OH... WHAT'S THIS?
SOME KIND OF PARADE? OR WAIT... IS IT A PROTEST? I CAN'T TELL! WHAT DO THOSE SIGNS SAY?
ARE YOU SERIOUS?! WHAT DO I DO? ANY MISSTEP COULD BE EMBARRASSING... IF NOT OFFENSIVE!
BUT HAVING NO REACTION COULD BE EVEN WORSE! FUCK, I'M TRAPPED! I'M AN IGNORANT, UGLY AMERICAN, AND I'M TRAPPED!
NO TIME TO THINK! MUST... MAKE... **SOME** KIND OF FACIAL EXPRESSION **RIGHT NOW**!

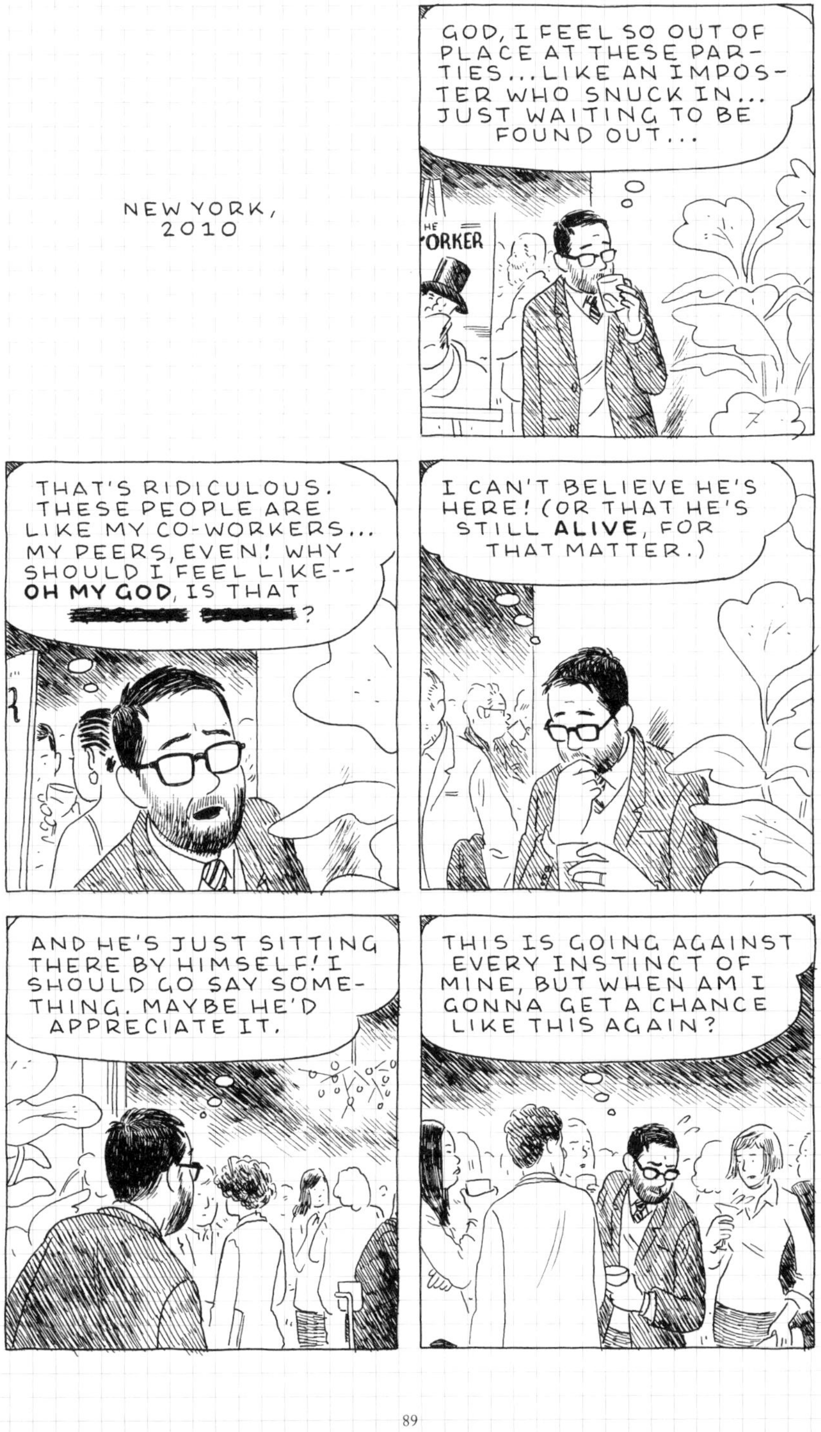
NEW YORK, 2010
GOD, I FEEL SO OUT OF PLACE AT THESE PARTIES... LIKE AN IMPOSTER WHO SNUCK IN... JUST WAITING TO BE FOUND OUT...
THAT'S RIDICULOUS. THESE PEOPLE ARE LIKE MY CO-WORKERS... MY PEERS, EVEN! WHY SHOULD I FEEL LIKE-- **OH MY GOD**, IS THAT [redacted]?
I CAN'T BELIEVE HE'S HERE! (OR THAT HE'S STILL **ALIVE**, FOR THAT MATTER.)
AND HE'S JUST SITTING THERE BY HIMSELF! I SHOULD GO SAY SOMETHING. MAYBE HE'D APPRECIATE IT.
THIS IS GOING AGAINST EVERY INSTINCT OF MINE, BUT WHEN AM I GONNA GET A CHANCE LIKE THIS AGAIN?

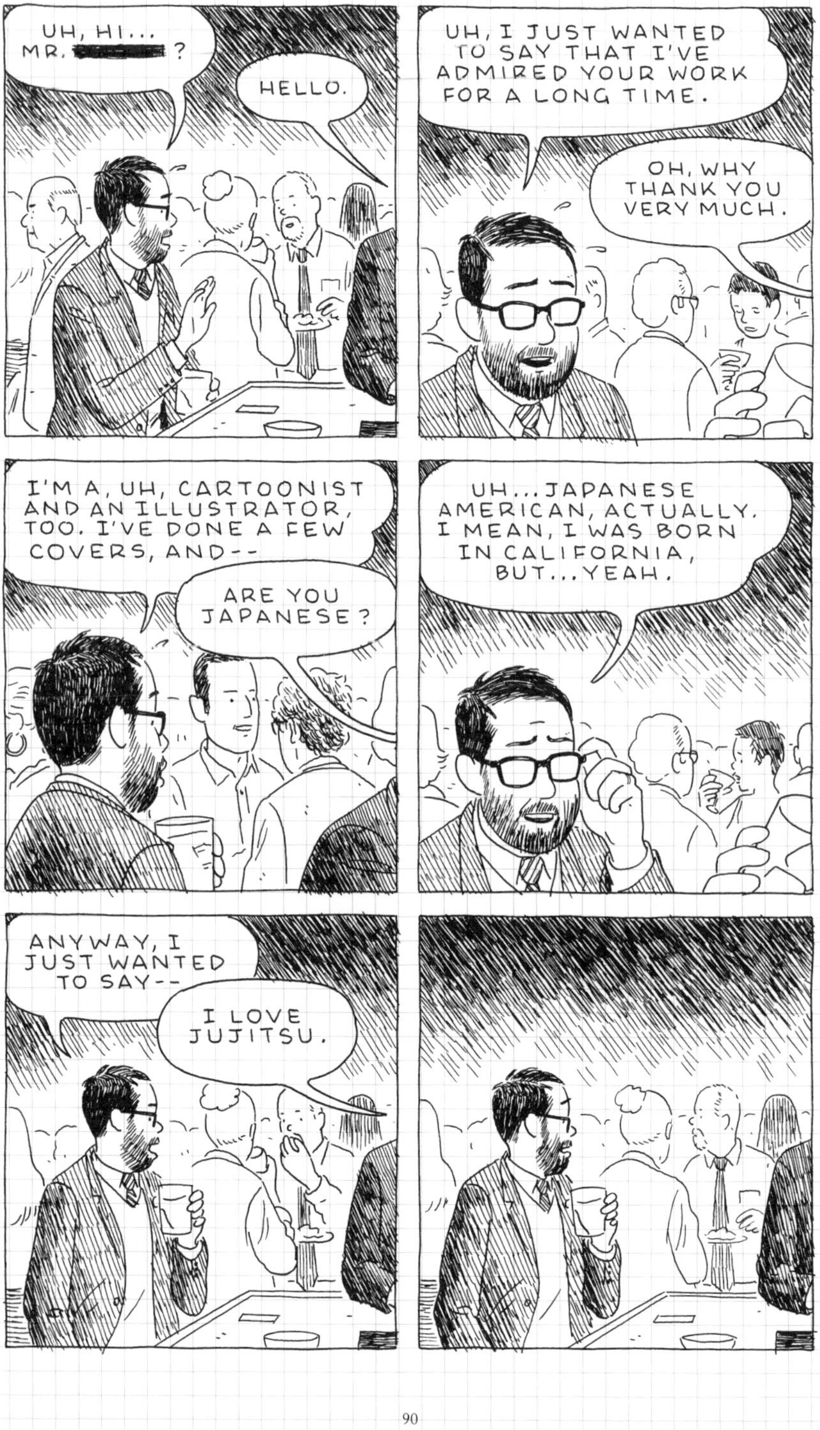
UH, HI... MR. [redacted]?
HELLO.
UH, I JUST WANTED TO SAY THAT I'VE ADMIRED YOUR WORK FOR A LONG TIME.
OH, WHY THANK YOU VERY MUCH.
I'M A, UH, CARTOONIST AND AN ILLUSTRATOR, TOO. I'VE DONE A FEW COVERS, AND--
ARE YOU JAPANESE?
UH... JAPANESE AMERICAN, ACTUALLY. I MEAN, I WAS BORN IN CALIFORNIA, BUT... YEAH.
ANYWAY, I JUST WANTED TO SAY--
I LOVE JUJITSU.

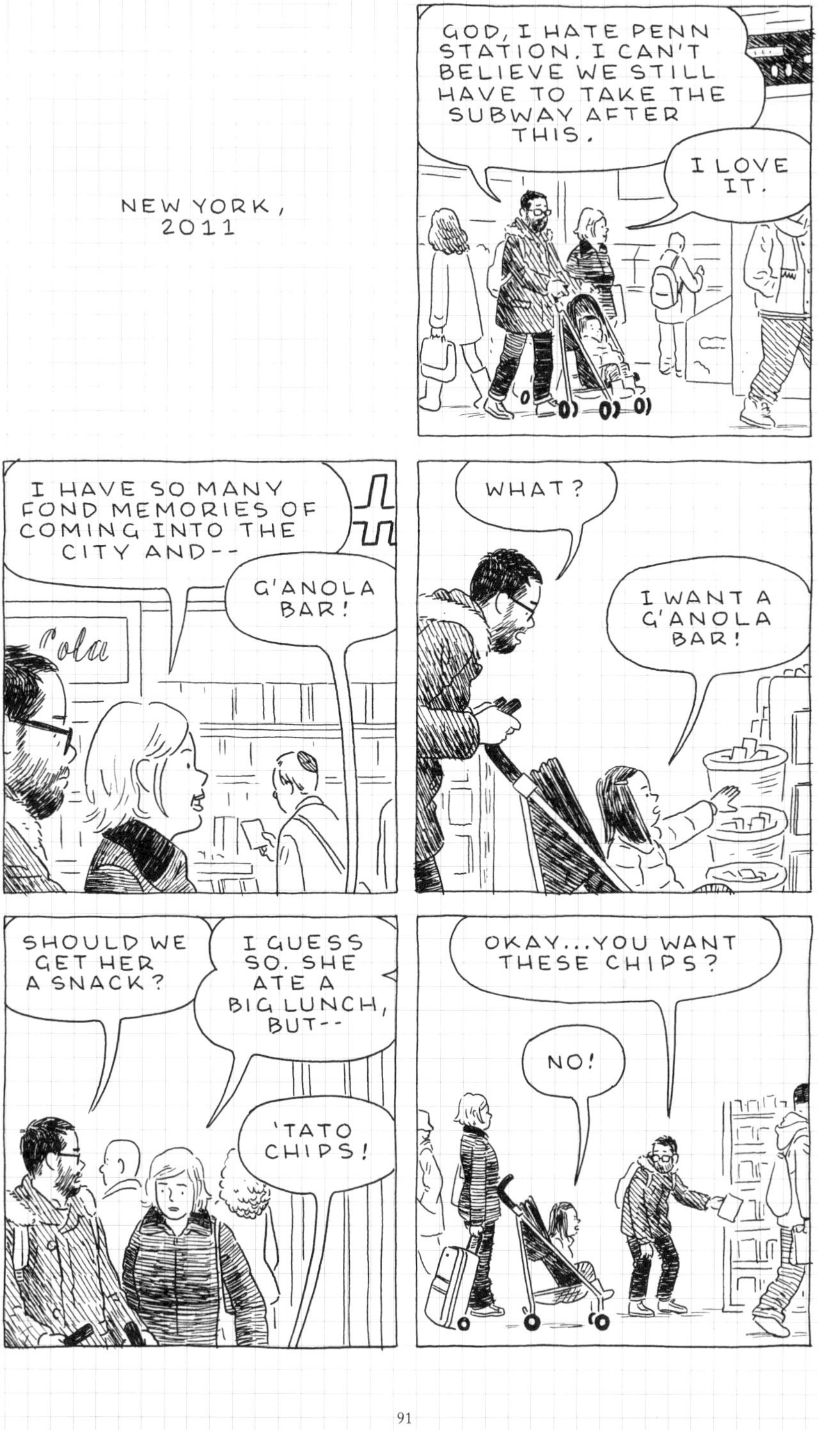
NEW YORK, 2011
GOD, I HATE PENN STATION. I CAN'T BELIEVE WE STILL HAVE TO TAKE THE SUBWAY AFTER THIS.
I LOVE IT.
I HAVE SO MANY FOND MEMORIES OF COMING INTO THE CITY AND--
G'ANOLA BAR!
WHAT?
I WANT A G'ANOLA BAR!
SHOULD WE GET HER A SNACK?
I GUESS SO. SHE ATE A BIG LUNCH, BUT--
'TATO CHIPS!
OKAY...YOU WANT THESE CHIPS?
NO!

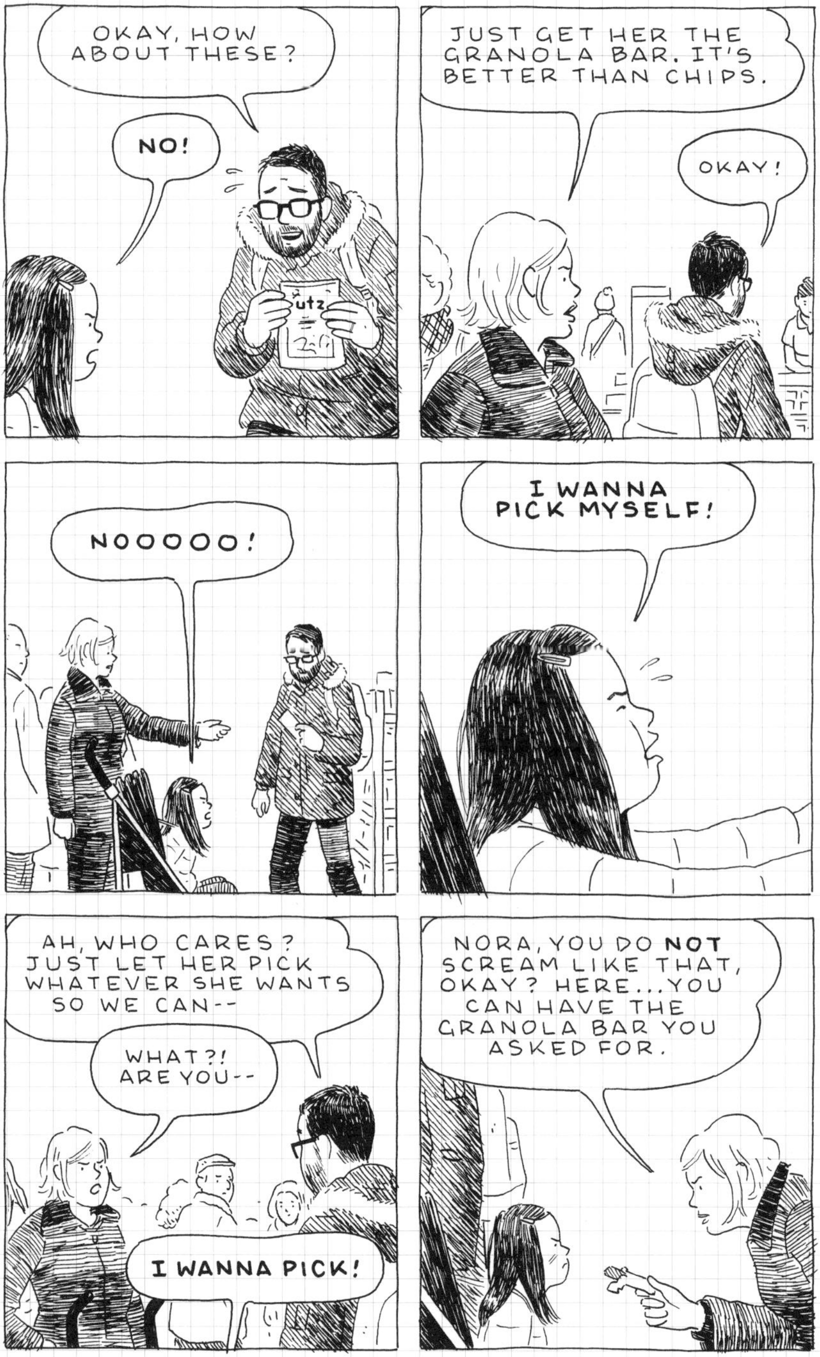
OKAY, HOW ABOUT THESE?
NO!
utz
JUST GET HER THE GRANOLA BAR. IT'S BETTER THAN CHIPS.
OKAY!
NOOOOO!
I WANNA PICK MYSELF!
AH, WHO CARES? JUST LET HER PICK WHATEVER SHE WANTS SO WE CAN--
WHAT?! ARE YOU--
I WANNA PICK!
NORA, YOU DO **NOT** SCREAM LIKE THAT, OKAY? HERE... YOU CAN HAVE THE GRANOLA BAR YOU ASKED FOR.

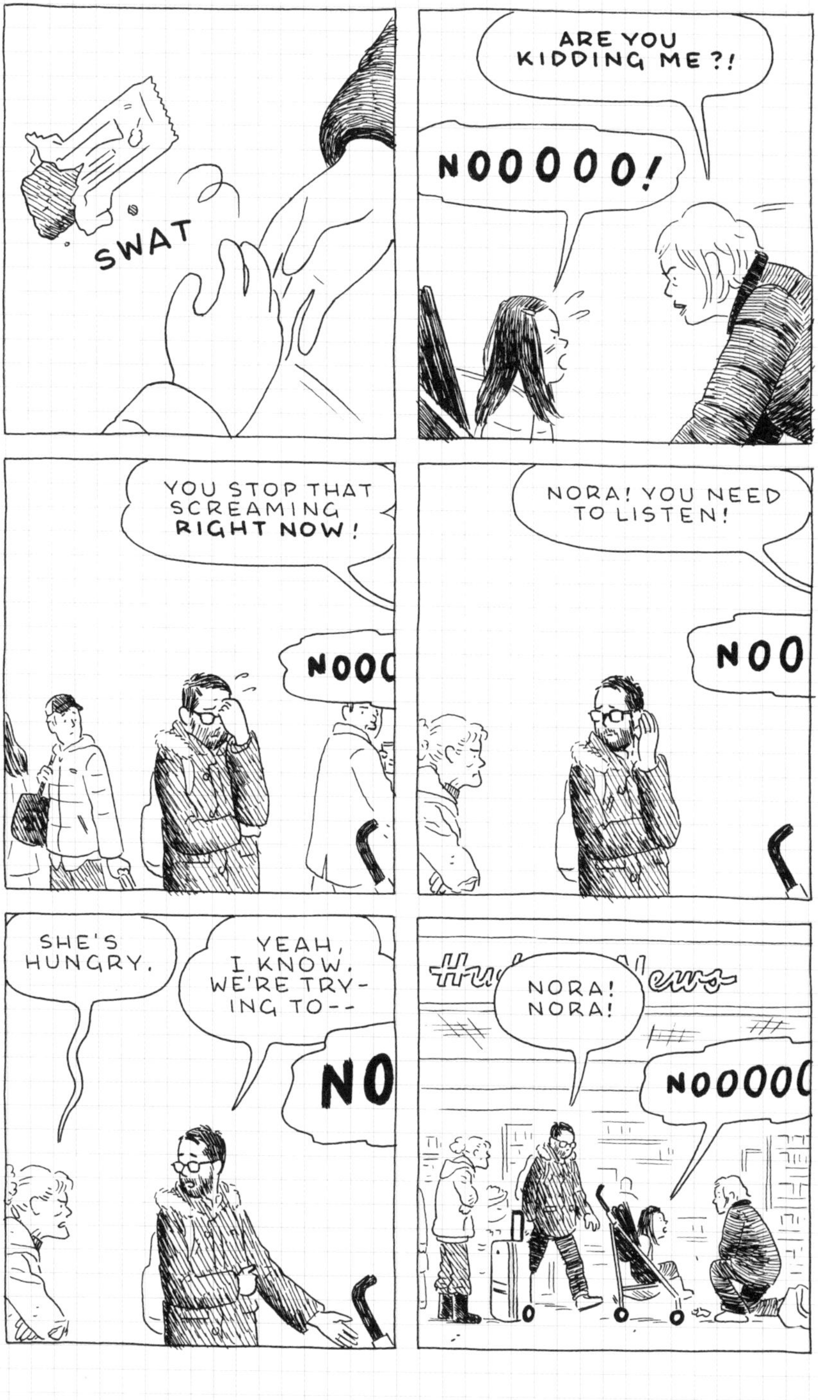
SWAT
ARE YOU KIDDING ME?!
NOOOOO!
YOU STOP THAT SCREAMING RIGHT NOW!
NOOO
NORA! YOU NEED TO LISTEN!
NOO
SHE'S HUNGRY.
YEAH, I KNOW. WE'RE TRY-ING TO--
NO
NORA! NORA!
NOOOOO

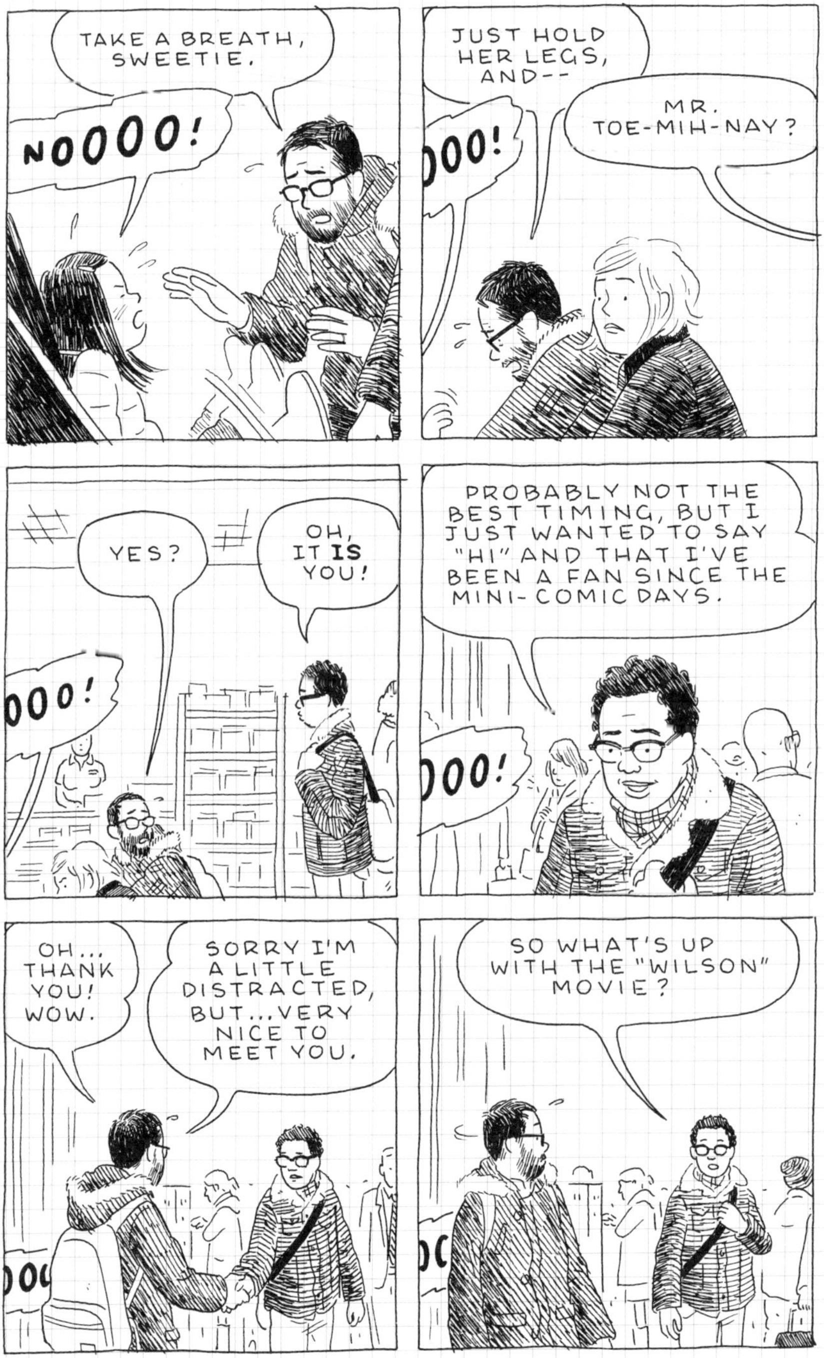
TAKE A BREATH, SWEETIE.
NOOOO!
JUST HOLD HER LEGS, AND--
OOO!
MR. TOE-MIH-NAY?
YES?
OH, IT **IS** YOU!
OOO!
PROBABLY NOT THE BEST TIMING, BUT I JUST WANTED TO SAY "HI" AND THAT I'VE BEEN A FAN SINCE THE MINI-COMIC DAYS.
OOO!
OH... THANK YOU! WOW.
SORRY I'M A LITTLE DISTRACTED, BUT... VERY NICE TO MEET YOU.
SO WHAT'S UP WITH THE "WILSON" MOVIE?

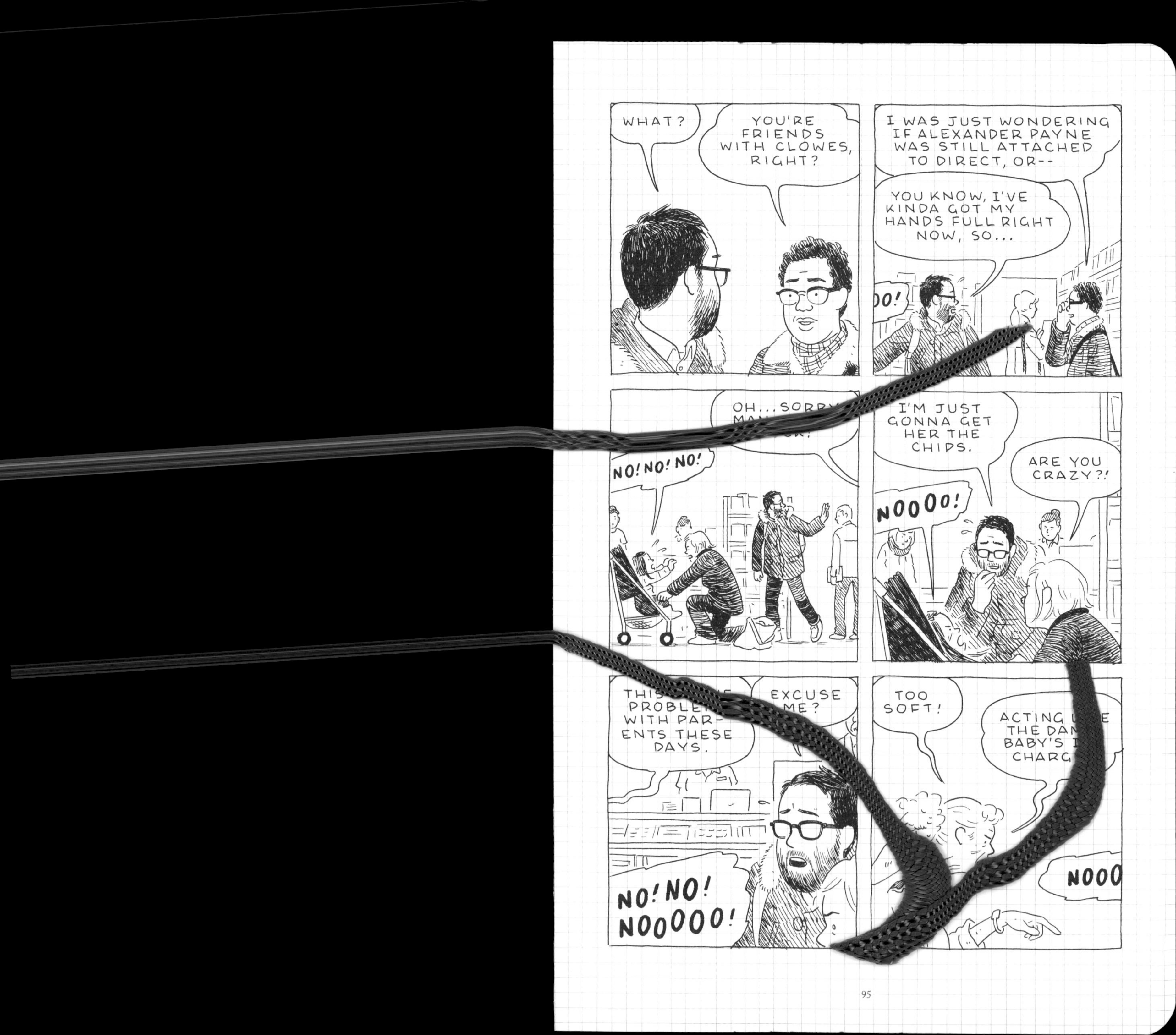
WHAT?
YOU'RE FRIENDS WITH CLOWES, RIGHT?
I WAS JUST WONDERING IF ALEXANDER PAYNE WAS STILL ATTACHED TO DIRECT, OR--
YOU KNOW, I'VE KINDA GOT MY HANDS FULL RIGHT NOW, SO...
OO!
OH...
NO! NO! NO!
I'M JUST GONNA GET HER THE CHIPS.
NOOOO!
ARE YOU CRAZY?!
THIS
WITH PAR- ENTS THESE DAYS.
EXCUSE ME?
NO! NO! NOOOOO!
TOO SOFT!
ACTING
BABY'S
NOOO

THANK YOU! THANKS FOR THAT--
SHE'S NOT GOING TO CALM DOWN UNLESS WE RESTRAIN HER!
NOOOO!
NOOOOOO!
KICK!
SHIT!
NOOOOOO!
SEE? NOW IF THAT WAS MY KID, I'D SPANK THAT ASS!
WILL YOU PLEASE LEAVE US ALONE?
FINE! BUT EVERYONE IN THIS DAMN STATION KNOWS YOU NEED TO PICK THAT BABY UP AND SPANK THAT ASS!

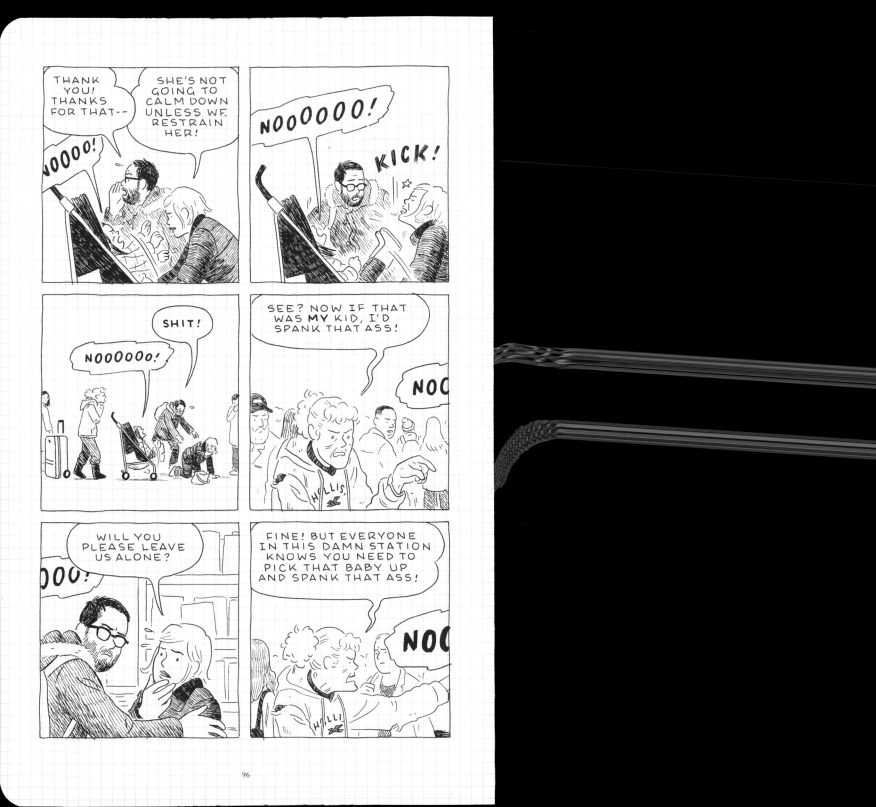

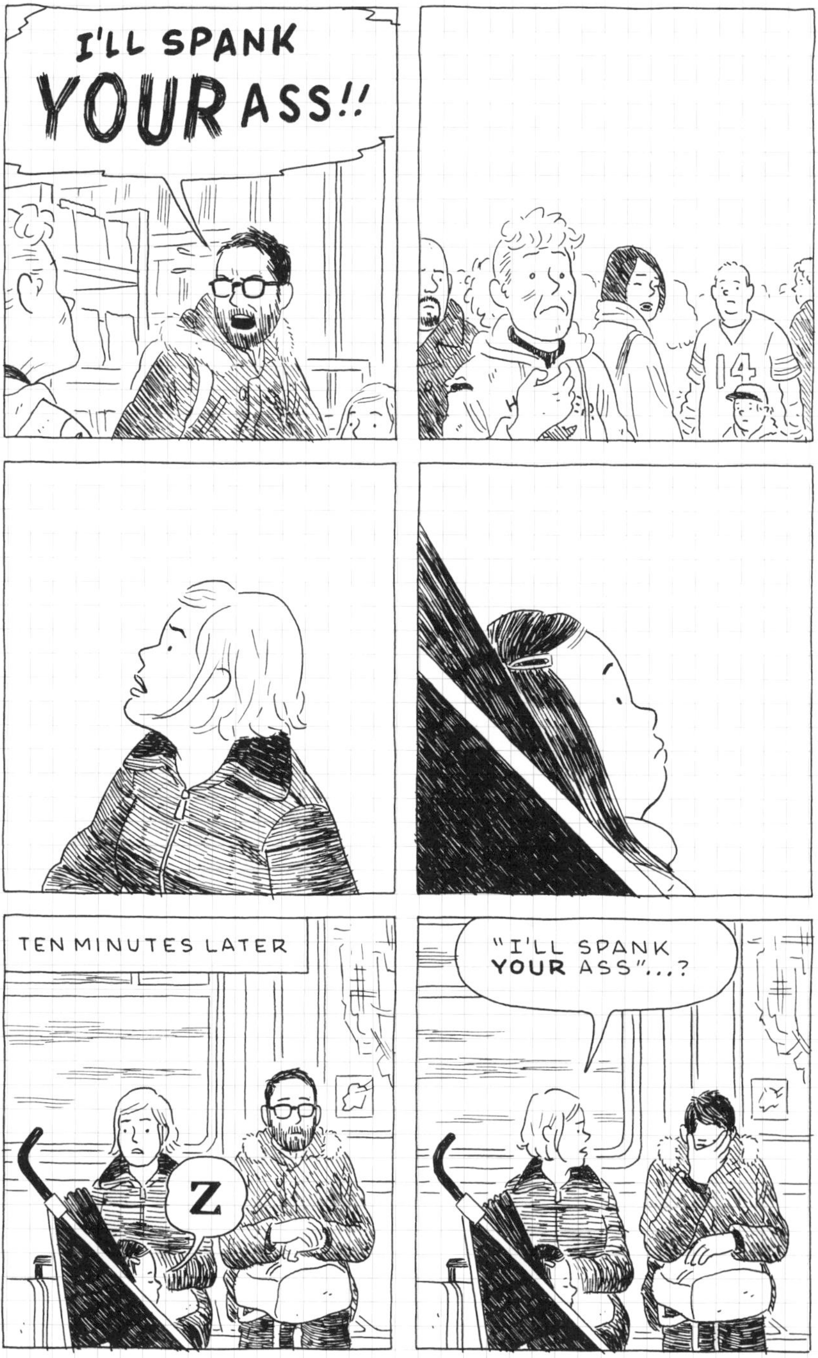
I'LL SPANK YOUR ASS!!
14
TEN MINUTES LATER
Z
"I'LL SPANK YOUR ASS"...?

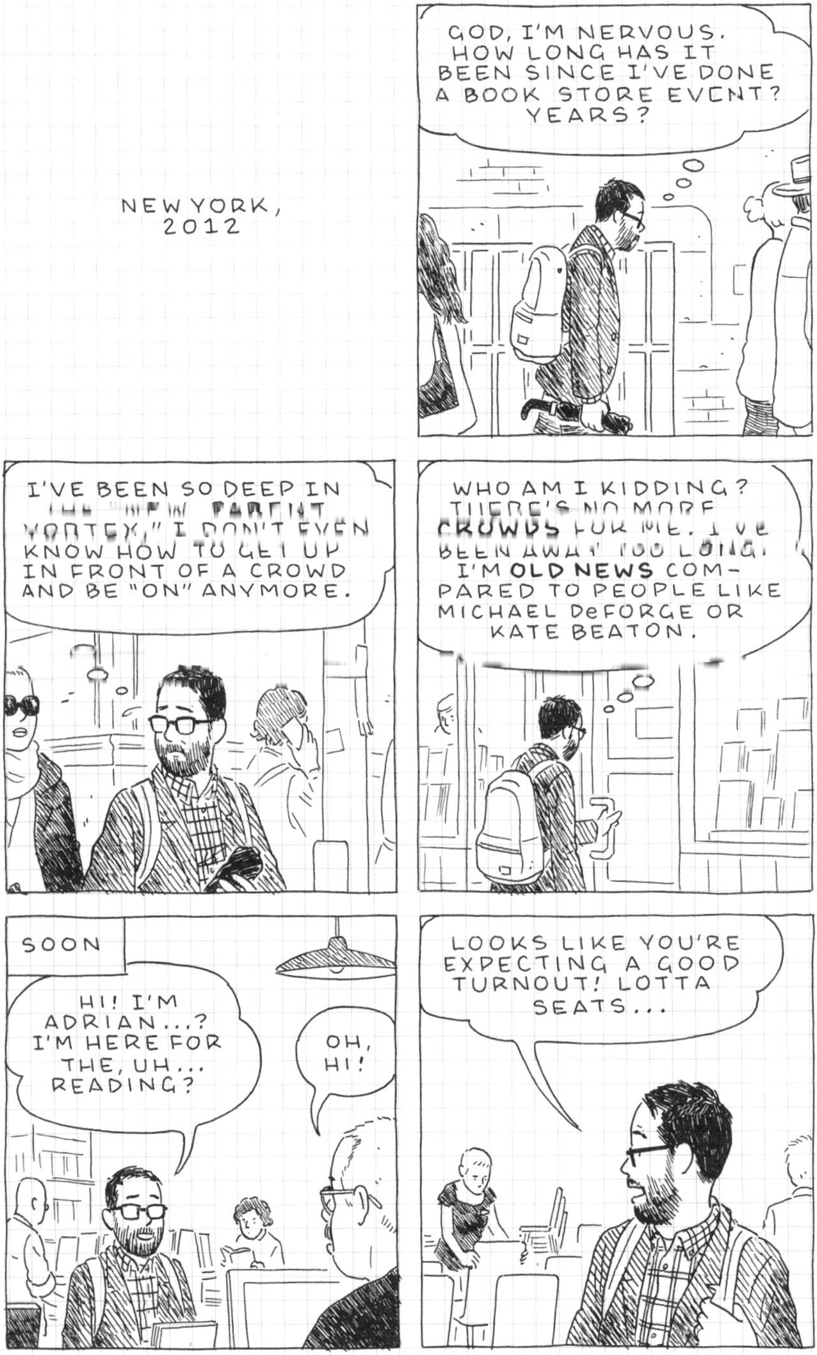
NEW YORK, 2012
GOD, I'M NERVOUS. HOW LONG HAS IT BEEN SINCE I'VE DONE A BOOK STORE EVENT? YEARS?
I'VE BEEN SO DEEP IN THE "NEW PARENT VORTEX," I DON'T EVEN KNOW HOW TO GET UP IN FRONT OF A CROWD AND BE "ON" ANYMORE.
WHO AM I KIDDING? THERE'S NO MORE **CROWDS** FOR ME. I'VE BEEN AWAY TOO LONG. I'M **OLD NEWS** COMPARED TO PEOPLE LIKE MICHAEL DeFORGE OR KATE BEATON.
SOON
HI! I'M ADRIAN...? I'M HERE FOR THE, UH... READING?
OH, HI!
LOOKS LIKE YOU'RE EXPECTING A GOOD TURNOUT! LOTTA SEATS...

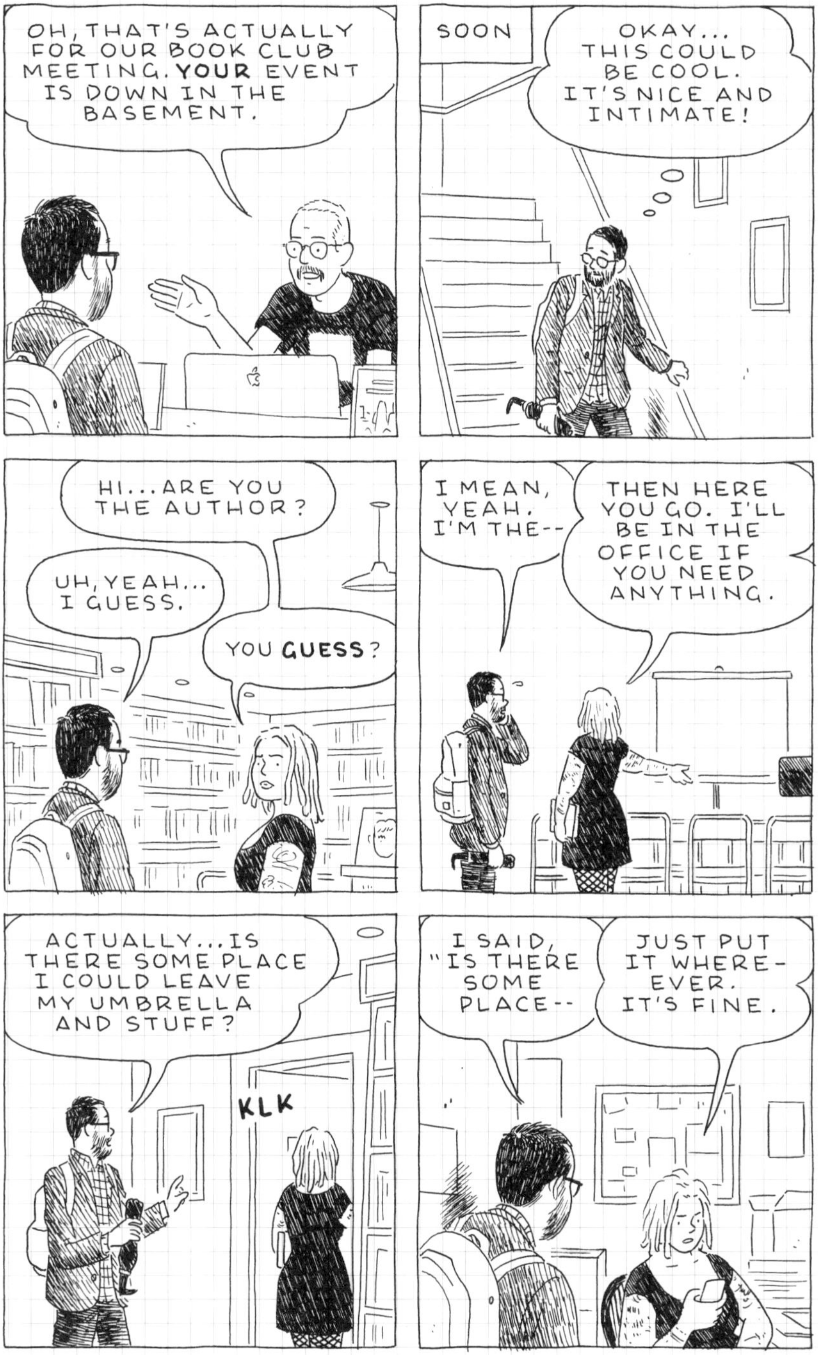
OH, THAT'S ACTUALLY FOR OUR BOOK CLUB MEETING. **YOUR** EVENT IS DOWN IN THE BASEMENT.
SOON
OKAY... THIS COULD BE COOL. IT'S NICE AND INTIMATE!
HI... ARE YOU THE AUTHOR?
UH, YEAH... I GUESS.
YOU **GUESS**?
I MEAN, YEAH. I'M THE--
THEN HERE YOU GO. I'LL BE IN THE OFFICE IF YOU NEED ANYTHING.
ACTUALLY... IS THERE SOME PLACE I COULD LEAVE MY UMBRELLA AND STUFF?
KLK
I SAID, "IS THERE SOME PLACE--
JUST PUT IT WHERE-EVER. IT'S FINE.

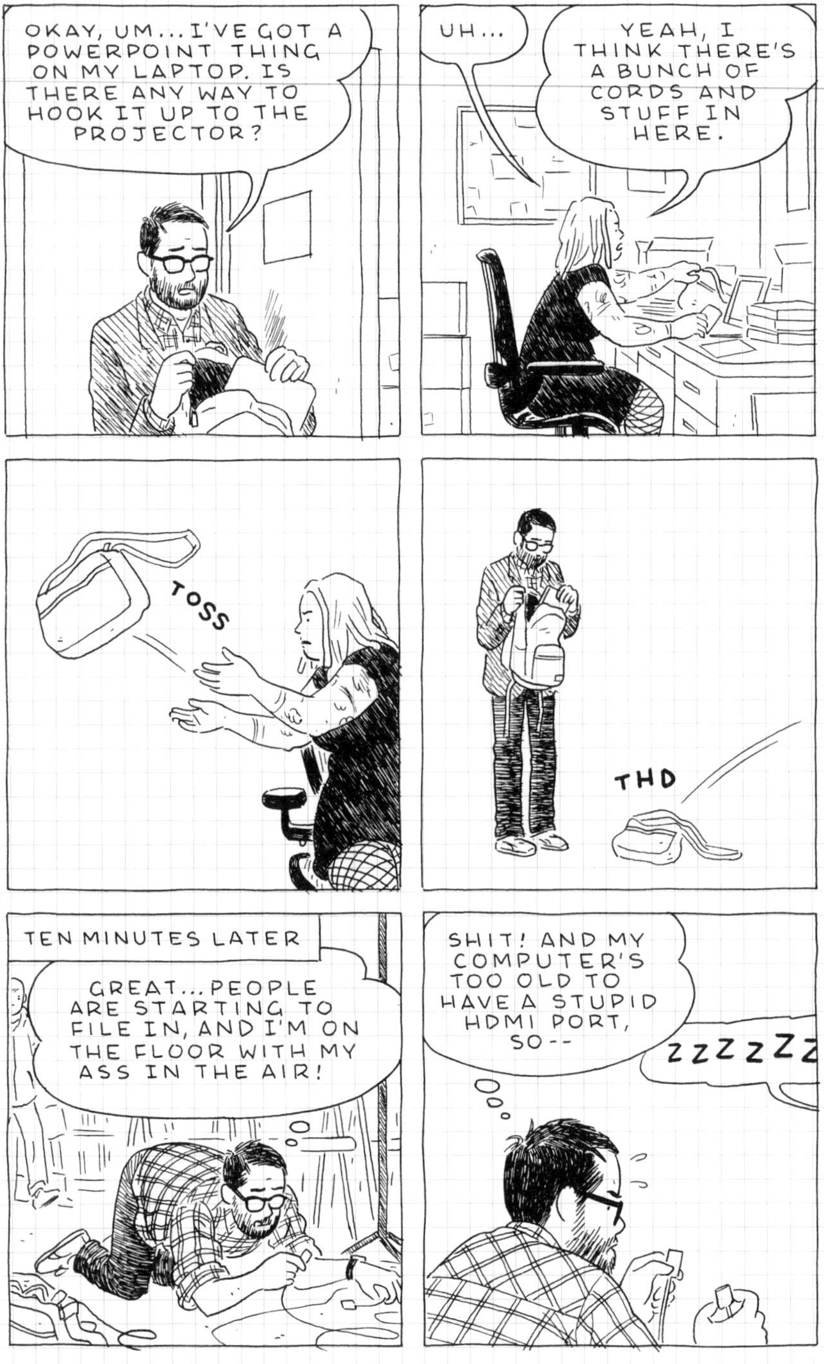
OKAY, UM... I'VE GOT A POWERPOINT THING ON MY LAPTOP. IS THERE ANY WAY TO HOOK IT UP TO THE PROJECTOR?
UH...
YEAH, I THINK THERE'S A BUNCH OF CORDS AND STUFF IN HERE.
TOSS
THD
TEN MINUTES LATER
GREAT... PEOPLE ARE STARTING TO FILE IN, AND I'M ON THE FLOOR WITH MY ASS IN THE AIR!
SHIT! AND MY COMPUTER'S TOO OLD TO HAVE A STUPID HDMI PORT, SO--
ZZZZZZ

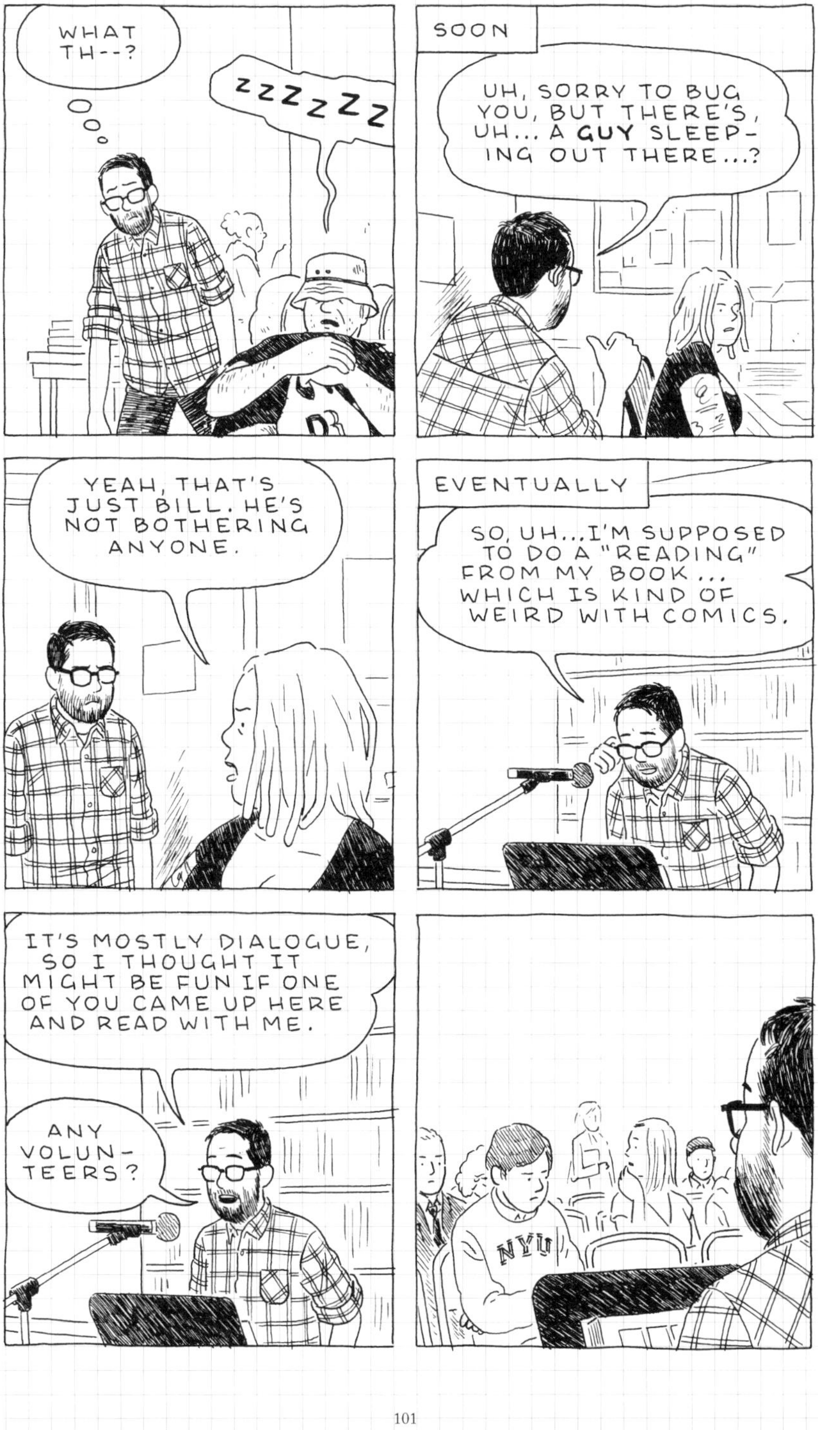
WHAT TH--?
ZZZZZZZ
SOON
UH, SORRY TO BUG YOU, BUT THERE'S, UH... A **GUY** SLEEPING OUT THERE...?
YEAH, THAT'S JUST BILL. HE'S NOT BOTHERING ANYONE.
EVENTUALLY
SO, UH...I'M SUPPOSED TO DO A "READING" FROM MY BOOK... WHICH IS KIND OF WEIRD WITH COMICS.
IT'S MOSTLY DIALOGUE, SO I THOUGHT IT MIGHT BE FUN IF ONE OF YOU CAME UP HERE AND READ WITH ME.
ANY VOLUNTEERS?
NYU

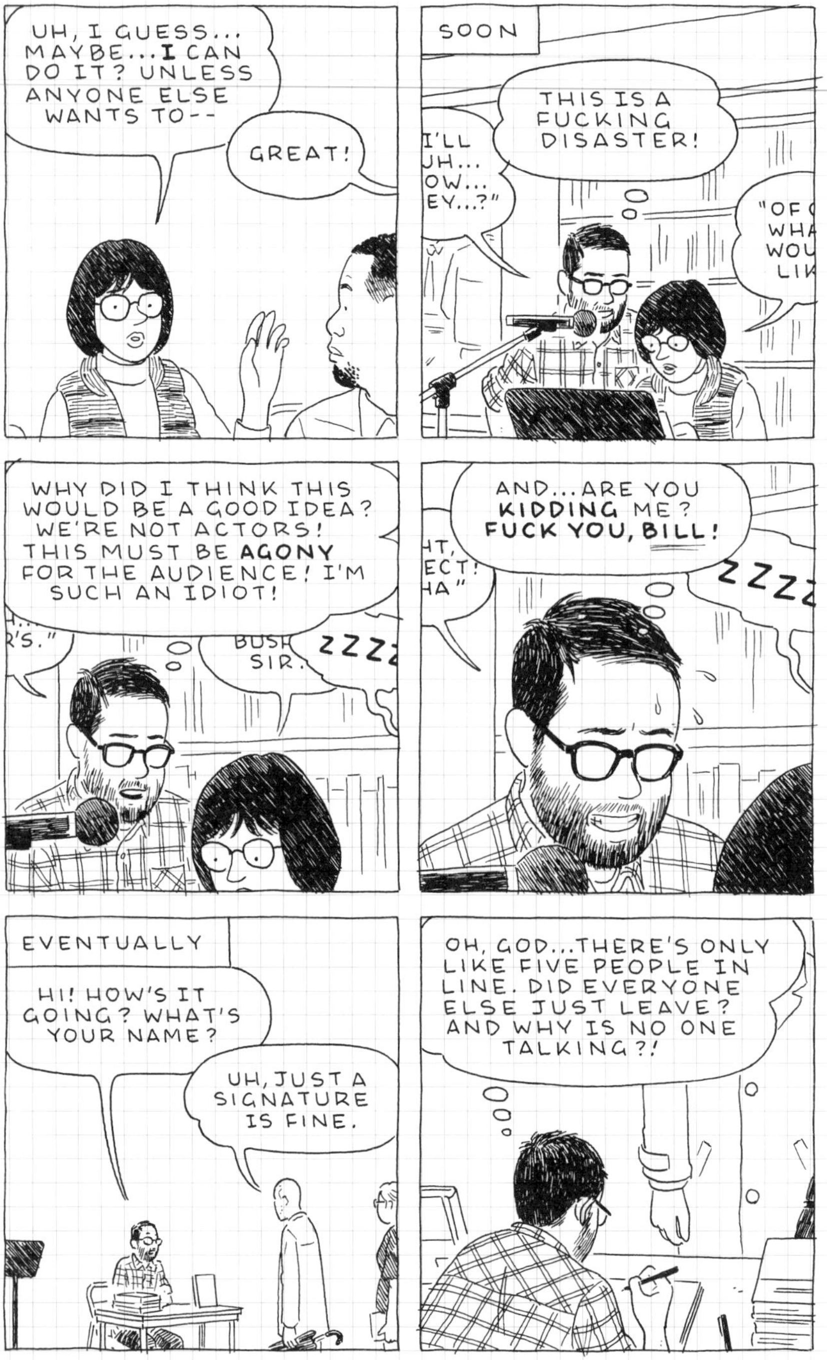
UH, I GUESS... MAYBE... **I** CAN DO IT? UNLESS ANYONE ELSE WANTS TO--
GREAT!
SOON
THIS IS A FUCKING DISASTER!
WHY DID I THINK THIS WOULD BE A GOOD IDEA? WE'RE NOT ACTORS! THIS MUST BE **AGONY** FOR THE AUDIENCE! I'M SUCH AN IDIOT!
ZZZZ
AND... ARE YOU **KIDDING** ME? **FUCK YOU, BILL!**
ZZZZ
EVENTUALLY
HI! HOW'S IT GOING? WHAT'S YOUR NAME?
UH, JUST A SIGNATURE IS FINE.
OH, GOD... THERE'S ONLY LIKE FIVE PEOPLE IN LINE. DID EVERYONE ELSE JUST LEAVE? AND WHY IS NO ONE TALKING?!

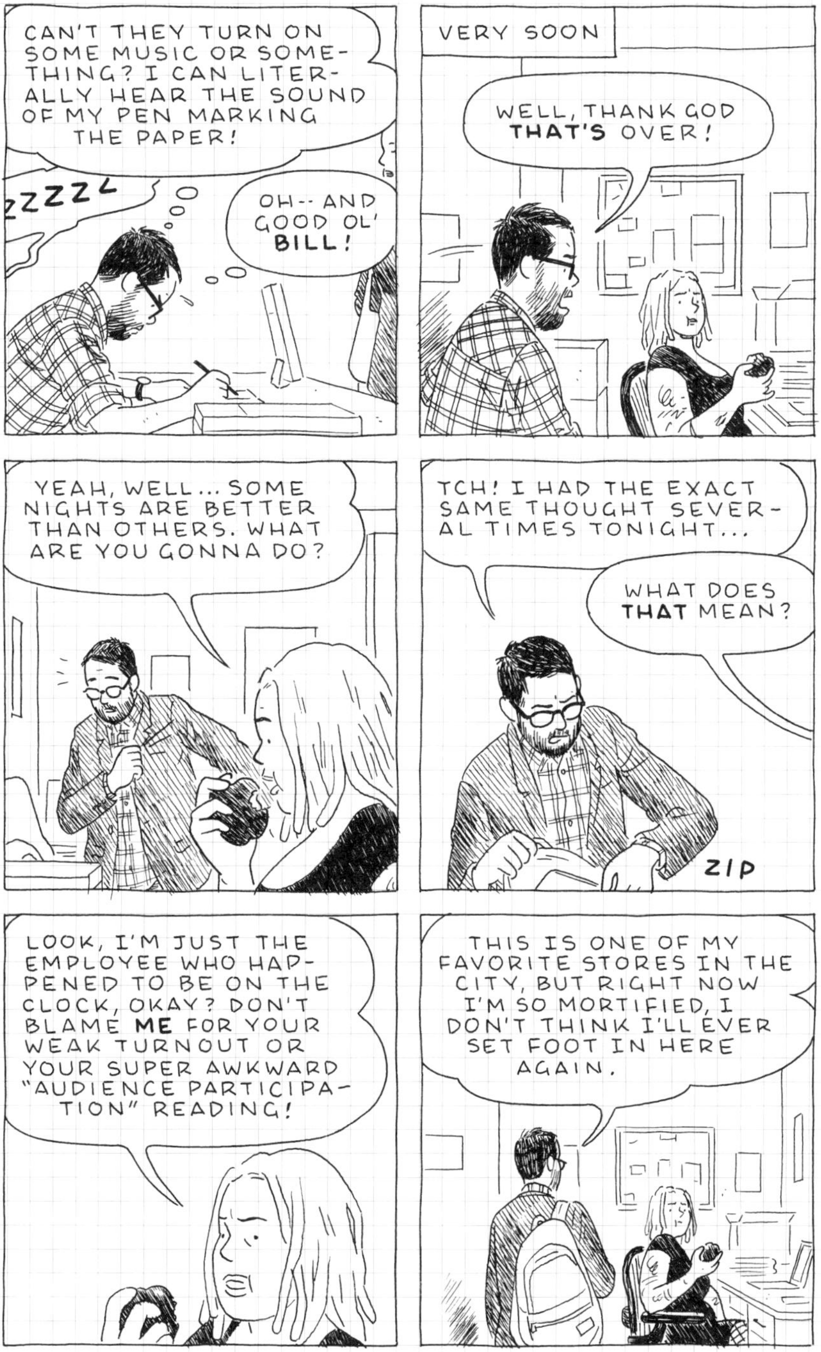
CAN'T THEY TURN ON SOME MUSIC OR SOMETHING? I CAN LITERALLY HEAR THE SOUND OF MY PEN MARKING THE PAPER!
ZZZZZ
OH-- AND GOOD OL' **BILL**!
VERY SOON
WELL, THANK GOD **THAT'S** OVER!
YEAH, WELL... SOME NIGHTS ARE BETTER THAN OTHERS. WHAT ARE YOU GONNA DO?
TCH! I HAD THE EXACT SAME THOUGHT SEVERAL TIMES TONIGHT...
WHAT DOES **THAT** MEAN?
ZIP
LOOK, I'M JUST THE EMPLOYEE WHO HAPPENED TO BE ON THE CLOCK, OKAY? DON'T BLAME **ME** FOR YOUR WEAK TURNOUT OR YOUR SUPER AWKWARD "AUDIENCE PARTICIPATION" READING!
THIS IS ONE OF MY FAVORITE STORES IN THE CITY, BUT RIGHT NOW I'M SO MORTIFIED, I DON'T THINK I'LL EVER SET FOOT IN HERE AGAIN.

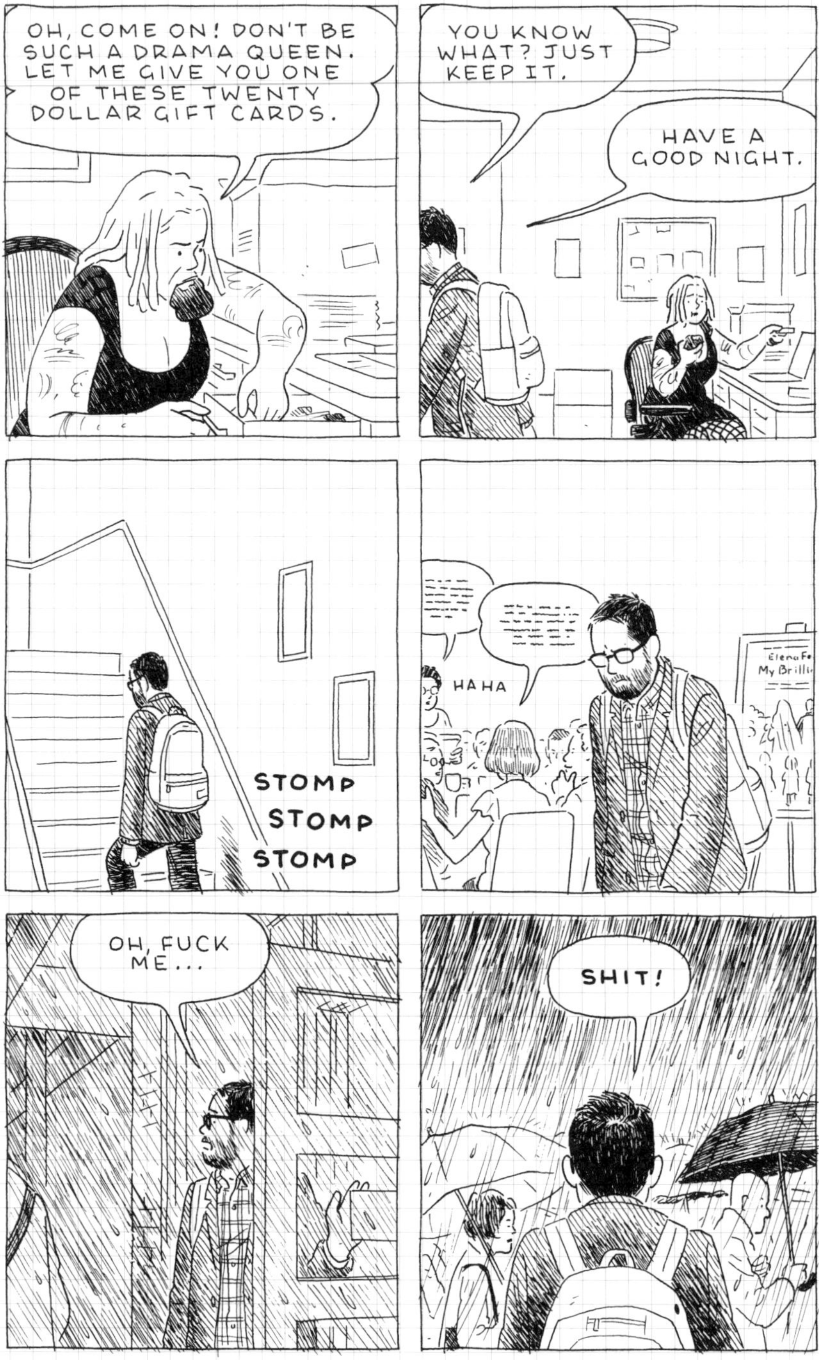
OH, COME ON! DON'T BE SUCH A DRAMA QUEEN. LET ME GIVE YOU ONE OF THESE TWENTY DOLLAR GIFT CARDS.
YOU KNOW WHAT? JUST KEEP IT.
HAVE A GOOD NIGHT.
STOMP
STOMP
STOMP
HAHA
OH, FUCK ME...
SHIT!

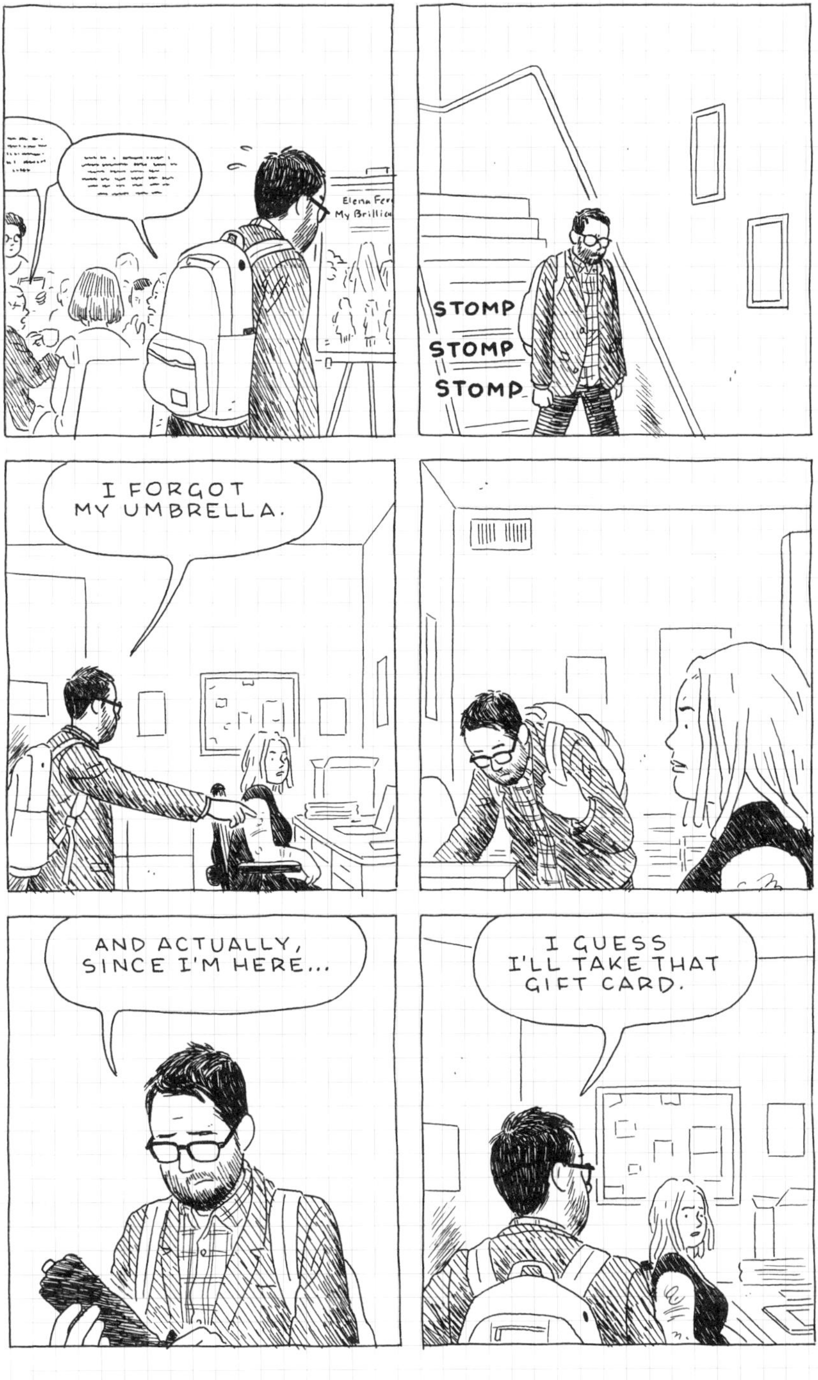
STOMP
STOMP
STOMP
I FORGOT MY UMBRELLA.
AND ACTUALLY, SINCE I'M HERE...
I GUESS I'LL TAKE THAT GIFT CARD.

BROOKLYN,
2014

GOOD MORNING,
CLASS! TODAY WE
HAVE A SPECIAL
VISITOR.

PLEASE SAY "HI"
TO...**NORA'S DAD!**

HI, EVERY-
BODY!

CLAP
CLAP
CLAP
AP

CLA
CL

SO...I'M HERE TO TALK
TO YOU GUYS BECAUSE
I'M A **CARTOONIST.**
DO YOU KNOW WHAT
THAT MEANS?

YOU DRAW
STUFF!

YEAH...
CARTOONS!

LIKE
"DORA"!

OR
"WILD
KRATTS"!

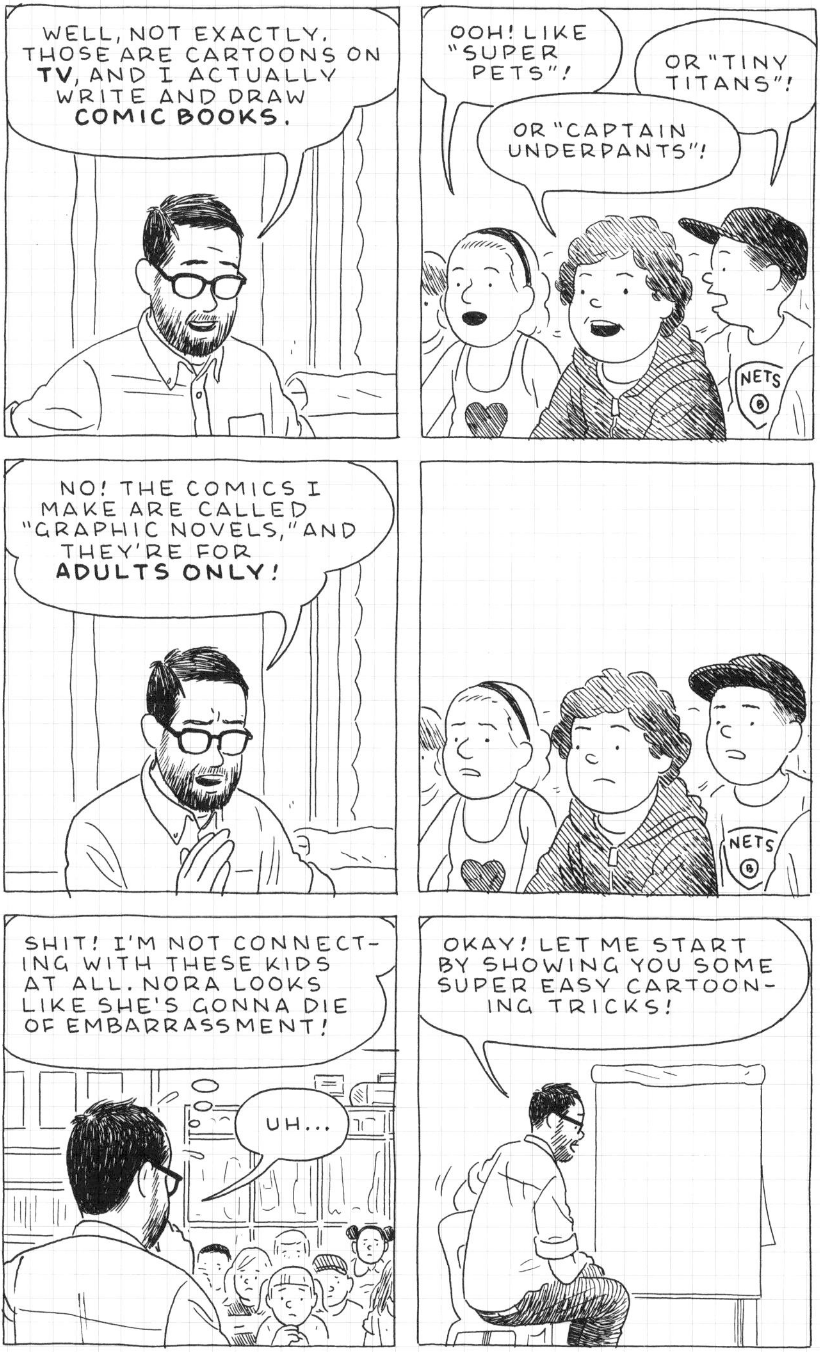
WELL, NOT EXACTLY. THOSE ARE CARTOONS ON TV, AND I ACTUALLY WRITE AND DRAW COMIC BOOKS.
OOH! LIKE "SUPER PETS"!
OR "TINY TITANS"!
OR "CAPTAIN UNDERPANTS"!
NO! THE COMICS I MAKE ARE CALLED "GRAPHIC NOVELS," AND THEY'RE FOR ADULTS ONLY!
SHIT! I'M NOT CONNECTING WITH THESE KIDS AT ALL. NORA LOOKS LIKE SHE'S GONNA DIE OF EMBARRASSMENT!
UH...
OKAY! LET ME START BY SHOWING YOU SOME SUPER EASY CARTOONING TRICKS!
NETS

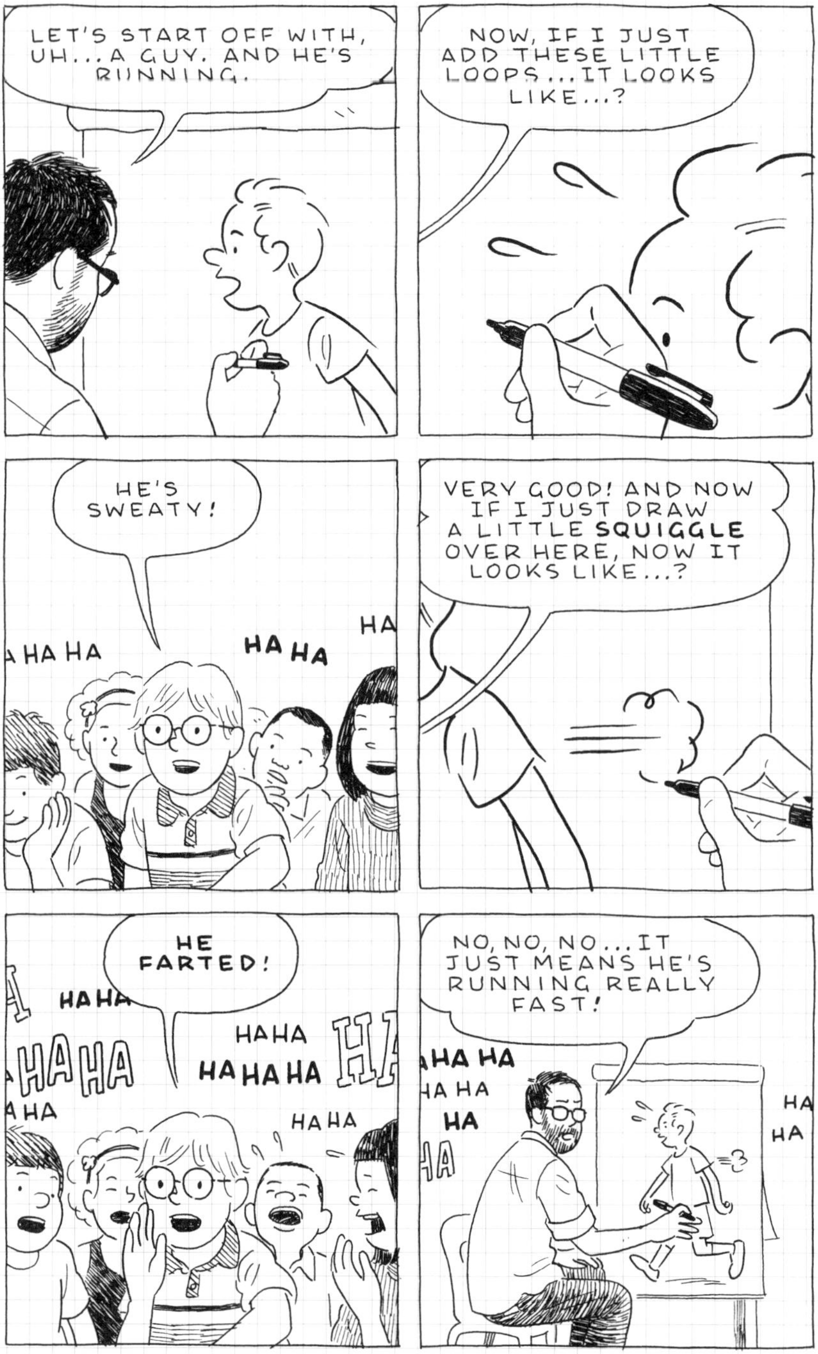
LET'S START OFF WITH, UH... A GUY. AND HE'S RUNNING.
NOW, IF I JUST ADD THESE LITTLE LOOPS... IT LOOKS LIKE...?
HE'S SWEATY!
HA HA
HA HA
HA
VERY GOOD! AND NOW IF I JUST DRAW A LITTLE **SQUIGGLE** OVER HERE, NOW IT LOOKS LIKE...?
HE FARTED!
HA HA
HA HA
HA HA HA
HA HA
NO, NO, NO... IT JUST MEANS HE'S RUNNING REALLY FAST!
HA HA
HA
HA

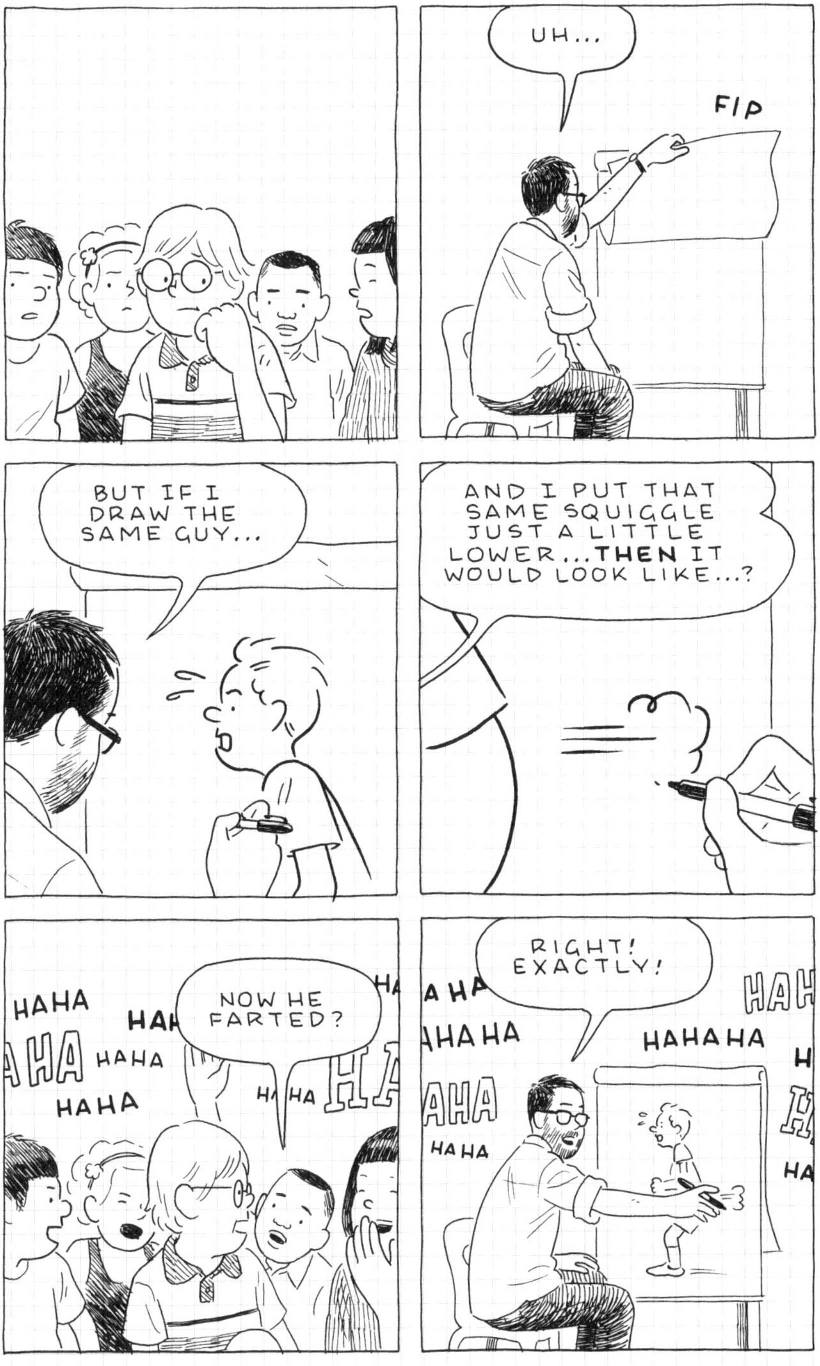
UH...
FIP
BUT IF I DRAW THE SAME GUY...
AND I PUT THAT SAME SQUIGGLE JUST A LITTLE LOWER... **THEN** IT WOULD LOOK LIKE...?
HAHA
HAHA
HAHA
HAHA
NOW HE FARTED?
RIGHT! EXACTLY!
HAHAHA
HAHA

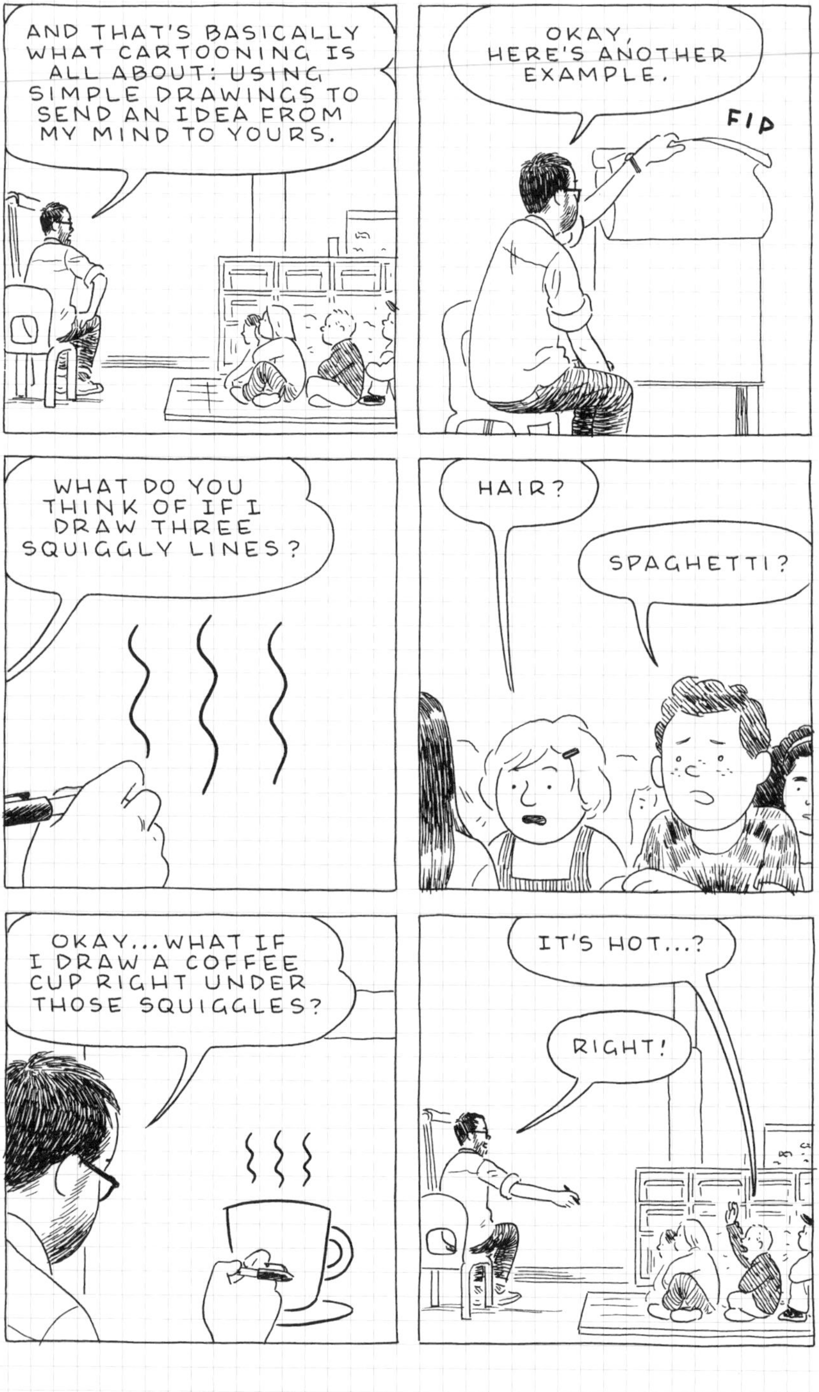
AND THAT'S BASICALLY WHAT CARTOONING IS ALL ABOUT: USING SIMPLE DRAWINGS TO SEND AN IDEA FROM MY MIND TO YOURS.
OKAY, HERE'S ANOTHER EXAMPLE.
FIP
WHAT DO YOU THINK OF IF I DRAW THREE SQUIGGLY LINES?
HAIR?
SPAGHETTI?
OKAY... WHAT IF I DRAW A COFFEE CUP RIGHT UNDER THOSE SQUIGGLES?
IT'S HOT...?
RIGHT!

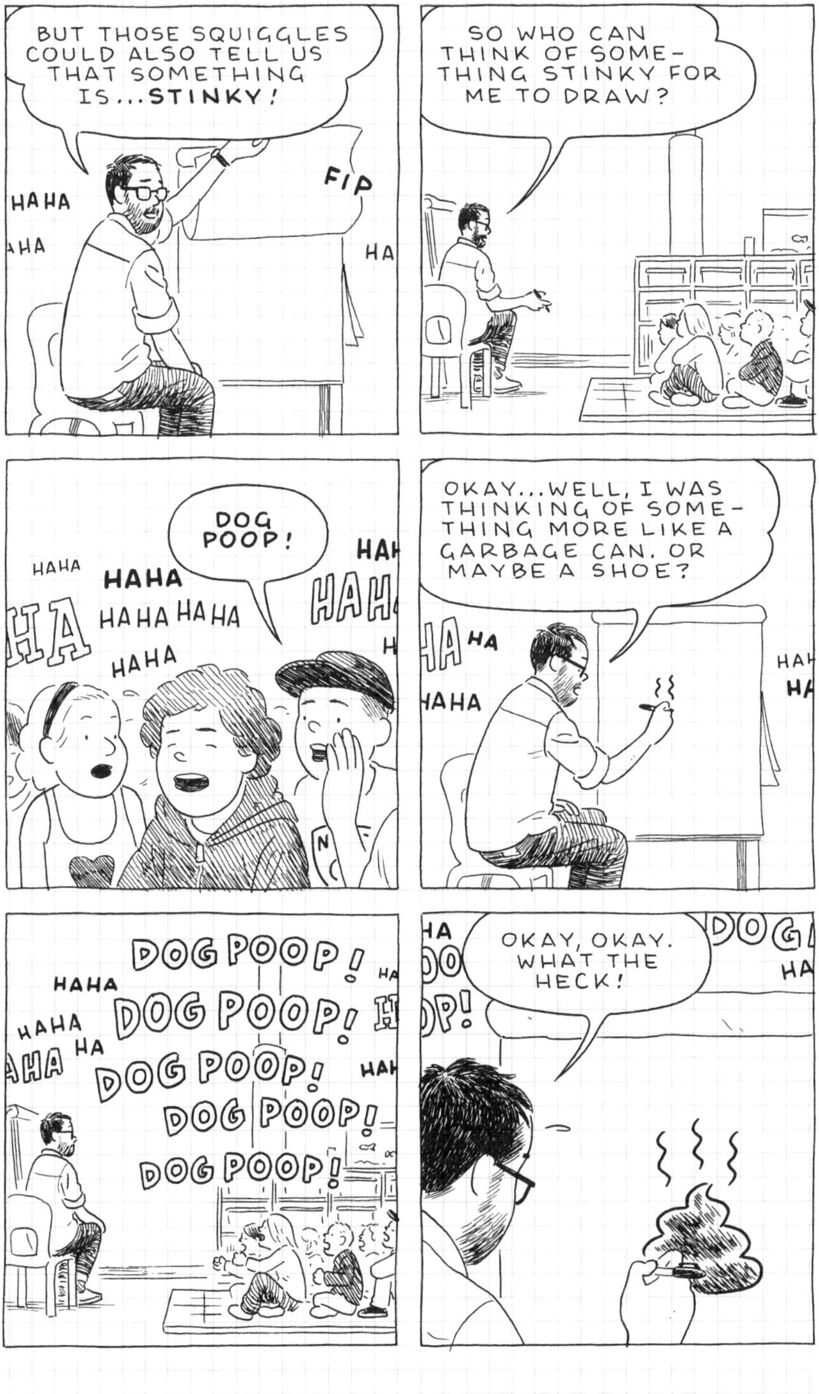
BUT THOSE SQUIGGLES COULD ALSO TELL US THAT SOMETHING IS...STINKY!
HAHA
FIP
HA
SO WHO CAN THINK OF SOME-THING STINKY FOR ME TO DRAW?
HAHA
HAHA
HAHA HAHA HAHA
HAHA
DOG POOP!
OKAY...WELL, I WAS THINKING OF SOME-THING MORE LIKE A GARBAGE CAN. OR MAYBE A SHOE?
HA
HAHA
DOG POOP!
HAHA
DOG POOP!
HAHA
HA
DOG POOP!
DOG POOP!
DOG POOP!
OKAY, OKAY. WHAT THE HECK!

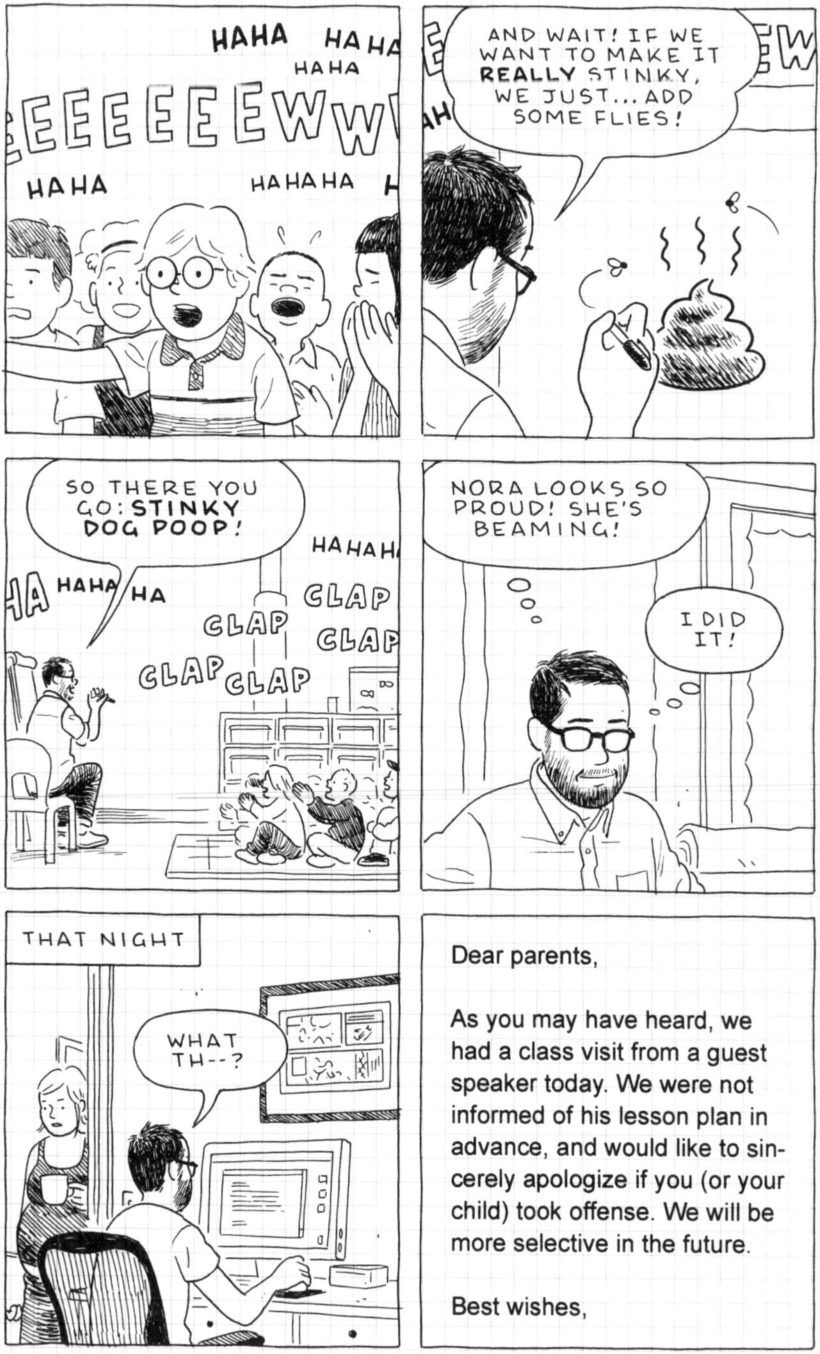
HAHA HAHA
HAHA
EEEEEEEEWW
HAHA
HAHAHA
AND WAIT! IF WE WANT TO MAKE IT REALLY STINKY, WE JUST... ADD SOME FLIES!
SO THERE YOU GO: STINKY DOG POOP!
HAHAHA
HAHA HA
CLAP
CLAP
CLAP
CLAP CLAP
NORA LOOKS SO PROUD! SHE'S BEAMING!
I DID IT!
THAT NIGHT
WHAT TH--?
Dear parents,
As you may have heard, we had a class visit from a guest speaker today. We were not informed of his lesson plan in advance, and would like to sincerely apologize if you (or your child) took offense. We will be more selective in the future.
Best wishes,

NEW YORK,
2015

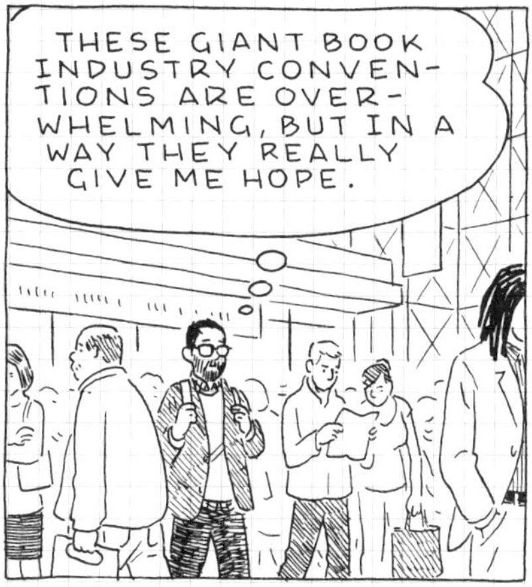
THESE GIANT BOOK INDUSTRY CONVENTIONS ARE OVERWHELMING, BUT IN A WAY THEY REALLY GIVE ME HOPE.

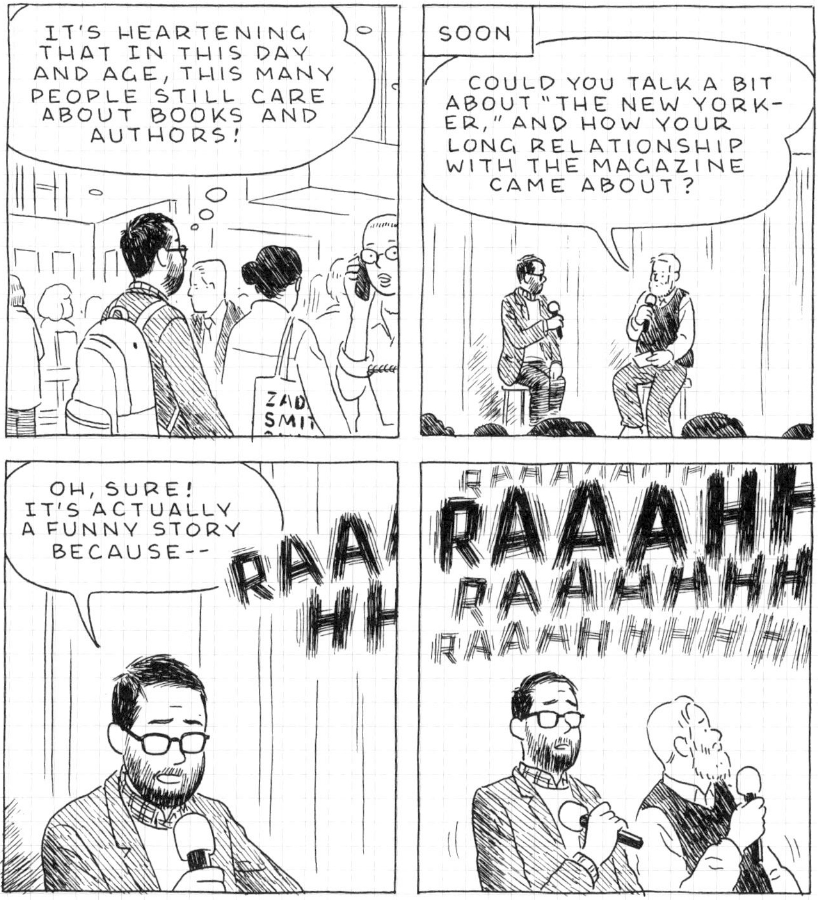
IT'S HEARTENING THAT IN THIS DAY AND AGE, THIS MANY PEOPLE STILL CARE ABOUT BOOKS AND AUTHORS!
SOON
COULD YOU TALK A BIT ABOUT "THE NEW YORKER," AND HOW YOUR LONG RELATIONSHIP WITH THE MAGAZINE CAME ABOUT?
OH, SURE! IT'S ACTUALLY A FUNNY STORY BECAUSE--
RAAAHH
RAAAHH

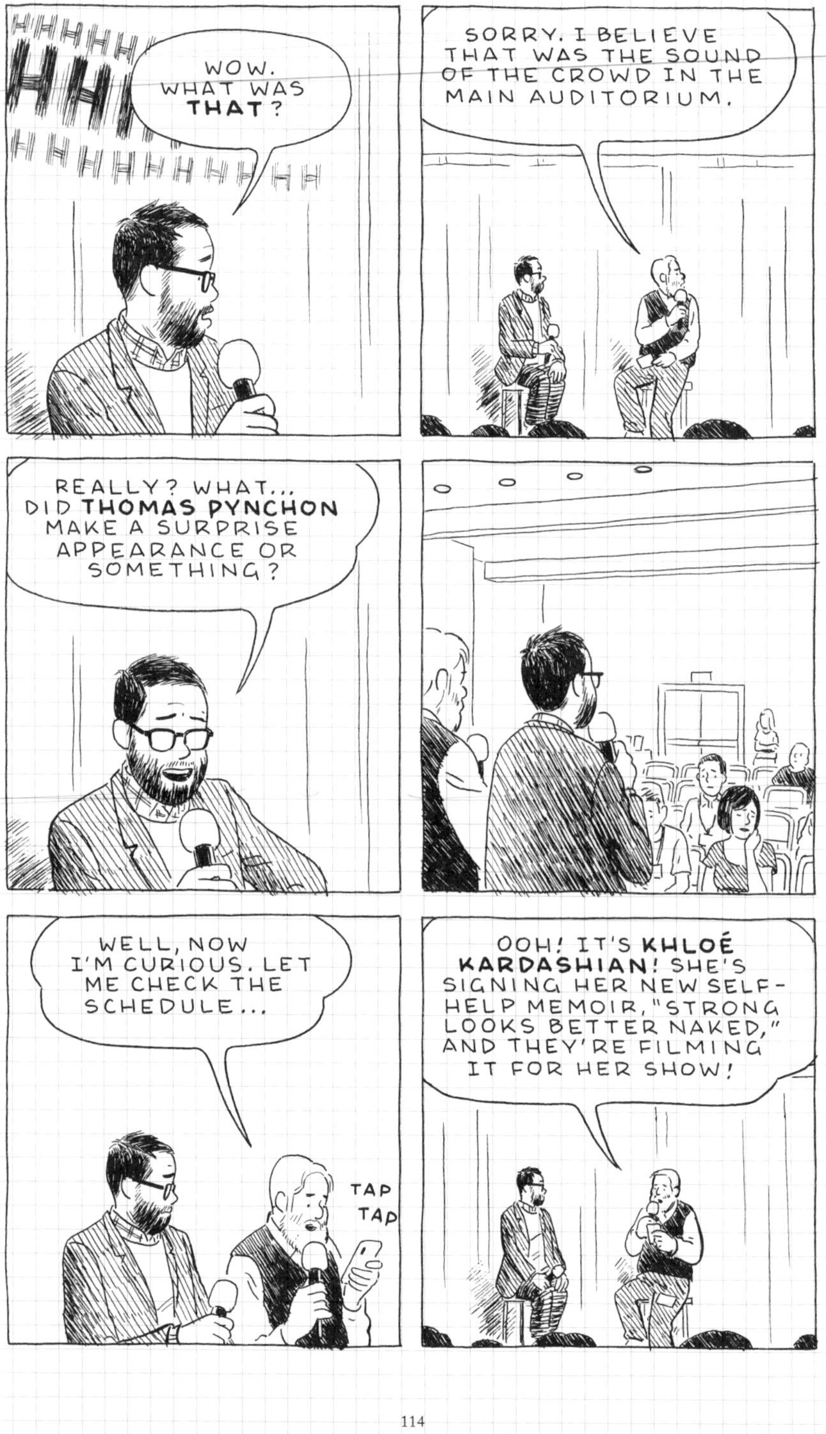
HHHHHHHHHHHHHHHH
WOW. WHAT WAS **THAT**?
SORRY. I BELIEVE THAT WAS THE SOUND OF THE CROWD IN THE MAIN AUDITORIUM.
REALLY? WHAT... DID **THOMAS PYNCHON** MAKE A SURPRISE APPEARANCE OR SOMETHING?
WELL, NOW I'M CURIOUS. LET ME CHECK THE SCHEDULE...
TAP TAP
OOH! IT'S **KHLOÉ KARDASHIAN**! SHE'S SIGNING HER NEW SELF-HELP MEMOIR, "STRONG LOOKS BETTER NAKED," AND THEY'RE FILMING IT FOR HER SHOW!

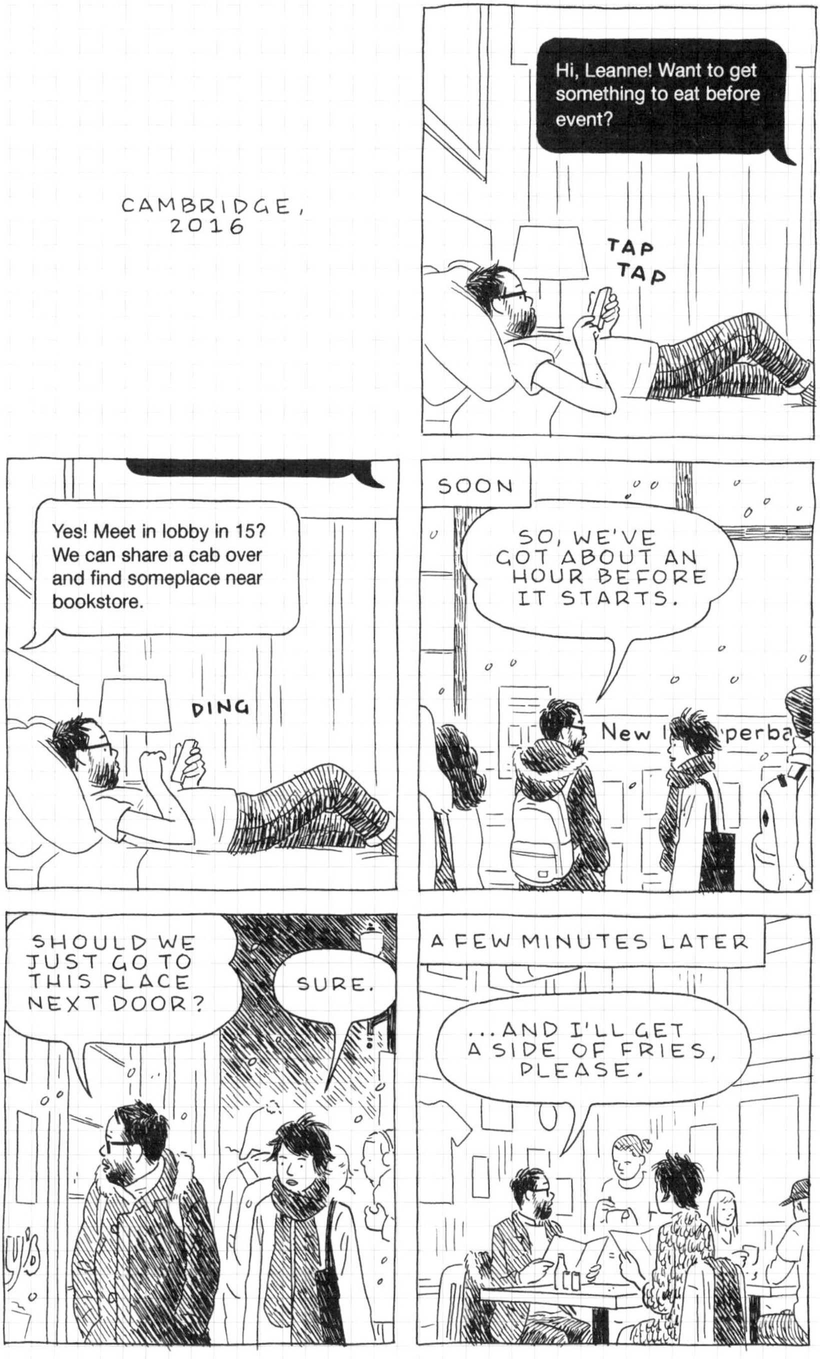
CAMBRIDGE, 2016
Hi, Leanne! Want to get something to eat before event?
TAP TAP
Yes! Meet in lobby in 15? We can share a cab over and find someplace near bookstore.
DING
SOON
SO, WE'VE GOT ABOUT AN HOUR BEFORE IT STARTS.
SHOULD WE JUST GO TO THIS PLACE NEXT DOOR?
SURE.
A FEW MINUTES LATER
...AND I'LL GET A SIDE OF FRIES, PLEASE.

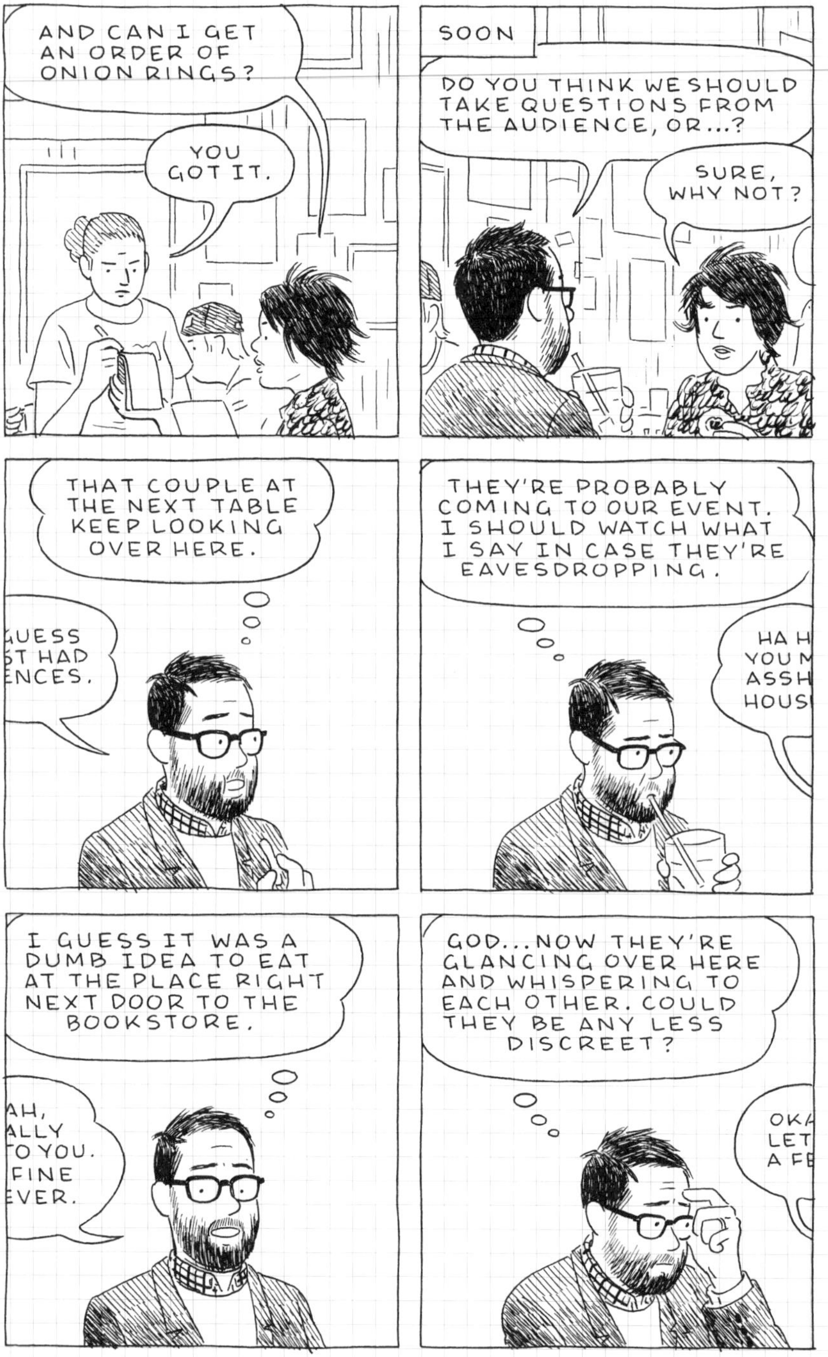
AND CAN I GET AN ORDER OF ONION RINGS?
YOU GOT IT.
SOON
DO YOU THINK WE SHOULD TAKE QUESTIONS FROM THE AUDIENCE, OR...?
SURE, WHY NOT?
THAT COUPLE AT THE NEXT TABLE KEEP LOOKING OVER HERE.
UESS
T HAD
NCES.
THEY'RE PROBABLY COMING TO OUR EVENT. I SHOULD WATCH WHAT I SAY IN CASE THEY'RE EAVESDROPPING.
HA H
YOU M
ASSH
HOUS
I GUESS IT WAS A DUMB IDEA TO EAT AT THE PLACE RIGHT NEXT DOOR TO THE BOOKSTORE.
AH,
ALLY
O YOU.
FINE
EVER.
GOD...NOW THEY'RE GLANCING OVER HERE AND WHISPERING TO EACH OTHER. COULD THEY BE ANY LESS DISCREET?
OK
LET
A F

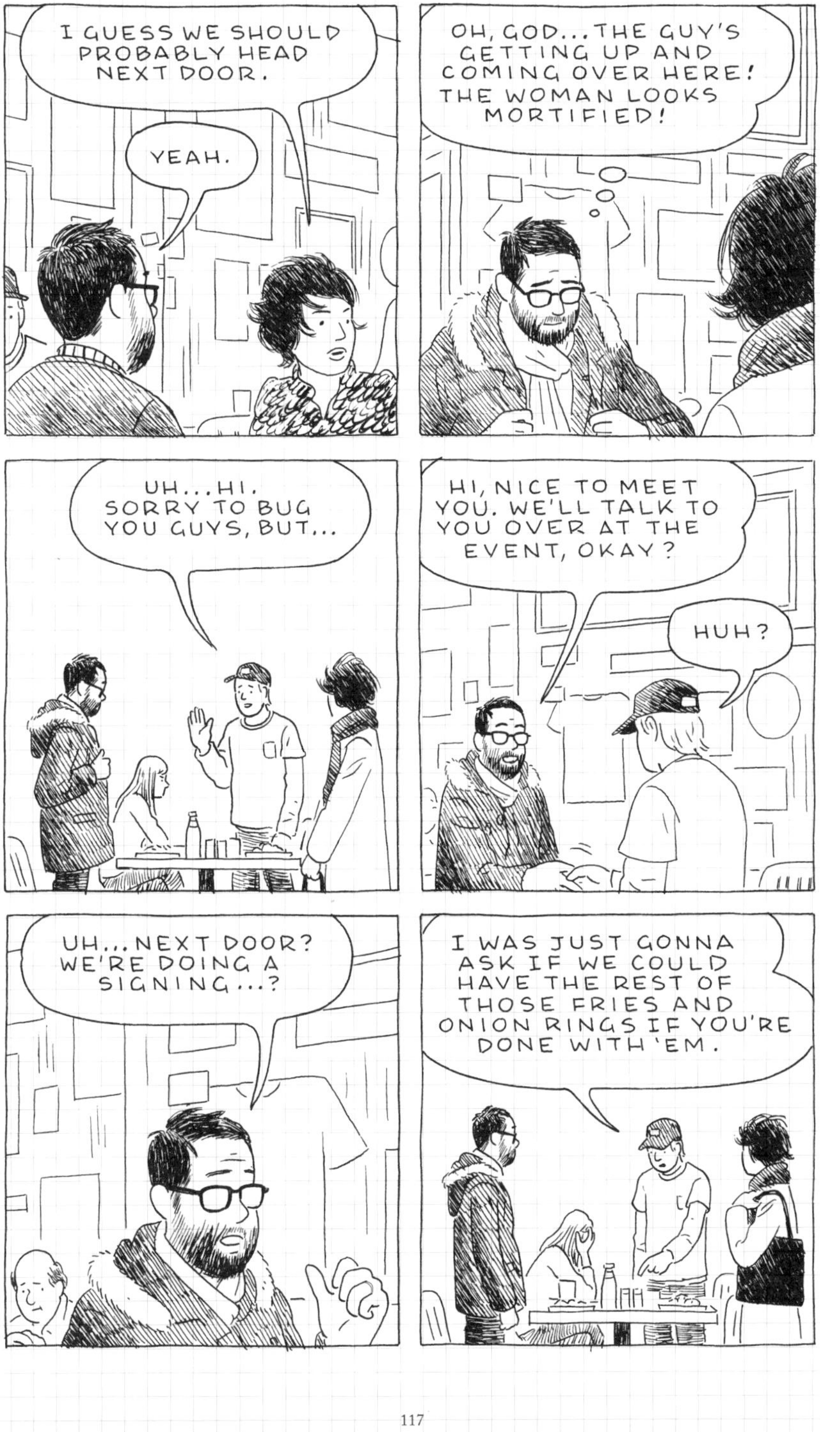
I GUESS WE SHOULD PROBABLY HEAD NEXT DOOR.
YEAH.
OH, GOD... THE GUY'S GETTING UP AND COMING OVER HERE! THE WOMAN LOOKS MORTIFIED!
UH...HI. SORRY TO BUG YOU GUYS, BUT...
HI, NICE TO MEET YOU. WE'LL TALK TO YOU OVER AT THE EVENT, OKAY?
HUH?
UH...NEXT DOOR? WE'RE DOING A SIGNING...?
I WAS JUST GONNA ASK IF WE COULD HAVE THE REST OF THOSE FRIES AND ONION RINGS IF YOU'RE DONE WITH 'EM.

BROOKLYN, 2016

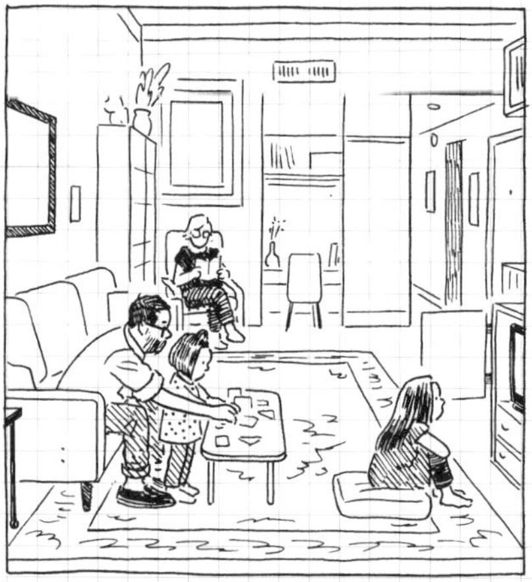

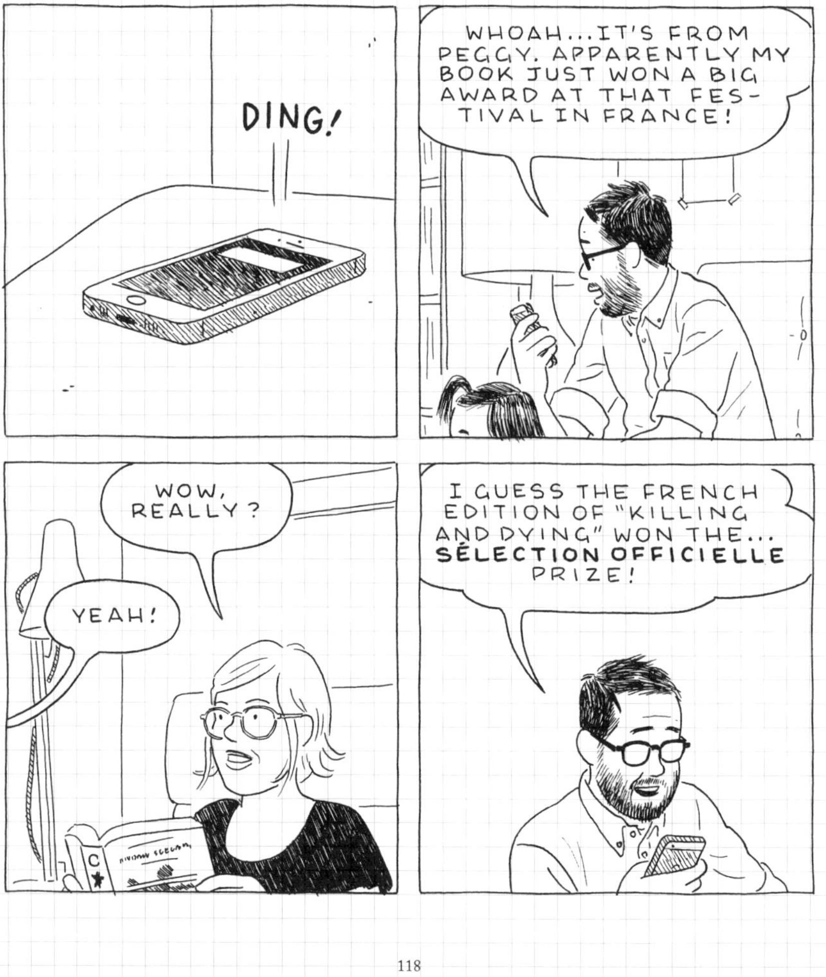
DING!
WHOAH...IT'S FROM PEGGY. APPARENTLY MY BOOK JUST WON A BIG AWARD AT THAT FES-TIVAL IN FRANCE!
WOW, REALLY?
YEAH!
I GUESS THE FRENCH EDITION OF "KILLING AND DYING" WON THE... SÉLECTION OFFICIELLE PRIZE!

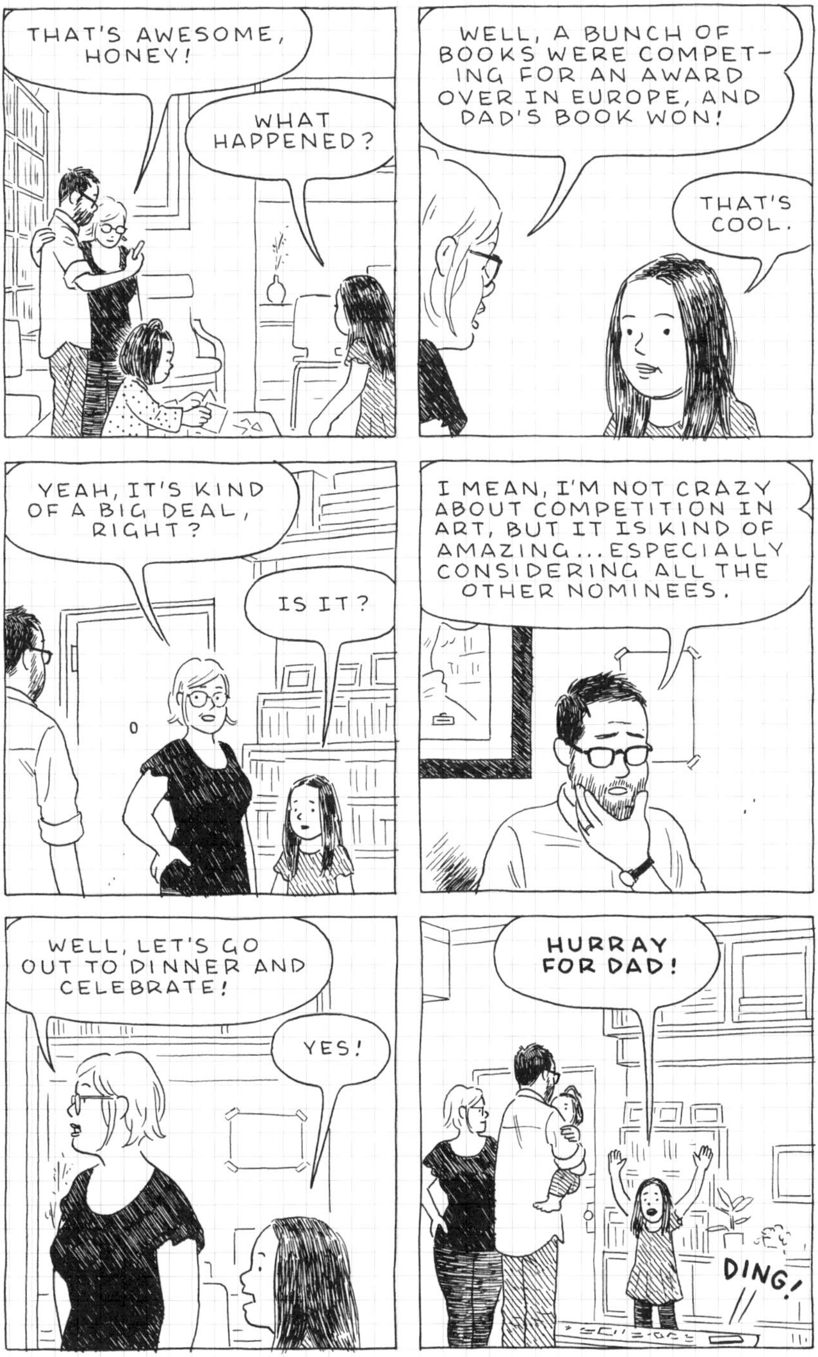
THAT'S AWESOME, HONEY!
WHAT HAPPENED?
WELL, A BUNCH OF BOOKS WERE COMPETING FOR AN AWARD OVER IN EUROPE, AND DAD'S BOOK WON!
THAT'S COOL.
YEAH, IT'S KIND OF A BIG DEAL, RIGHT?
IS IT?
I MEAN, I'M NOT CRAZY ABOUT COMPETITION IN ART, BUT IT IS KIND OF AMAZING... ESPECIALLY CONSIDERING ALL THE OTHER NOMINEES.
WELL, LET'S GO OUT TO DINNER AND CELEBRATE!
YES!
HURRAY FOR DAD!
DING!

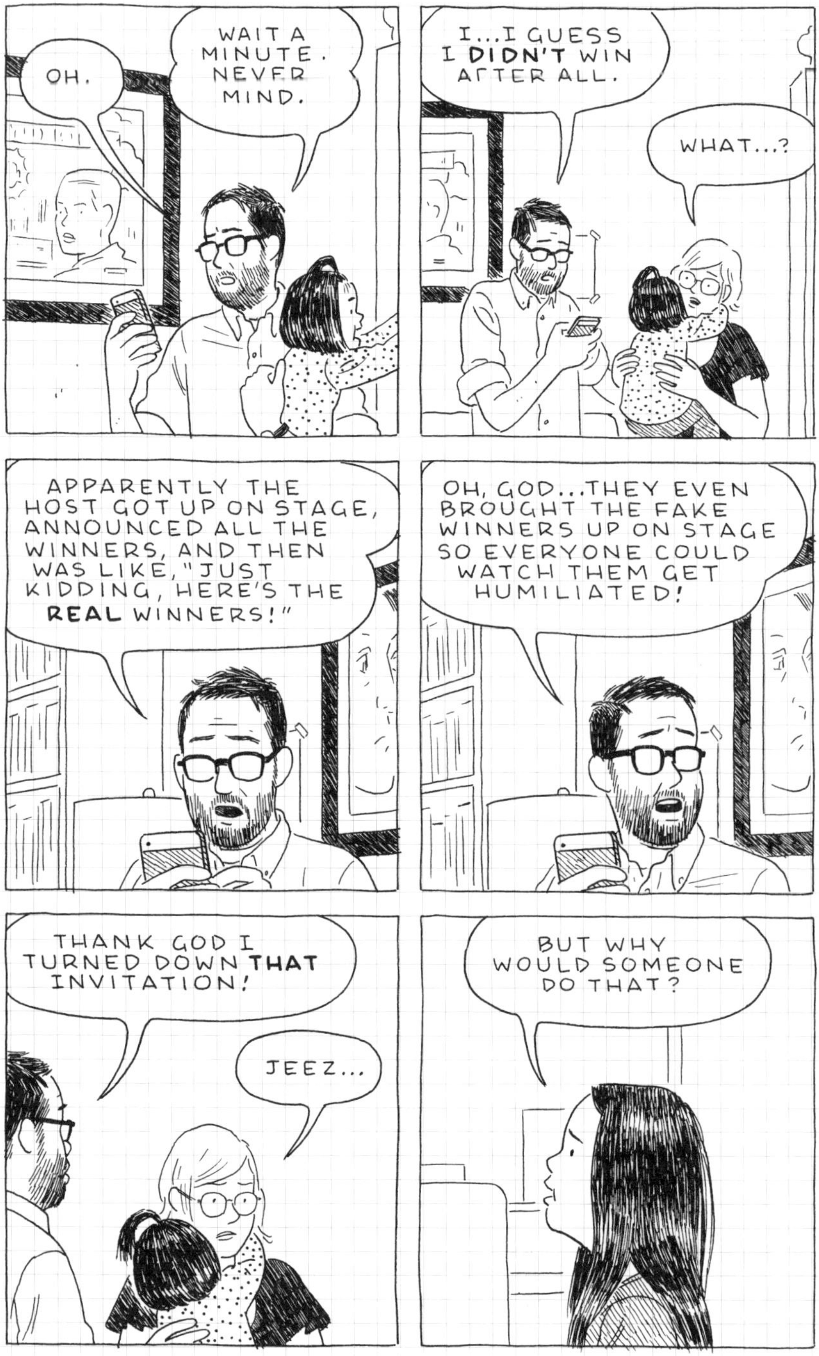
OH.
WAIT A MINUTE. NEVER MIND.
I...I GUESS I **DIDN'T** WIN AFTER ALL.
WHAT...?
APPARENTLY THE HOST GOT UP ON STAGE, ANNOUNCED ALL THE WINNERS, AND THEN WAS LIKE, "JUST KIDDING, HERE'S THE **REAL** WINNERS!"
OH, GOD...THEY EVEN BROUGHT THE FAKE WINNERS UP ON STAGE SO EVERYONE COULD WATCH THEM GET HUMILIATED!
THANK GOD I TURNED DOWN **THAT** INVITATION!
JEEZ...
BUT WHY WOULD SOMEONE DO THAT?

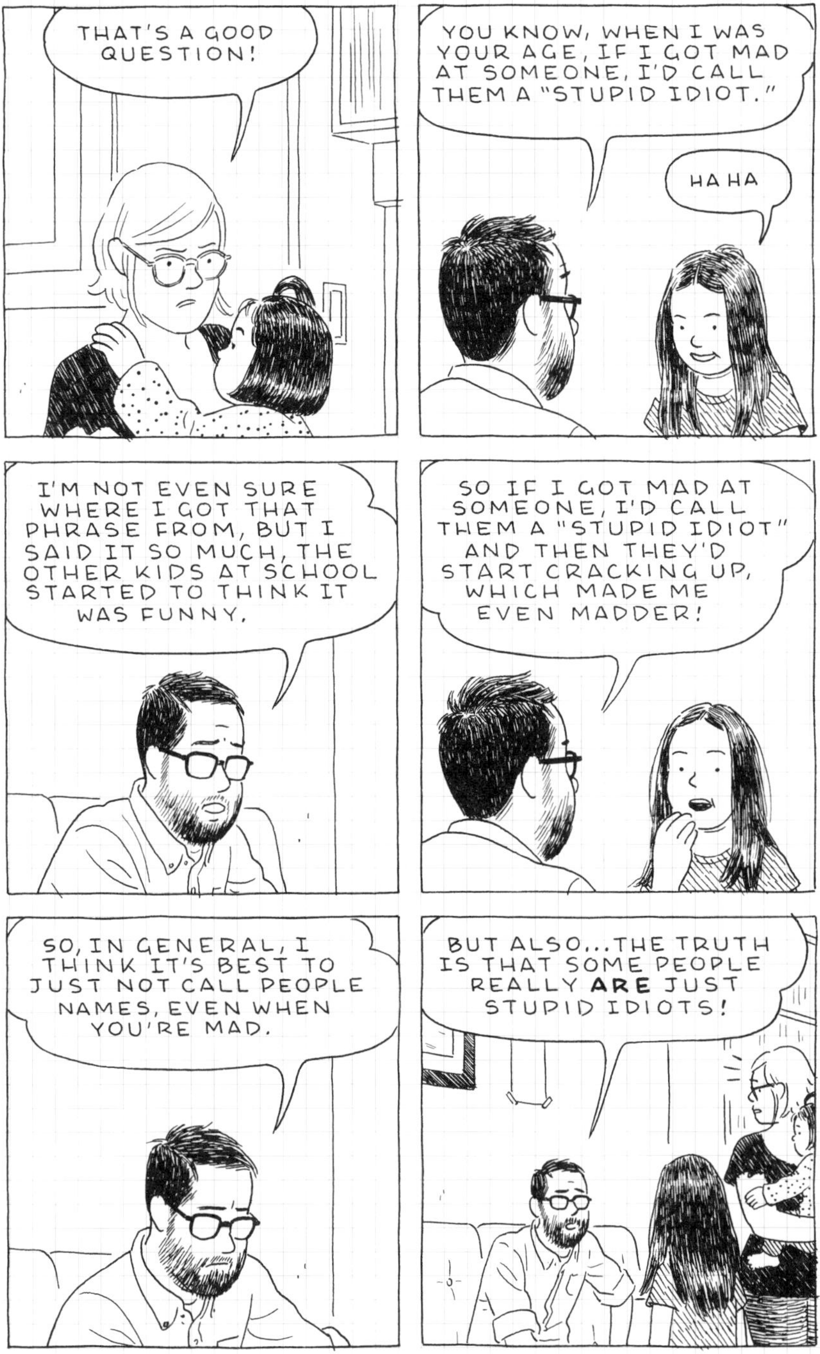
THAT'S A GOOD QUESTION!
YOU KNOW, WHEN I WAS YOUR AGE, IF I GOT MAD AT SOMEONE, I'D CALL THEM A "STUPID IDIOT."
HA HA
I'M NOT EVEN SURE WHERE I GOT THAT PHRASE FROM, BUT I SAID IT SO MUCH, THE OTHER KIDS AT SCHOOL STARTED TO THINK IT WAS FUNNY.
SO IF I GOT MAD AT SOMEONE, I'D CALL THEM A "STUPID IDIOT" AND THEN THEY'D START CRACKING UP, WHICH MADE ME EVEN MADDER!
SO, IN GENERAL, I THINK IT'S BEST TO JUST NOT CALL PEOPLE NAMES, EVEN WHEN YOU'RE MAD.
BUT ALSO...THE TRUTH IS THAT SOME PEOPLE REALLY **ARE** JUST STUPID IDIOTS!

PHILADELPHIA, 2017

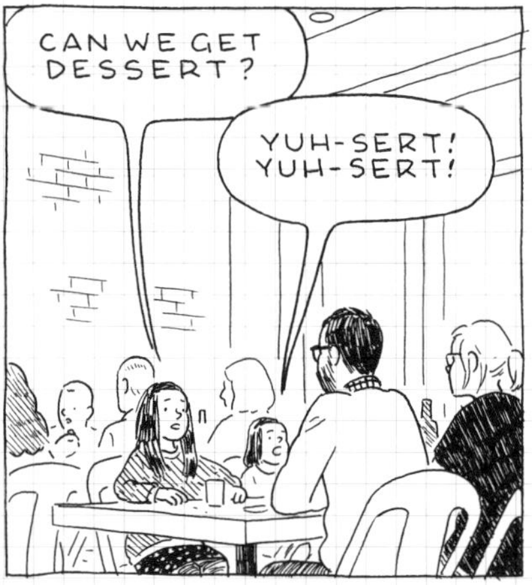
CAN WE GET DESSERT?
YUH-SERT! YUH-SERT!

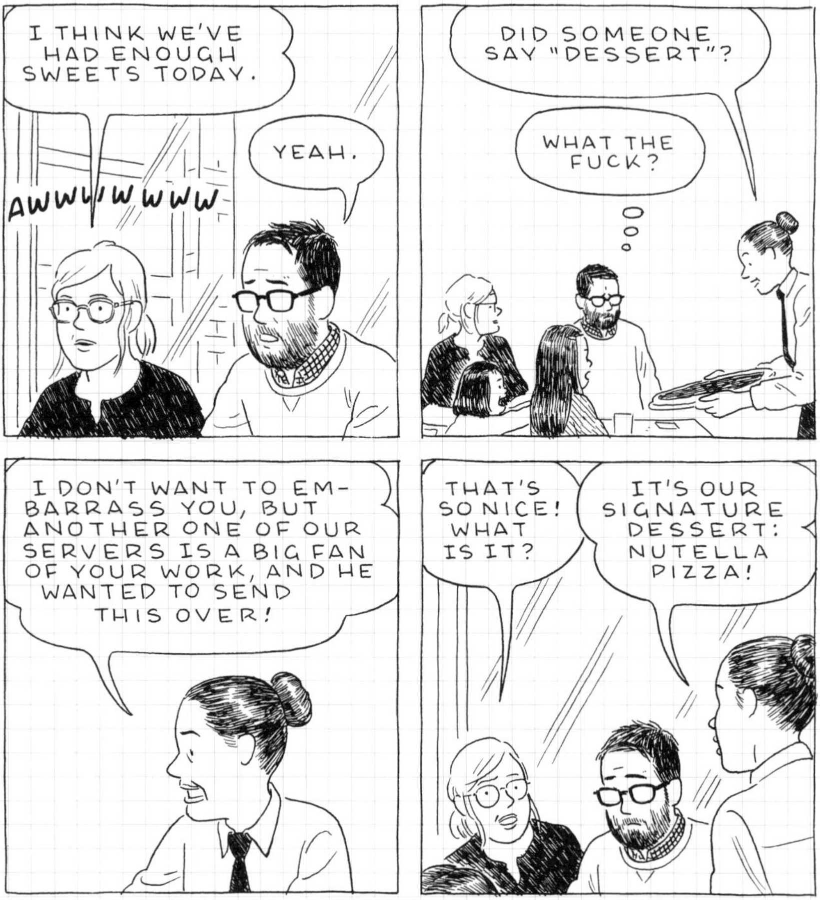
I THINK WE'VE HAD ENOUGH SWEETS TODAY.
AWWWWWWW
YEAH.
DID SOMEONE SAY "DESSERT"?
WHAT THE FUCK?
I DON'T WANT TO EM-BARRASS YOU, BUT ANOTHER ONE OF OUR SERVERS IS A BIG FAN OF YOUR WORK, AND HE WANTED TO SEND THIS OVER!
THAT'S SO NICE! WHAT IS IT?
IT'S OUR SIGNATURE DESSERT: NUTELLA PIZZA!

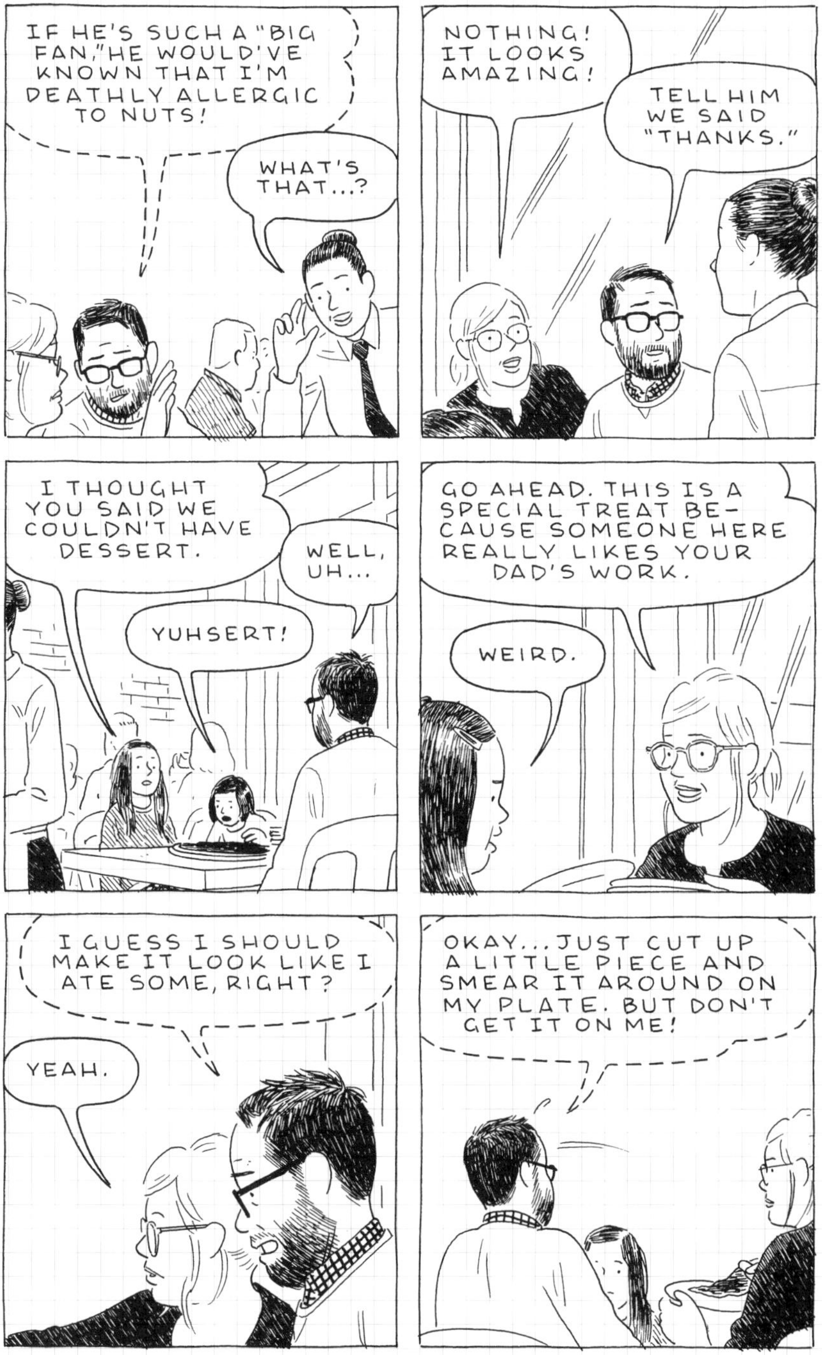

IF HE'S SUCH A "BIG FAN," HE WOULD'VE KNOWN THAT I'M DEATHLY ALLERGIC TO NUTS!
WHAT'S THAT...?
NOTHING! IT LOOKS AMAZING!
TELL HIM WE SAID "THANKS."
I THOUGHT YOU SAID WE COULDN'T HAVE DESSERT.
WELL, UH...
YUHSERT!
GO AHEAD. THIS IS A SPECIAL TREAT BE-CAUSE SOMEONE HERE REALLY LIKES YOUR DAD'S WORK.
WEIRD.
I GUESS I SHOULD MAKE IT LOOK LIKE I ATE SOME, RIGHT?
YEAH.
OKAY... JUST CUT UP A LITTLE PIECE AND SMEAR IT AROUND ON MY PLATE. BUT DON'T GET IT ON ME!

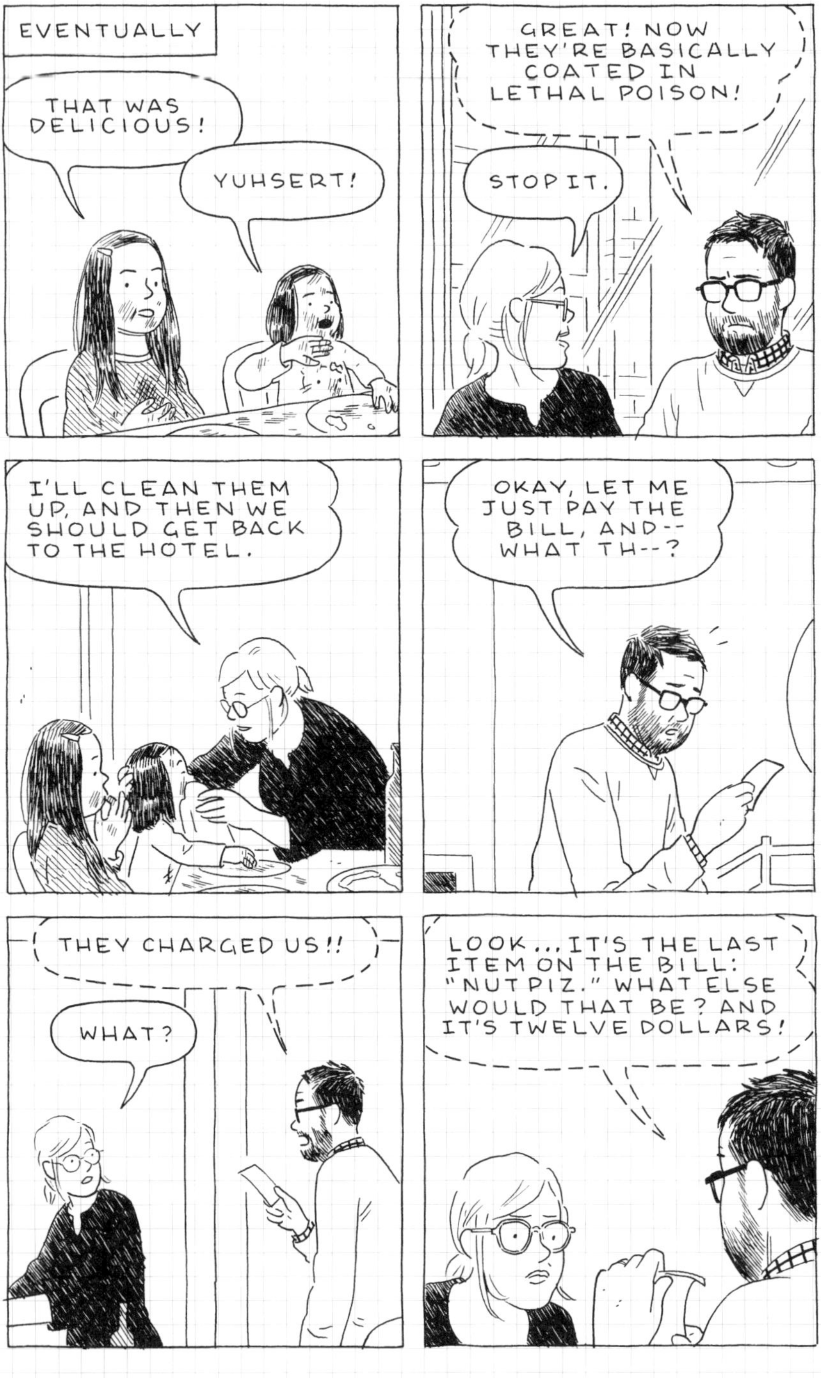
EVENTUALLY
THAT WAS DELICIOUS!
YUHSERT!
GREAT! NOW THEY'RE BASICALLY COATED IN LETHAL POISON!
STOP IT.
I'LL CLEAN THEM UP, AND THEN WE SHOULD GET BACK TO THE HOTEL.
OKAY, LET ME JUST PAY THE BILL, AND-- WHAT TH--?
THEY CHARGED US!!
WHAT?
LOOK... IT'S THE LAST ITEM ON THE BILL: "NUTPIZ." WHAT ELSE WOULD THAT BE? AND IT'S TWELVE DOLLARS!

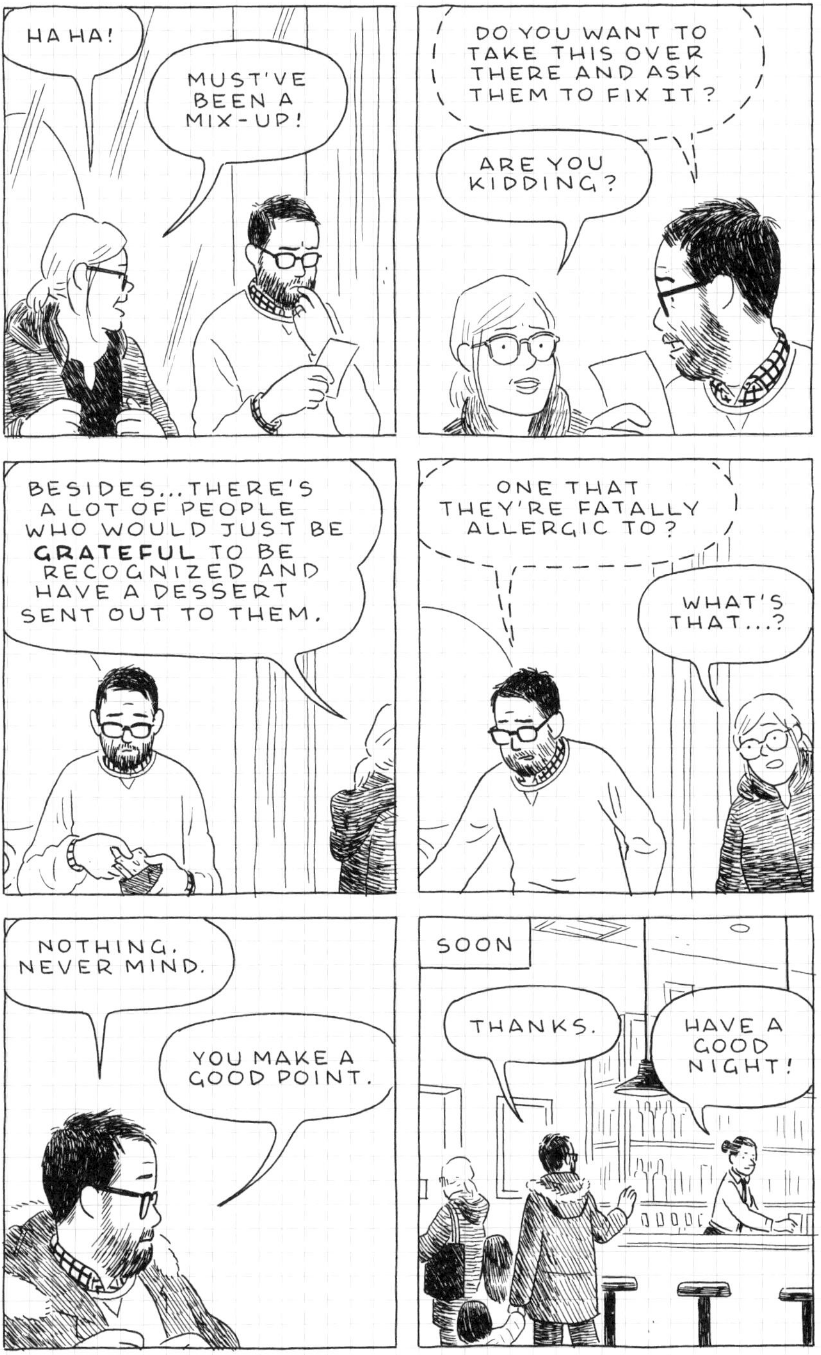
HA HA!
MUST'VE BEEN A MIX-UP!
DO YOU WANT TO TAKE THIS OVER THERE AND ASK THEM TO FIX IT?
ARE YOU KIDDING?
BESIDES... THERE'S A LOT OF PEOPLE WHO WOULD JUST BE GRATEFUL TO BE RECOGNIZED AND HAVE A DESSERT SENT OUT TO THEM.
ONE THAT THEY'RE FATALLY ALLERGIC TO?
WHAT'S THAT...?
NOTHING. NEVER MIND.
YOU MAKE A GOOD POINT.
SOON
THANKS.
HAVE A GOOD NIGHT!

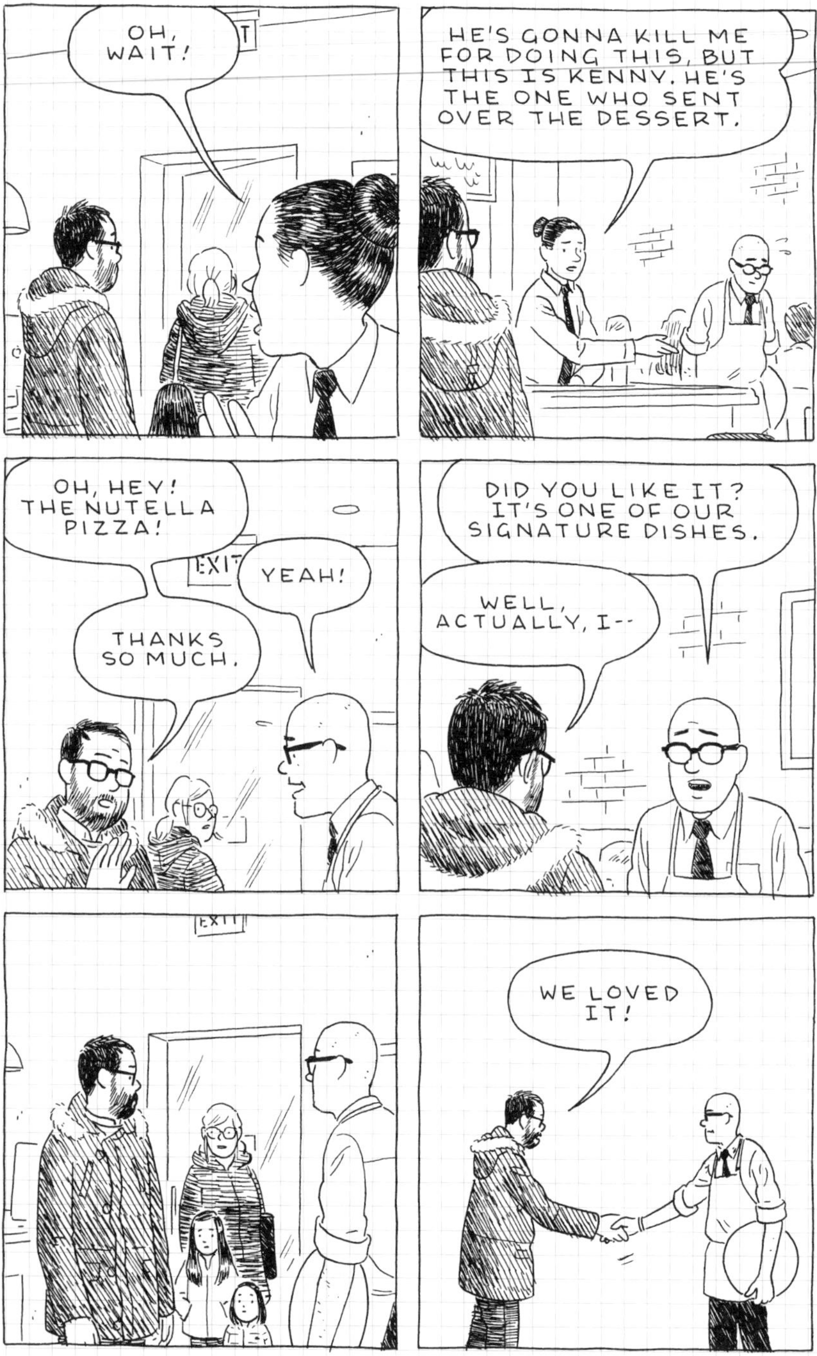
OH, WAIT!
HE'S GONNA KILL ME FOR DOING THIS, BUT THIS IS KENNY. HE'S THE ONE WHO SENT OVER THE DESSERT.
OH, HEY! THE NUTELLA PIZZA!
YEAH!
THANKS SO MUCH.
DID YOU LIKE IT? IT'S ONE OF OUR SIGNATURE DISHES.
WELL, ACTUALLY, I--
WE LOVED IT!

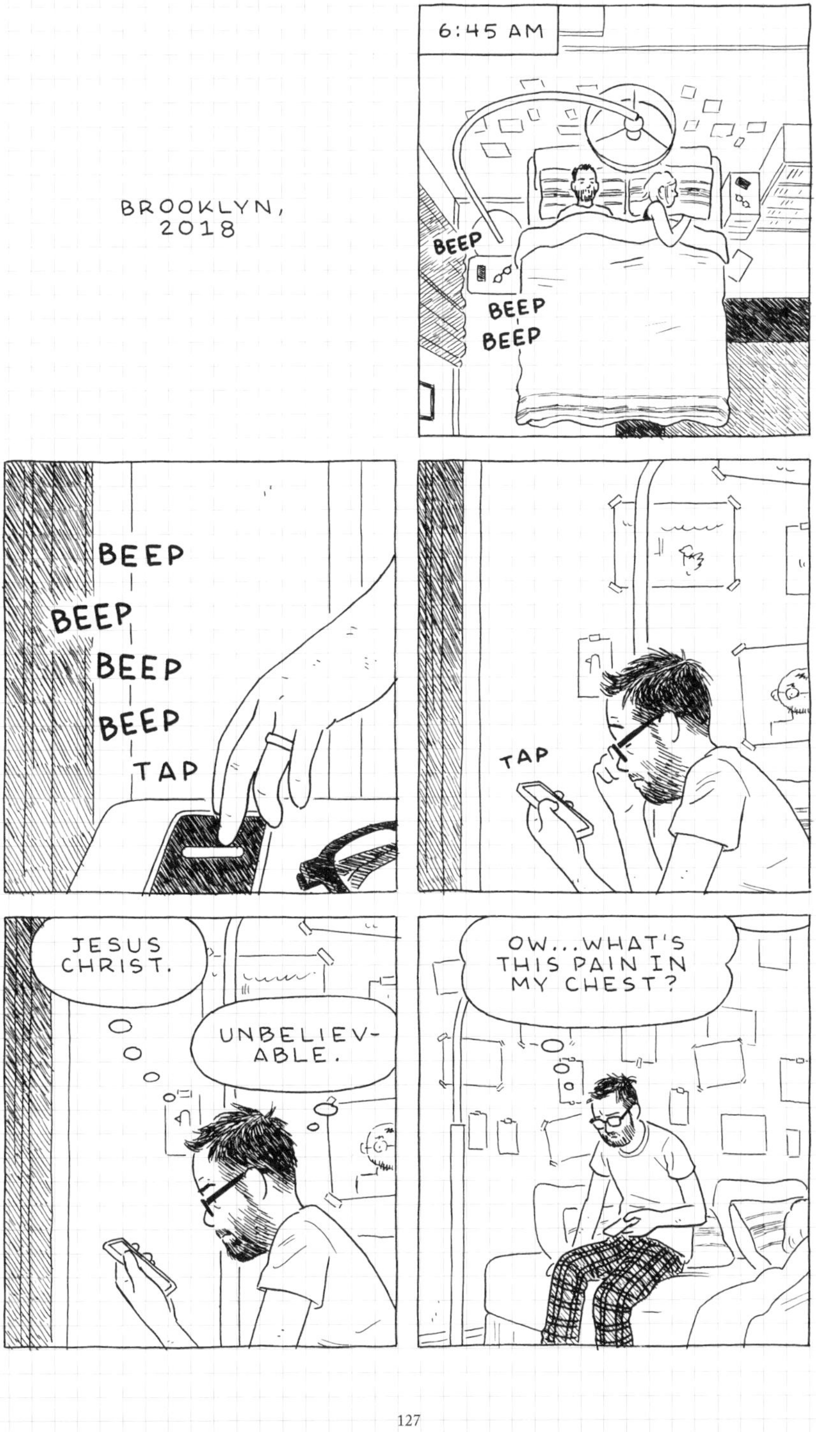
BROOKLYN, 2018
6:45 AM
BEEP
BEEP
BEEP
BEEP
BEEP
BEEP
BEEP
TAP
TAP
JESUS CHRIST.
UNBELIEV-ABLE.
OW...WHAT'S THIS PAIN IN MY CHEST?

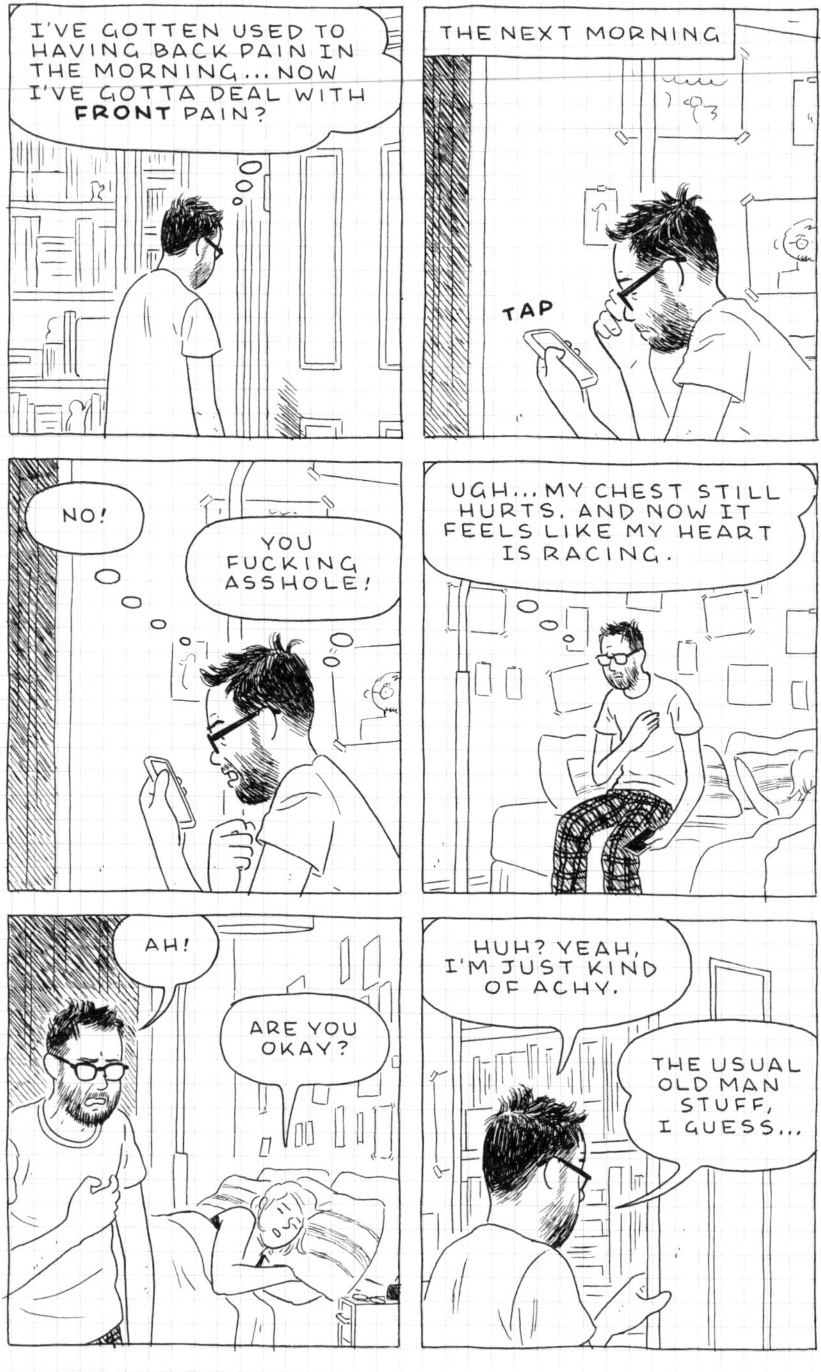

I'VE GOTTEN USED TO HAVING BACK PAIN IN THE MORNING... NOW I'VE GOTTA DEAL WITH **FRONT** PAIN?
THE NEXT MORNING
TAP
NO!
YOU FUCKING ASSHOLE!
UGH... MY CHEST STILL HURTS. AND NOW IT FEELS LIKE MY HEART IS RACING.
AH!
ARE YOU OKAY?
HUH? YEAH, I'M JUST KIND OF ACHY.
THE USUAL OLD MAN STUFF, I GUESS...

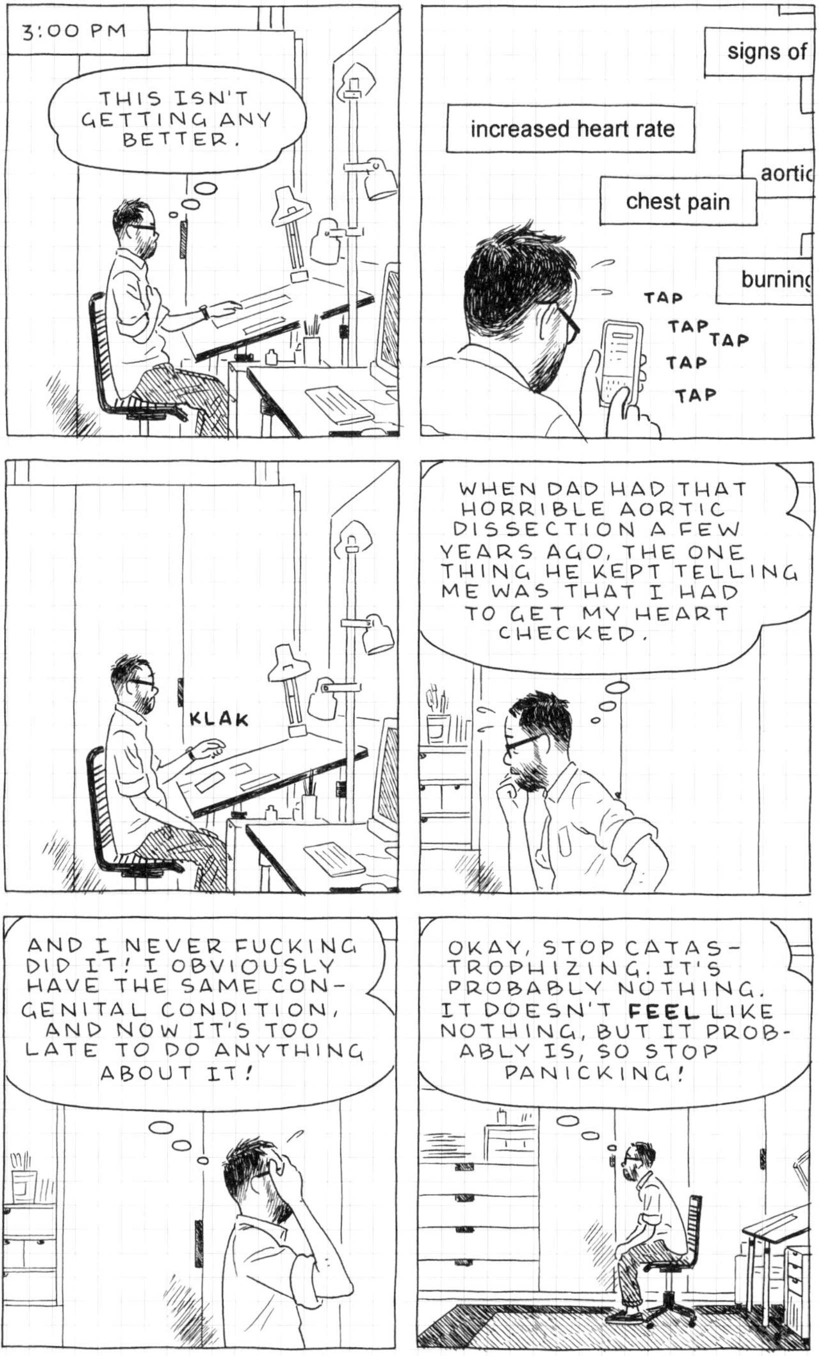
3:00 PM
THIS ISN'T GETTING ANY BETTER.
signs of
increased heart rate
aortic
chest pain
burning
TAP TAP TAP TAP TAP
KLAK
WHEN DAD HAD THAT HORRIBLE AORTIC DISSECTION A FEW YEARS AGO, THE ONE THING HE KEPT TELLING ME WAS THAT I HAD TO GET MY HEART CHECKED.
AND I NEVER FUCKING DID IT! I OBVIOUSLY HAVE THE SAME CON-GENITAL CONDITION, AND NOW IT'S TOO LATE TO DO ANYTHING ABOUT IT!
OKAY, STOP CATAS-TROPHIZING. IT'S PROBABLY NOTHING. IT DOESN'T FEEL LIKE NOTHING, BUT IT PROB-ABLY IS, SO STOP PANICKING!

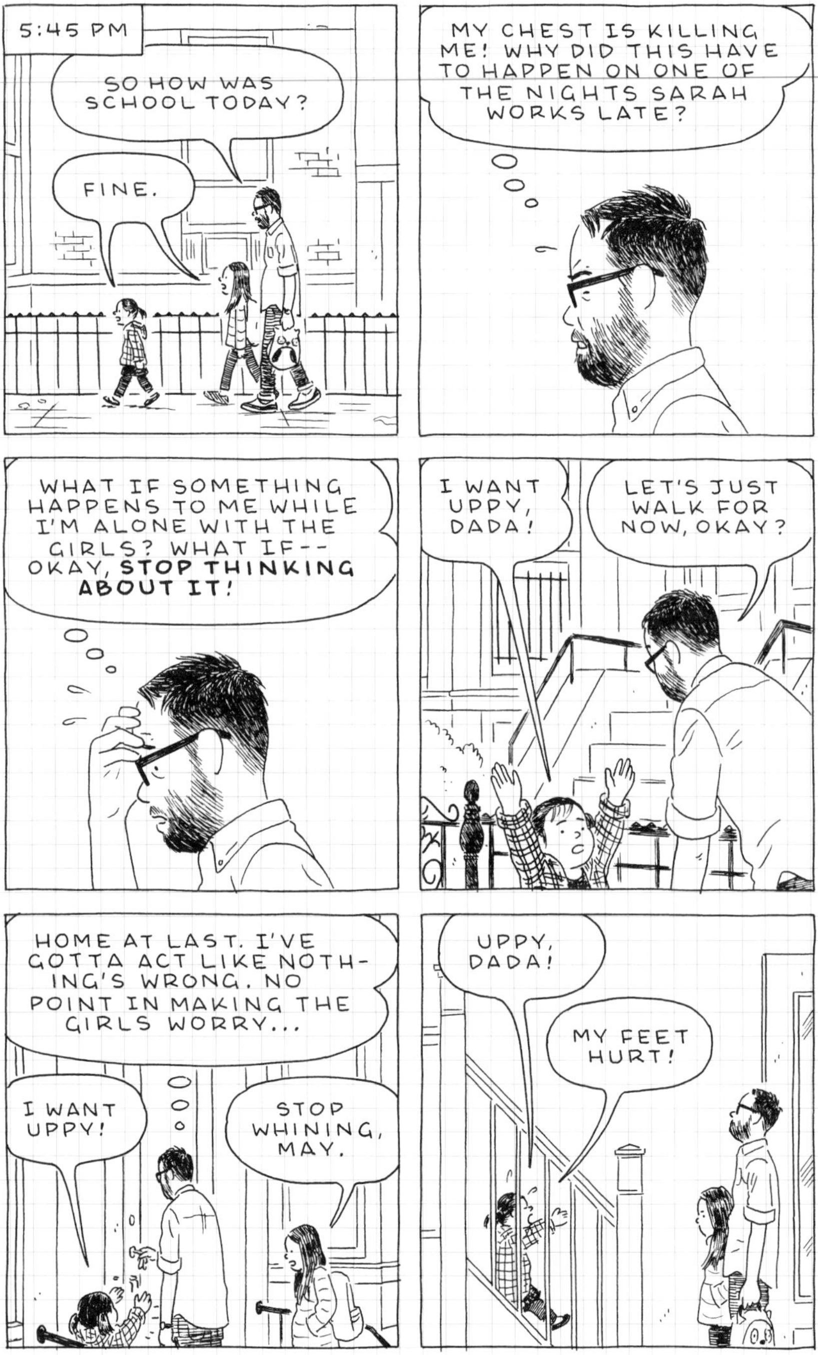
5:45 PM
SO HOW WAS SCHOOL TODAY?
FINE.
MY CHEST IS KILLING ME! WHY DID THIS HAVE TO HAPPEN ON ONE OF THE NIGHTS SARAH WORKS LATE?
WHAT IF SOMETHING HAPPENS TO ME WHILE I'M ALONE WITH THE GIRLS? WHAT IF-- OKAY, STOP THINKING ABOUT IT!
I WANT UPPY, DADA!
LET'S JUST WALK FOR NOW, OKAY?
HOME AT LAST. I'VE GOTTA ACT LIKE NOTHING'S WRONG. NO POINT IN MAKING THE GIRLS WORRY...
I WANT UPPY!
STOP WHINING, MAY.
UPPY, DADA!
MY FEET HURT!

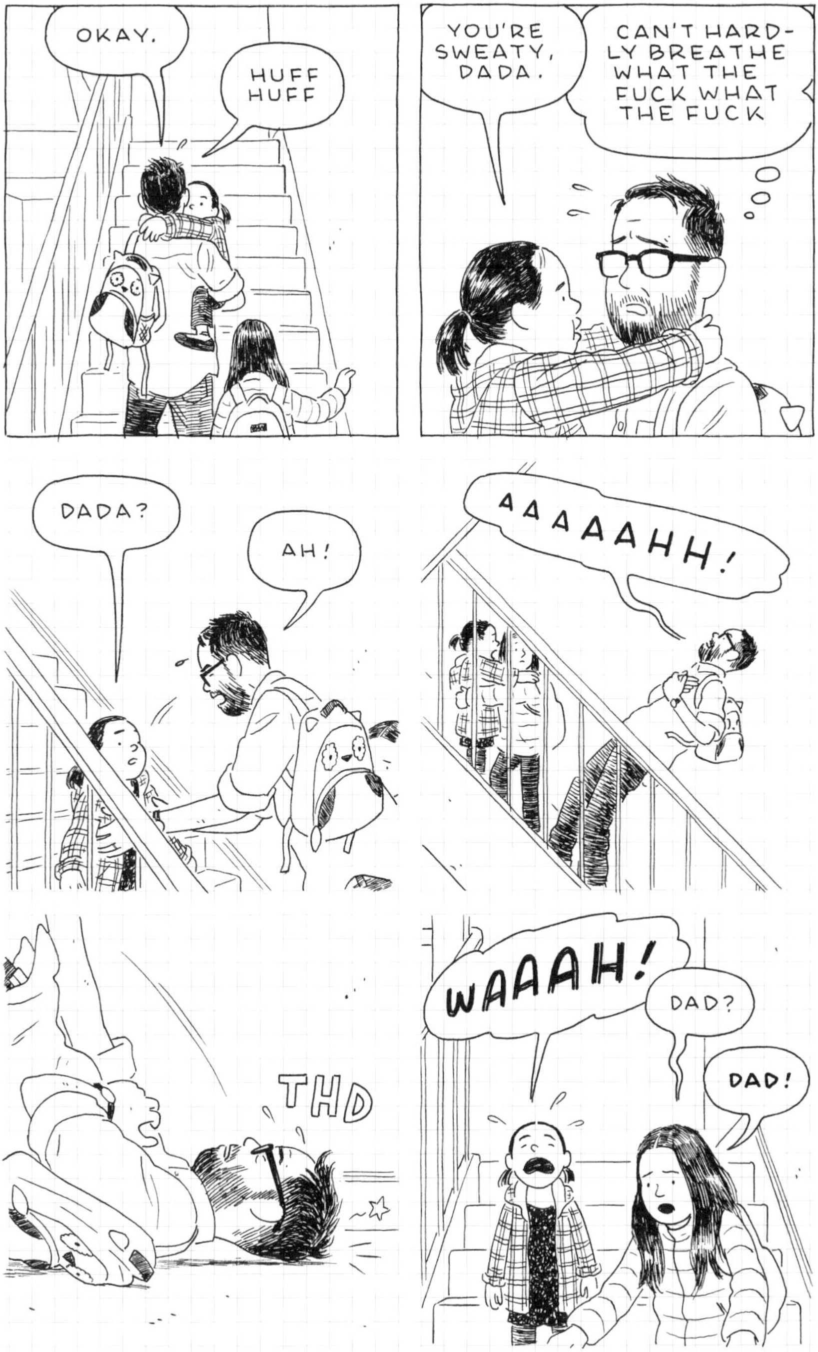
OKAY.
HUFF HUFF
YOU'RE SWEATY, DADA.
CAN'T HARDLY BREATHE WHAT THE FUCK WHAT THE FUCK
DADA?
AH!
AAAAAHH!
THD
WAAAH!
DAD?
DAD!

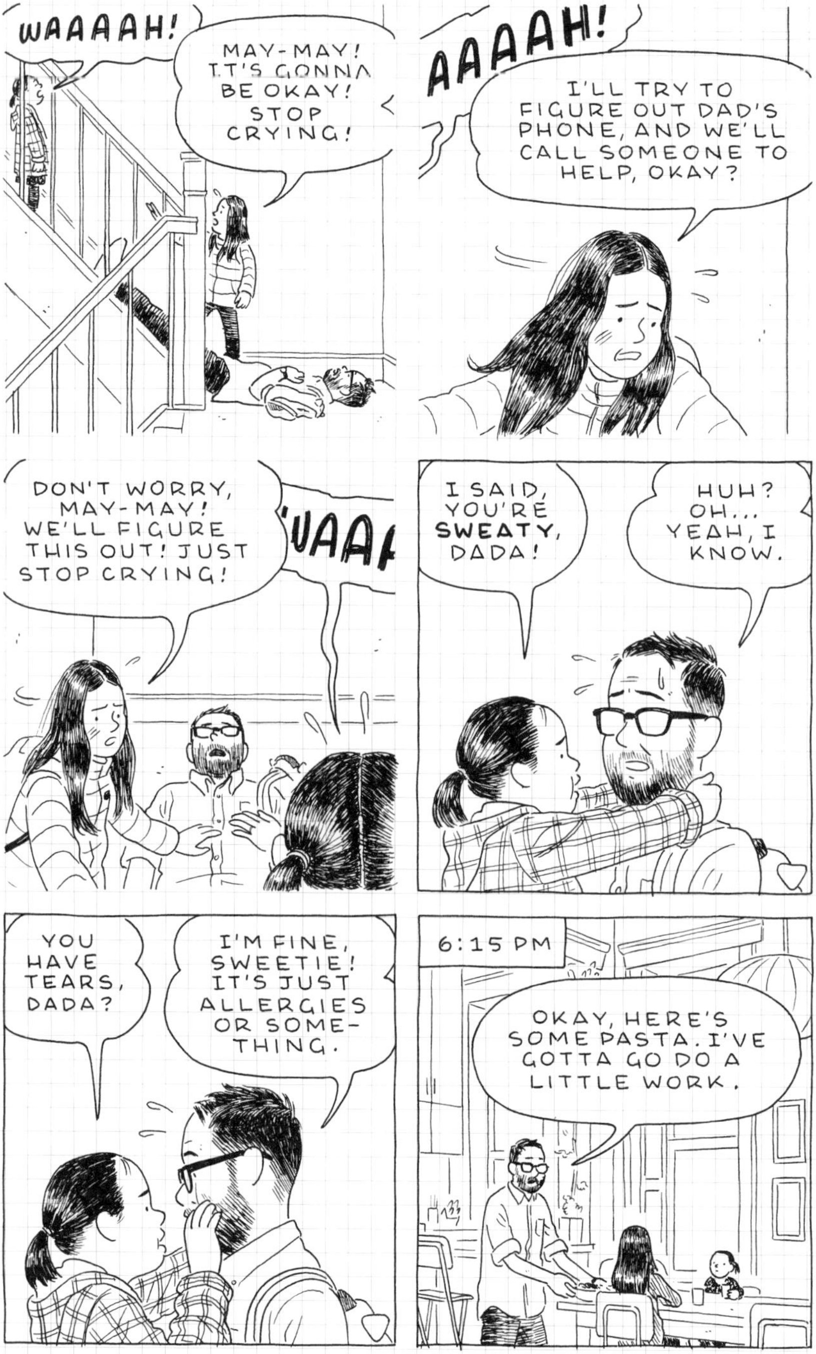

WAAAAH!
MAY-MAY! IT'S GONNA BE OKAY! STOP CRYING!
AAAAH!
I'LL TRY TO FIGURE OUT DAD'S PHONE, AND WE'LL CALL SOMEONE TO HELP, OKAY?
DON'T WORRY, MAY-MAY! WE'LL FIGURE THIS OUT! JUST STOP CRYING!
I SAID, YOU'RE SWEATY, DADA!
HUH? OH... YEAH, I KNOW.
YOU HAVE TEARS, DADA?
I'M FINE, SWEETIE! IT'S JUST ALLERGIES OR SOME-THING.
6:15 PM
OKAY, HERE'S SOME PASTA. I'VE GOTTA GO DO A LITTLE WORK.

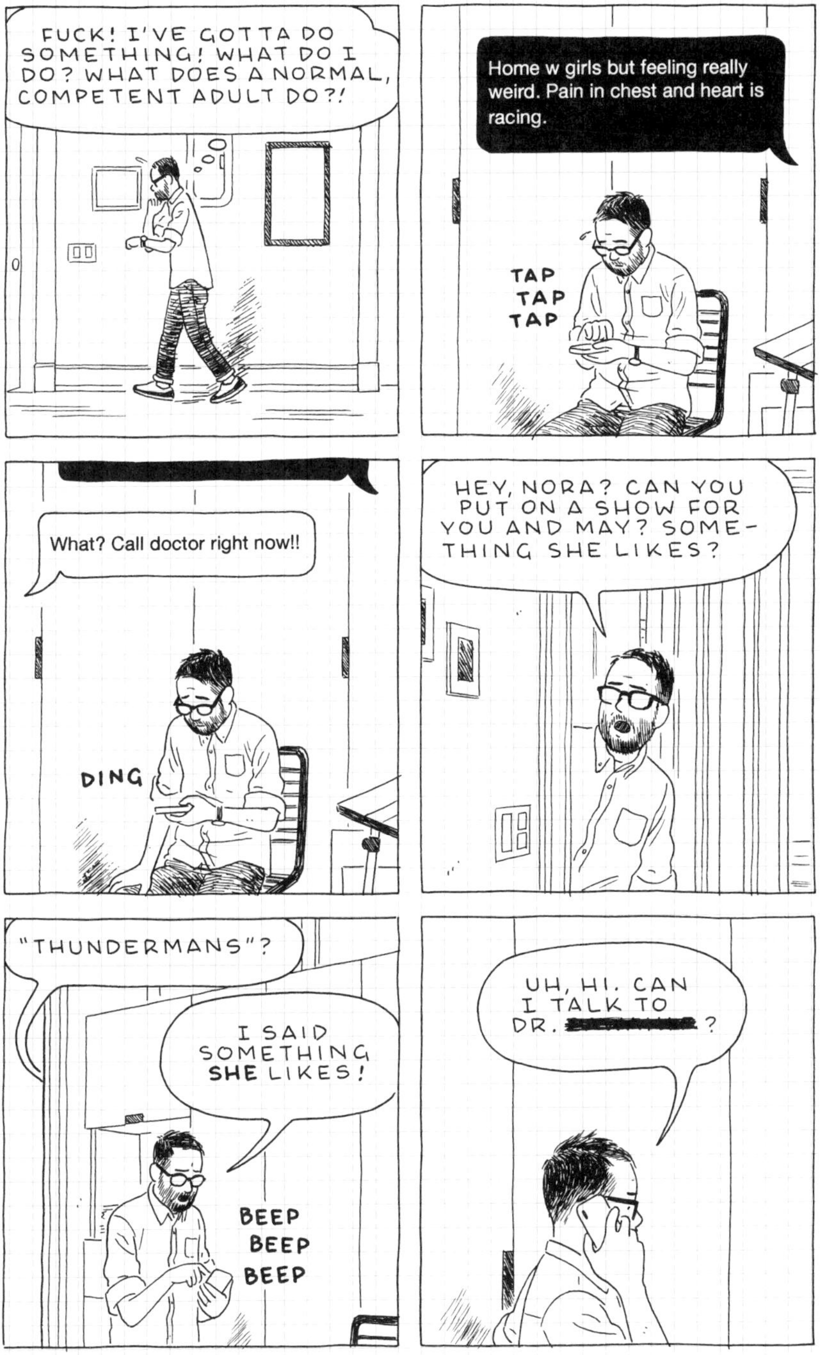
FUCK! I'VE GOTTA DO SOMETHING! WHAT DO I DO? WHAT DOES A NORMAL, COMPETENT ADULT DO?!
Home w girls but feeling really weird. Pain in chest and heart is racing.
TAP TAP TAP
What? Call doctor right now!!
DING
HEY, NORA? CAN YOU PUT ON A SHOW FOR YOU AND MAY? SOMETHING SHE LIKES?
"THUNDERMANS"?
I SAID SOMETHING **SHE** LIKES!
BEEP BEEP BEEP
UH, HI. CAN I TALK TO DR. [redacted]?

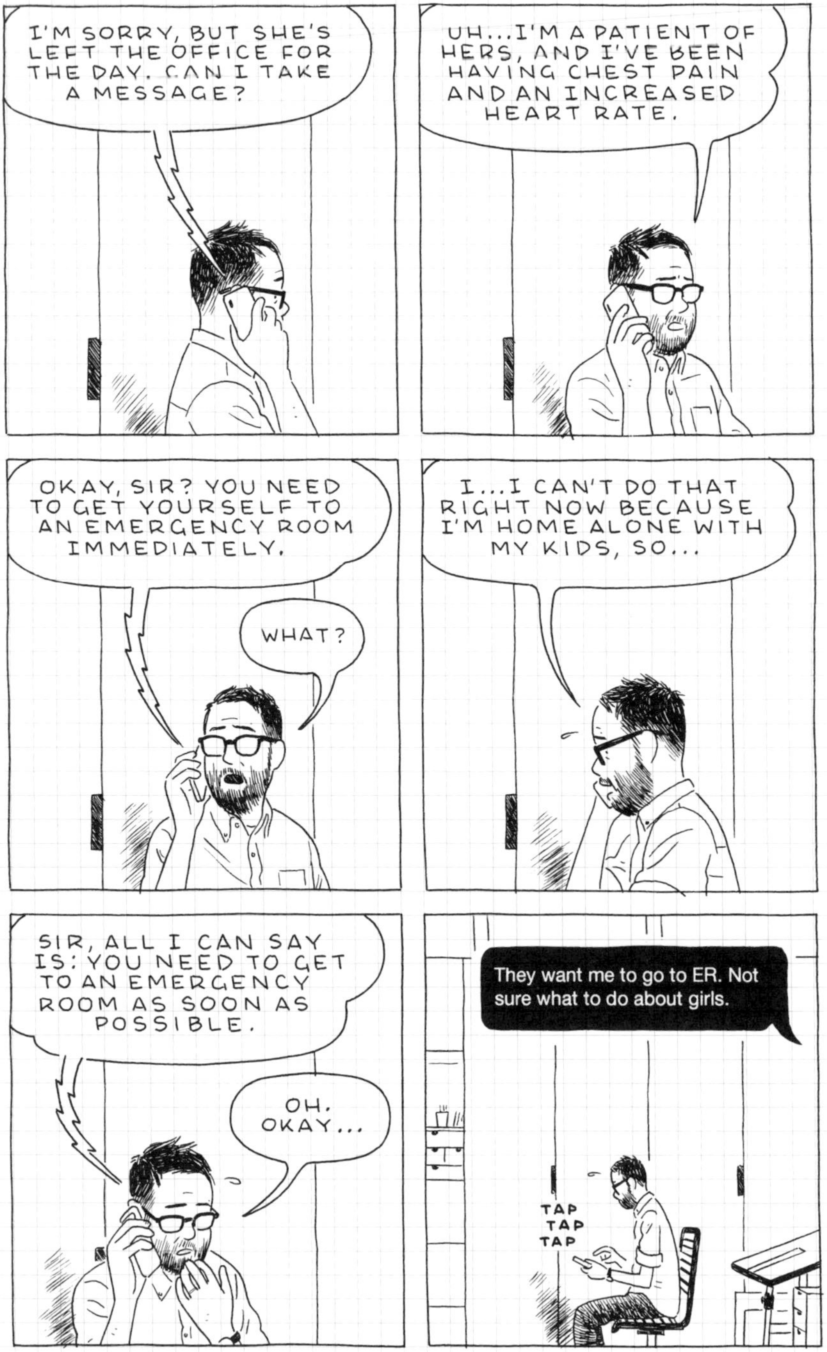
I'M SORRY, BUT SHE'S LEFT THE OFFICE FOR THE DAY. CAN I TAKE A MESSAGE?
UH...I'M A PATIENT OF HERS, AND I'VE BEEN HAVING CHEST PAIN AND AN INCREASED HEART RATE.
OKAY, SIR? YOU NEED TO GET YOURSELF TO AN EMERGENCY ROOM IMMEDIATELY.
WHAT?
I...I CAN'T DO THAT RIGHT NOW BECAUSE I'M HOME ALONE WITH MY KIDS, SO...
SIR, ALL I CAN SAY IS: YOU NEED TO GET TO AN EMERGENCY ROOM AS SOON AS POSSIBLE.
OH. OKAY...
They want me to go to ER. Not sure what to do about girls.
TAP TAP TAP

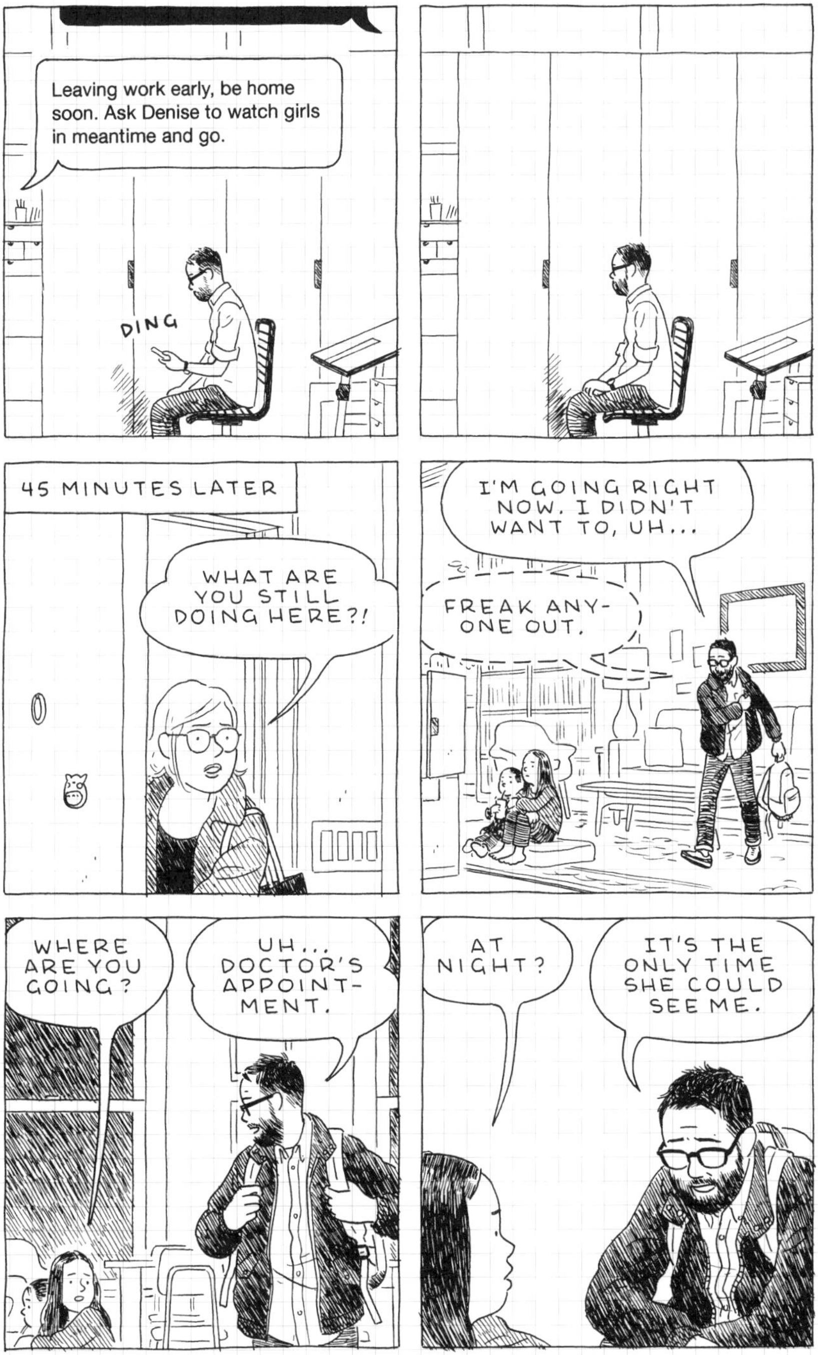
Leaving work early, be home soon. Ask Denise to watch girls in meantime and go.
DING
45 MINUTES LATER
WHAT ARE YOU STILL DOING HERE?!
I'M GOING RIGHT NOW. I DIDN'T WANT TO, UH...
FREAK ANY-ONE OUT.
WHERE ARE YOU GOING?
UH... DOCTOR'S APPOINT-MENT.
AT NIGHT?
IT'S THE ONLY TIME SHE COULD SEE ME.

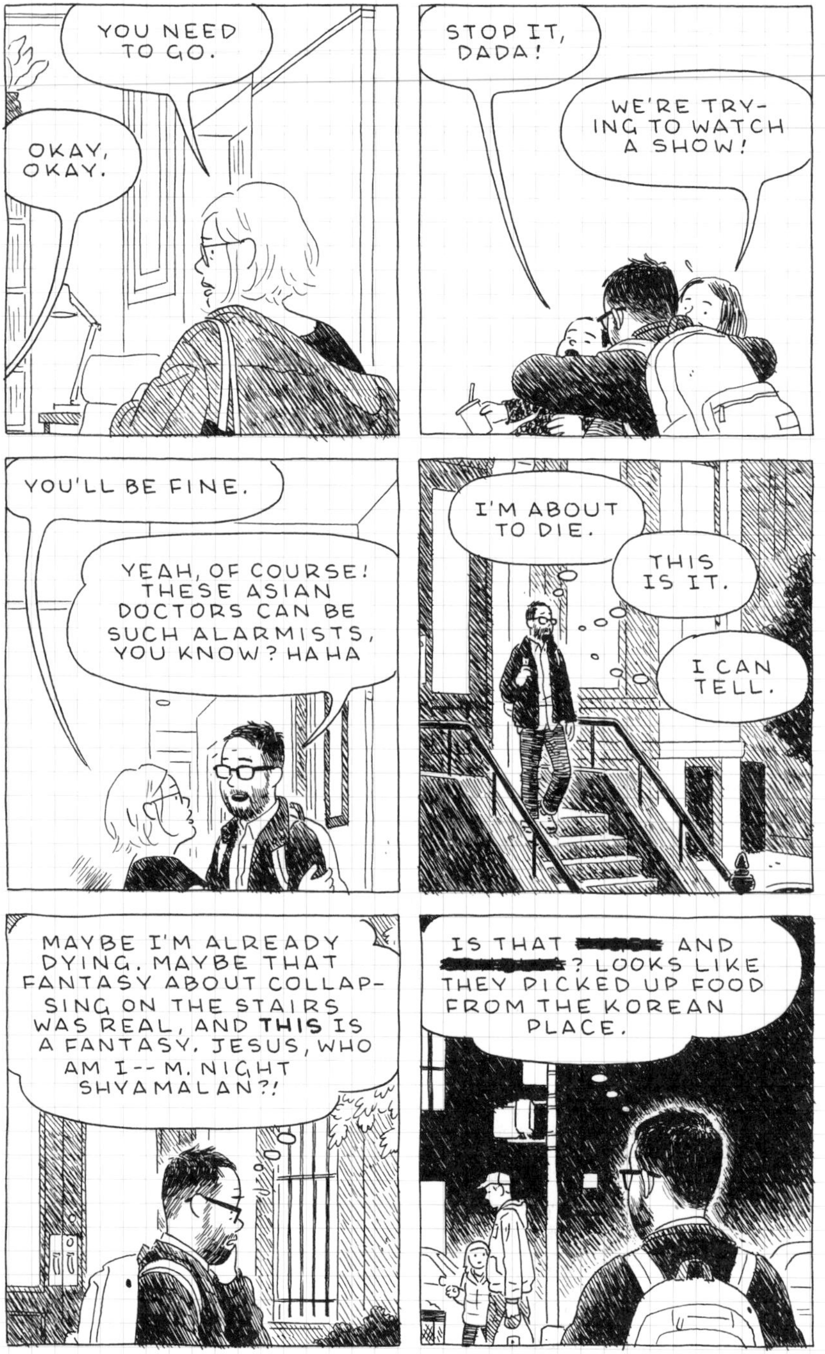
YOU NEED TO GO.
OKAY, OKAY.
STOP IT, DADA!
WE'RE TRY-ING TO WATCH A SHOW!
YOU'LL BE FINE.
YEAH, OF COURSE! THESE ASIAN DOCTORS CAN BE SUCH ALARMISTS, YOU KNOW? HA HA
I'M ABOUT TO DIE.
THIS IS IT.
I CAN TELL.
MAYBE I'M ALREADY DYING. MAYBE THAT FANTASY ABOUT COLLAP-SING ON THE STAIRS WAS REAL, AND **THIS** IS A FANTASY. JESUS, WHO AM I-- M. NIGHT SHYAMALAN?!
IS THAT [redacted] AND [redacted]? LOOKS LIKE THEY PICKED UP FOOD FROM THE KOREAN PLACE.

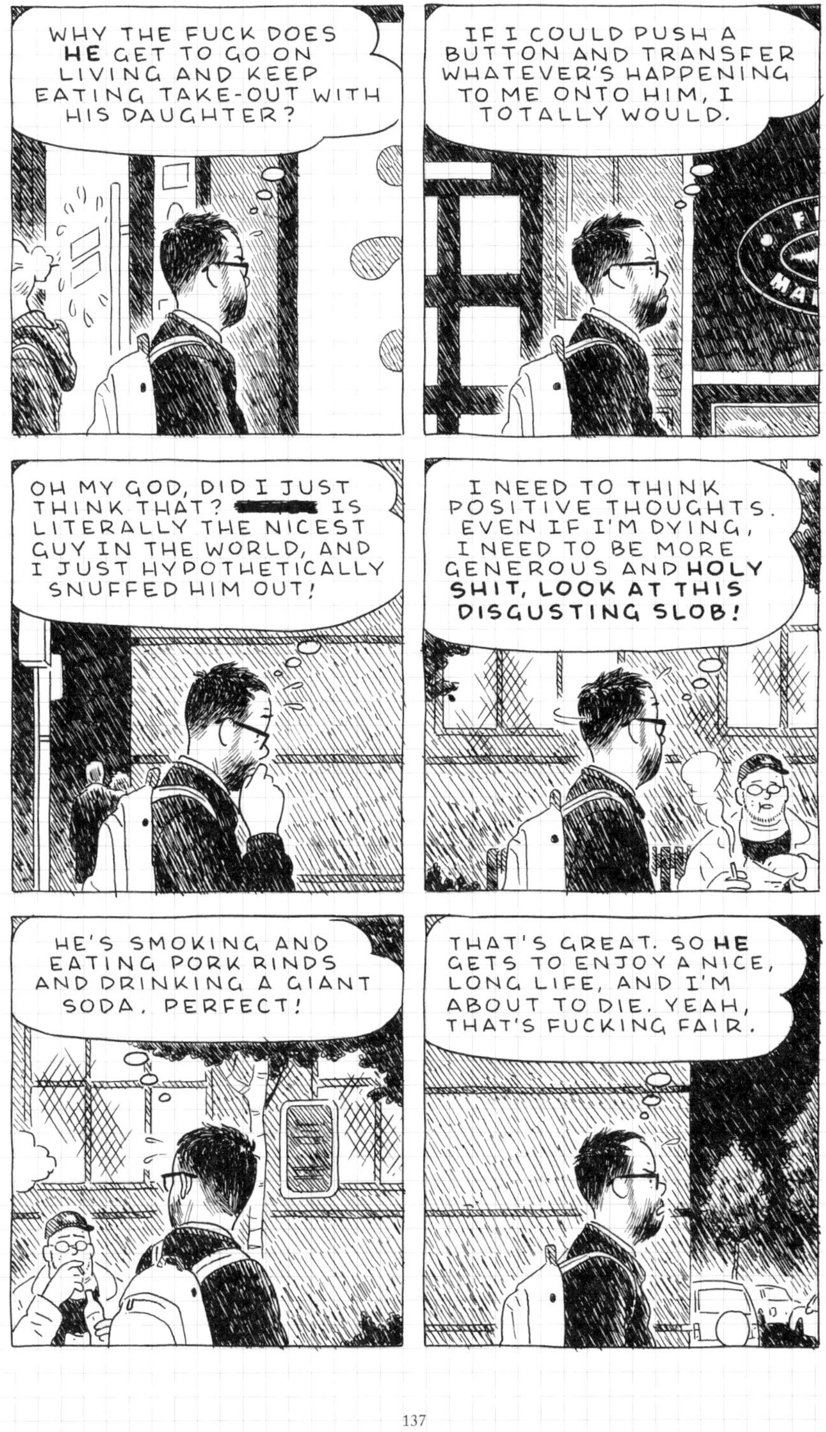
WHY THE FUCK DOES HE GET TO GO ON LIVING AND KEEP EATING TAKE-OUT WITH HIS DAUGHTER?
IF I COULD PUSH A BUTTON AND TRANSFER WHATEVER'S HAPPENING TO ME ONTO HIM, I TOTALLY WOULD.
OH MY GOD, DID I JUST THINK THAT? [redacted] IS LITERALLY THE NICEST GUY IN THE WORLD, AND I JUST HYPOTHETICALLY SNUFFED HIM OUT!
I NEED TO THINK POSITIVE THOUGHTS. EVEN IF I'M DYING, I NEED TO BE MORE GENEROUS AND HOLY SHIT, LOOK AT THIS DISGUSTING SLOB!
HE'S SMOKING AND EATING PORK RINDS AND DRINKING A GIANT SODA. PERFECT!
THAT'S GREAT. SO HE GETS TO ENJOY A NICE, LONG LIFE, AND I'M ABOUT TO DIE. YEAH, THAT'S FUCKING FAIR.

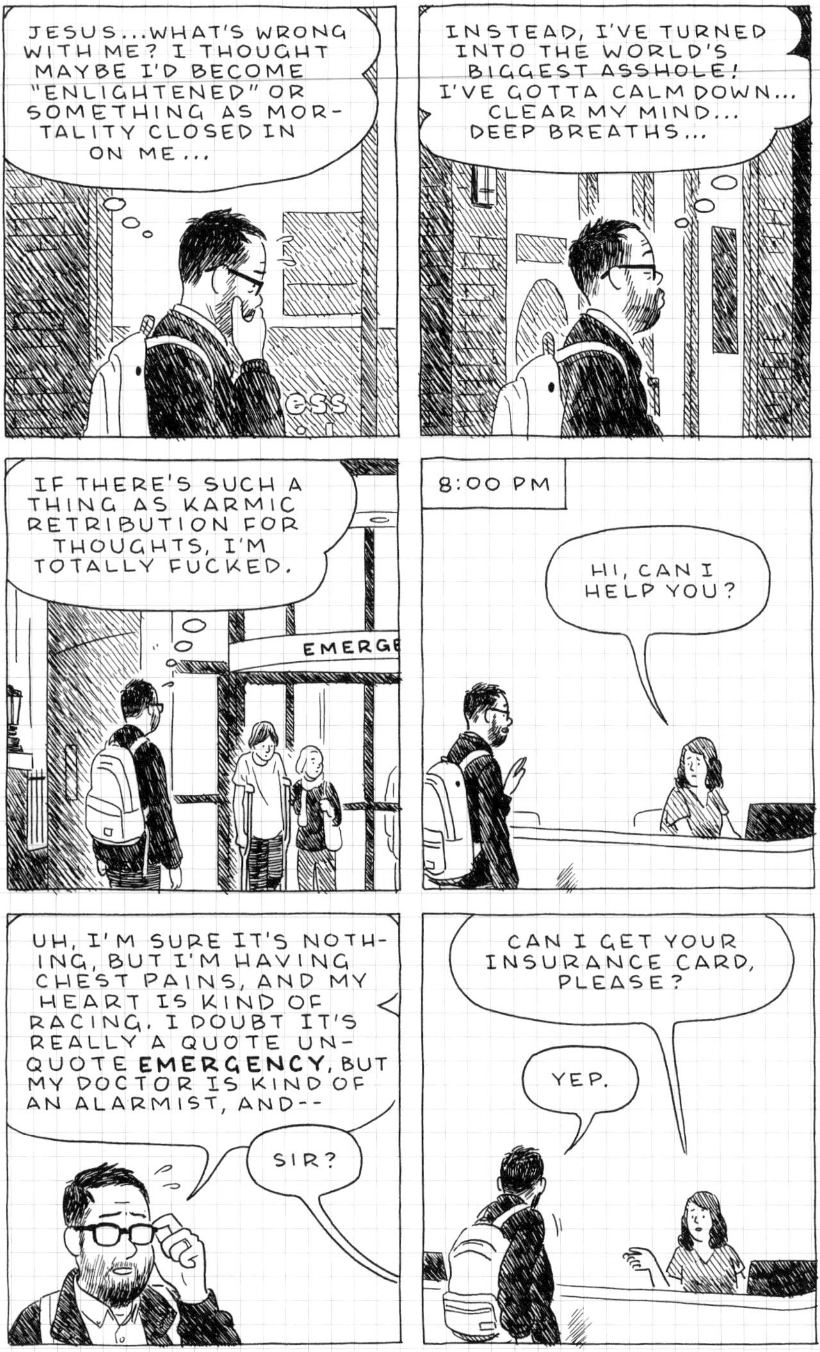
JESUS...WHAT'S WRONG WITH ME? I THOUGHT MAYBE I'D BECOME "ENLIGHTENED" OR SOMETHING AS MORTALITY CLOSED IN ON ME...
INSTEAD, I'VE TURNED INTO THE WORLD'S BIGGEST ASSHOLE! I'VE GOTTA CALM DOWN... CLEAR MY MIND... DEEP BREATHS...
IF THERE'S SUCH A THING AS KARMIC RETRIBUTION FOR THOUGHTS, I'M TOTALLY FUCKED.
EMERGE
8:00 PM
HI, CAN I HELP YOU?
UH, I'M SURE IT'S NOTHING, BUT I'M HAVING CHEST PAINS, AND MY HEART IS KIND OF RACING. I DOUBT IT'S REALLY A QUOTE UNQUOTE **EMERGENCY**, BUT MY DOCTOR IS KIND OF AN ALARMIST, AND--
SIR?
CAN I GET YOUR INSURANCE CARD, PLEASE?
YEP.

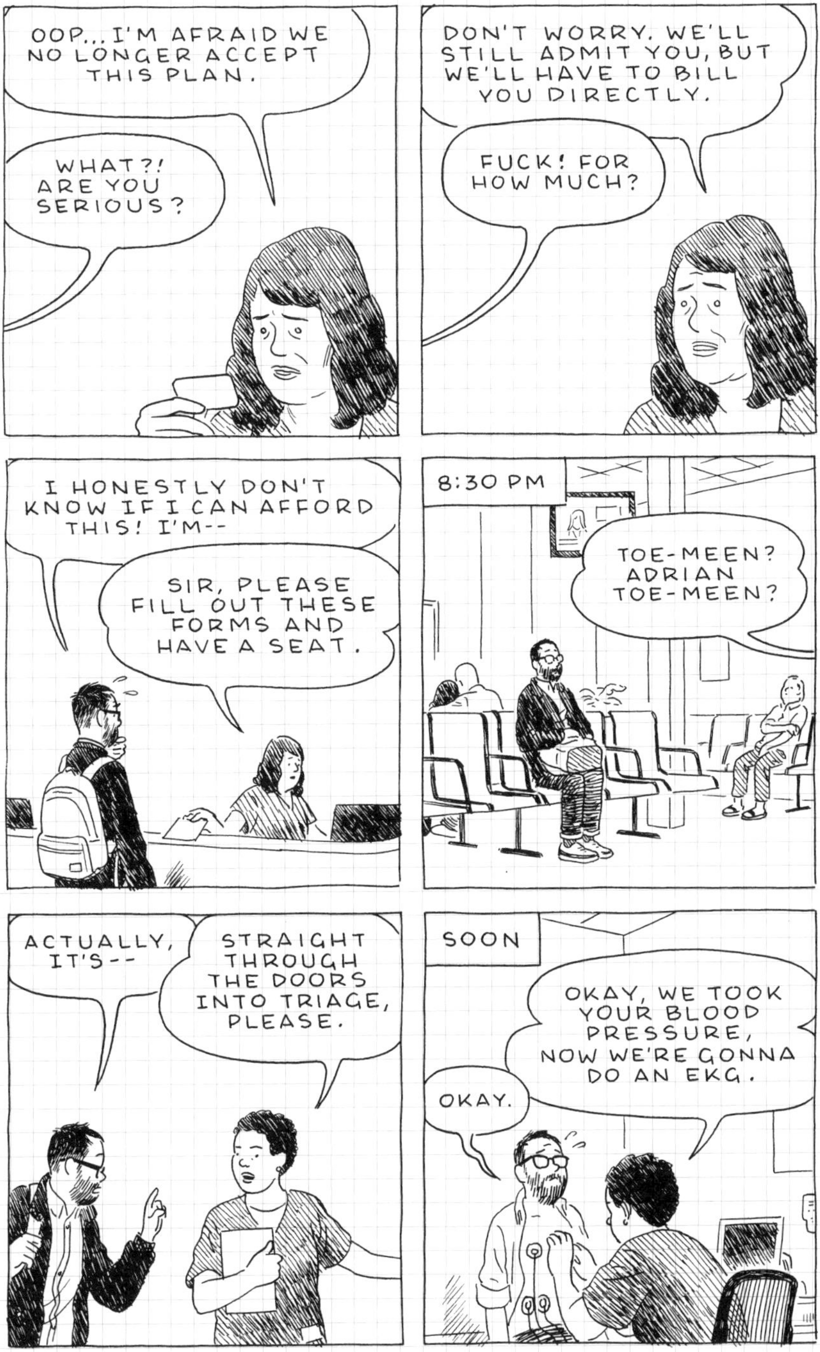
OOP... I'M AFRAID WE NO LONGER ACCEPT THIS PLAN.
WHAT?! ARE YOU SERIOUS?
DON'T WORRY. WE'LL STILL ADMIT YOU, BUT WE'LL HAVE TO BILL YOU DIRECTLY.
FUCK! FOR HOW MUCH?
I HONESTLY DON'T KNOW IF I CAN AFFORD THIS! I'M--
SIR, PLEASE FILL OUT THESE FORMS AND HAVE A SEAT.
8:30 PM
TOE-MEEN? ADRIAN TOE-MEEN?
ACTUALLY, IT'S--
STRAIGHT THROUGH THE DOORS INTO TRIAGE, PLEASE.
SOON
OKAY, WE TOOK YOUR BLOOD PRESSURE, NOW WE'RE GONNA DO AN EKG.
OKAY.

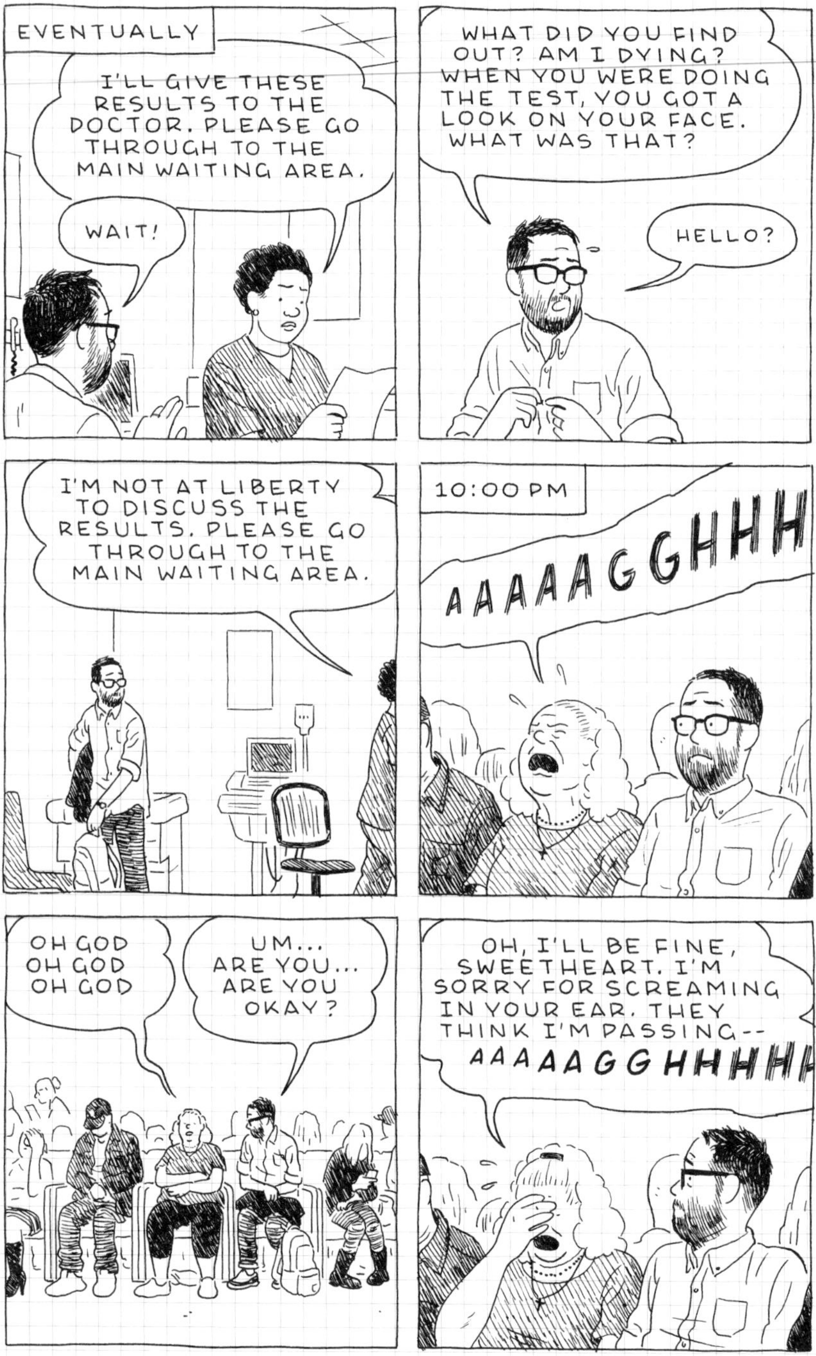
EVENTUALLY
I'LL GIVE THESE RESULTS TO THE DOCTOR. PLEASE GO THROUGH TO THE MAIN WAITING AREA.
WAIT!
WHAT DID YOU FIND OUT? AM I DYING? WHEN YOU WERE DOING THE TEST, YOU GOT A LOOK ON YOUR FACE. WHAT WAS THAT?
HELLO?
I'M NOT AT LIBERTY TO DISCUSS THE RESULTS. PLEASE GO THROUGH TO THE MAIN WAITING AREA.
10:00 PM
AAAAAGGHHH
OH GOD OH GOD OH GOD
UM... ARE YOU... ARE YOU OKAY?
OH, I'LL BE FINE, SWEETHEART. I'M SORRY FOR SCREAMING IN YOUR EAR. THEY THINK I'M PASSING--
AAAAAGGHHHH

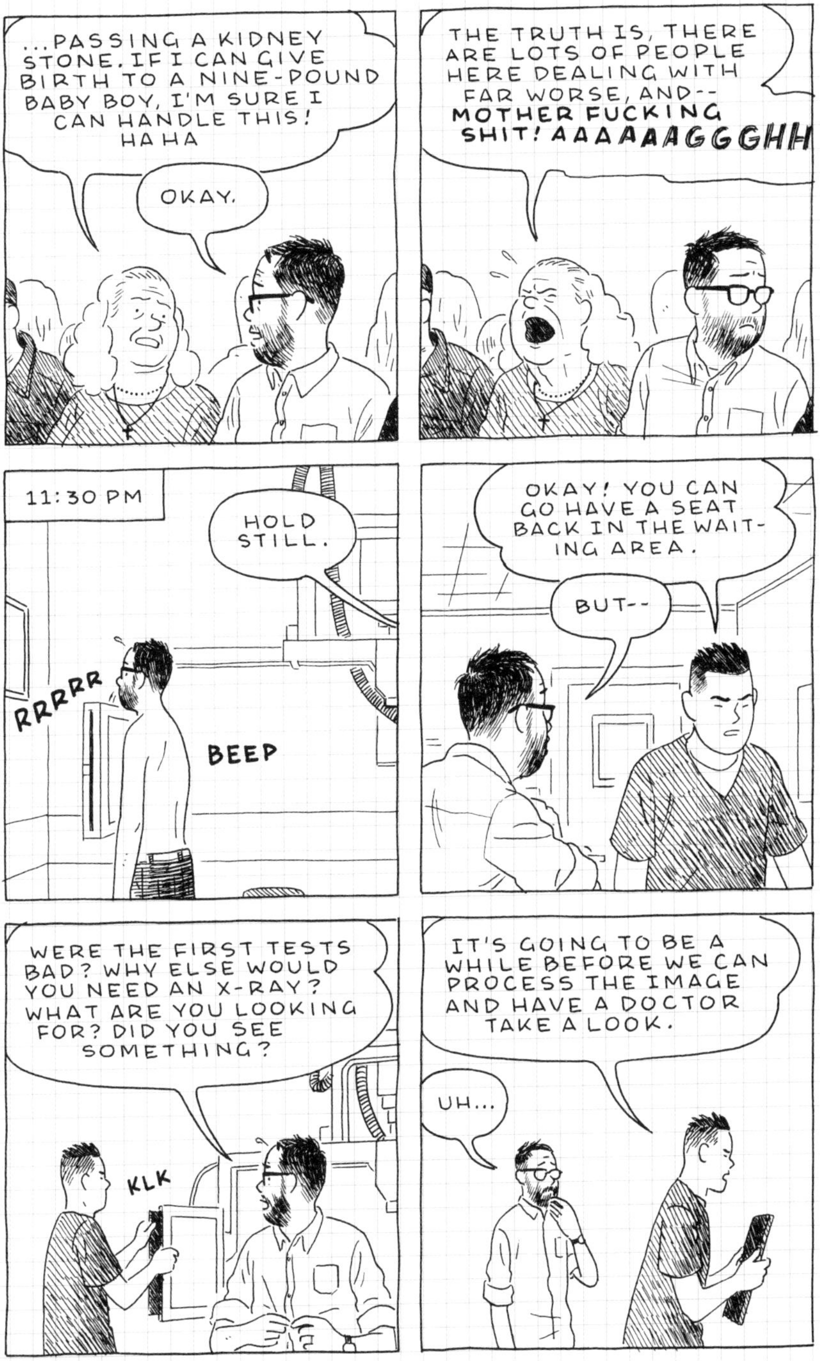
...PASSING A KIDNEY STONE. IF I CAN GIVE BIRTH TO A NINE-POUND BABY BOY, I'M SURE I CAN HANDLE THIS! HA HA
OKAY.
THE TRUTH IS, THERE ARE LOTS OF PEOPLE HERE DEALING WITH FAR WORSE, AND-- MOTHER FUCKING SHIT! AAAAAAGGGHH
11:30 PM
HOLD STILL.
RRRRR
BEEP
OKAY! YOU CAN GO HAVE A SEAT BACK IN THE WAIT-ING AREA.
BUT--
WERE THE FIRST TESTS BAD? WHY ELSE WOULD YOU NEED AN X-RAY? WHAT ARE YOU LOOKING FOR? DID YOU SEE SOMETHING?
KLK
IT'S GOING TO BE A WHILE BEFORE WE CAN PROCESS THE IMAGE AND HAVE A DOCTOR TAKE A LOOK.
UH...

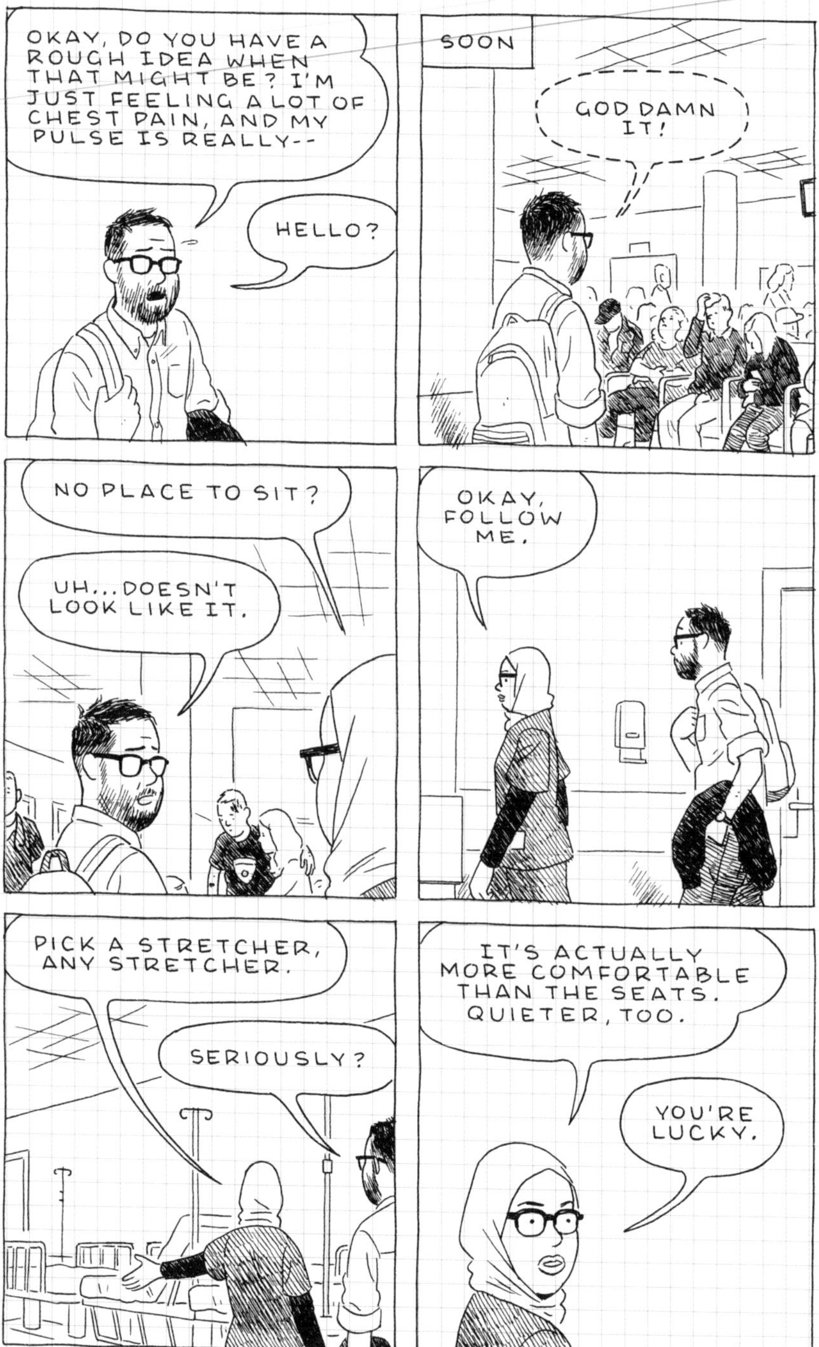
OKAY, DO YOU HAVE A ROUGH IDEA WHEN THAT MIGHT BE? I'M JUST FEELING A LOT OF CHEST PAIN, AND MY PULSE IS REALLY--
HELLO?
SOON
GOD DAMN IT!
NO PLACE TO SIT?
UH...DOESN'T LOOK LIKE IT.
OKAY, FOLLOW ME.
PICK A STRETCHER, ANY STRETCHER.
SERIOUSLY?
IT'S ACTUALLY MORE COMFORTABLE THAN THE SEATS. QUIETER, TOO.
YOU'RE LUCKY.

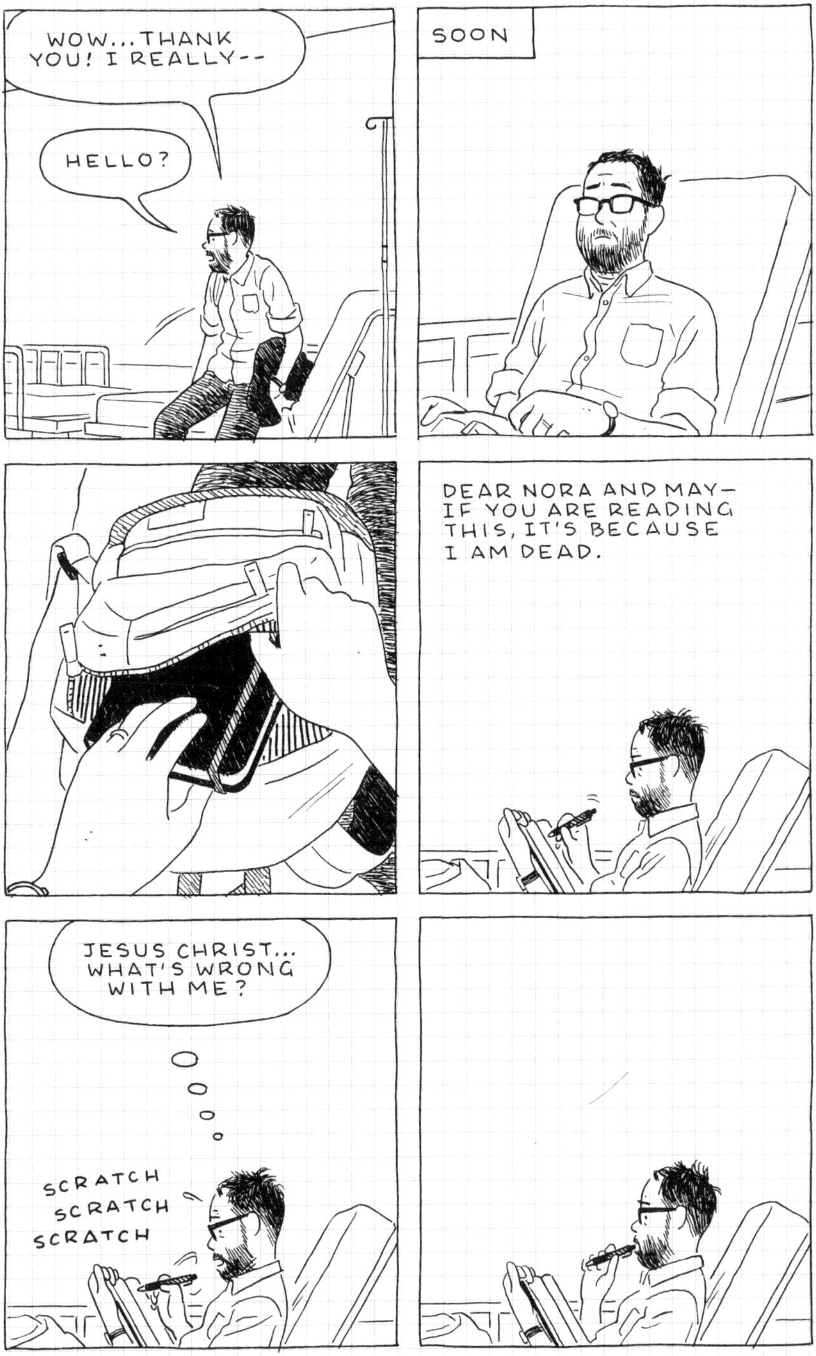
WOW... THANK YOU! I REALLY--
HELLO?
SOON
DEAR NORA AND MAY— IF YOU ARE READING THIS, IT'S BECAUSE I AM DEAD.
JESUS CHRIST... WHAT'S WRONG WITH ME?
SCRATCH SCRATCH SCRATCH

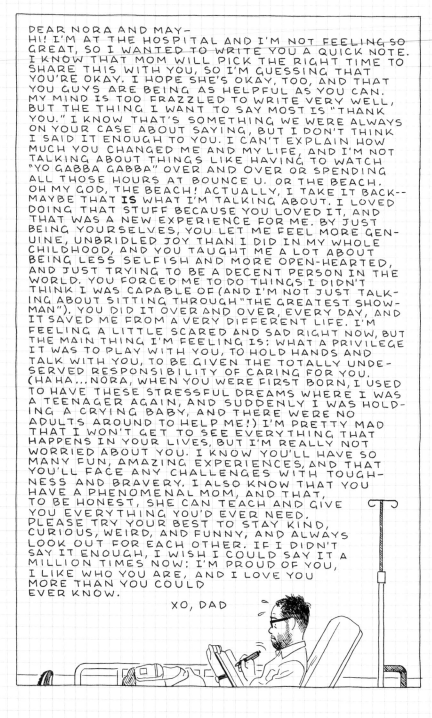

DEAR NORA AND MAY—
HI! I'M AT THE HOSPITAL AND I'M NOT FEELING SO
GREAT, SO I WANTED TO WRITE YOU A QUICK NOTE.
I KNOW THAT MOM WILL PICK THE RIGHT TIME TO
SHARE THIS WITH YOU, SO I'M GUESSING THAT
YOU'RE OKAY. I HOPE SHE'S OKAY, TOO, AND THAT
YOU GUYS ARE BEING AS HELPFUL AS YOU CAN.
MY MIND IS TOO FRAZZLED TO WRITE VERY WELL,
BUT THE THING I WANT TO SAY MOST IS "THANK
YOU." I KNOW THAT'S SOMETHING WE WERE ALWAYS
ON YOUR CASE ABOUT SAYING, BUT I DON'T THINK
I SAID IT ENOUGH TO YOU. I CAN'T EXPLAIN HOW
MUCH YOU CHANGED ME AND MY LIFE, AND I'M NOT
TALKING ABOUT THINGS LIKE HAVING TO WATCH
"YO GABBA GABBA" OVER AND OVER OR SPENDING
ALL THOSE HOURS AT BOUNCE U. OR THE BEACH.
OH MY GOD, THE BEACH! ACTUALLY, I TAKE IT BACK--
MAYBE THAT **IS** WHAT I'M TALKING ABOUT. I LOVED
DOING THAT STUFF BECAUSE YOU LOVED IT, AND
THAT WAS A NEW EXPERIENCE FOR ME. BY JUST
BEING YOURSELVES, YOU LET ME FEEL MORE GEN-
UINE, UNBRIDLED JOY THAN I DID IN MY WHOLE
CHILDHOOD, AND YOU TAUGHT ME A LOT ABOUT
BEING LESS SELFISH AND MORE OPEN-HEARTED,
AND JUST TRYING TO BE A DECENT PERSON IN THE
WORLD. YOU FORCED ME TO DO THINGS I DIDN'T
THINK I WAS CAPABLE OF (AND I'M NOT JUST TALK-
ING ABOUT SITTING THROUGH "THE GREATEST SHOW-
MAN"). YOU DID IT OVER AND OVER, EVERY DAY, AND
IT SAVED ME FROM A VERY DIFFERENT LIFE. I'M
FEELING A LITTLE SCARED AND SAD RIGHT NOW, BUT
THE MAIN THING I'M FEELING IS: WHAT A PRIVILEGE
IT WAS TO PLAY WITH YOU, TO HOLD HANDS AND
TALK WITH YOU, TO BE GIVEN THE TOTALLY UNDE-
SERVED RESPONSIBILITY OF CARING FOR YOU.
(HA HA...NORA, WHEN YOU WERE FIRST BORN, I USED
TO HAVE THESE STRESSFUL DREAMS WHERE I WAS
A TEENAGER AGAIN, AND SUDDENLY I WAS HOLD-
ING A CRYING BABY, AND THERE WERE NO
ADULTS AROUND TO HELP ME!) I'M PRETTY MAD
THAT I WON'T GET TO SEE EVERYTHING THAT
HAPPENS IN YOUR LIVES, BUT I'M REALLY NOT
WORRIED ABOUT YOU. I KNOW YOU'LL HAVE SO
MANY FUN, AMAZING EXPERIENCES, AND THAT
YOU'LL FACE ANY CHALLENGES WITH TOUGH-
NESS AND BRAVERY. I ALSO KNOW THAT YOU
HAVE A PHENOMENAL MOM, AND THAT,
TO BE HONEST, SHE CAN TEACH AND GIVE
YOU EVERYTHING YOU'D EVER NEED.
PLEASE TRY YOUR BEST TO STAY KIND,
CURIOUS, WEIRD, AND FUNNY, AND ALWAYS
LOOK OUT FOR EACH OTHER. IF I DIDN'T
SAY IT ENOUGH, I WISH I COULD SAY IT A
MILLION TIMES NOW: I'M PROUD OF YOU,
I LIKE WHO YOU ARE, AND I LOVE YOU
MORE THAN YOU COULD
EVER KNOW.
            XO, DAD

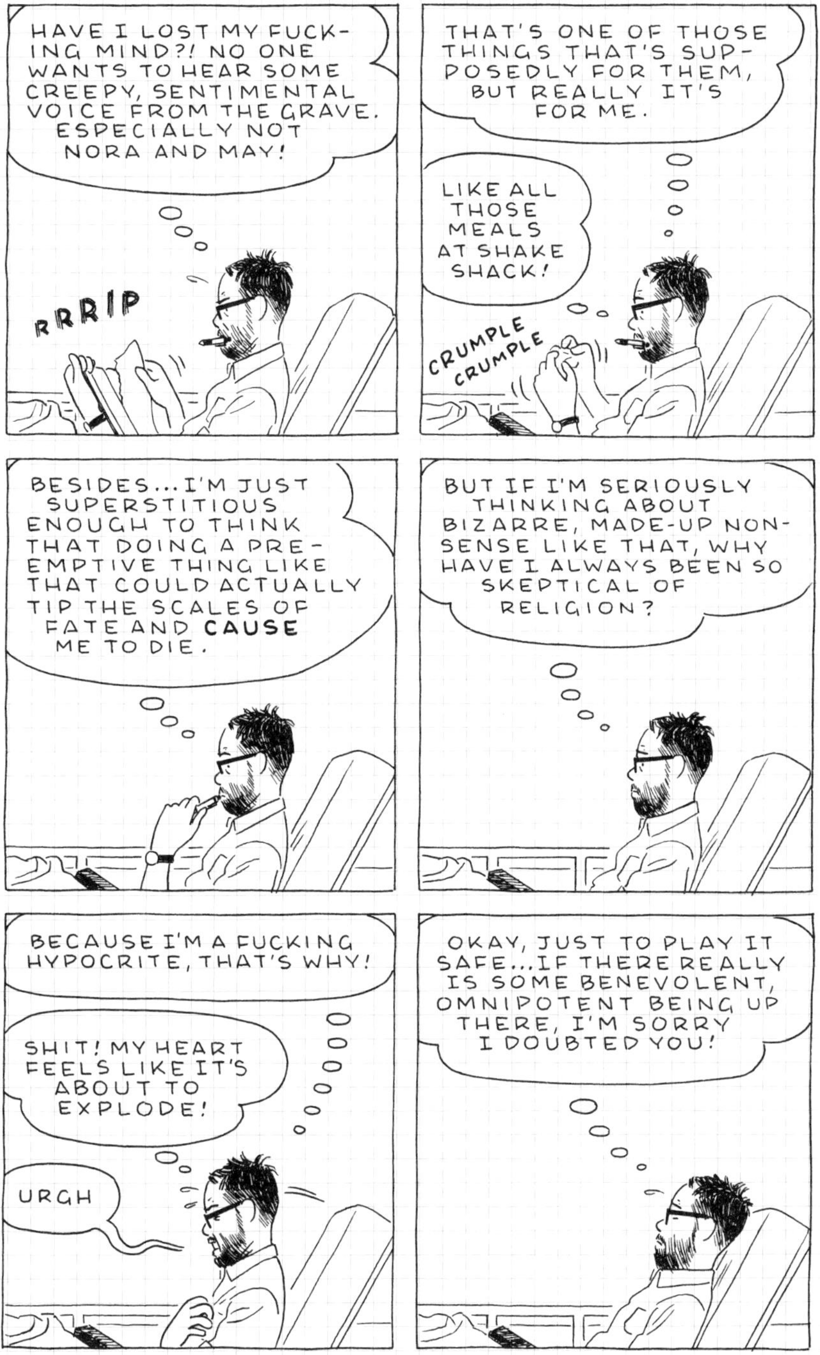
HAVE I LOST MY FUCKING MIND?! NO ONE WANTS TO HEAR SOME CREEPY, SENTIMENTAL VOICE FROM THE GRAVE. ESPECIALLY NOT NORA AND MAY!
RRRIP
THAT'S ONE OF THOSE THINGS THAT'S SUPPOSEDLY FOR THEM, BUT REALLY IT'S FOR ME.
LIKE ALL THOSE MEALS AT SHAKE SHACK!
CRUMPLE CRUMPLE
BESIDES... I'M JUST SUPERSTITIOUS ENOUGH TO THINK THAT DOING A PRE-EMPTIVE THING LIKE THAT COULD ACTUALLY TIP THE SCALES OF FATE AND **CAUSE** ME TO DIE.
BUT IF I'M SERIOUSLY THINKING ABOUT BIZARRE, MADE-UP NONSENSE LIKE THAT, WHY HAVE I ALWAYS BEEN SO SKEPTICAL OF RELIGION?
BECAUSE I'M A FUCKING HYPOCRITE, THAT'S WHY!
SHIT! MY HEART FEELS LIKE IT'S ABOUT TO EXPLODE!
URGH
OKAY, JUST TO PLAY IT SAFE... IF THERE REALLY IS SOME BENEVOLENT, OMNIPOTENT BEING UP THERE, I'M SORRY I DOUBTED YOU!

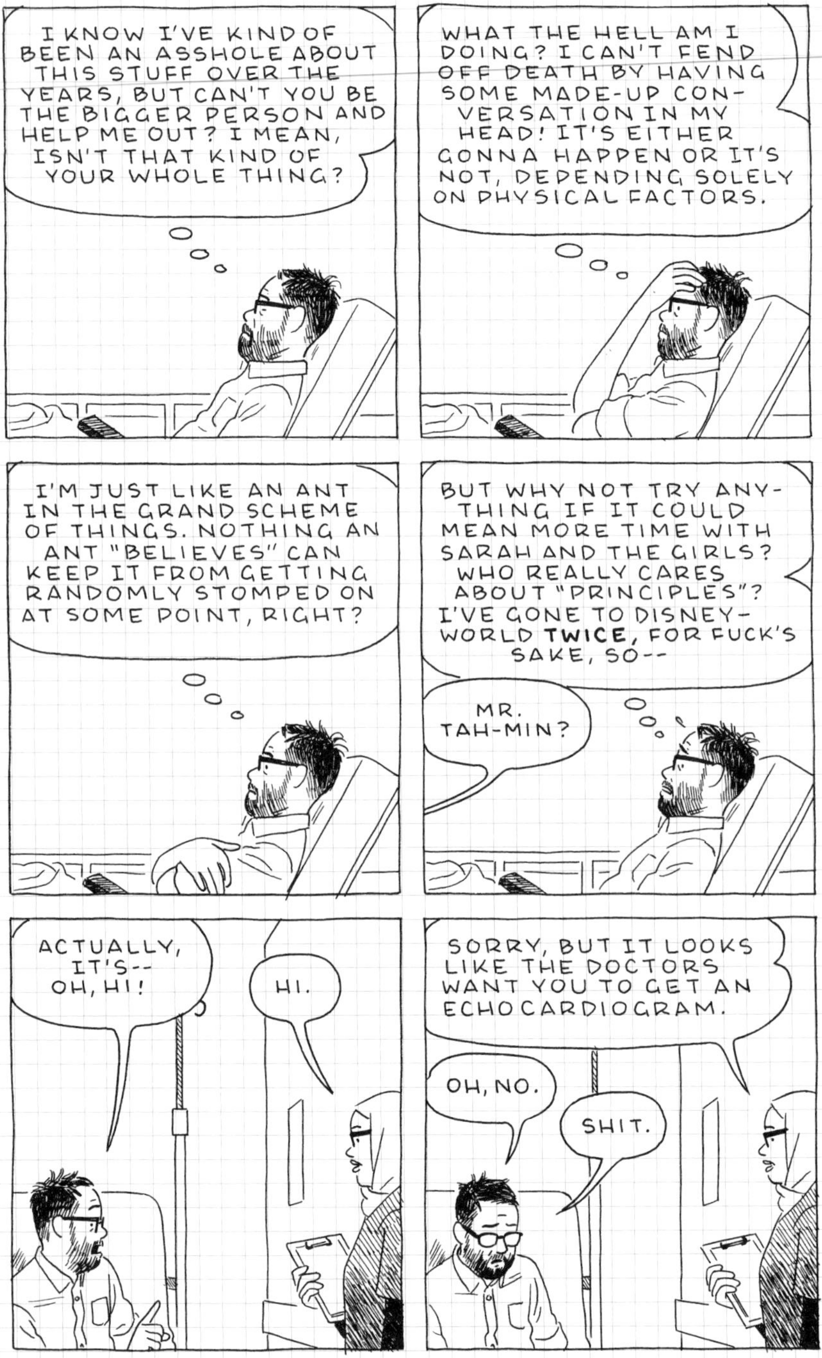
I KNOW I'VE KIND OF BEEN AN ASSHOLE ABOUT THIS STUFF OVER THE YEARS, BUT CAN'T YOU BE THE BIGGER PERSON AND HELP ME OUT? I MEAN, ISN'T THAT KIND OF YOUR WHOLE THING?
WHAT THE HELL AM I DOING? I CAN'T FEND OFF DEATH BY HAVING SOME MADE-UP CONVERSATION IN MY HEAD! IT'S EITHER GONNA HAPPEN OR IT'S NOT, DEPENDING SOLELY ON PHYSICAL FACTORS.
I'M JUST LIKE AN ANT IN THE GRAND SCHEME OF THINGS. NOTHING AN ANT "BELIEVES" CAN KEEP IT FROM GETTING RANDOMLY STOMPED ON AT SOME POINT, RIGHT?
BUT WHY NOT TRY ANYTHING IF IT COULD MEAN MORE TIME WITH SARAH AND THE GIRLS? WHO REALLY CARES ABOUT "PRINCIPLES"? I'VE GONE TO DISNEYWORLD **TWICE**, FOR FUCK'S SAKE, SO--
MR. TAH-MIN?
ACTUALLY, IT'S-- OH, HI!
HI.
SORRY, BUT IT LOOKS LIKE THE DOCTORS WANT YOU TO GET AN ECHOCARDIOGRAM.
OH, NO.
SHIT.

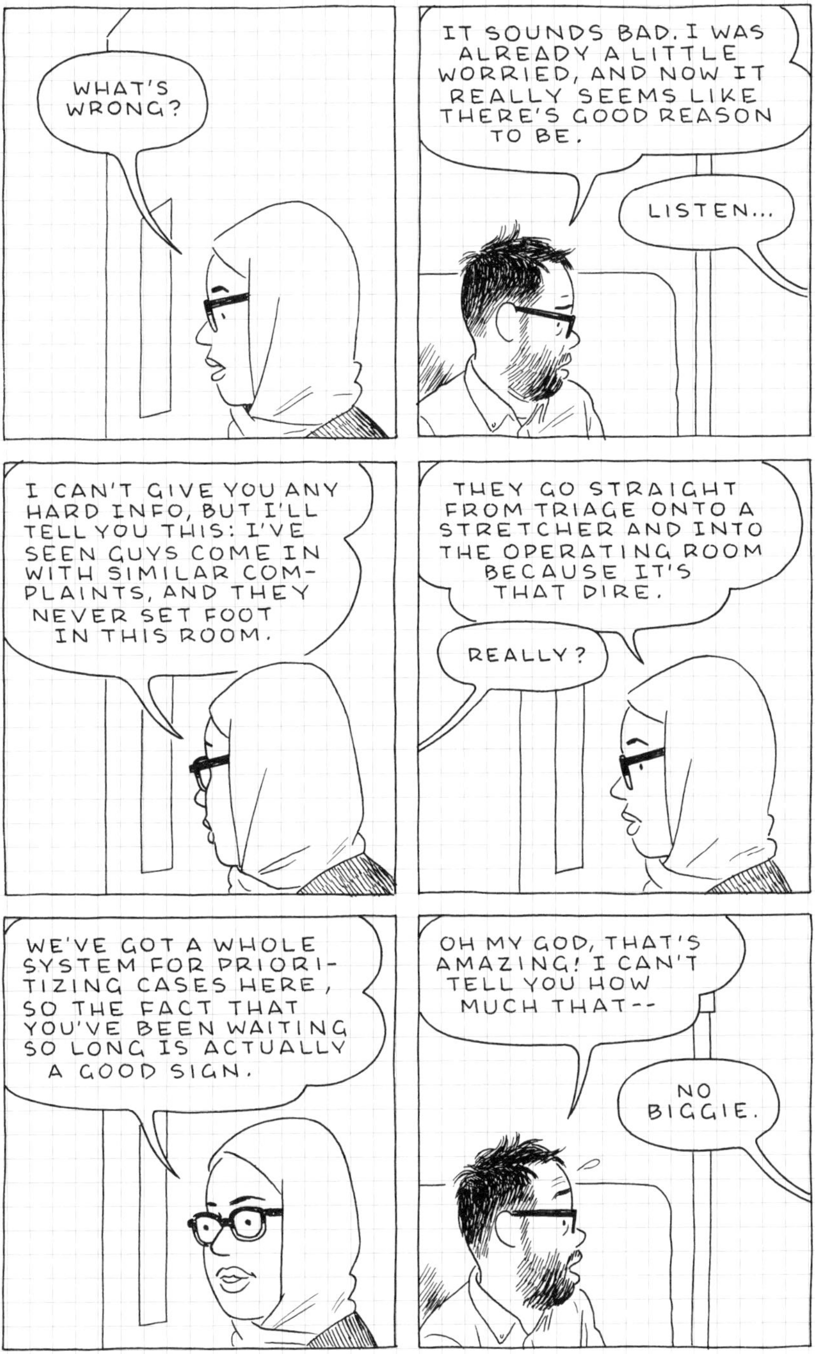
WHAT'S WRONG?
IT SOUNDS BAD. I WAS ALREADY A LITTLE WORRIED, AND NOW IT REALLY SEEMS LIKE THERE'S GOOD REASON TO BE.
LISTEN...
I CAN'T GIVE YOU ANY HARD INFO, BUT I'LL TELL YOU THIS: I'VE SEEN GUYS COME IN WITH SIMILAR COM-PLAINTS, AND THEY NEVER SET FOOT IN THIS ROOM.
THEY GO STRAIGHT FROM TRIAGE ONTO A STRETCHER AND INTO THE OPERATING ROOM BECAUSE IT'S THAT DIRE.
REALLY?
WE'VE GOT A WHOLE SYSTEM FOR PRIORI-TIZING CASES HERE, SO THE FACT THAT YOU'VE BEEN WAITING SO LONG IS ACTUALLY A GOOD SIGN.
OH MY GOD, THAT'S AMAZING! I CAN'T TELL YOU HOW MUCH THAT--
NO BIGGIE.

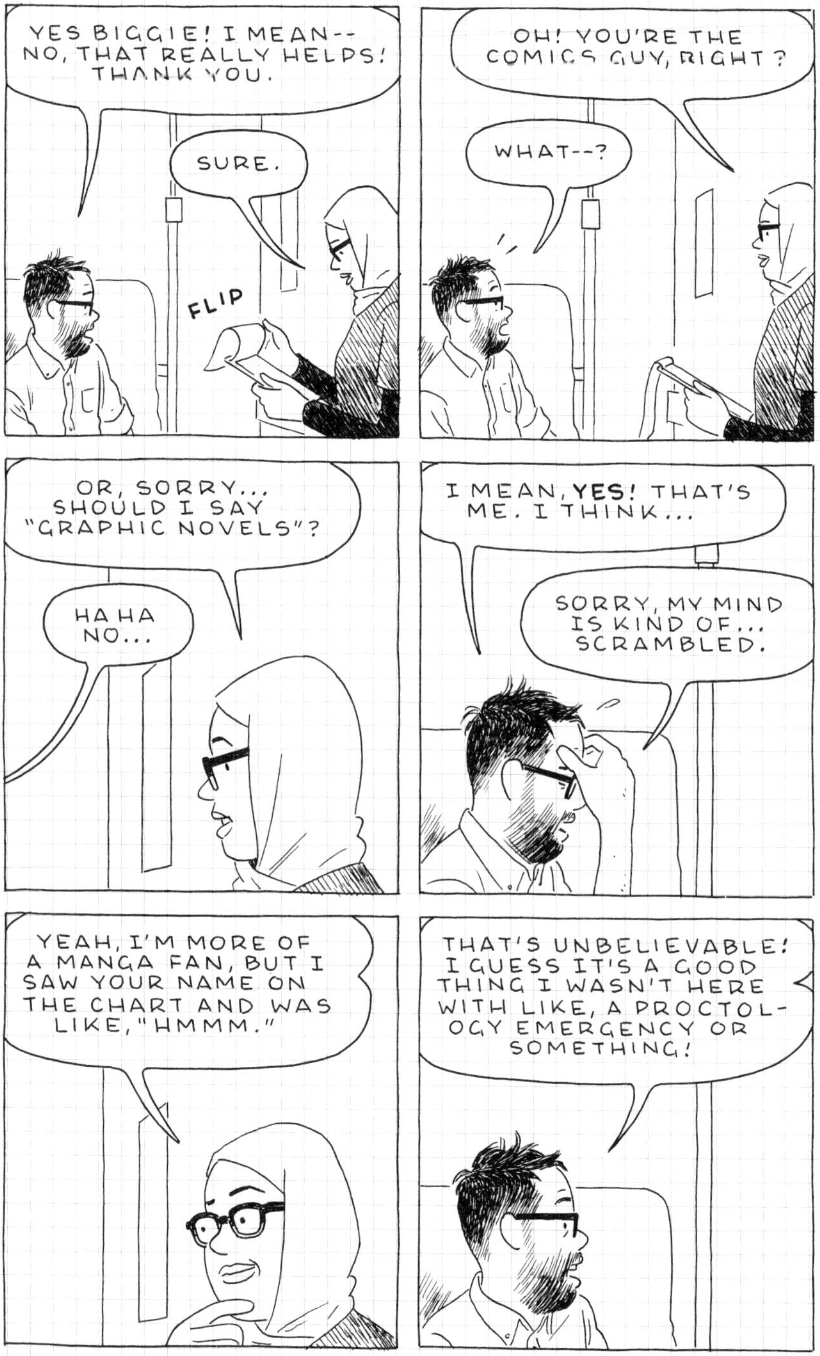
YES BIGGIE! I MEAN-- NO, THAT REALLY HELPS! THANK YOU.
SURE.
FLIP
OH! YOU'RE THE COMICS GUY, RIGHT?
WHAT--?
OR, SORRY... SHOULD I SAY "GRAPHIC NOVELS"?
HA HA NO...
I MEAN, YES! THAT'S ME. I THINK...
SORRY, MY MIND IS KIND OF... SCRAMBLED.
YEAH, I'M MORE OF A MANGA FAN, BUT I SAW YOUR NAME ON THE CHART AND WAS LIKE, "HMMM."
THAT'S UNBELIEVABLE! I GUESS IT'S A GOOD THING I WASN'T HERE WITH LIKE, A PROCTOLOGY EMERGENCY OR SOMETHING!

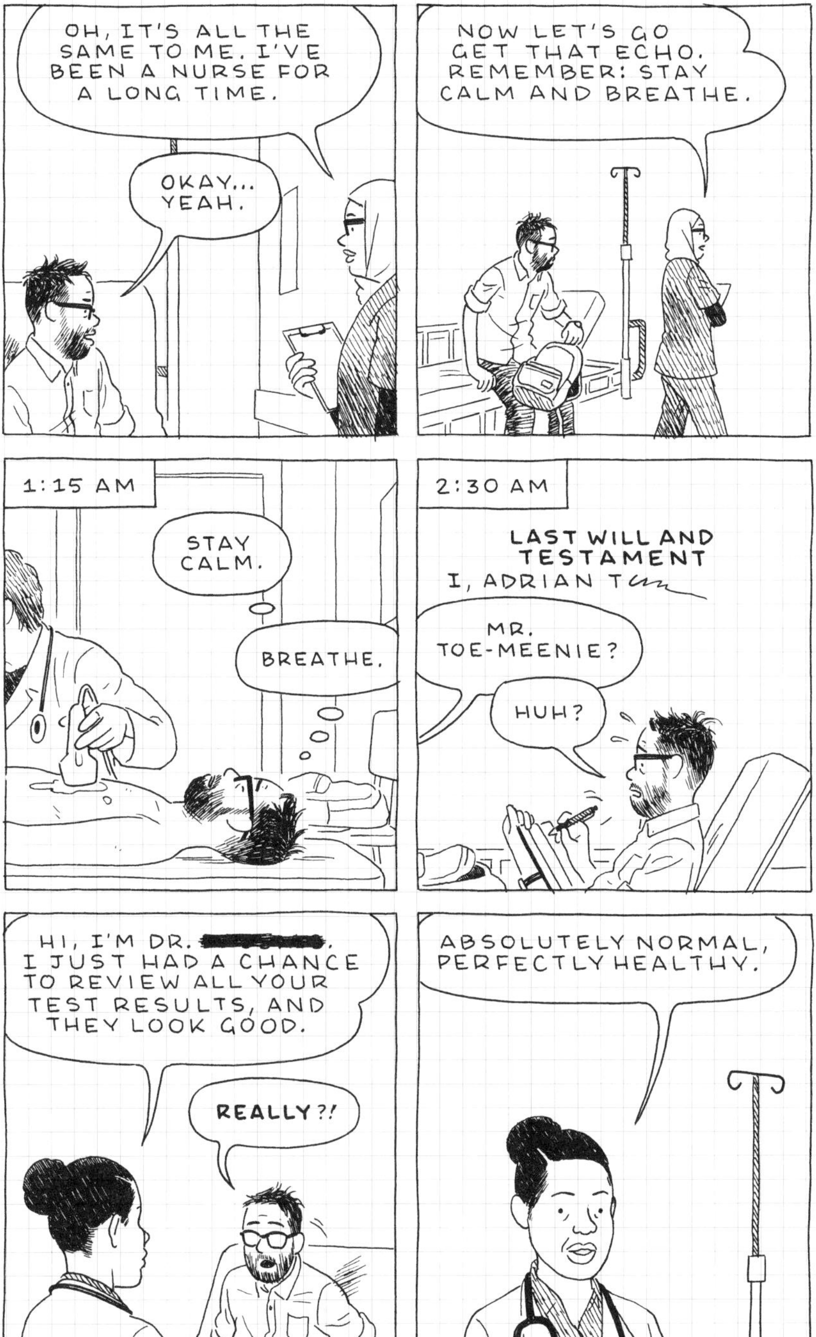
OH, IT'S ALL THE SAME TO ME. I'VE BEEN A NURSE FOR A LONG TIME.
OKAY... YEAH.
NOW LET'S GO GET THAT ECHO. REMEMBER: STAY CALM AND BREATHE.
1:15 AM
STAY CALM.
BREATHE.
2:30 AM
LAST WILL AND TESTAMENT
I, ADRIAN T
MR. TOE-MEENIE?
HUH?
HI, I'M DR. [redacted]. I JUST HAD A CHANCE TO REVIEW ALL YOUR TEST RESULTS, AND THEY LOOK GOOD.
REALLY?!
ABSOLUTELY NORMAL, PERFECTLY HEALTHY.

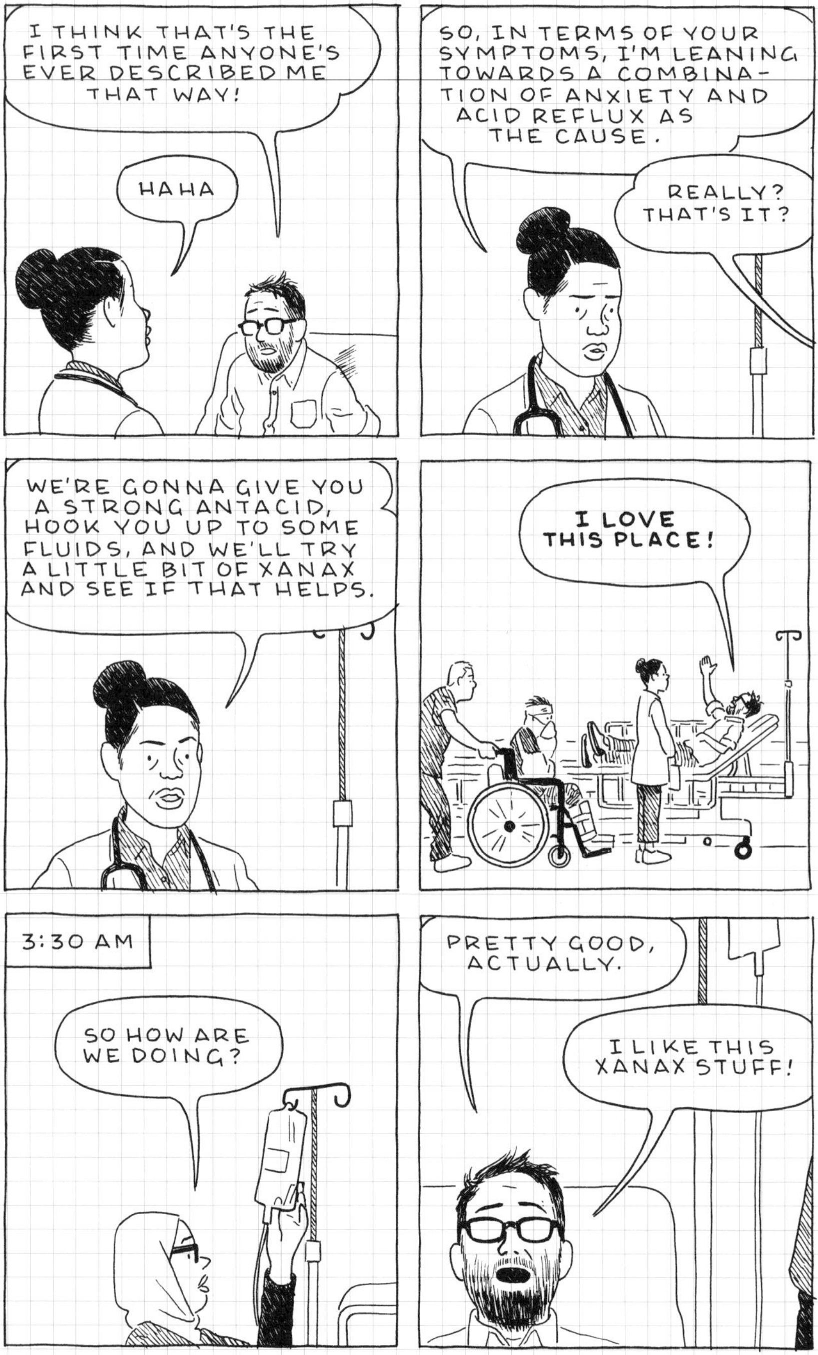
I THINK THAT'S THE FIRST TIME ANYONE'S EVER DESCRIBED ME THAT WAY!
HAHA
SO, IN TERMS OF YOUR SYMPTOMS, I'M LEANING TOWARDS A COMBINATION OF ANXIETY AND ACID REFLUX AS THE CAUSE.
REALLY? THAT'S IT?
WE'RE GONNA GIVE YOU A STRONG ANTACID, HOOK YOU UP TO SOME FLUIDS, AND WE'LL TRY A LITTLE BIT OF XANAX AND SEE IF THAT HELPS.
I LOVE THIS PLACE!
3:30 AM
SO HOW ARE WE DOING?
PRETTY GOOD, ACTUALLY.
I LIKE THIS XANAX STUFF!

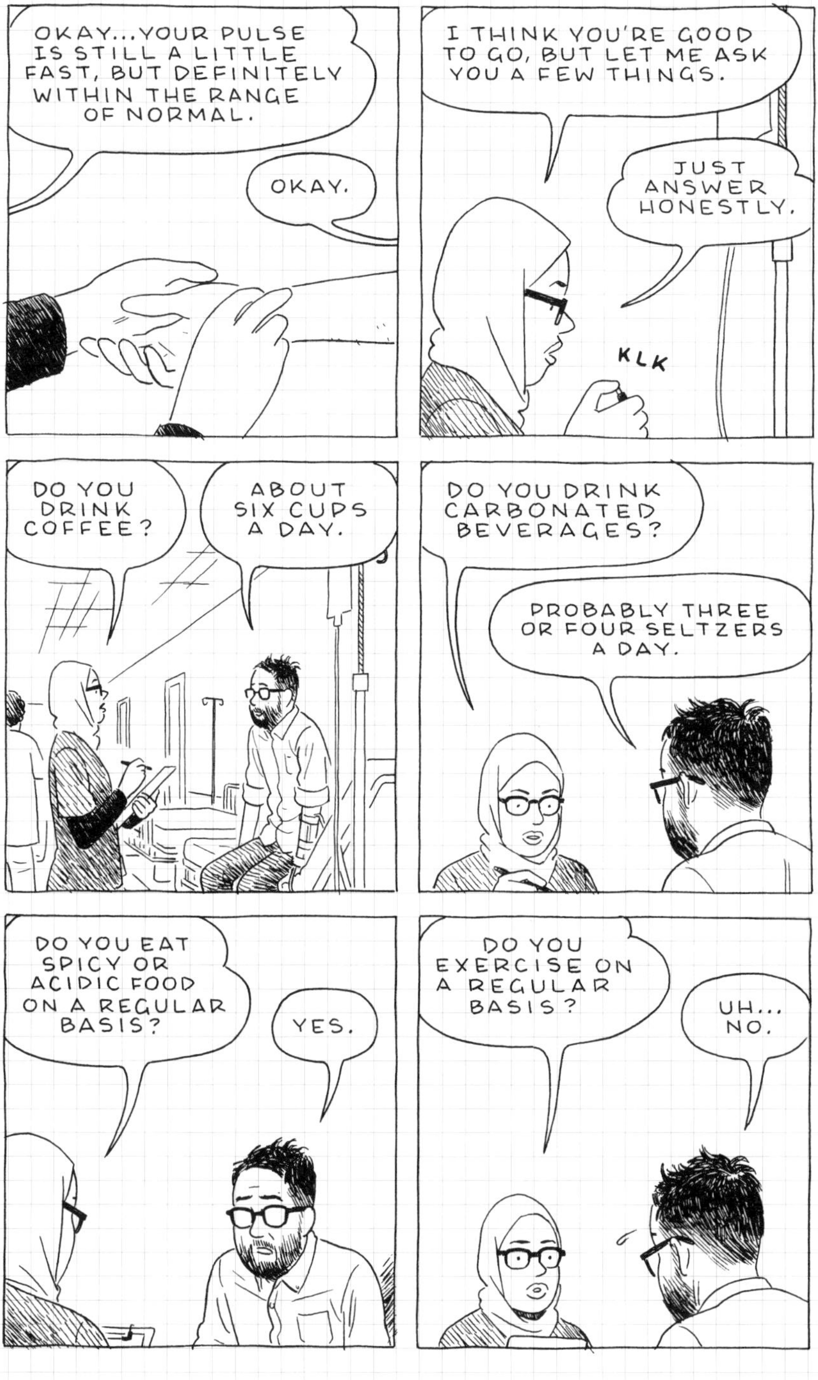
OKAY... YOUR PULSE IS STILL A LITTLE FAST, BUT DEFINITELY WITHIN THE RANGE OF NORMAL.
OKAY.
I THINK YOU'RE GOOD TO GO, BUT LET ME ASK YOU A FEW THINGS.
JUST ANSWER HONESTLY.
KLK
DO YOU DRINK COFFEE?
ABOUT SIX CUPS A DAY.
DO YOU DRINK CARBONATED BEVERAGES?
PROBABLY THREE OR FOUR SELTZERS A DAY.
DO YOU EAT SPICY OR ACIDIC FOOD ON A REGULAR BASIS?
YES.
DO YOU EXERCISE ON A REGULAR BASIS?
UH... NO.

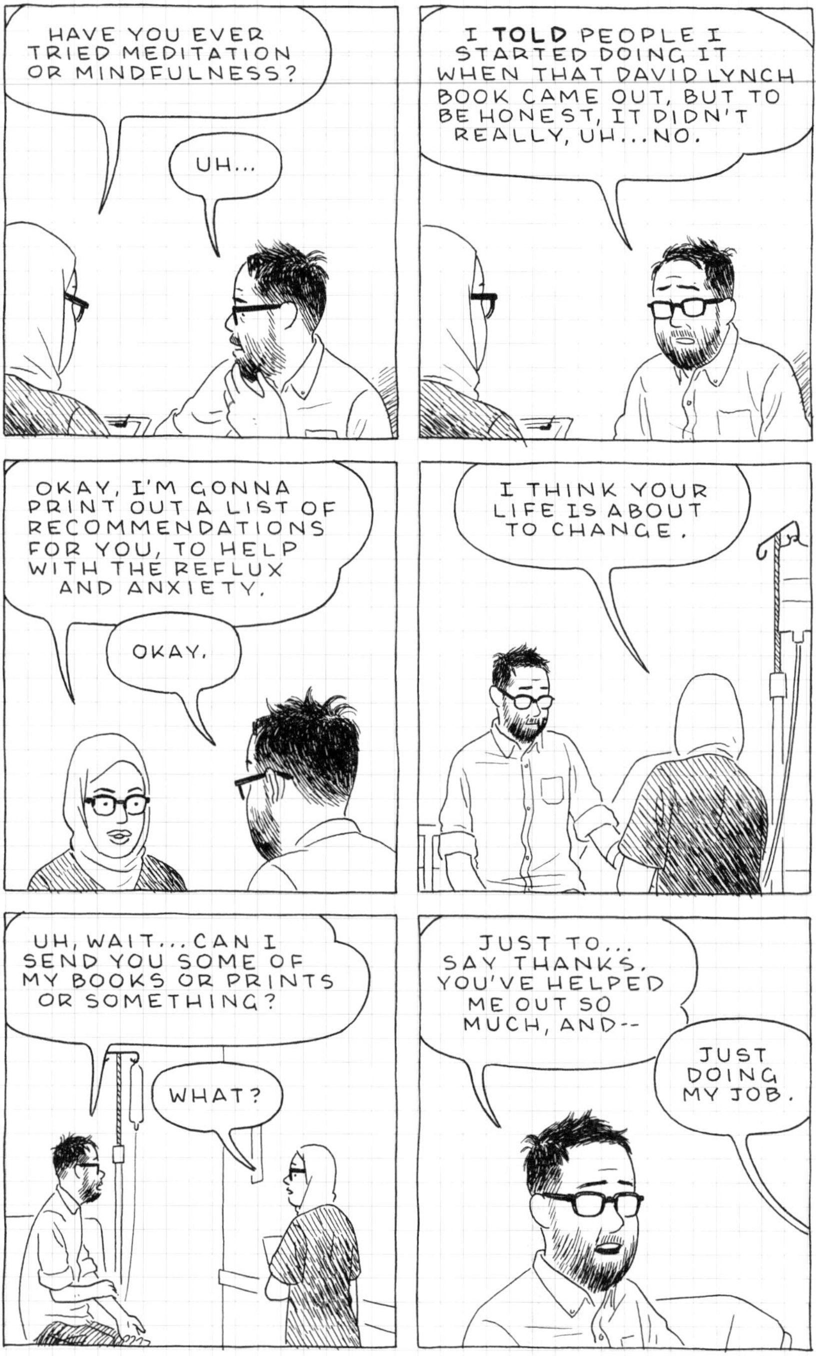
HAVE YOU EVER TRIED MEDITATION OR MINDFULNESS?
UH...
I **TOLD** PEOPLE I STARTED DOING IT WHEN THAT DAVID LYNCH BOOK CAME OUT, BUT TO BE HONEST, IT DIDN'T REALLY, UH... NO.
OKAY, I'M GONNA PRINT OUT A LIST OF RECOMMENDATIONS FOR YOU, TO HELP WITH THE REFLUX AND ANXIETY.
OKAY.
I THINK YOUR LIFE IS ABOUT TO CHANGE.
UH, WAIT... CAN I SEND YOU SOME OF MY BOOKS OR PRINTS OR SOMETHING?
WHAT?
JUST TO... SAY THANKS. YOU'VE HELPED ME OUT SO MUCH, AND--
JUST DOING MY JOB.

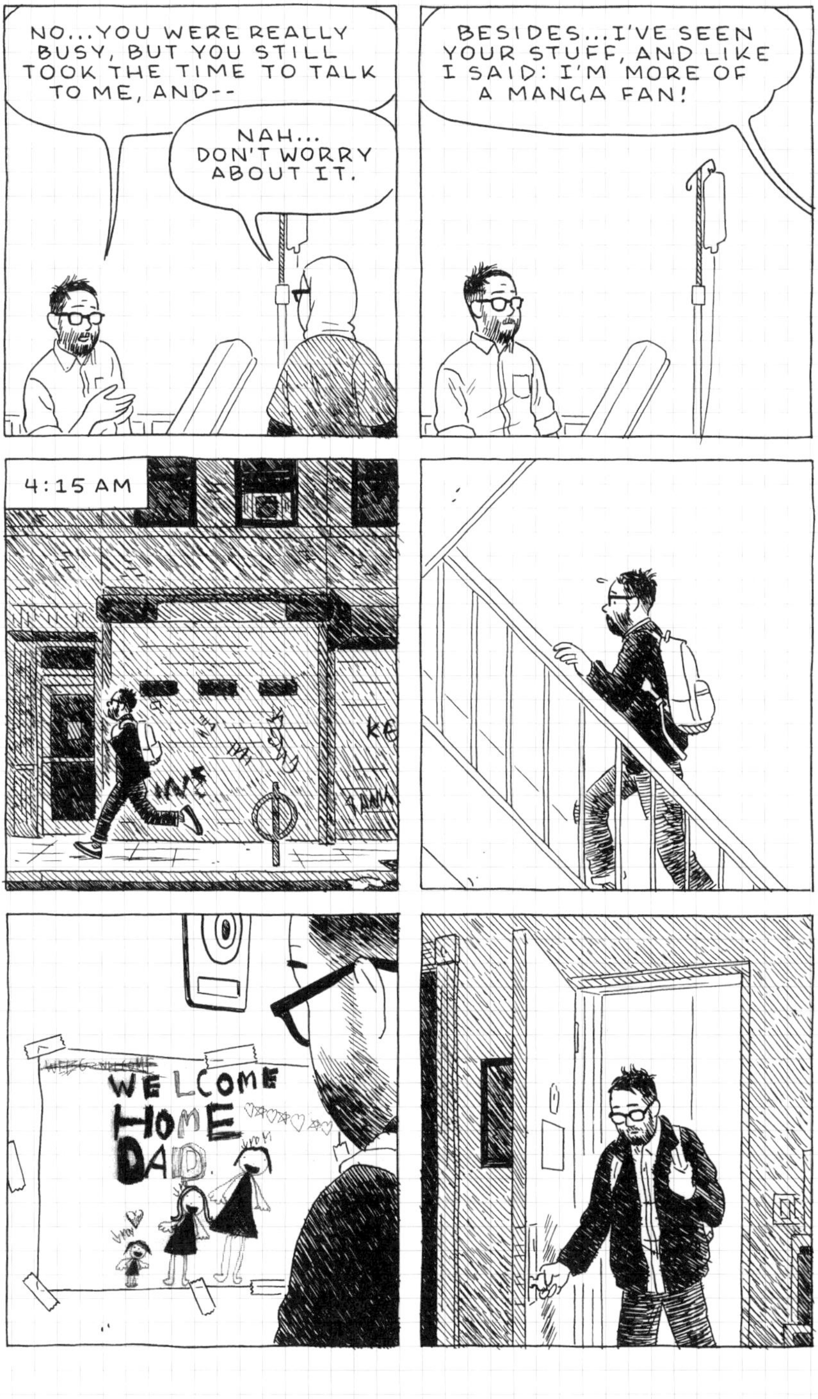
NO...YOU WERE REALLY BUSY, BUT YOU STILL TOOK THE TIME TO TALK TO ME, AND--
NAH... DON'T WORRY ABOUT IT.
BESIDES...I'VE SEEN YOUR STUFF, AND LIKE I SAID: I'M MORE OF A MANGA FAN!
4:15 AM
WELCOME HOME DAD.

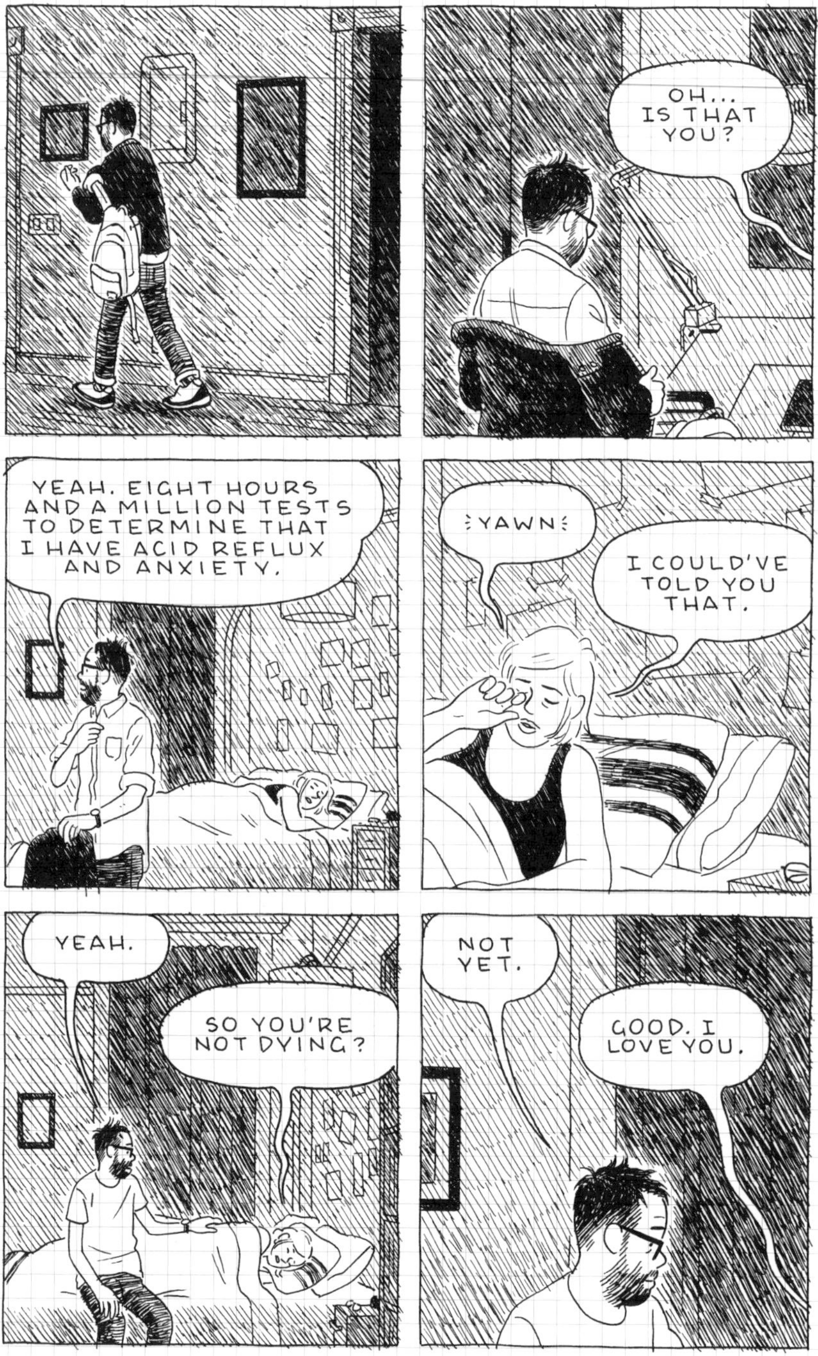
OH... IS THAT YOU?
YEAH. EIGHT HOURS AND A MILLION TESTS TO DETERMINE THAT I HAVE ACID REFLUX AND ANXIETY.
YAWN
I COULD'VE TOLD YOU THAT.
YEAH.
SO YOU'RE NOT DYING?
NOT YET.
GOOD. I LOVE YOU.

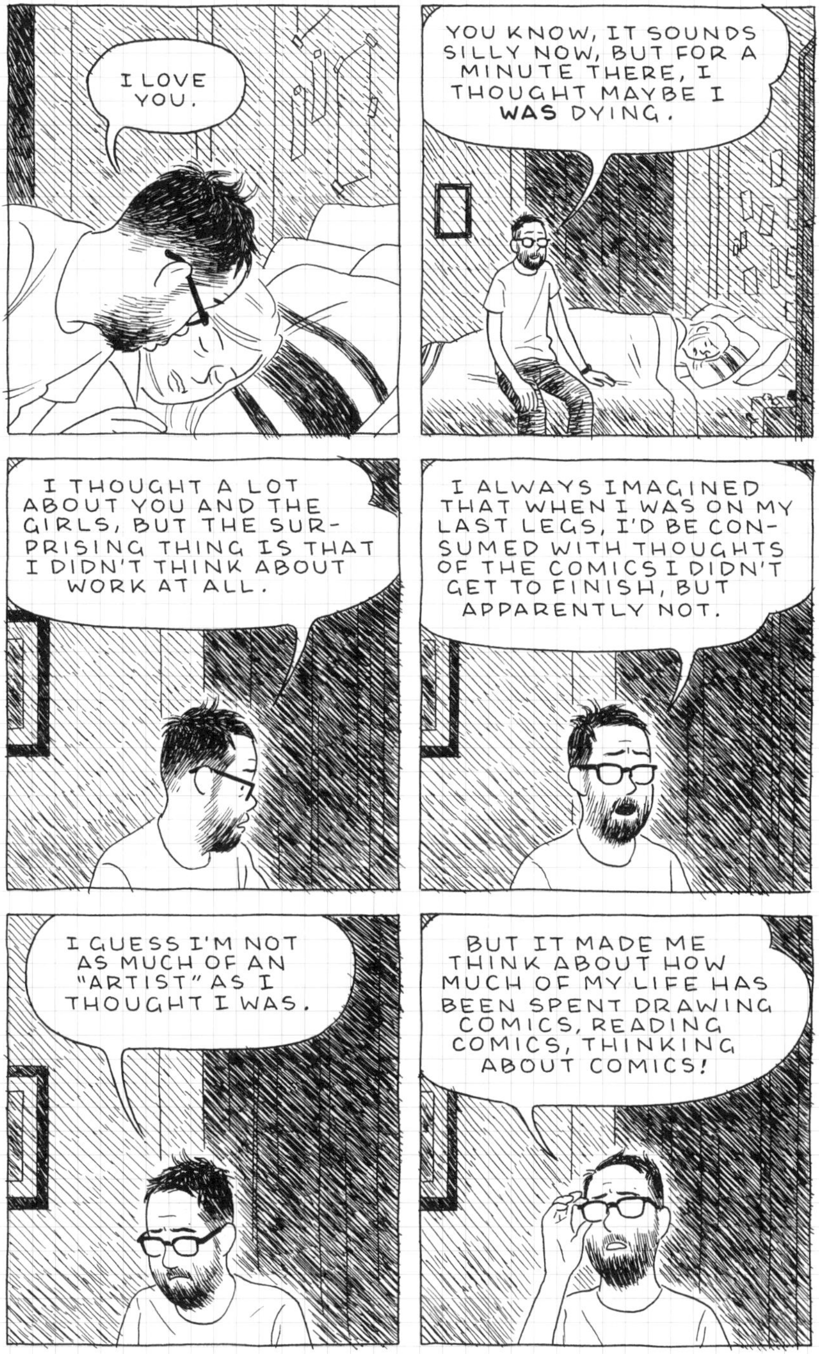
I LOVE YOU.
YOU KNOW, IT SOUNDS SILLY NOW, BUT FOR A MINUTE THERE, I THOUGHT MAYBE I **WAS** DYING.
I THOUGHT A LOT ABOUT YOU AND THE GIRLS, BUT THE SURPRISING THING IS THAT I DIDN'T THINK ABOUT WORK AT ALL.
I ALWAYS IMAGINED THAT WHEN I WAS ON MY LAST LEGS, I'D BE CONSUMED WITH THOUGHTS OF THE COMICS I DIDN'T GET TO FINISH, BUT APPARENTLY NOT.
I GUESS I'M NOT AS MUCH OF AN "ARTIST" AS I THOUGHT I WAS.
BUT IT MADE ME THINK ABOUT HOW MUCH OF MY LIFE HAS BEEN SPENT DRAWING COMICS, READING COMICS, THINKING ABOUT COMICS!

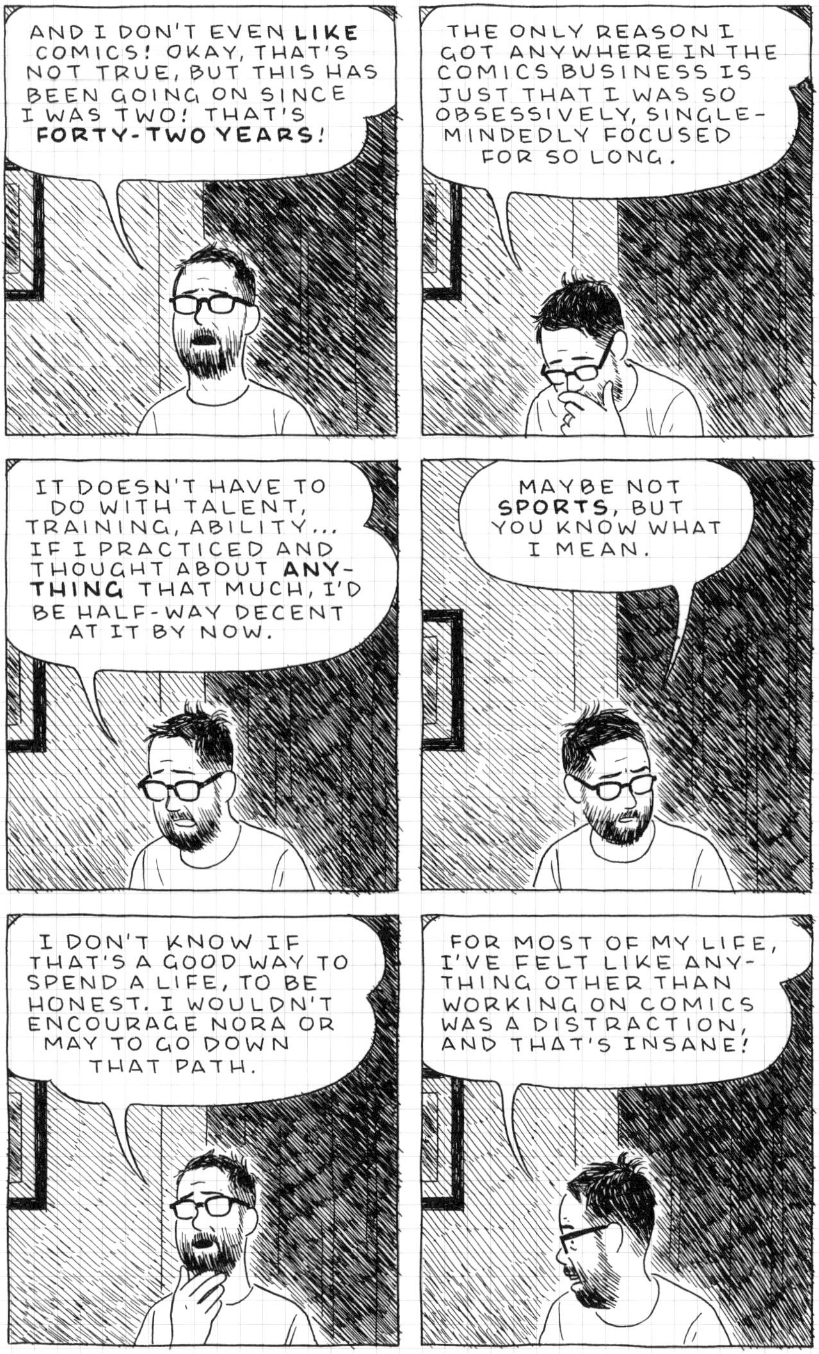
AND I DON'T EVEN **LIKE** COMICS! OKAY, THAT'S NOT TRUE, BUT THIS HAS BEEN GOING ON SINCE I WAS TWO! THAT'S **FORTY-TWO YEARS**!
THE ONLY REASON I GOT ANYWHERE IN THE COMICS BUSINESS IS JUST THAT I WAS SO OBSESSIVELY, SINGLE-MINDEDLY FOCUSED FOR SO LONG.
IT DOESN'T HAVE TO DO WITH TALENT, TRAINING, ABILITY... IF I PRACTICED AND THOUGHT ABOUT **ANYTHING** THAT MUCH, I'D BE HALF-WAY DECENT AT IT BY NOW.
MAYBE NOT **SPORTS**, BUT YOU KNOW WHAT I MEAN.
I DON'T KNOW IF THAT'S A GOOD WAY TO SPEND A LIFE, TO BE HONEST. I WOULDN'T ENCOURAGE NORA OR MAY TO GO DOWN THAT PATH.
FOR MOST OF MY LIFE, I'VE FELT LIKE ANYTHING OTHER THAN WORKING ON COMICS WAS A DISTRACTION, AND THAT'S INSANE!

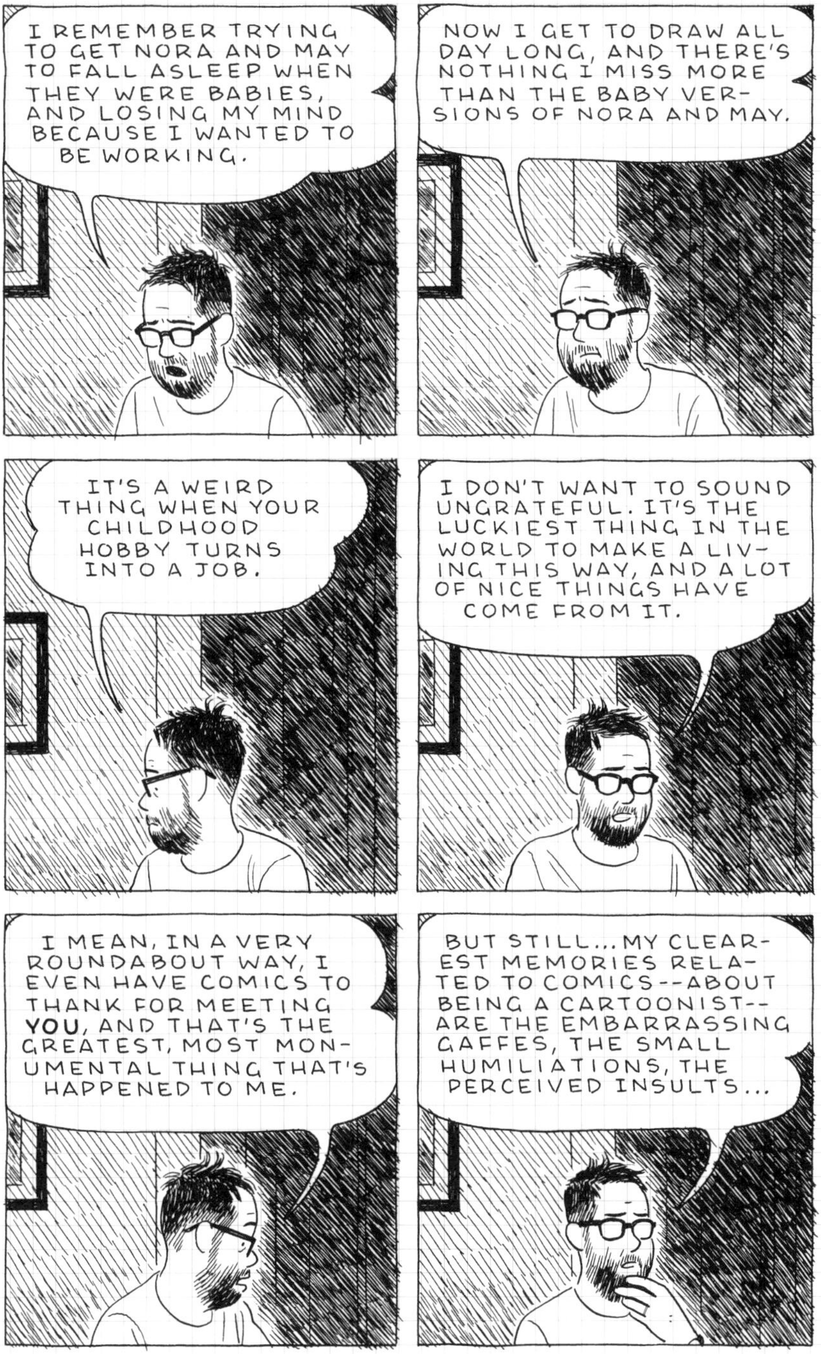
I REMEMBER TRYING TO GET NORA AND MAY TO FALL ASLEEP WHEN THEY WERE BABIES, AND LOSING MY MIND BECAUSE I WANTED TO BE WORKING.
NOW I GET TO DRAW ALL DAY LONG, AND THERE'S NOTHING I MISS MORE THAN THE BABY VERSIONS OF NORA AND MAY.
IT'S A WEIRD THING WHEN YOUR CHILDHOOD HOBBY TURNS INTO A JOB.
I DON'T WANT TO SOUND UNGRATEFUL. IT'S THE LUCKIEST THING IN THE WORLD TO MAKE A LIVING THIS WAY, AND A LOT OF NICE THINGS HAVE COME FROM IT.
I MEAN, IN A VERY ROUNDABOUT WAY, I EVEN HAVE COMICS TO THANK FOR MEETING **YOU**, AND THAT'S THE GREATEST, MOST MONUMENTAL THING THAT'S HAPPENED TO ME.
BUT STILL... MY CLEAREST MEMORIES RELATED TO COMICS--ABOUT BEING A CARTOONIST--ARE THE EMBARRASSING GAFFES, THE SMALL HUMILIATIONS, THE PERCEIVED INSULTS...

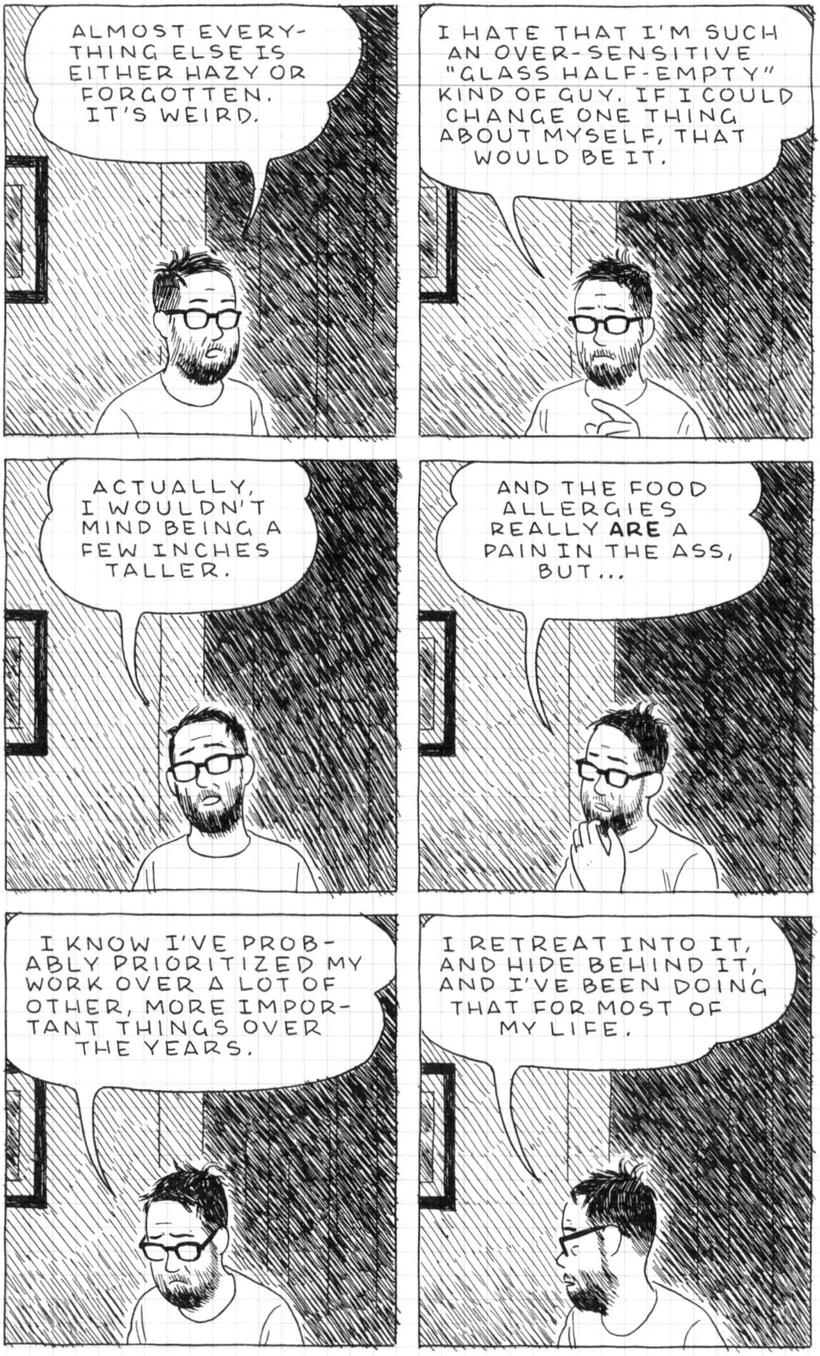
ALMOST EVERY-THING ELSE IS EITHER HAZY OR FORGOTTEN. IT'S WEIRD.
I HATE THAT I'M SUCH AN OVER-SENSITIVE "GLASS HALF-EMPTY" KIND OF GUY. IF I COULD CHANGE ONE THING ABOUT MYSELF, THAT WOULD BE IT.
ACTUALLY, I WOULDN'T MIND BEING A FEW INCHES TALLER.
AND THE FOOD ALLERGIES REALLY ARE A PAIN IN THE ASS, BUT...
I KNOW I'VE PROB-ABLY PRIORITIZED MY WORK OVER A LOT OF OTHER, MORE IMPOR-TANT THINGS OVER THE YEARS.
I RETREAT INTO IT, AND HIDE BEHIND IT, AND I'VE BEEN DOING THAT FOR MOST OF MY LIFE.

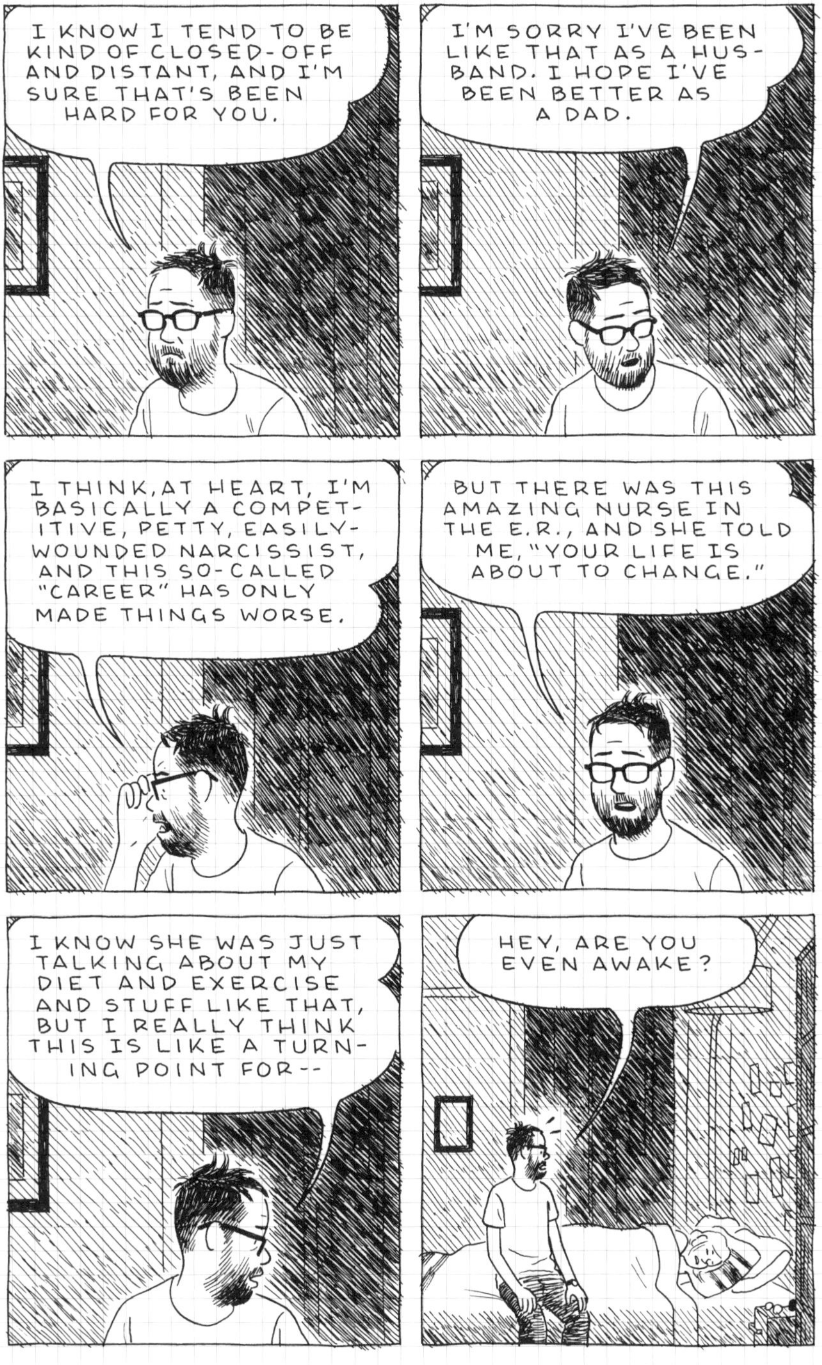
I KNOW I TEND TO BE KIND OF CLOSED-OFF AND DISTANT, AND I'M SURE THAT'S BEEN HARD FOR YOU.
I'M SORRY I'VE BEEN LIKE THAT AS A HUS-BAND. I HOPE I'VE BEEN BETTER AS A DAD.
I THINK, AT HEART, I'M BASICALLY A COMPET-ITIVE, PETTY, EASILY-WOUNDED NARCISSIST, AND THIS SO-CALLED "CAREER" HAS ONLY MADE THINGS WORSE.
BUT THERE WAS THIS AMAZING NURSE IN THE E.R., AND SHE TOLD ME, "YOUR LIFE IS ABOUT TO CHANGE."
I KNOW SHE WAS JUST TALKING ABOUT MY DIET AND EXERCISE AND STUFF LIKE THAT, BUT I REALLY THINK THIS IS LIKE A TURN-ING POINT FOR--
HEY, ARE YOU EVEN AWAKE?

THE LONELINESS OF THE LONG–DISTANCE CARTOONIST

The quote on page five is from an interview with Andrea Juno in *Dangerous Drawings* (Juno Books, 1997). The quotes on page 18 are from a review by Jordan Raphael in *The Comics Journal*, issue 179 (Fantagraphics Books, 1995). Dialogue translation on pages 61 and 62 by Mina Kaneko. Inset drawing on page 153 by Nora and May Tomine. Cover design by Adrian Tomine and Tracy Hurren.

www.drawnandquarterly.com
www.adrian-tomine.com

ISBN 978-1-77046-395-0
First edition: June 2020
Printed in Italy
10 9 8 7 6 5 4 3 2 1

Cataloguing data available from Library and Archives Canada

Published in the USA by Drawn & Quarterly,
a client publisher of Farrar, Straus and Giroux.

Published in Canada by Drawn & Quarterly,
a client publisher of Raincoast Books.

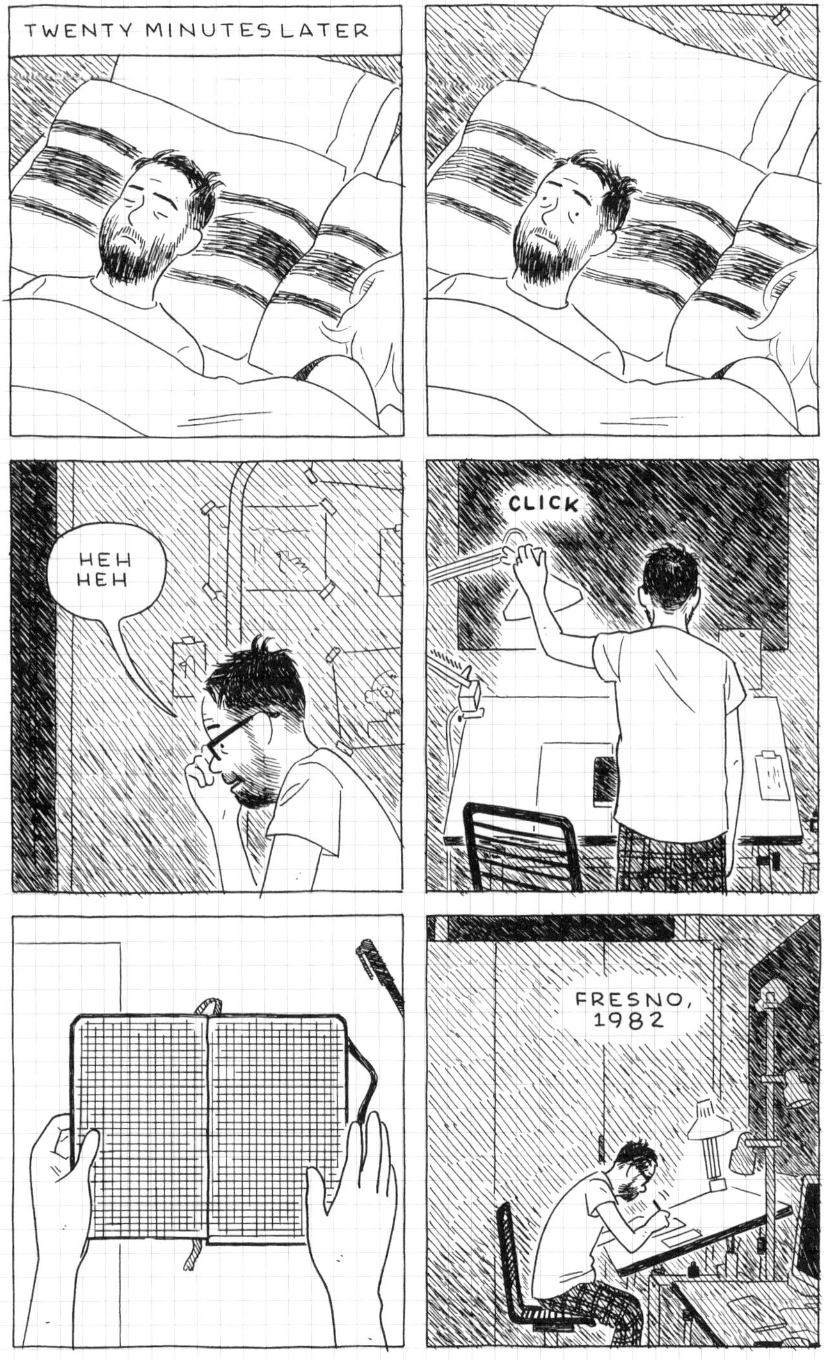
TWENTY MINUTES LATER
HEH HEH
CLICK
FRESNO, 1982

ACKNOWLEDGMENTS

Thanks to Adam Baumgold, Maggie Brennan, Angus Cargill, Denise Goldberg, Samantha Haywood, Todd Hignite, Mina Kaneko, Françoise Mouly, Ken Parille, Mark Parker, Eric Reynolds, and of course, Sarah, Nora, and May.

Thank you to Peggy Burns, Ann Cunningham, Tom Devlin, Lucia Gargiulo, Tracy Hurren, Alison Naturale, Chris Oliveros, Julia Pohl-Miranda, Megan Tan, and all at Drawn & Quarterly.

Thanks most of all to the long-distance cartoonists who, through their work, advice, and example, taught me everything.